The Voluntourist

The Voluntourist

A SIX-COUNTRY TALE OF LOVE,
LOSS, FATHERHOOD, FATE,
AND SINGING BON JOVI
IN BETHLEHEM

KEN BUDD

WILLIAM MORROW

An Imprint of HarperCollins*Publishers*

THE VOLUNTOURIST. Copyright © 2012 by Ken Budd. All rights reserved. Printed in the United States of America. No part of this book may be used or reproduced in any manner whatsoever without written permission except in the case of brief quotations embodied in critical articles and reviews. For information address Harper-Collins Publishers, 10 East 53rd Street, New York, NY 10022.

HarperCollins books may be purchased for educational, business, or sales promotional use. For information please write: Special Markets Department, HarperCollins Publishers, 10 East 53rd Street, New York, NY 10022.

FIRST EDITION

Designed by Kathryn Parise

Library of Congress Cataloging-in-Publication Data has been applied for.

ISBN 978-0-06-194646-2

12 13 14 15 16 OV/RRD 10 9 8 7 6 5 4 3 2 1

For my wife—
now and forever,
the love of my life

Jeffrey Lebowski: "Is it being prepared to do the right thing? Whatever the price? Isn't that what makes a man?"

The Dude: "Sure. That and a pair of testicles."

—*The Big Lebowski*

The Voluntourist

Prologue

Dad's last photo—the day he hit a hole in one—June 2005.

I WANT TO LIVE a life that matters. I realize that's a sickeningly self-important, obnoxiously earnest thing to say, so if you're feeling queasy, or you want to sneer and make a snide comment, I understand. Hell, I'm tempted to make a snide comment myself. But for too long now—long before I began my six-country do-gooder quest—I've felt that my life *doesn't* matter. That if I were to die today, if my heart were to implode in a life-ending instant, no one would ponder my time on Earth and say—

That man made me a better me.

Folks have said this about my father. *I've* said this about my father, though never, of course, to him. We're similar in temperament—both introverted, both reserved—yet far different in experience. I've never raised a son or daughter. I didn't rise from poverty. My middle-class upbringing came from his lower-class trials. And so the challenge, I find, is simply trying to measure up: to be more than a poor imitation—the lite beer to his stout ale.

About twenty-five years ago, when Dad was fifty-two, he traveled through China on business: a road trip from Hong Kong to Guangdong. Dad was a VP with the medical division of a Japanese electronics company. This was his only trip to China, and driving through the green countryside with his team, seeing China's poverty and immense potential, finding himself plucked from his comfort zone . . . it was the most memorable trip of his life.

Now I'm in China on a journey of my own. For two hectic weeks, I'm volunteering at La La Shou, a special-needs school in the gritty, growing city of Xi'an. I have no teaching skills or relevant experience. I do whatever the teachers need. The classroom is on the seventh floor of an old tea distributor's building, and the dull walls boom with colliding sounds: the children's giggles, chirps, and sobs; the teachers' instructions in indecipherable Chinese; the kiddie songs blaring on a tinny stereo.

On my first day, an eleven-year-old autistic boy, chubby but solid, already taller than one of the teachers, grabs a clump of my hair and screams—

MMMMMMMMMMMMMMMMM!

He yanks my hair with one hand, as though pulling stubborn weeds, pinching my arm with the other as he shrieks. Moments earlier he'd been silent, leaning in a tipped-back chair against the wall, his eyes hazy like the gray sky in the open window. Stitched on his long-sleeved shirt are grinning bears, each proclaiming in English: "I'm a happy bear!"

I grab his wrist. "It's okay," I tell him in a soothing soft-jazz DJ voice, hoping the tone will compensate for my lack of Chinese. "Relax—it's okay."

"Okay!" says a short-haired girl.

One of the class's three teachers rushes to us, barking at the boy in Chinese, prying his hand from my head. She calms him, returns him to his wood chair. He tips back against the wall again, crying. "He pinch," the teacher warns me with a smile.

A pincher. Yes. Good to know.

Later that afternoon, a university student asks me a question. She's volunteering at the school for the day, and like every college student I meet, she speaks good English, then quickly apologizes for not speaking good English.

"Why you do this?" she asks.

She looks more concerned than puzzled, wondering why I've flown sixteen hours to spend my free time on a "voluntourism" trip—a mini Peace Corps–like program; most of them run a week to three months—toiling at a noisy special-needs school where I don't speak the language, where children may yank my hair with Moe-from-the-Three-Stooges vigor, and where I'm not only working for free, I'm paying for the privilege.

I answer in the clear, me-Tarzan way I've taken to speaking: "Most Americans come to China, sit on tour buses. Only see other Americans. When I come to China, I meet you. I meet teachers. I meet children."

All of which is true without being the truth. I'm as evasive with this pleasant young student as I am with my wife, Julie, back home. I've known Julie since the sixth grade, though she's surely wondered lately how well she really knows me. First it was my solo trip to a volunteer rebuilding project in New Orleans, nine months after Hurricane Katrina. Three months later I convinced her to spend our vacation time teaching English at a rural elementary school in Costa Rica. Soon I'll be working at a climate change project in the remote Andes Mountains of Ecuador, and I'll spend Christmas— Julie's birthday—without her, toiling for two weeks in a Palestinian refugee camp. After that, assuming she hasn't left me, Julie will join me at an orphanage in Kenya.

So I don't tell this student that I want to live a life that matters. I don't tell her I'm in China because my childless life lacks meaning, because I'm struggling to answer questions that have plagued me for nearly five years—

How can I live up to my father's life when I'll never be a father myself?

What am I supposed to *be*?

PART ONE

New Orleans

THE EFFECTS OF HURRICANE KATRINA, NINE MONTHS AFTER THE STORM. (AMY GREBER)

MY FATHER'S FIRST CAR could only turn in one direction. It was a 1940 Plymouth, and whenever Dad turned left, the right front wheel would suddenly lurch, the bald tire tilting, the car stopping fast. Dad bought the old clunker in '56, shortly after his sixteenth birthday, and only a mix of creativity and teenage resourcefulness kept it running. The gas pedal was a beer can. The gear shift was a screwdriver. The upper front frame was held together with a men's leather belt. When the car hit high speeds—or turned left—the belt would slide from the frame, and the wheel would slide from the car. So it was right turns only. *Slow* right turns. In Arlington, Virginia, the urban Washington, D.C., suburb where Dad spent his high school years, he'd make three right turns to avoid going left.

"You'd be surprised," he once told me, "how far you can go turning just one direction."

I was thirty-nine when Dad collapsed. He'd finished eighteen holes of golf when he fell outside the clubhouse, his buddies inside ordering late morning beers. I've often wondered if Dad's life flashed before his eyes, though I know it's a foolish notion: the body doesn't respond to cardiac arrest with a montage of classic clips. And yet as soon as I got the call, his life flashed before *my* eyes—or at least the parts of his life that I knew. The old Plymouth with the unreliable wheel. My parents' honeymoon at an Arlington pizza joint after the courtroom ceremony. The time as a farm boy when he fell from the roof of a barn.

I thought back to his retirement party the summer before in San Francisco, one of the great nights of his life. What made that party so remarkable wasn't simply the throng of guests—colleagues from twenty years earlier attended—or the happy buzz in the restaurant party room. What made the evening so memorable, so stunning, even, was that Dad had laid off at least a third of the jolly guests a few months before. The company was moving its manufacturing operation back to Japan, and Dad went from overseeing production of MRI units to closing the facility. Which is why the crowded room of pink-slipped partiers was so odd. Who celebrates the guy who killed your job? Who poses for pictures with him, hugs him, shares old war stories? Who gives their hard-earned cash to buy him a freaking gift? It's beyond my comprehension. Like your ex-wife marrying your divorce attorney and you being so delighted to attend the wedding.

I watched Dad laugh with old colleagues when his friend Kevin, an ex-cop with fullback shoulders, corralled me for a chat. It was Kevin, a member of Dad's leadership team, who noted all the recently-let-go workers in the room. Until I spoke with Kevin, I'd never known about Dad's long battles to protect employees, to keep them on the payroll as long as possible, to preserve jobs as part of a small research-and-development operation that would remain behind.

"I was in a lot of the meetings," Kevin said. "The Japanese wanted to give everyone a basic severance package. But Bob—your dad—he has this blue-collar compassion. He kept pushing and pushing for something better. And just about every employee got a management-level severance package. If they didn't get that, they got more than they would have otherwise."

The postbuffet, postdessert speechifying had a tone similar to Kevin's. Colleagues praised Dad's generosity and work ethic. Mr. Yakamura, Dad's bespectacled, gray-haired Japanese boss, recalled my father's Zen-like calm during emergencies. Dad always joked that the only Japanese words he knew were *dai mondai*—"big problem." When those *dai mondai*s surfaced—they weren't infrequent given the cultural differences—the Japanese execs would summon Dad, asking: "Where is Bob-san!"

Finally it was Dad's turn to speak. He held the microphone but said nothing, staring at the floor. A few weeks earlier he'd shaved off the mustache he'd worn for twenty years. Without it his eyes seemed wider behind his glasses.

He shuffled a bit, put a hand in his pocket. He thanked everyone.

"I've been so lucky," he said, looking out over the gathering, at the white icicle lights gleaming against the walls. "Everywhere I've worked, someone took a chance on me. People saw something in me. They believed in me."

Few people in the room knew it, but Dad never went to college. He was embarrassed by this hole in his résumé, though it fueled his drive and ambition, his quiet empathy. Dad knew what it was like to be unemployed—it happened for an uncomfortable spell when I was in high school. He knew what it was like to work two jobs—he did it while my mom was pregnant with my sister. He knew what it was like to work twice as hard as the other guy because *that* guy had a master's degree and *you* had a certificate from a correspondence course.

The next morning, Dad was still glowing. We sipped coffee on the patio of my parents' home near San Jose, me and Dad and Julie, my mom enjoying her traditional morning Diet Pepsi. Julie inspected the digital camera Dad received as a gift.

I told him what Kevin told me; how Dad had helped those who'd lost their jobs. He shrugged it off, but I pressed him, and he told me something I'd heard him say before. That you can't just look at things from your perspective. That you can't really understand people if you don't put yourself in their position. Then he sipped his coffee, and he said something I *hadn't* heard him say. "Remember, Budo"—my old family nickname—"*you* succeed when others succeed."

The night of the party, amid all the good vibes and food and laughs, Kevin mentions something in confidence that surprises me.

"Your dad has some serious regrets," he says in low tones. "He thinks he didn't spend enough time with you and your sister because he worked so much."

"Really? He thinks that?"

"Yeah."

Really?

It's like saying, *Your dad regrets having eyeballs and nostrils and testicles.* This is who he was. He'd sit on the couch at night, manila folders spread on the cushions, a report in his lap, open briefcase on the floor. He'd work late, he'd work weekends. He had a zest for spreadsheets that most people reserve for heroin or chocolate cake. So yes—Dad worked a lot. And Mom, as most moms do, bore the everyday labors of parenting: feeding us, dressing us, disciplining us. But Dad never skipped Christmas plays or Pinewood Derbies—he slaved over our little red car with the nail for a steering wheel—and I knew, always, I was more important than his work.

Maybe I should ease his regrets. You know—some mushy Hallmark moment where I say, "You've always been an amazing dad." Where I tell him he's not just the smartest man I know, he's the best man I know. But I say nothing because . . . C'mon. We're *guys*. We're not weepy, confessional types. Besides—he's retired now. My parents sold their house in California. They're coming home to Virginia. He'll be close.

It's the weekend after Father's Day: I make a dinner reservation at Dad's favorite restaurant—our belated gift—then walk to the pool in the townhouse community where Julie and I live. It's hot out. Humid hot. Miserable hot. Dad is playing golf that morning with his usual Saturday foursome and I think—

How in the hell can he play in such God-awful heat?

The golf has been good for him, slimming his belly. He looks fit, trim from the walking and working on their new house: painting, building shelves, landscaping. His golfer's tan is a deep bronze, his arms abruptly pale at the sleeves. I'd thought he'd struggle with retirement, but he has enough projects, for now, to stay busy. "It wasn't fun anymore," he says of his career. "If it was still fun, it would have been harder to retire."

I'm sweating when I return home—so much for the refreshing swim—and the air-conditioned foyer feels like another, better world. Julie walks from the kitchen and stops me as I close the door.

"Your mom just left a really weird message."

I take off my sunglasses, hit "play" on the answering machine. Mom's message is unintelligible. I call her at home. No answer.

I grab my cell phone. Water rolls from my bathing suit to my ankles.

She's crying on the voice mail message.

I wonder if she's sick. I was just telling Dad last week that I worry about her. She smokes—though Dad does, too—she doesn't eat right, she doesn't exercise. Amid her heaves and sputtering I hear only a few words, like a distress call that's largely static: Dad has collapsed.

I call my sister. Dad was rushed from the golf course to Fair Oaks Hospital. I scramble to put on dry clothes, throwing on a T-shirt from a park in West Virginia where Julie and I went mountain biking. I know I wore that shirt because I couldn't bring myself to wear it again for more than a year.

Julie and I hop in the car. We don't speak the entire drive. *It could be anything*, I tell myself. Probably heatstroke. Dehydration. Dad had experienced some light-headedness of late—probably tied to a new blood pressure medicine, his doctor said—but a week ago he easily passed a stress test.

It could be anything. Relax.

We arrive at the ER. Mom is outside, talking on her cell phone, smoking. I jump out of the car. Julie moves to the driver's seat to park.

Mom rushes toward me, throwing herself against me, sobbing into my chest.

"Daddy died," she moans.

I hold her. I stroke her head as she cries. But for a moment it's like I don't exist. No thoughts, no nerves . . . nothing.

Mom and I walk toward the ER doors like survivors of a bombing, holding each other up. A stocky cop offers his condolences and shakes my hand. The hospital pastor does the same. It's been two minutes since I heard the news.

We're led to a small, indiscriminate room; a room of bland white paint, the bland furniture of interstate hotels. Every table has a box of tissues. The tragedy room. A place for instant grief and long forms on clipboards.

I want a moment alone with Dad. A nurse leads me past imposing wood doors down a white hall. His body is on a gurney, half surrounded by a curtain, a white sheet up to his chest, his red golf shirt still damp.

I stand by him. I speak. I make promises.

Everything changed for me that day.

It wasn't just that I lost my father. When life works the way it's supposed to, your parents die before you. I know that. I'm glad he died quickly, doing something he loved. I'm glad he never suffered the indignities of old age, the pain of cancer, the horrible haze of Alzheimer's. I tell myself that frequently, and yet beyond just missing him, and mourning him, I'm forever jarred by the way we lost him. The morbid speed of it all. His memories, his hopes—everything—gone. Extinguished. The time it takes to clutch your chest and crumple to the earth.

My father and both his parents died suddenly in their sixties. They all led harder lives than me. And yes, they all smoked. The risk factors were higher. But who knows? Maybe a coronary time bomb is ticking in my chest, too. Maybe a genetic "off" switch lurks in my heart, programmed for my sixty-fifth year.

It's not even dying that bothers me. It's dying without making a difference in the world. Without doing a damn thing that matters. After Dad died—"The big sad news," as one of his former Japanese colleagues put it—we received heartfelt letters and e-mails from the people who loved him, and I read and reread them all.

"When I think of Bob, as I do frequently these days, I recall him as a great influence on my life," wrote Will, the HR director where Dad worked.

"I don't think I would be the person that I am today without knowing him," said Steve, another of Dad's employees.

"I may dream to play golf with him at *ano-yo* [heaven] some day," wrote Kyoto Tanaka, one of Dad's first Japanese bosses and his close friend. "His score will be 95 and my score will be 96."

By saying Dad will have the better score, Mr. Tanaka said his friend was the better man.

I read these letters and wondered: *What will people say when I'm gone? What if my own life ends in an instant? What have I accomplished?* These feelings weren't new. Dad's death simply ignited them, exposed them, ripped them from my secret shell. I've long wanted children, and in the weeks after the funeral I made my most emphatic case to Julie. It's not too late, I said. We'll conceive. We'll adopt. We'll build a child from a kit. We're cheating ourselves out of the central experience of life.

She agreed to consider it, but I became morose. I found myself acting like things were normal—still smiling at work, still soldiering through middle-class routines—but I was lost. My life didn't stand for anything. I had no purpose, no passion, no mission.

Months later, Julie's sister gave birth to a son. When her mother left the happy message on our answering machine, I felt . . . anger. Long-submerged anger. Anger that surprised me with its intensity; jealousy that startled me with its bite.

"What's bothering you?" Julie asked the next day.

"I don't want to talk about it," I snapped. But I knew that we must.

Late that night, Julie was in bed, under the covers, reading a mystery. I paced downstairs before heading up and entering the bedroom. I sat beside her. We've been friends since the sixth grade. Married for fifteen years. I've loved her for all that time put together. We talked. She had thought about children many times since we'd last discussed it. But . . .

But.

She looked at the book in her hands.

"I just don't have maternal feelings," she said.

Sorrow softened her voice. A sadness that seemed to say, *I want so badly to do this for you, but I can't.*

When Julie was about three years old, a drunk driver killed her older sister. That day—the anguish of that day—is one of her earliest memories. I've always believed, though Julie disagrees, that something happened that day. That somewhere inside, that stunned little girl determined that she would never, *ever* subject herself to that kind of pain. The pain of grieving parents.

On the day Dad died, I never cried. I wanted to be strong for Mom. It was only the next day that I wandered away from visiting relatives, walked out of my sister's house, made the five-minute trek in the heat to my parents' nearby home, sat on their bed, alone, and wept. I could only lose control if I was *in* control. I could only cry on my own terms. But on this night, sitting on the edge of the bed with Julie, I finally—unwillingly—lost that carefully maintained control.

I needed an escape. I needed an outlet for wasted energies. I needed a way to tackle my grief: my grief at losing my father, my grief at not *being* a father.

A few months later the e-mail arrived. The subject: "Katrina Relief Volunteer Opportunities." My employer was working with Rebuilding Together, an organization that repairs homes owned by low-income older Americans. Rebuilding Together was managing projects in New Orleans and throughout Louisiana, and ten to fifteen slots were available for volunteers to do hot, hard work for one week in the Big Easy, nine months after Hurricane Katrina had devastated the city.

"Employee volunteers will work under hardship conditions," the announcement said. "Accommodations will be provided in a tent city and/or on cots in facilities such as church basements. Three simple meals will be provided daily, and dietary restrictions cannot be met. Employee volunteers must be in good health and capable of hard physical work."

Without discussing it with Julie—without even knowing what the job would be—I signed up.

From the window of a cramped airport shuttle van, as I travel east on Interstate 10—a route that nine months earlier was underwater— the city of New Orleans seems almost healthy. Through smudged glass I see a few crude plywood patches on the roofs of houses, the occasional abandoned strip mall, the silhouettes of workers on the Superdome's half-repaired roof. In the French Quarter, the old homes with their long shutters and iron gates seem free of Katrina's scars. "You're standing in the twenty percent of New Orleans that didn't get any flooding," the owner of Crescent City Books tells me that afternoon in his shop. On Canal Street, the reopened Harrah's casino beckons gamblers to eat, drink, and lose money; dirty Bourbon Street entices out-of-town drunks with stiff Hurricanes and big-boobed contortionists on trapeze swings.

Now that I'm here, I'm not sure why I'm here. I have no talents to offer the city. My primary professional skills—writing and editing—aren't exactly in high demand. ("Thank God the editor's here—we've got one hell of a compound modifier problem . . .") Not that any of this occurred to me when I signed up. I was aware of my feeble ability in all things hardware, but only when I spoke by phone with Cynthia, Rebuilding Together's disaster relief coordinator, about two weeks before the trip, did I realize this was an issue.

"So," Cynthia asked me, "what kinds of skills do you have?"

Skills?

No one said anything about needing skills.

I spared Cynthia the long, bullshitty answer—"Well, that all depends, of course, on how you define *skills*"—but my "skills" are basically limited to this:

1. Sarcasm
2. Spinning a basketball on my right middle finger for upwards of ten seconds
3. Quoting large sections of old *Simpsons* episodes

And that, sadly—*really* sadly, I realized, during our long-distance silence—is pretty much it. I can handle a drill and a hammer, I'm decent at replacing the innards of toilet tanks, but I'm about as qualified to operate a band saw as I am to give birth.

"That's okay," Cynthia said. "We have plenty of work for unskilled people."

As Cynthia explained it, rebuilding projects seesaw between skilled and unskilled labor. The unskilled folks start first on a broken-down home, tearing down moldy drywall, ripping up floors;

work that could be done by anyone with two hands and half a brain (me). After that, the skilled people—contractors and construction pros who volunteer their services—arrive to rewire homes, rebuild roofs, replace appliances, reinstall torn-out drywall and floors, and do any other jobs best performed by nonamateurs who know what they're doing. Unskilled volunteers then return to paint, haul trash, and help residents move back in.

I tell Cynthia that I'm pretty confident in my ability to haul trash.

Our accommodations are lovely, which is disappointing. I was welcoming hardship conditions, because when you're trying to figure out your life, severity is more illuminating than comfort (and when you're trying to help those who have suffered, you want to know what they've endured). But we the eager volunteers—about fifty of us are here from around the country—are *not* staying in a tent city as we'd originally been told. Nor are we sleeping in church basements, like many other volunteer groups, or in cramped, no-frills trailers.

We're staying at the New Orleans Marriott.

I know. There's something deeply wrong about this. It's like the Buddha seeking enlightenment in a limo.

The Marriott rooms are courtesy of the Order of Malta, a Roman Catholic organization that is some nine hundred years old and—I suspect—has *Da Vinci Code*–like plans for world domination. Based in Rome, the order is led by a Grand Master and Knights of Justice, and its red-and-white logo resembles a medieval shield (the Malta fleet waged war throughout the Crusades to "defend the Christian territories in the Holy Land"). As a sovereign subject of international law, it issues its own passports. The major flaw in my take-over-the-world theory is that the order's altruistic mission, *Tuitio Fidei et Obsequium Pauperum*—"defense of the faith and assistance to the suffering"—has inspired centuries of good deeds. Here in New Orleans, the Maltas are providing not only unskilled older labor—many of the volunteers appear to be over the age of sixty-five—but also $1.3 million in a partnership with Rebuilding Together. We've all received red or blue Malta baseball caps, and our new yellow-and-white work T-shirts prominently display the Malta logo. As for the hotel rooms, apparently a high-ranking Marriott executive is a Malta, and rumor has it he worked out a deal: volunteers can stay for free if Rebuilding Together rebuilds homes for some Marriott employees.

The only inconvenience—a minor one, I grant you—is that I have a roommate. Obviously this doesn't qualify as a hardship given the agony this city has suffered and since, I'm guessing, the tent city doesn't have cable television or those cute little bottles of hotel shampoo. But there *is* something awkward about sleeping and showering in a modest-sized hotel room with a total stranger.

That stranger is a Californian named Antonio, and we work for the same nonprofit, which has donated money to Rebuilding Together. Antonio works in accounting outside of Los Angeles, while I'm an editor with the organization's magazine in D.C. The good news—aside from the fact that the room has two beds—is that Antonio is an affable guy (not that one expects humanitarian projects to attract serial killers). We meet when I return to the room after strolling the city, still full from a shrimp po'boy at a nearby dive.

"Hey, buddy!" says Antonio with a firm handshake, dropping the remote control as he hops up from the bed.

Antonio exudes energy. He's thin: a hiker and a beach volleyball player back in Long Beach. As we make small talk of the "how was your flight" variety, I realize we're total opposites: I'm tall, he's not; I'm an introvert, he's an extrovert; I'm married, he's single; I'm East Coast, he's West Coast (though a native of Colombia who grew up in Puerto Rico). Antonio is one of those guys who enter a crowded room and within fifteen minutes know everyone's name. He is out-going, upbeat, charismatic, enthusiastic, and a real people lover. Despite that I think we'll get along fine.

Any illusions about the health of New Orleans are shattered on the first morning's bus ride to our work site. We drive through the Lower Ninth Ward and stare at empty apocalyptic neighborhoods, deserted homes with brown watermarks like grim tattoos, bitter graffiti with messages like:

Fix
Everything
My
Ass

The dingy siding of one home is a makeshift billboard in sprawling white paint: "Our government cares more about foreign countries than us."

Watermarks line most homes three feet or so above the dirt and clumps of uncut weeds, but that's simply where the floodwater settled. In many areas the water rose up to ten feet higher. Some homes have multiple watermarks as the water lowered then settled, lowered then settled.

We pass the occasional FEMA camp: fenced-in trailer parks with trailer offices and residences. Trailers also sit in random front yards, serving as temporary homes for residents. For every home being rebuilt, endless others sit eerily abandoned, phantom neighborhoods in a silent, vacant sprawl. Spray-painted by front doors is an X mark. On the right and left of the X are dates showing when rescue workers inspected the home. In the bottom of the X is a number: how many bodies were found.

Windows are boarded, mounds of trash heaped at the ends of

driveways. Stores and strip malls are empty as well, and may never come back.

"This looks a lot better," says Luther, our bus driver, as we pull through a deserted neighborhood. "A lot of the trash has been cleaned up."

Trash is good. The nicely collected piles mean people are coming back and cleaning up. Where there is trash, there are people. "That's why there aren't any rat problems," says Luther, who's also a minister. "No people, no rats."

The houses don't seem too battered on the outside, but they're unlivable on the inside, wracked with mold and water damage. Building supplies are limited. Rebuilding Together's warehouse was flooded and later looted. Mark, a thirtysomething guy who works for the Order of Malta, says it took four weeks to find kitchen cabinets for one home. "You can't just go to Home Depot," he said at an orientation dinner at the Marriott. "Nothing is normal here." The city fell from 460,000 residents to 180,000 after the floods, so many businesses are understaffed: stores, restaurants, hotels.

"Think of it this way," said Mark. "You're in a huge construction site of one hundred thousand homes. You'll be driving down the road—this happened to me—and suddenly there's a hole the size of a car; something the city dug to restore water. And traffic is insane because of the construction and closed roads and people coming back in the evening to work on their homes."

Underneath an overpass are abandoned cars. The vehicles are dented, dirty from submersion in muddy water, broken windshields and brown waterlines along the windows; stretching in rows, like weary soldiers in formation, for what seems like miles. Imagine a long, open garage for ghost cars—"The world's largest junkyard," as Luther calls it. We drive past them twice a day. After a while, they become a rusted blur.

"They're not organized in any way, so it's just about impossible for people to find their cars," says Luther. "Not that they would run anyway."

The bus drops us off at a single-level brick house on Coronado Street in New Orleans East, which is where we'll work. Our merry band of volunteers is split into two groups—the red team and blue team (hence our different colored Malta hats, I realize)—and sent to two different projects. Antonio and I are on the red team. A white trailer sits in the front yard, along with assorted odds and ends—an old stationary bike, a faded black tarp covering who knows what—but overall the home is in good shape. Much of the interior work is finished, from new walls to new ceilings. The main priority is interior and exterior painting, though some volunteers will rip out the dingy kitchen floor. A Porta-Potty stands at attention next to the driveway.

There's a mad, enthusiastic scramble to grab paintbrushes and tools as we descend from the bus. Two college girls are ostensibly in charge and divvying up assignments, though they lack the you-do-this, you-do-that management skills of a foreman. At the blue team site, within the first hour, a college guy gets smacked in the mouth with a two-by-four, knocking out a tooth and sending him to the ER.

I receive my first task: scraping white paint from a wood workshop out back. It's the kind of stimulating work one normally associates with prison road crews, but it's work that needs to be done, and it's a good match for my skills (or lack thereof). So I stand in the small backyard, alone, and I scrape, scrape, scrape, and though it's simple work, it's hard work, because if this cracked paint could endure one of the five most lethal hurricanes to strike the United States, it certainly isn't daunted by unskilled me.

The sun roasts my neck and arms as I scrape. I'm a lifelong Virginian, so I'm conditioned to humidity, but the steamy May heat feels like July back home. Except the clouds seem more scarce, the sun more intense. My morning goes like this:

Scrape, scrape, scrape.

Sweat, sweat, sweat.

Scrape.

Sweat.

Wipe face with shirt.

Chug water.

Repeat.

It's easy to think paint scraping is futile given the scale of the destruction. But one thing I've slowly learned in the ten months since Dad died, something I'm still only beginning to grasp, is the significance of small gestures. On the evening of Dad's death his friend Joe drove me to the golf course, the now infamous golf course where Dad died, to pick up my father's car. Here was a task, one of many, that would never have occurred to me when I woke that morning.

If your father's heart implodes, you'll need to get his car.

Joe drove fast, too fast, face ashen, zooming down a twisty two-lane road in his convertible. The top was down; Joe's graying hair flapped in the wind. Over the past year, Joe had gone from distant acquaintance—my sister's boss's husband—to Dad's golfing buddy and good friend when my parents moved home. Dad filled a hole in Joe's Saturday foursome; Joe filled a hole in Dad's postretirement life. He was there when Dad collapsed.

"We'd all gone to the clubhouse to get a beer," Joe told me, yelling over the wind and the engine as we drove. "Your dad sat down on a bench outside. We thought he'd gone to the bathroom. Some guy saw him sitting there and said, 'Hey—I think there's something wrong with your friend.'"

The car hugged a curve; Joe shifted gears and roared down a straightaway, the trees a blur on either side. It was like being in a cop movie.

"He'd been joking about how healthy he was after acing his stress test," Joe yelled. "He was so relieved."

The parking lot was largely empty when we arrived. Joe got out and lit a cigarette, paced a bit, then stared at the spot in the green grass where the crowd had formed. I thought about asking him to show me the exact spot, to re-create the incident, to satisfy my sudden detective hunger. Instead I watched him, the cigarette smoke rising from crossed arms. It only occurred to me much later, given my own shell-shocked state, that this was the last place Joe wanted to be. It was too soon to be here; to be where his friend died only hours before. He was here purely to help. And it was something I'll never forget.

Small gestures.

And so I think about Joe, and I think about Dad, and I scrape harder.

As will become our nightly routine, Antonio and I lie in our separate beds, tired, pillows propped up, watching the NBA playoffs. It's a fitting TV choice, since my full stomach resembles a basketball. We ate dinner earlier with the volunteers in a Marriott ballroom: grilled salmon with stewed tomatoes on a bed of potatoes, plus two pre-dinner beers for me. I told Mark I felt guilty staying here instead of the tent city.

"Actually the tent city is quite nice," he said. "The food is good, they have washing machines, showers . . ."

Yeah, sure. It may be nice, but it's still a tent city. I doubt the folks there enjoyed a delightful raspberry tart with coffee for dessert.

Before dinner, while I nursed my beer, Antonio mingled with the other volunteers, as if every stranger were a friend.

"I never thought I'd be meeting knights and dames," he says back in the room, talking about the esteemed elder Malta volunteers. "That Margaret sure is interesting."

"Which one is Margaret?"

"You know: Margaret. Worked at ABC News and was married to a senator. She was sitting there with Jim."

Jim . . .

"The guy who was a developer."

On the TV screen, Steve Nash shoots a free throw. I pick up my cell phone.

"Louisiana is on Central time, right?"

"Central time," he says.

"So we're an hour behind home. I wonder if I should call my wife."

"Hey, you don't want to get in trouble with your wife." He clicks channels during a commercial. "So what's your wife's name?"

"Julie," I say, realizing how little I've revealed of myself. "She's a nurse practitioner. Which means she does more diagnosis stuff than an RN, and she can write prescriptions. She works at a university, in the student health office."

"Man, I couldn't be a nurse or a doctor."

"Me neither. You gotta have the right personality. I couldn't do any job that involves phlegm."

Sometimes if I call Julie at work I'll jokingly ask, "So—have you healed anyone today?" But she really is a healer, even if she doesn't see herself that way. Recently our dog, Molly, developed a nasty sore near one of her back paws. Every night, Julie sits on the floor and soaks it, and cleans it, and wraps it in gauze.

I don't talk with many people about our kid quandary, but I once told a friend of mine about Julie's dog care. "Sounds to me like she has maternal feelings," she said. "She just has a four-legged outlet for those feelings."

Antonio flips back to the game. I look down at my phone. It's too late to call.

It's our second day of work and by lunchtime I've already gulped down three bottles of water. Yesterday I drank six bottles, but thanks to the heat and my energetic sweat glands I made just one trip to the driveway Porta-Potty. And that, believe me, is a blessing, since the Porta-Potty bakes all day in the Louisiana sun.

I spend most of my morning painting the carport ceiling and all its upper carport crannies, a natural job for my long arms. As I dip my roller in a tray of white paint, the homeowner, Lucille, and her two middle-aged daughters make a surprise appearance to check the progress and say hello. Lucille is a tiny woman, probably approaching eighty (though I have more gray than she does), and her arrival is greeted with rock-star excitement. Susan, a volunteer who's been painting shutters with a precision normally reserved for wristwatch repairs or circumcisions, rushes toward her with white-stained fingers and hugs her. Cameras come out. Mom and the daughters grin, arms around each other, posing for our paint-streaked paparazzi. For all the hardships these three good people have suffered—they endured the Superdome in the aftermath of the storm before relocating to Austin, Texas—they're glowing, not just because Lucille will soon have a house again, *her* house (one of her daughters lives in the refurbished house next door), but because of the staggering generosity that rebuilt it. There's a wonderment in their smiles that says—

All of these people—these strangers—have come from across the country to help us. Us! Can you believe it?

I've seen this grateful reaction throughout the city. The hotel staff seemed so damned happy when I arrived. Not the phony, robotic "How may I help you" happy you normally receive. This was *thank you, thank you, we need people to visit our city, please tell your friends.* The doorman's smile made me feel like a long-lost brother. (Anna, a colleague from D.C., meets a probably not-uncommon exception, talking one day with a tattooed waiter in a French Quarter café who is sick of volunteers. "All the do-gooders are driving me crazy," he says. "They don't realize that things move here at a certain pace.")

At lunchtime we grab box lunches and spread out around the house, from the carport to the backyard. The hardier folks sit in the grass under the front-yard sun, a terrific idea if you like a bit of heatstroke after dessert, but not appealing to a shade guy like me. I opt for the cooler front walkway. My neck is stiff from looking up at the ceiling for hours while painting, and I'm embarrassed to admit that my shoulder is a little sore from yesterday's scraping, and from applying primer on the workshop. Complaining about it seems unthinkable. Seeing Lucille and her daughters, and their deserted neighborhood . . . I admire these determined homeowners who have the guts to rebuild and move back; the guts to endure such stress and doubt and uncertainty. I'm not sure I could do it.

Earlier that morning, Mark told one of many survival stories we will hear during the course of the week. "There was this old man," he said. "I mean, really old. He was asleep on his couch when the levees broke. He woke up and the water was up to the cushions. So he went to his attic. A lot of people used hatchets to hack their way through the roof, but this guy didn't have one. So he was trapped in the attic with no way out; his home was completely flooded. Think about the heat—it must have been unbearable. And yet somehow he survived. He just endured until someone found him."

Not everyone was so lucky. Two months after I return home, New Orleans firefighters will find the skeletal remains of a Katrina victim in a Lower Ninth Ward home. It will happen again in December, when workers uncover another skeleton while demolishing a house.

I came here because I felt miserable, but now that I see other people's misery—not misery because their suburban middle-class lives lack purpose, or because life hasn't turned out the way they hoped, but *real* misery; the misery that comes from homelessness, from death and despair, from unthinkable loss—I feel ashamed for feeling miserable. Which, of course, makes me feel more miserable.

I sit on the cement and eat my turkey breast on white bread

in silence. Antonio plops down next to me, gives me an elbow to the arm.

"Hey buddy," he says, winking, then peering into his boxed lunch. "Whew! Man, when we got here that first night, and I saw how old some of these volunteers were, I thought you and I were gonna do all the work. These people work hard! But you know—it's just good to be helping people, isn't it?"

I munch on an apple from the box. Maybe he's right. And then a little thought creeps into my sweat-drenched head.

Remember, Budo—you succeed when others succeed.

A coach-style bus takes us to and from the work sites, the air-conditioning a blessing at the end of the hot days. In the mornings, everyone is groggy, the coffee yet to provide its caffeine spark. In the afternoons, everyone is exhausted. We gaze out the windows at the injured city, finding some previously missed detail—I watch the watermarks rise and fall from one neighborhood to the next—and we ask questions of Luther, the minister–bus driver who enlightens us with his sermons on the city and the hurricane.

"Katrina was God's punishment for the city's sins," Luther proclaims from his steering wheel pulpit. "This city did wrong for too long. So God sent us a flood to sweep up all the murderers and the drug dealers. That's not to say they won't be back. Some of them already *are* back. But God was sending a message."

God has plenty of reasons to be irked with humanity, but the flooding was the work of man. Overdevelopment eliminated marshlands that once served as natural drainage areas. The levees failed, as did the floodwalls—which the U.S. Army Corps of Engineers had predicted could happen twenty years earlier. As for the criminals, fifteen convicts escaped from Orleans Parish Prison in the post-flood chaos. Eighty percent of New Orleans' police officers lost their homes. Another 30 percent suffered post-traumatic stress disorder.

Luther's life has been affected as well. He lives in Baton Rouge, and the drive to New Orleans that once took ninety minutes now takes up to two hours, since so many people now live outside the city and commute to work. His sister, he tells us, used to live in New Orleans—she and her family had sat down to dinner when the levees broke, sending them scrambling to the attic in terror.

"Next time there's a hurricane, they'll bus you out the second they hear the *word* 'hurricane,'" says Luther. His description of the state's post-Katrina recovery efforts: "Louisiana has a way of saying, 'Leave it up to me and I can screw it up.'"

Tracy, a fiftyish volunteer from Sacramento, laughs and nods. I'm sitting next to her on the bus. She has an impressively intellectual résumé: for twenty years she led a bipartisan California think tank before becoming a university professor. I suspect, however, that she's secretly a therapist, because she has this annoying talent for getting reticent, tight-lipped, closed-off people like myself to discuss things we don't really want to discuss.

"You never told me why you're volunteering here," says Tracy. I've ducked the question for days, but now I'm trapped: we're twenty minutes from the hotel.

"Well," I say, "I turned forty a few months ago, and, you know . . ."

"So what was it about turning forty that bothered you?"

I see what she's trying to do. She's pressing me for specifics, because the more specific I get, the more I reveal. Well, it's not going to work. I'm not going to start blabbing like some reality-show idiot and share my existential doubts and disappointments about life and not having kids. I don't care if she is incredibly friendly, or if she looks like a happy elementary school teacher behind her dark-frame, smart-person eyeglasses, or if she has the type of calm, persuasive nature that encourages you to lie down and pour out your life's secrets. I'm cleverer than that. In fact, *she* winds up talking about children, roughly ten minutes after I start blabbing like some reality-show idiot and sharing my existential doubts and disappointments about life and not having kids.

"For a long time I wasn't sure I wanted children," she says. "And then I'd see diaper ads on TV, and I'd start crying. That's when I knew it was time."

"I haven't seen Julie crying during diaper ads," I say.

I fell in love with Julie in the sixth grade: her family moved to Virginia from California, just outside of Pasadena. We lived on the same green-grass suburban court, four houses apart. For years I liked her, liked her in that prepubescent way that's more intense, more desperate, more painful than mere love. To her I was simply her brother Tom's friend, but I knew that one day Julie and I would be together. I can remember hearing Bob Seger on my clock radio as a dopey fourteen-year-old, convinced the song was right: *Someday lady you'll accomp'ny me.*

Our first date was my junior prom. 1982. Julie was a sophomore. She's two weeks older than me, but I was a grade ahead: in kindergarten I was promoted to first grade because I could read *Green Eggs and Ham*. Sadly, I reached my academic peak as a five-year-old.

For the prom, I wore a tan corduroy three-piece suit from JCPenney. Julie looked beautiful in a pink-and-white gown, which by today's thin-strap, look-at-my-cleavage standards seems almost Victorian. I drove us in my mom's *Smokey and the Bandit*–style Trans Am, a silver car with the big-winged orange-and-red bird on the hood, a cool-at-the-time improvement over my humble Volkswagen squareback.

We broke up after my senior year in 1983: Julie started dating the manager of the McDonald's where she worked. He drove a Firebird, certainly sportier than my VW, though it didn't have a hood. (Let me repeat: *it didn't have a hood.*) About a year later we reconnected. We were married in 1991.

I always assumed we'd have kids. My parents had kids, her parents had kids—it seemed like a natural. An inevitable progression in life. We started with houseplants, graduated to fish, made the leap to a dog. A tiny human would surely be next.

But then we hit thirty, and thirty-five, and still no little one was scurrying through the house; no child to love us, infuriate us, worry us. Julie worked in a pediatric office, which didn't help. When you handle sick, screaming kids eight hours a day, you generally don't race home and say, *I beg you: impregnate me—NOW.* As the years passed, I struggled to discuss the issue, perhaps because I knew its conclusion: Julie, whether because of her sister's long-ago death or because she wanted her freedom, was content with a childless life. And a silent sadness took hold of me, a malaise dragged to the surface by the slightest events: birthday parties for our friends' kids, soccer games at the field near our house. That should be us, I'd think. Why the hell isn't it us? And it would hit me, like a type of paralysis—

We may never have children. I may live my entire life without holding a son. Without holding a daughter. I may never have a relationship with a child like the one I had with my dad.

Julie and I are forty. The clock isn't just ticking; it's shaking us by the shoulders and screaming, "I'm ticking, you idiots! Can't you hear me ticking!?"

I don't have maternal feelings, she'd said. I respect those feelings. And I'm glad we never conceived a half-wanted child. Julie is a wonderful woman. She has devoted her career to caring for others. When my mother needed surgery for pancreatitis, Julie accompanied her to talk with the surgeon. When my grandmother needed monthly B_{12} shots, Julie would jab her arm, sparing her a trip to the doctor. I receive more from her than I give in return. She is the best part of me. And yet knowing all this doesn't make it easier.

Cindy, one of the college-age quasi-foremen, needs a few volunteers to help install a laminate floor at a house down the street. I quickly raise my hand. It's a chance to do something different, see a new home, learn a new skill.

Four of us work on the floor. The unskilled laborers are me and Keith, a volunteer from Sacramento who looks vaguely like Billy Carter. The skilled half of the team are Justin and Frank, two California contractors. Justin shows us how to install the rectangular floor pieces, which fit together with grooves. To knock them in place, we put a block against the open side, then tap the block with a hammer. Striking it too hard, as Keith and I discover, damages the wood grooves. We scrap several pieces due to not-gentle-enough tapping, but our efficiency soon improves, and by late morning we're like a seasoned railroad crew laying track. Justin and Frank handle the corners and odd-sized end pieces, sawing the slabs to the right size, while Keith and I handle the easy stuff.

"This is kind of fun," I tell Keith as we crawl across the floor, tapping.

"Yeah—nice change of pace. And it's good to be away from the Paint Nazi."

I look up from all fours. "The Paint Nazi?"

"You know—Bruce. The guy who doesn't do any work. All he does is stir paint. And he keeps barking out orders like he's in charge."

Bruce has indeed decreed himself the unofficial paint stirrer, probably because it's the only job that requires extended sitting. He plants himself on a knee-high overturned white plastic bucket like it's a throne. And now that I think about it, he is a bossy son of a bitch for someone with no authority.

"I guess he *is* kind of a paint Nazi," I say.

"Oh yeah. He's a paint Nazi. 'No paint for you!'" says Keith, mimicking the famous *Seinfeld* episode.

The homeowner, Sherry, pops in to say hello. She and her dog live in a trailer in the front yard. Keith, Justin, Frank, and I are eating lunch in the shade on the cement back patio; she brings us each a cold Pepsi. Sherry was forced to evacuate her home after Katrina. She traveled to Texas, where her son is a priest. When she returned home, two months later, her house was ravaged by mold. She shows us photos.

"It was on the walls, the furniture—everything," she says, handing us one dismal pic after another. "All the food in the refrigerator . . . mold. I didn't have time to take anything out."

It's hard to imagine, given the newly painted walls, the new bathroom fixtures, the new lights, the new everything. In the photos the house seems infected with plague.

"The smell would about knock you over," says Sherry. "I tried all sorts of cleaning stuff, but the only thing that got rid of it was gutting the house."

Like Luther, Sherry believes Katrina was God's will. A message. And being a devout Catholic, she sees another message in the photos.

"It got everything I own," she says of the mold. "But there wasn't a single bit of mold on my Jesus and Mary statues."

By the end of the afternoon, we stand—me, Keith, Justin, and Frank—admiring our now-installed living room floor. It's dark brown fake wood, and it looks damn good. I assume it's not a big deal for Justin and Frank, since they're contractors, but even they pull out cameras for a group shot. We pose in the empty room, proudly, like hunters with a deer.

As cleanup work begins, I grab a broom and sweep the adjacent dining room, which is empty but loaded with dust from its own new floor and lights, including a very modern, very sleek hanging lamp. I picture the dining room table that will soon be underneath; imagine Sherry and her family enjoying a well-deserved meal.

The floor is similar to one Julie and I recently had installed in our basement. We'd overhauled the room, and Dad helped me in the months before he died. I was determined to do most of the work myself—all the painting, installing new ceiling lights, replacing the outlets—but we bought new doors, one for the room and one for the closet. As usually happens with home improvement projects, we hit a snag: the new doors didn't quite fit the new frames.

"We can replace that one door frame," Dad said with confidence. "We'll adjust the other one. I did it in California. It won't be a problem."

He did research, of course. Spent an afternoon at the bookstore reading about door frames. "Nothing is worth doing unless you're gonna do it right," he said, another of his favorite phrases. We installed the frame, and I thought it looked good, but Dad checked it with the level, and the frame was a thousandth of a degree off, so we fiddled with it again, and he grabbed the level again, and we fiddled with it some more until it was perfect.

Dad could fix and build anything, just as his father could fix and build anything. (The handyman gene seems to be missing from my DNA.) As a kid, he took apart and rebuilt old tractor engines on the farms where my grandfather worked. After high school, he earned his certificate for a National Radio Institute correspondence course in electronics (sample question on the first quiz: "If a full-wave rectifier is used in a 25-cycle circuit, how many pulses will there be per second in the output?"). Soon he was assembling circuit boards for minimum wage, and eventually moved to a small start-up, building check-processing machines for banks. From there he worked his way up to management and then medical electronics, overseeing the production of ultrasound units and MRIs.

I can barely change the wiper blades on my car.

The mechanical miracles that most impressed me were his least sophisticated work. As a kid I had a bunch of superhero action figures—from Aquaman to Spider-Man—all with removable polyester tights, all anatomically incorrect. Their limbs were connected to their torsos by a nylon band, and inevitably, after overuse, the band would break, and Superman would go from Man of Steel to Pile of Body Parts. I had a shoe box that resembled a superhero trauma unit, filled with naked limbs and masked faces. Dad would repair them, rebuilding the bodies with rubber bands and paper clips, making each hero whole again. Superman still survives in my closet, and he's still in one piece.

And so I'm thinking about dismembered superheroes as I sweep near the stunning new lamp, which hangs from the fresh white ceiling. And I'm feeling so very, very proud of this newly installed floor.

Which is when it happens. *How* it happens, I'm not sure. Meaning I'm not sure how the lamp goes from hanging to not hanging. I know, as I am so vigorously sweeping, that the top of my broom handle whacks the hanging lamp. And the lamp becomes dislodged. And that its descent seems to take *hours*.

Imagine a small nuclear weapon implanted in a lamp. That's how it sounds when it hits the beautiful new laminate floor. Every other sound in the house—the banter and last-minute work, the dumping of tools in toolboxes—stops. Total, terrible, mortifying, I'm-a-complete-jackass silence. Volunteers and Rebuilding Together staff rush to see what happened. And I stand with my broom, chunks of glass at my feet, feeling so . . . unskilled.

I'll pay for the lamp, I tell Brian, one of the Rebuilding Together staffers. No, no, he says—these things happen. Keith helps me clean, and says the lamp shouldn't have been installed yet with so much work going on. He's right, I suppose, but as I look down at the chunks of broken glass, this doesn't *feel* right. I pick up the big pieces, dropping them into an empty paint bucket, then sweep the tiny ones in a sparkling pile, wishing I could fix the lamp the way that Dad used to fix Spider-Man.

Given how much I'm sweating, my work shorts are developing a gym locker funk. I could wash them in the hotel washing machine, but that seems like a waste of water, so before dinner I shower with my shorts on, scrubbing them with shampoo as I bathe. Washing proves easier than drying, alas: the shorts are dripping as I blast them with a hair dryer over the tub.

So now I'm feeding dollar bills into the clothes dryer near the soda machines. As the dryer hums, I call Julie on my cell phone. She thinks I'm cracking up. She hasn't said that, but I'm convinced that's what she's thinking, since over the last few weeks she's seen me: 1) become surly over the joyous birth of our nephew; 2) engage in an uncontrollable late-night crying fit; 3) withdraw even more than usual after the aforementioned late-night crying fit; and 4) abandon her for a week in New Orleans to do work for which I'm unqualified.

Sixteen years ago—about a year before our wedding—Julie volunteered for a medical mission in Haiti (a job for which she *was* qualified), working with a team of Virginia nurses and doctors. The two-story hospital looked more like a run-down garage than a medical facility, but the trip brought much-needed, highly skilled care to people who otherwise wouldn't receive it. Typical for a medical person, her photos included not simply locals and landscapes, but also a twenty-pound tumor that looked like an uncooked turkey.

I hope we can remove whatever tumors are lurking in our marriage. Julie and I are similar in personality, which is the strength and weakness of our relationship. We're both mellow. Easygoing. We've known each other almost thirty years, yet we've never once fought. Which isn't healthy. Because rather than tell her what I'm feeling—*I understand why you don't want children but I'm pissed and I'm sad and I'm lost and I'm trying to compensate for the void*—I become more distant, more locked in my thoughts. And she doesn't say, *Snap out of it, you secretive, self-absorbed, self-pitying jerk. Your life is good.* And so the bad feelings rankle.

The conversation is awkward. I ask her what's happening at home. Nothing much. She walked the dog. She's trying to find something for dinner.

I used to make her laugh, I think. I can't think of a way to make her laugh.

She tells me a few work-related tidbits. I tell her about New Orleans.

"Well . . . I miss you," I finally say.

"I miss you, too."

I think about it, and I wonder if she misses me, or the me she fell in love with.

Each morning starts with a boxed breakfast, which includes a bottle of orange juice and three snacks: a pastry, a pastry, and—for the main course—a pastry. "A carton of carbs," as Anna calls it. The question is what to eat first. Should I start with a pastry and save the pastries, or save the pastries and devour the pastry?

Actually, the pastries are tasty: one oozes with cherry filling, another is more from the muffin family. We eat them, half awake, at tables in the hotel lobby. Anna notes that some of the insulin-challenged Maltas have retreated to the restaurant for meals that won't send them into diabetic shock.

When it's time to leave for work, the bus travels a different route, stopping first in Gentilly, a neighborhood bordering the breached London Avenue Canal. This is ground zero of the flooding, one of the hardest-hit areas. We're brought here, I assume, to satisfy the disaster voyeurism we all feel. (Bus tours take gawking tourists to the worst-hit locations.) But we're also brought here so we'll share what we see; so we'll go home and tell our friends that we can't forget New Orleans, because it's even worse than they think.

We clamber off the bus. It feels like a *Star Trek* scene; like we're the lone life-forms on an alien planet, observers of vacant streets and a vacant civilization. The neighborhood, Mark says, was blasted with a wall of water when the levees broke. The canal is about forty or fifty feet away. On many of the one-story homes, the waterline is just below the roof, near the gutter, meaning the homes were completely submerged.

"Most people had already evacuated," says Mark. "But if you were here, you were dead."

Owners' cell phone numbers are spray-painted on garage doors. Other messages are from inspectors: "Natural gas leak" or "One dog rescued" with a phone number. Windows are missing. We pass a home with two boards nailed in a crooked X across the doorless front entryway. "Keep out!!!" is scrawled against one board, as if anyone would be tempted to go in. The same message is on a board across the bay window and its black-stained white curtains. The front yard, like every front yard, is covered with sand and sediment, the odd weed shooting through.

A muddy stroller lies on its side in front of a gutted home. A mangy teddy bear is sprawled atop a pile of trash. Many of these homes, says Mark, will be demolished. They're structurally unsound. Beyond saving.

Construction crews work on the canal walls, the arms of cranes rising behind empty houses. I see what looks like a metal Band-Aid patch on the canal wall. I wonder if it's strong enough to survive another Katrina.

We walk to a battered single-level home. Multiple watermarks stain the siding, like rings in a cut tree. The windows and doors are gone. Three tires lie scattered in the middle of the sandy front yard, not far from a white four-door car, the roof and hood crumpled, rust devouring the hubcaps. On the driver's side door, painted in yellow like graffiti, are the letters *DB*. I ask Mark what it means.

"Dead body," he tells me.

We stare for a while, and then we file back on the bus.

My mother says she dreams about Dad almost every night. She felt his presence in the bedroom one morning when she woke up. I've dreamed about him periodically since his sudden death: in each dream we're driving somewhere, or watching TV—something ordinary—and then I remember . . . he shouldn't be here. I struggle to figure out *why* he's here, and *how* he's here. Sometimes I wake up, thinking it's real, until my half-awake brain says, *Wait, hang on, no—he's gone.*

In one dream we're at my grandparents' old ground-floor apartment in Arlington. We're in the tiny kitchen—me, Dad, my grandparents—sitting at the round table where I'd eat grilled cheese sandwiches as a boy. We're laughing. I'm so thrilled to see them; my grandparents have been dead for almost thirty years. And then I'm quiet, because I know this can't be. And then *they* become quiet. We sit in silence.

In my past nocturnal encounters with Dad, we haven't talked. But this time I look at him, and with all the seriousness I can muster, I ask a single question.

What is it like?

I mean death. But I also mean, what is it like to know the answers: to know the age-old questions of why the hell we're here, and what we're supposed to do with ourselves, and how to live a meaningful life.

I look up at Dad as if I'm a child again. He smiles softly, sympathetically.

"I can't tell you," he says.

I'd like to take a moment to formally apologize to the Paint Nazi.

I'm sorry.

I'm sorry for saying that you're bossy and that you spend the day on your tuchis stirring paint. Hey—who am I to judge? Because *you*, Paint Nazi, blessed our tired red team bus with a grand humanitarian gesture, a gesture that may not seem that grand to you but was exceedingly grand to me.

Here's the scene:

At the end of another dirty day of sanding and painting and

lugging supplies in the thick New Orleans heat, we wait on the bus for the last few red team volunteers before driving back to the hotel. My white Malta shirt is soaked, and I can't tell if I'm smelling me or Antonio or some unpleasant combination of both. That's when the Paint Nazi comes on board, holding two silver briefcase-sized boxes.

A cheer erupts. Beer! *Frosty* beer!

"Hey, all right!" says Antonio, applauding. The Paint Nazi rips the top off the first box and pulls out beer cans one by one, like an alcoholic Santa reaching into his perforated sack. The cans travel down the aisle, each so wonderfully sweaty and cold. I place mine against my forehead, rub it against my cheeks, and I smile at Antonio, and he smiles at me, and when I pop the top and gulp that first bubbly swig . . . after the heat and the sweat and the grime and hard work, this is *the* best beer of my life.

Okay, so buying beer doesn't make the Paint Nazi the Paint Saint. And I won't question how he found the time to not only sneak off and buy beer, but to find an open market in this largely deserted neighborhood. But it's a thoughtful gesture, a nice morale boost, and far more than I've done for any of these volunteers. And so a toast to the Paint Nazi: may your paints be well stirred and your beer always cold.

At the end of the week, I hear the sound I will most associate with New Orleans. It's not the hammering of nails or the whirring of drill bits through drywall, or a trumpeter's wail in the French Quarter. It's Antonio screaming.

We're at a new site in the Ninth Ward. I'm one of several volunteers working on the back of the house, first putting on primer, then paint. It's a two-story home, so I stand high on a ladder near the roof's peak, awkwardly painting around a power line connected to the house. I can hear the cable buzzing. There's no insulation, no protection, so the prospect of touching it and getting zapped with however many volts is real and a bit worrisome. Even more worrisome: getting zapped and falling twenty-five feet off a ladder. I would rather not die in a way that reminds witnesses of a Road Runner cartoon.

"It's not worth it," says Keith, who's painting below and watching me stretch to extend my brush around the cable. "No one can tell if you miss a spot."

He's right. But I keep thinking of Dad's favorite line—

Nothing is worth doing unless you're gonna do it right.

And so I keep straining. As I listen to the hum of the cables, I wonder if there's a secondary clause to Dad's statement—

Nothing is worth doing unless you're gonna do it right, or unless you're going to get electrocuted and fall twenty-five feet off a ladder.

I climb down, lug the ladder a bit closer to the cables, climb back up, then carefully paint around the power line connection. Dad, I hope, would be pleased.

After lunch, Antonio and I take a quick walk around the block. He delivers a few of our extra box lunches to workers at a house two doors down. The workers are gutting the place, and it's our first exposure to the rancid, rank, putrescent smell of out-of-control mold. The only scent I can compare it to is horseshit. Except more intense. Like extra-strength horseshit. From a really big horse.

When we return, Antonio and I clean out trash that's accumulated in the bedraggled side yard, the grass mangy and tall. We drop the small stuff in bags, drag the big stuff to the curb. The more trash we pull, the more we realize it's the muddy remnants of people's lives, carried here by the flood. A Playskool hammer. Assorted Tupperware containers and muddy cups. A black plastic ball from a kiddie bowling set.

Antonio rakes some of the trash out of tall, unruly weeds near the fence.

Which is when he screams.

He sliced an artery. That's my first thought. Or that he somehow impaled himself with the rake. The real reason for the scream isn't quite so terrifying: he smacked a plastic bowl while raking. The bowl is filled with funky, slimy brown water; the water sprayed his arms and face. It surprised him, and it stunk, almost as bad as the horseshitty mold. I don't blame him for screaming. To this day, Antonio won't even call it water. He was hit, he says, by a "liquid substance."

"I yelped like a little girl," he says back in the hotel that night. "I thought it was urine or toxic waste or some kind of bacteria-infested gunk."

But Antonio's yelp wasn't the cry of some trivial mishap, the *whoooaaa* you shout as you slip on ice or slam on brakes. This was a scream of terror. Like this "liquid substance" was a relic of the flood and the blood of the city's twelve hundred dead; the human waste and industrial waste possibly lurking in this morbid stew; like death itself was creeping in the water. Which, maybe, it was.

A bit melodramatic, perhaps. Maybe the scale of the devastation finally got to us. But this I know: I'll never forget the sound of that scream.

On our last workday, we help a family move back into their home. Most of the volunteers have left for the airport, so only a small group of stragglers remains. Antonio, Keith, Anna, and I ride in the back of a pickup driven by Brian, the Rebuilding Together guy. I take pictures as we cruise down Canal Street. Anna smiles beneath a baseball hat. Antonio flashes a peace sign.

Inside the house—a white shotgun home—Anna and I wipe the baseboards and walls, which are grungy from workers and work. Later, Antonio and I haul lingering trash to the street and load supplies in the truck to return to the warehouse: barrels of paint, brushes and rollers, assorted tools. When the moving truck arrives, we lug furniture and boxes inside. After Katrina, the family was displaced to Paris, Texas, and city residents donated this furniture.

"Really *sweet* furniture," Anna says, admiring the large framed Florentine paintings, the overstuffed tan sofa and armchairs, the bright decorative pillows.

Antonio and I carry a couch up the driveway. He backs in through the front door with one end, I walk up the concrete steps holding the other. We move gingerly, trying not to drip sweat on the upholstery or nick the newly painted walls inside. Voices echo as boxes and box springs, tables and chairs, mattresses and knick-knacks stream into the house; as volunteer contractors install a new toilet and sink.

As we move this family into their rebuilt home, my mom, back in Virginia, is sorting through Dad's things: sifting through closets and drawers, reviewing the objects of a life. The clothes were difficult. What if he comes back? If he comes back he'll need his clothes. She knows it's illogical, yet the clothes remain in the closet.

In a junk drawer of papers and coins, right below his sock drawer, she finds a six-page letter Dad had started, then stashed, six years earlier. She'll find several letters like this: monologues from long flights to Tokyo or when Mom was in Virginia visiting the grandkids. He'd jot down his thoughts, his feelings, then tuck them away. I never considered Dad a religious man—he seemed more interested in science than spirituality—but in his letter he invokes God and envisions his sudden death.

My dear family,

I always fear that someday the Lord will suddenly call for me and I will not have told you how much I love you. I guess I worry because that is exactly what happened with my own mother and father. So, I love all of you so much. I often pray to the Lord to let me carry your burdens, give you good health, and happiness. I also ask Him to allow you the opportunity to use your talents for the good of the world. All I ask of you is to be your best and do your best. Always look at the other side— often you don't fully understand things unless you put yourself in the other person's shoes.

I tried to do my best here in New Orleans, though I'm under no delusions that our red and blue teams contributed much in five short days. What New Orleans needed after Katrina was a bayou Marshall Plan. What it got instead, largely, was people like me and Anna and Antonio. Eager volunteers with noble intentions. But the solution is inadequate for the problem, as inadequate as the flood-walls against Katrina's waves.

Our greatest contribution is simply being here, spending money, seeing the problems, showing that people care. The day I scraped paint, sweating in the humid heat and wondering if my efforts really mattered, I told myself this: If someone doesn't scrape, the house doesn't get painted. If the house doesn't get painted, the house doesn't get finished. If the house doesn't get finished, the owner doesn't move back in. If the owner doesn't move back in, he or she is still homeless—and Rebuilding Together can't proceed to a new project.

I always fear that someday the Lord will suddenly call for me.

I often pray to the Lord to let me carry your burdens.

On the day Dad died, I was at my sister's house when the hospital called.

We can't keep the body, a woman told me. Where should the body go?

All day: questions. About an autopsy. Casket. Death notice. Burial plot. And then another call.

"Do you want to donate your father's organs," a hospital administrator asked. "We need to know."

I lowered the phone to my chest.

"Who is it," Mom asked from my sister's kitchen table.

"The hospital. They want to know about Dad's organs."

She started crying.

"I can't deal with that," she said, shaking her head. "I can't deal with that."

"I'll call you back," I told the administrator.

I never did. And I've always regretted it. I wish we had created something good from something bad. That's what I hoped to do here in New Orleans: channel grief into action. Worthy action. As simple as lugging trash.

All I ask of you is to be your best and do your best.

Use your talents for the good of the world.

I land in D.C. the next day and throw my bag in the backseat of Julie's car. We kiss. She asks about the trip, and I tell her I painted ceilings and helped install a floor (I don't tell her I shattered a lamp). I'm glad I went, I say. I'm glad I offered my labor and limited skills to three resilient families, because it's impossible to walk the Lower Ninth Ward's barren neighborhoods, to see the spray-painted rants and muddy scars, and not feel changed. To not feel humbled, and angry, and baffled, and sad.

We drive home, a route we've taken many times before. I'm not sure what's next. Sometimes, in life, you can drive a familiar road and still not know where you're going.

PART TWO

Costa Rica

Teaching English—and learning about life—at Escuela Cuestillas.

A BREEZE TICKLES SCRUFFY grass, the turf tough from soccer games and small feet. Palm trees and fruit trees shade tin roofs. It's our first day teaching English at Escuela Cuestillas, an elementary school in rural Costa Rica, and Julie and I are screwed, so very, very screwed, though we don't know it yet as we walk from the gravel road to a one-level building, home to six rooms and 110 students, most from low-income families, many of them Nicaraguan immigrants.

Children in uniforms—short-sleeve white dress shirts, blue pants—descend on us as we walk: they are whispering, giggling, inspecting the gringos. We're escorted into the center classroom by Maria, the local program director for Cross-Cultural Solutions (CCS), our volunteer organization. The cinder-block school seems tidy and well kept, though this particular room is like a long-neglected garage. A discarded couch and dinged-up file cabinets are stashed against the walls. The chalkboard has a large, scablike hole. Centered above it is a gold-framed painting of Jesus and what I assume is God—white beard, flowing robes, air of confidence—though neither is identified, not that identification is necessary: Roman Catholicism is Costa Rica's official religion.

Grinning children, third graders (I think), sit in groups of three and four, fidgeting and snickering behind benchlike desks, staring at us with tiny, curious eyes. Maria introduces us in Spanish. We stand in the humid room, already sweating—I have no clue what she's telling them—and I wonder . . . where, exactly, is the teacher we're assisting?

The kids pull pencils and papers from backpacks; we talk with them as best we can given our very limited Spanish. Maria hangs with us a bit, then wishes us luck. We watch her walk back to the waiting van. We watch the van turn around, dust rising behind it. And that's when we realize it. We *are* the teachers.

We gaze at each other, Julie and I, just for an instant—there's too much noise and too many boisterous children—but our thoughts are the same.

We are so, so screwed.

Over the next two weeks, as we scramble to develop multiple lesson plans for multiple classes, as we learn new Spanish phrases for high-energy children (*Por favor, siéntense*—"Sit down, please"), as we struggle to ensure that we don't make their limited English *worse*, I'll think back to the day we arrived, to a young woman we met at the airport. She was a fellow volunteer, overweight, frizzy-haired, no more than twenty years old; so uncomfortable she stood out, though wanting only to blend in. About twenty volunteers arrived the same day, and we congregated on a busy sidewalk outside the terminal in the capital city of San José, chatting, introducing ourselves, ignoring the calls of taxi drivers, waiting for other volunteers to land before riding to Ciudad Quesada, the town where we're staying.

The young woman stood with crossed arms across her big belly, rubbing her left elbow with her right hand, a sad, scared look that said—

Oh shit oh shit oh shit—I've made a HUGE mistake—oh shit oh shit . . .

Maybe it was the two-hour tummy-churning, winding van ride over swooping green hills, through rusted-tin and stray-dog towns.

Maybe it was the afternoon downpour, which lingered into a soggy, sloggy night. Maybe it was the skinny, bubbly college-age women who fill the dormlike home where we'll stay. But the next morning, after hours of traveling—flying from the U.S. to Costa Rica, waiting at the airport, driving to Ciudad Quesada—the overweight girl with the overwhelmed look was gone. On her way back to the airport. On her way back home. Before any of us had eaten breakfast. She spent more time traveling *to* the town than she spent *in* the town.

On more than one occasion, when Julie and I are at the school, I'll wonder if she was the smartest one of us all.

I can't tell Julie that coming here was a mistake, because coming here was my idea. Julie knew from her medical stint in Haiti how exhausting these gigs can be. But I cheerfully spouted info from the CCS website: We'll only work in the mornings! We'll have our afternoons free! We'll be good people!

Unlike Julie, who'll work here for two weeks and then immediately return to her job, I'm off for six weeks. Around the time I went to New Orleans, my employer introduced a "renewal" program: after seven years of service to the organization you can take a four-week leave, fully paid, and add up to two weeks of vacation time. Given my new I-could-die-instantly-like-Dad approach to life, I signed up fast, determined to do something meaningful, though never believing I'd embarked on some larger quest. I certainly didn't return from New Orleans three months earlier and think—

I've got it! I'll be a daring do-gooder spreading happy fairy dust on every place I visit . . .

But I *was* formulating an idea that maybe, as a man without children—if that indeed is my destiny—I should use my time for activities other than reading the sports page and watching *South Park*. Both of which are happy pursuits, just not the achievements you want in your eulogy ("And so we remember Ken as a man who watched a lot of television . . ."). Plus . . . Julie and I need this trip. Travel is our spark. We rediscover one another away from home, where I sometimes fear we live separate lives. She takes classes, goes on dog walks with her sister and our infant nephew; I drift deeper into my what-am-I-doing-with-myself cocoon.

"It's like you're in your own world," she once told me, "and I'm not invited in."

We were so close in the months after Dad's death. As close as we've ever been. And now . . . distance. Distance I've created. Distance from loving my life with her and hating the life I'll never have.

The CCS house, alas, is unlikely to reignite passion. Julie and I are sleeping in bunk beds. Bunk beds are cool if you're four, ridiculous if you're forty, which is why no steamy romance novel has ever included the line *Descend the little ladder to the bottom bunk so I may ravish you.*

Our room is the size of a walk-in closet, with just enough space for the bunk bed, a few shelves, and a floor fan. I can stand in the middle of the room, extend my arms, and touch two of the walls, though I'm not complaining—we're thrilled to have a room to ourselves. The house is overloaded with people, this being August, a peak time for college student volunteers. (Right now: around fifty volunteers. In two weeks: fourteen volunteers.)

After a blast of Costa Rican coffee and an energizing breakfast—fresh rolls, scrambled eggs, local pineapple so good it'll make you cry—we take a first-morning stroll through town. Ciudad Quesada is not a destination; it's a launching point for destinations more interesting than Ciudad Quesada. The town has everything you need—clothing, appliances, groceries—but outside of the sweet fresh-bread smell of the *panaderías* (bakeries) and the shady green square in the center of town, Ciudad Quesada is more functional than charming. Which is not to say I don't grow fond of it. The people are friendly. Sunsets flare pink and red behind green mountains. The nearby land is rich with streams and cattle-filled pastures. Visitors do not outnumber the thirty-five thousand residents. I never see any Americans or Europeans other than CCS volunteers (locals call the CCS house "the gringo house").

That afternoon we attend a mandatory orientation led by Juan, CCS's country director. He explains the program's rules. Everyone washes and dries their own dishes after meals. Volunteers are forbidden to drink alcohol in Ciudad Quesada, not even wine: CCS doesn't want its local image tarnished by drunken, barfing foreigners. You get caught with a joint, a beer, a shot, probably even NyQuil—you're gone. (After Julie and I return home, one long-term volunteer—I'm convinced he's a fugitive hiding from the FBI—is kicked out for smoking pot and, oddly enough, for wearing another volunteer's clothes.)

So this trip isn't for the room service, cocktails-with-little-umbrellas crowd. Personally, I like the spare accommodations. This is what I wanted in New Orleans. "Most people come to Costa Rica, they never see the real country," says Juan. "They leave their air-conditioned plane, they get on an air-conditioned bus, they go to an air-conditioned resort." Not us. We will eat like locals, work like locals, and—the worrisome part—try to teach the local children.

After discovering that we're the teachers, which is like some schmuck who can make toast suddenly running a restaurant, the first hour of our first day goes surprisingly well. We review the alphabet, numbers, nouns; I hold up flash cards with one group and they shout the words with gusto.

Blue card—*Blue!!*

Green card—*Green!!*

Brown card—*Red!!*—*Green!!*—*Blue!!*—*Uhhhh . . .*

We're assessing their English skills. They can count, as high as one hundred in some cases, and they know basic nouns, but they don't know verbs, so they can't string words into sentences. They have English workbooks, though we never use them—one workbook will be nearly completed and another barely used, so we're not sure where to start—which is unfortunate since we quickly exhaust our limited bag of teacher tricks.

"Let's have them write their names on the board," says Julie, resorting to educational improv.

Yes—perfect. We teach them "My name is" and they write with chalk—

My name is Enrique
My name is Tabitha
My name is Carlos . . .

Which kills about ten minutes.

Shit.

"Maybe they can write their birthdays," I say.

They do that as well. Our blackboard activities work okay at first, but then one child wants to play tic-tac-toe, which leads to sudden swarms of children drawing tic-tac-toe grids. I play multiple games at once. Bend down and write an *X*. Straighten up and write an *O*. Turn right and write an *X*. As Julie says later, "We need more structured activities—otherwise they're gonna run us over."

By the end of the morning, a few scary facts are apparent:

Scary Fact #1

Because we'll be teaching three different age groups, we'll need to develop three different lesson plans. What works for second graders—say, drawing pictures—won't work for sixth graders.

Scary Fact #2

No one at the school speaks English. Not the principal, not the other teachers. So we can't ask for help. We can't ask for insights. We can't ask for mercy.

Scary Fact #3

Our class isn't really a class. It's more like an English club—and a forty-minute quasi break. Some students attend every day. Some pop in and out. It's chaos.

Scary Fact #4

We have no idea what we're doing.

At the end of the morning, as the children leave for lunch, a little sandy-blond girl with pigtails walks up and hugs me around my leg. She smiles and waves, clutching the backpack that fits snug against her tiny back as she skips out the door. And then another girl hugs me. And another one. Julie gets hugs as well. Well, at least they like us.

I find it surreal that I'm suddenly a teacher, given that twenty years earlier I was kicked out of college. Suspended, actually. For nine months. It was George Mason University's way of saying, "You should take some time off and really reflect on what a dipshit you are."

The suspension was one of the few things in life I'd actually earned, because attaining a 1.91 GPA requires a level of laziness and indifference that most responsible people lack. Some students graduate magna cum laude; I was magna cum quat: a pathological procrastinator who never studied and rarely attended class. As a sophomore, I tried to learn an entire semester of accounting ten hours before the final exam (which would be my entire grade since I hadn't attended class in three months). Around midnight, after channel surfing for, oh, two hours, I downed some NoDoz and a few cans of Mountain Dew, opened the fat red textbook for the first time in months, and said to myself—out loud—in a pep-talk tone, "Okay—it's time to learn accounting."

About 5:30 a.m. I realized I was *not* going to learn accounting in time for the exam. It was the only thing I got right all day.

My lack of motivation would make more sense if I were a pot-head or a crack addict (I've often thought of saying I was a crack addict because it sounds like a better explanation). But I was simply uninterested. As early as elementary school, a series of teachers made the same disappointed comment: "Kenny isn't living up to his potential."

All of which logically culminated in my suspension from college. And the worst part was knowing I had to call Dad. When *he* was twenty, he was a new husband, a new father, working two jobs to support his family, and taking his correspondence course at night.

You can do anything in life if you work hard enough. Dad said this repeatedly to me and my sister when we were young. I had twisted this—

You can fail at anything in life if you're lazy enough.

I called him the next day. I was on the east coast, he was on the west. His secretary, Susie, answered the phone. "Bob Budd's office . . ." If I was lucky he'd be in a meeting. A *long* meeting. I could leave a message with Susie: "Yeah—just tell him I've been suspended from college for nine months and I have no immediate plans."

Please be in a meeting. Please, please, please.

"He's here," Susie chirped. "Hang on a minute."

She transferred the call.

"Budo," he said. "What's up."

"I have a problem," I said.

He stayed silent as I explained, feebly, that I had attained con-secutive "less than satisfactory" performances. That I was forbidden from enrolling for two academic periods. That my classes would be canceled for the spring semester, my parents' money refunded.

That the word *suspended* would be imprinted forever on my record like an academic cattle brand.

A weighty cross-country silence sat between us.

"Well," he said finally. "What's the next step?"

That was it. No lecture. Just . . . how we do move forward.

When Dad was a boy, his family moved constantly, uprooted when the rent came due, drifting through shabby homes and small Virginia towns. They moved from Delaplane to Middleburg, from Middleburg to The Plains, from The Plains to Marshall, from Marshall to The Plains—all in one year. He was quiet, shy from the moves, hiding when family visited, eating his dinner outside.

At the age of seven, he attended seven different schools in one year. Imagine always being the new kid, always ahead or behind the class. It could make you angry, or bored, or defiant, but Dad always swore it made him strong. On the day I told him about my suspension, it was never clearer to me: He *was* strong. I was weak. I was a fuckup. And I'd never really viewed myself that way.

After I was kicked out of college, I worked two jobs, including a sales gig at an electronics store. Selling batteries and widgets for minimum wage was a sobering experience, and though Julie and I hadn't yet discussed marriage, it occurred to me that she might not want to spend the rest of her life with a widget salesman. Perhaps, I thought, while vacuuming the store's worn carpet at closing time, a college degree might have its benefits. And so I went back to college. I graduated. And a few years later, I took night classes to get my master's degree—earning straight A's—mainly to prove I could do it. To prove I had just a whiff of my father's fortitude.

Full from lunchtime beans and rice, motivated by fear, Julie and I walk to an Internet café in town and scan a kiddie-song website. Music, we've decided, is a fun, loud, active way to engage the children while teaching them English. So we scroll the online list, jotting down songs with potential. "Eensy, Weensy Spider." "Old MacDonald." "The Hokey Pokey." Julie clicks on "If You're Happy and You Know It." We read the bubbly lyrics; she hums the impossible-to-forget tune.

If you're happy and you know it clap your hands (clap clap) . . .

"It might be fun to teach it wrong," I say.

If you're crappy and you know it take a pill (gulp gulp) . . .

"You're so helpful," she says.

One song is a definite: "Head, Shoulders, Knees, and Toes." First off, it's easy—the lyrics to "Head, Shoulders, Knees, and Toes" are "Head, shoulders, knees, and toes"—and it involves movement (touching your head, shoulders, knees, and toes). Most of the kids already know the tune: it's to international English classrooms what "Take Me Out to the Ball Game" is to baseball stadiums.

"Ooo—click on that one," I say, pointing at the screen. It's "On Top of Spaghetti," one of my childhood favorites. Cheeses and sneezes, a mushed meatball that grows into a tree . . . *this*, to me, is poetry.

Julie sings a line softly, in a silly cartoonish voice.

The tree was all covered, all covered with moss . . .

I join her, quietly, to avoid the stares of the far-more-serious-looking Costa Rican Web users.

And on it grew meatballs, all covered with sauce.

That evening, back at the house, full from a rice-and-beans dinner, we're still figuring out our lesson plans, sitting at one of the long cafeteria-style tables in the outdoor group dining area. A steady rain raps the roof. Julie has ideas: a word search puzzle, fill-in-the-blank phrases. Two other volunteers are working on plans as well, assisted by Hannah, a loud and lively forty-year-old Spanish teacher from New Jersey. We listen in—and beg her to help us when she's done.

She sits across from us a few minutes later, asks about our classes, then churns out advice. "Make things active and funny," she says. "Do either/or stuff. Point at one of the kids and say, 'Is this a boy or a girl?' 'Is this a desk or a dog?' 'Is this a pencil or a house?' And you've got songs, right? Good. Sing songs." She looks at our list. " 'The Hokey Pokey.' Perfect. Lets them move around. You could also give them cards with words on them and have them put the card on the object."

It's a ten-minute teaching tutorial that sparks ideas and boosts our shaky confidence. As I write down her suggestions, our new hero bemoans our situation.

"I don't know why the fuck you got put in that class without any help," she says. "I mean, you don't even speak the same fucking language as the other teachers."

The fucking amazing Hannah has entered our lives.

When I saw Hannah for the first time, wearing white sun-glasses with rhinestones and demonstrating tae kwon do moves—*Turn! Spin! Thrust! Kick!*—I assumed I would *not* be spending a lot of time with this woman. She's my opposite even more than Antonio was in New Orleans: four feet, eleven inches of raised-in-Queens toughness and relentless energy who never fails to shock with her jaw-dropping honesty about every intimacy in her loco life. In an atmosphere oozing with earthy PC earnestness, Hannah pines for her battery-operated boyfriend, shares every emotion in every moment—"I'm shvitzing from the fucking heat"—and drops f-bombs like a comedian at a Friars Club roast.

After the first-day orientation, Julie and I went for a quick swim at a nearby pool. Hannah joined us, as did Jonathan, another member of the very exclusive volunteers-over-the-age-of-forty club. Jonathan lives in Birmingham, England; he recently took a buyout after twenty-eight years as a communications officer for a bank. Coming here was a once-in-a-lifetime opportunity to tackle the unknown and help others—"I wanted to be selfless instead of selfish," he told me. So he's here for twelve weeks, away from his partner, William, who's back home.

The four of us entered the cool water, wading more than swimming, laughing as Hannah told stories about her foulmouthed students, introducing us to teenage terms like *snowballing*. (Which, let's just say, involves oral sex, and the transfer of certain bodily fluids from the giver to the receiver, and back to the giver.) Jonathan, already the droll counterpart to the talkative Hannah, recoiled in mock horror: "OH my *God* . . ."

We exited the pool, and a dripping little girl with a towel over her shoulders talked to Jonathan and Hannah, who are both fluent in Spanish. They erupted in laughter.

"She wants to know if we're married," Hannah said, giggling.

From that moment forth, Jonathan and Hannah *were* married. "Where is my husband," Hannah says repeatedly. They become a unit, talking serious when alone, talking dirty when they're with us; joking, hugging, quarreling, and insulting each other, often at the same time.

"I'd like to grow my hair longer, but I don't want to look like a whore," Hannah says one evening.

"You don't need long hair to look like a whore, darling," Jonathan replies.

"Fuck you, you fuck. You're not my husband anymore."

In our classroom hangs a banner made from a bedsheet, a project led by college students who taught here a few weeks before. "Never

Give Up" is painted in Spanish and English, surrounded by the children's handprints in yellow, blue, and red. The intent, I assume, was to inspire the kiddies, but to me it's a cotton billboard trumpeting our inadequacies, since there's no way in hell we'll undertake something similar (although Julie encourages my "Always Give In" alternatives). Our goal, inspired by Hannah's tutelage, is to offer fun but effective lessons—simple pub grub rather than flashy nouvelle cuisine. And the children seem to like what we're serving, whether they're supposed to be in our class or not (and we're not always sure).

Our first class of students—we think they're about eight years old—are eager and businesslike. Tabitha, a round-cheeked Nicaraguan girl, becomes one of our favorites. She's always ready to laugh, like she just *knows* something funny is about to happen. After class she stays in the room, talking to us, giggling frequently. We can usually figure out what she's saying, though in some cases, as with all the kids, I consult the English-Spanish dictionary, scrolling the page for the word.

Tabitha is smart. We ask the children to draw their families, and label them in English: mother, father, uncle, etc. A few children draw unlabeled stick figures. In Tabitha's drawing the people are bigger, bolder, more defined. She labels everyone in English *and* Spanish. One morning she asks me my age—one of the few sentences I can quickly translate—and I make a frowny face, whisper my age in her ear, then hobble about like a geezer with a cane. She laughs, shakes her head no, walks to the board where Julie had written numbers and points at "30."

See? Smart kid.

Tabitha and the other children play intense soccer games during breaks. "Teacher, teacher!" they yell, waving me to the field. I'm the goalie, presumably because they'd rather run and slide and knock the snot out of their classmates than stand and defend the goal. They play rougher than overprotective parents and teachers would allow back home. Not mean or vicious, just physical, running in sock feet, I assume to reduce kick-related bruises and broken bones. The boys unbutton their white uniform shirts and fling them in the grass, playing in their undershirts.

My goalie skills are roughly equivalent to my teaching skills, and a few shots zip past my long arms for goals. One comes from Adrian, a terrifically smart boy and gifted goal scorer. He's the type of student—brains, athletic ability, good looks—about whom, even though he's eight, I think: I should remember this kid's name because someday he's going to be Costa Rica's first combination President/Soccer MVP/Astronaut/Movie Star/Nobel Prize Winner.

Adrian blasts a shot past my outstretched foot, and a little boy approaches as I retrieve the ball. I toss it to him, but he holds it, waiting as I walk. His Spanish is rapid, so I can't understand, but I sense he's suggesting a few improvements to my game, along the lines of "Listen—I realize you're American, I know soccer isn't your game, but dude, seriously—you have *got* to do better than this."

I agree with whatever he's saying, even though I don't know what he's saying.

"*Sí, sí, sí,*" I reply.

"When a player is dribbling toward you, don't just stand here— charge him. Cut down the angle—make yourself big."

"*Ahhhhh—sí, sí, sí . . .*"

He appears to be Nicaraguan. Many Nicaraguans migrated south to Costa Rica in the 1980s, escaping their war-battered country, searching for stability and prosperity, but finding poverty still hard to escape. Soccer goals, perhaps, are one thing he can control.

A community of Nicaraguan immigrants live in a nearby shantytown called Bajo de Meco. On a day when the schools are closed—Virgen de los Angeles Day, celebrating the country's patron saint—Julie and I go with eleven other volunteers to play with the kids. Bajo de Meco is a rural dirt road village, each home a square hodgepodge of discarded plywood and rusted metal scraps.

The CCS van chugs down a steep road, the mountains leafy and wet before us. As we squeeze out of the van, the children run to us, smiling and squealing. We walk to a dirt square, a former trash dump recently cleared of brush and debris by CCS. Julie notices occasional bits of broken glass.

The square is now a makeshift playground, blessed with the shade of a few tall trees. Andrew, a CCS staffer, unloads a burlap bag of outdoor toys. The result is semi-organized mayhem: a dodgeball game intersects a soccer game; the soccer ball zips past kids on a tree swing; the swinging kids nearly nail the soccer players. Tennis balls whiz by kids and volunteers playing pattycake. Remarkably, collisions are few.

I throw a football with a shirtless boy named Julio. We imitate each other—when I throw it high, he throws it high—and we're soon sucked into the vortex of games, Julio switching to soccer, me moving to baseball. Julio's sister, who insists we call her Chicken Little, rests a plastic bat against her shoulder, surveying her would-be players and then deciding, like a manager plotting strategy, that instead of Chicken Little we should call her Garfield. Satisfied with her irreverence—which seems to interest her more than baseball—she names me Rambo.

Garfield organizes a system. I, Rambo, am the pitcher. Heather, an eighteen-year-old from Oregon whom Garfield dubs "Cheemah," is the catcher. The kids each get five at-bats, and when they're not swinging they're fielding, which is helpful, because a tennis ball smacked into tropical brush is hard to find, especially when your brush-clearing machete is a plastic bat.

After pitching for two hours to seemingly every child in Central America, I join Julie, who's been playing dodgeball, for a neighborhood tour with some of the volunteers. A few children join us, kindergarten age, holding our hands as we walk past puddles in the pocked dirt road. The neighborhood has no electricity. No running water. The patched-together houses cling to green hillsides on wood supports.

The poverty rate in Costa Rica, Andrew tells us, is under 20 percent, which is pretty good compared to its neighbors (in Nicaragua it's 48 percent). Costa Rica is essentially the Switzerland of Central America: the military was abolished after a coup in 1949, allowing the government to invest in health care and education. Nicaraguans now make up about 20 percent of the country's population, leading to increasing complaints about illegal immigrants. More than once we hear lighter-skinned Costa Ricans note, with a hint of matter-of-fact smugness, that Nicaraguans are darker.

The men of Bajo de Meco work mainly on nearby cattle and sugar farms. Because this particular land was useless for ranching or agriculture, squatters built shacks, and the landowner, a Señor Meco, Ciudad Quesada's richest man, never got around to kicking them out. Drugs, alcohol, and prostitution are common, and in an unfortunate cycle, the children often grow up to repeat their parents' lives. And yet as we walk, everyone smiles at us and nods. The children laugh. And as Julie notices, for a community with no electricity or water—and kids who get *really* dirty—the clothesline laundry is clean, the school shirts a sparkling white as they flap in the breeze.

In addition to Rambo, I gain another name in Costa Rica: Lord Kenneth of Fairfax. James, a thirty-four-year-old Brit who's volunteering for twelve weeks, tells me that Kenneth is a fine English name. He dubs me a lord, which means, he says, I'll need a country estate, a pipe, a hunting rifle, a tweed suit, and a manservant. Oh—and some "below-stairs staff," as he calls them.

James served in the Royal Air Force, in logistics, for seven years, and he remains a loyal subject of the British Crown, reserving a nook in the CCS kitchen for brewing proper English tea. When Hannah prods him to speak "normal fucking English" like her, he's royally defiant.

"The Queen's English will always prevail! In every corner of the globe there is always a piece of England!"

I do my best to encourage him. After awarding himself the title "Lord Juan of San Carlos"—the region where we're staying—he announces he'll write a royal decree instructing all residents of the CCS house that they are now loyal servants of the Crown. And that any inappropriate acts from the common ranks will be punishable by public flogging in the square followed by forceful consumption of rice and beans.

James is Jonathan's roommate, as well as his workmate: they work together two days a week at a recycling center run by local women, and three days in a class for troubled teens (where they wrap a condom over a cucumber while teaching sex ed). I assume they're paired together because they're English—they'd never met before arriving here—but apparently someone in CCS thought they were a couple. This bothers the heterosexual James less than Jonathan's disinterest in him physically.

"Why don't you fancy me?" says James.

"You're just not my type."

"You mean you don't find me attractive?"

"I'm sure plenty of women find you attractive. You're just not the type of man I fancy."

James is recently divorced, and this is the perfect place to be single: he's one of just three unattached heterosexual men among roughly forty-five college-age, earthily attractive single women. Over time, several women will offer to serve as short-term volunteers in the privacy of James's room, if you know what I mean.

James is also a master of the word-guessing game Taboo, which we find on a shelf in the main area of the CCS house. If you've never played Taboo, one person holds a card with a word on it. That person—in this case James—helps other players guess the word without actually using the word, or five other related words on the card.

We warp the game so every word is sexual. Why this happened, I don't recall, though I'm sure Hannah talked about missing Bob (her battery-operated boyfriend) and how much she interacts with Bob in a given week, and Jonathan said "OH my *God . . .*" and Hannah informed us that she and Bob are close because she hasn't had sex in nine months, and Jonathan suggested that this perhaps led to a marked decrease in New Jersey's venereal disease rate, and Hannah told Jonathan, "You are *such* a fucking asshole."

"This is a movie title," James announces, reading a Taboo card. "So this gent goes round to the pharmacy and buys some Viagra, because he's meeting a woman that night. And things go well—they go out to dinner—and later on he gets lucky and takes a Viagra. But then, during sex, he has a heart attack. And he keels over, right there in the bed, right during the sex."

We never guess the answer: *Die Hard.*

Our own perverted entertainment aside, CCS offers a variety of education sessions for volunteers, from Spanish classes to lectures on Costa Rican history to Wednesday afternoon field trips (including a visit to the Arenal volcano). As part of our cultural education, a woman who works at a nearby diner offers dance lessons. We fold up tables in the outdoor dining area to make room, and she winks and grins as she demonstrates salsa moves, her black hair bouncing, hips and shoulders shimmying to Latin boom-box music. As one of only two straight male participants—James is the other—I feel obligated to say that watching this woman dance is worth the expense of flying to Costa Rica.

About thirty of us stand behind her in five cramped rows. We're supposed to start with feet apart—open—then bring them together, moving to the left. She shouts instructions as she dances—

Open center center TAP

Open center center TAP

She adds a spin move—

Center TURN center TURN

From my back row perch I watch our attempts to mimic her sultry moves, and I'm impressed by how truly, truly awful we are. We look like narcotized robots. And our outdoor dining space wasn't designed for a large group to salsa dance: when we sashay to the right—I'm on the end of the back row—I run out of real estate well before we're done *center centering*, and since I'm watching my feet I barrel into the wall with a thud.

Our sizzling salsa teacher is oblivious, her back to us, sliding to the left, then to the right, as if the dance gods created Latin music and tight Levi's just for her. We're all drenched in sweat—I was sweating before we even started—yet she's pleasingly dry despite her long-sleeve sweater. We trudge behind her to the left, then lurch to the right.

Open center center TAP

Center TURN center TURN

It's a ceramic tile floor, and a back corner tile is loose, with some sort of pipe underneath. When I drop my foot for the *tap* it makes a *thwock* noise, which complements the thud as I hit the wall.

Open center center THUD

Center THWOCK! *center* THWOCK!

James, already a reluctant participant, smartly leaves his row and takes a seat. "It's like a bloody marching drill," he says.

Our teacher finally turns and sees our zombie dance team, her face a mix of sorrow and shock. Like seeing a pack of dogs pee on your favorite flower bed.

Our dancing may suck, but Julie and I are performing somewhat better at the school. Julie created a word search puzzle by hand, focusing on verbs, which the students devoured. A few even find a mistake: the word *read* appears twice.

I enjoy watching Julie with Roberto. He's a sweet, pudgy kid, not the brightest student at the school, but one of the friendliest. Roberto frequently lobbies Julie to play Go Fish with our deck of English-Spanish flash cards. The problem is that none of the cards match. And yet Julie still plays Go Fish with him, flipping through all sixty or so cards, appearing interested as Roberto holds up a picture of a fork.

"No," says Julie, checking her cards. "I don't have a fork. Do you have this?"

It's a card with a chicken. Nope—Roberto doesn't have a chicken.

Baseball?

No.

Umbrella?

No.

Clock?

No.

Because of our inadequate Spanish, she can't say to him: *Hey, Roberto—this is pointless. The cards DON'T MATCH.*

Finally, mercifully, they sift through the entire stack. And then Roberto tugs Julie's shirt and holds up the stack of cards. He wants to play again.

It's been enlightening to see Julie—to see us—pulled from our usual roles like the shuffled cards; to observe the person I know best in a new environment. To see her creativity. Her patience. She's so wonderful with children. Always has been. Watching her write and draw with the young girls, showing them how to make a cat's cradle with yarn . . . at times like these our childless life is a mystery to me.

Many of the kids, particularly the girls, ask if Julie is *mi esposa*— my wife. I say yes, fan my face, sigh dreamily. The girls cup their hands over their mouths and giggle. One day, after class finishes, Tabitha speaks to me in Spanish. She's asking, I think, if Julie and I have children. I grab a piece of chalk and draw male and female stick figures on the board. One is me and one is Julie. I draw a little kiddie stick figure next to us and point.

"*Yo tengo?*" I say.

I have?

She nods.

No, I say.

Tabitha thinks, then points at the chalkboard child. If we have a child, she says, and we have a girl, we could name her Tabitha.

Two days after national holiday number one is national holiday number two: Día de la Madre ("Mother's Day"), the Feast of the Assumption. Millions of people, we're told, walk to Cartago, east of San José, to see the apparition of the Virgin. With the schools closed again, we return to Bajo de Meco, Garfield waving as I squeeze my long legs out of the van. She again calls me Rambo, which leads to a chorus of greetings from the kids.

Hola Rambo!

Heyyyyy Rambo!

Rambo! Rambo! Rambo!

I spend most of my time playing baseball with a young boy. We play for close to two hours: I throw the tennis ball, he whacks it with a plastic bat. Over and over and over in the sticky heat, the ball slicing through mud puddles with each energetic swing. I'm pleased to say he gets tired first (I am Rambo, after all). He pats his stomach, runs to one of the patchwork shacks, and returns with a banana. I squat before him in the dirt road.

"*¿Como se llama?*" I ask.

"Rafael," he says.

He asks me my name. I tell him. I want to tell him what a good athlete he is: he rarely missed a pitch.

"*Tu juegas béisbol muy bien,*" I say in my meager Spanish.

He *beams*. It almost catches me off guard—his grin and his puffed-out chest—though this is one of the reasons we're here: to offer encouragement to those who rarely receive it. But somehow it seems so inadequate. I've never seen poverty this extreme. I suppose that's why the shirts sparkle on the clothesline. The people own nothing else. When we pull our bag of sports equipment from the van, you can tell the kids are thinking, *Holy shit . . . they have TEN-NIS BALLS*. And yet by global shantytown standards, I'm sure this is quite nice. The Bel Air of shantytowns.

Later I ask Mauricio, the program director, why we went to Bajo de Meco. Sure, we brought some morning fun to the kids, but how is that helpful?

"These children have no idea why they're there," Mauricio explains. "They never saw the war that drove their parents away. They've never seen their country and they don't know why they've been stigmatized for leaving there. They grow up feeling that they are not important; that it's normal to be pushed away or ignored.

"In our society, especially in rural areas, the highest social status is a gringo. Americans are considered wealthy and knowledgeable—which makes them important. Sending volunteers to this neighborhood has an effect on the adults, the other people in the community, and the children. Those children deserve to see something different than what they know. They need to understand that another way of living is possible. When all they've seen is that neighborhood, no one can blame them for not aspiring to something better. But when they feel important, welcomed, and acknowledged by others—especially those they consider important—it enhances their self-esteem. And it's a reminder to other community members—who know the gringos are visiting Bajo de Meco—that these children exist and they need someone to give them better opportunities."

When we toured Bajo de Meco, a little barefoot girl showed off a pet parrot. Several of the residents own birds. Maria tells Julie they catch the birds in the forest, then clip their wings so they can't fly away.

On Fridays after lunch, volunteers race out of the CCS house like soldiers with a weekend pass. It's your big chance to leave town and see the country, so we hire a local driver and travel with Hannah, Jonathan, James, and six others in a van for a weekend jaunt to an isolated cloud forest town called Monteverde.

Sure, it's a five-hour drive, but who cares! We're free! We can drink a beer! We're on an adventure! Woo hoo! And we sustain that merry mood for two laugh-filled hours until traffic stops on a narrow, twisty-turny rain forest mountain road.

We sit. Wide fern leaves press against the windows and roof. We sit some more. Marco, our driver, asks a few passersby what's happening. Hannah translates. Workers are replacing drainage pipes in a stream, which means a single-lane earth bridge has been obliterated. Why they picked a Friday afternoon for such work, I'm not sure.

We exit the van to stretch. A steam shovel covers two new concrete pipes with dirt and rocks, moving boulders on both sides to support them, then leveling them out and packing them in. Pedestrians stand within a few feet of the dinosaur-like machine as it loads and unloads boulders. James and I watch, then get soaked by a sudden downpour. It's the first time I've felt cool in a week.

After two long hours, the bridge is rebuilt. Traffic starts to move. Three hours to go. What we don't realize is that of two possible routes to Monteverde, our driver has chosen the longer, more scenic, yet far more roundabout route around Lake Arenal, instead of the shorter, still fairly scenic, less roundabout bypass. So that adds to our travel time. As does temporarily getting lost.

We stop at a pizza joint in a tiny, bustling-because-it's-Friday-night town, then embark on the most rugged stretch of the drive. The closer you get to Monteverde, the more ragged the roads become: a lunar-style mix of craters, gravel, and softball-sized rocks. For two hours we bump, bump, bump up the mountains, our rowdy banter silenced. Moods, and stomachs, turn sour. Heads bounce. James's seat squeaks. Twilight becomes night, the headlights squinting through dust, and still we crawl up the rocky road. It's like a two-hour earthquake on wheels.

Bump, bump, BUMP, bump . . .

Cindy, a twenty-six-year-old from England, announces that she *really* needs to pee. But Marco the driver doesn't speak English, and Hannah and Jonathan don't translate. Maybe they can't hear given the creaks and squeaks of the bouncing van, the thumps and grinds of the tires over stones.

A queasy James lowers his head out the window.

"I *really* have to go to the toilet," Cindy moans.

Bump, bump, BUMP, bump . . .

I begin to wonder if this is what hell is like: a never-ending claustrophobic ride in an old van with bad shocks on a bad road with a guy who might throw up and a woman who might have an accident, assuming that the van doesn't have one first.

"I'll go anywhere," she begs. "I can't hold on any longer."

After forty-five minutes of pee pleas, we pull over. Women scramble through darkness and cloud forest mist to crouch behind bushes on the side of the pitted gravel road. The men are less worried about privacy.

We get back in the van. "These are worse than the roads in Haiti," Julie says as we return to our now very familiar seats.

Bump, bump, BUMP, bump . . .

When we finally reach Monteverde, around midnight, we can't find our inn. When we *do* find it, the inn is dark. It looks closed for the night. Jonathan gets out to check, but Hannah doesn't like the looks of the place.

"No way—I'm not staying there."

"Why not?" says Cindy, with a hint of testiness.

"It looks like a shithole."

"Better a shithole than no place at all."

A mild argument ensues. Hannah wants someplace nice, and she wants privacy since she's been getting up at five in the fucking morning to avoid lines for the fucking shower, and she wants fucking space since she's in a claustrophobic two-bunk-bed room with three fucking roommates, one of whom has an ever-present boyfriend.

"No one's there," says Jonathan, climbing back in the van.

We're now faced with the terrifying prospect of sleeping in the van. Marco drives to see what else, if anything, is available. We find a hotel with lights on: El Sapo Dorado (The Golden Toad, named after Monteverde's most famous, and now extinct, amphibian). A security guard is shutting down. Hannah and Jonathan beg him to show compassion. The guard calls the manager. A minute later and we'd have been out of luck.

We rent cottages, sleep, and dream sweet dreams about smooth pavement.

Monteverde's primitive roads have one benefit: they discourage people from visiting Monteverde. Open a superhighway and the cloud forest would be packed with ecotourists. Already roughly a quarter million people a year endure the hemorrhoid-inducing trek to see its steep, biodiverse charms.

The weather is refreshingly cool, like a damp autumn day back home. We start at a zip-line park, whizzing like Spider-Man down cables at speeds approaching 45 miles per hour, soaring above the mist and the canopy. After that we swoop *waaay* into the air on a Tarzan swing. James screams from the speed and the height—around forty feet at its peaks—and from the tightness of the cables around his crotch.

"*Ohhhhh* my God!" he yells, approaching a block of trees.

"*Augggghhhh*—my bollocks!" he cries on the way back.

Hannah skips the Tarzan swing. She's freaked out by the zip-lining heights, so she rides with—and on—one of the hunky staff members, strapping her legs around him, as ordered, making no effort to conceal her pleasure.

"You're such a tart," says Jonathan, the shafted husband.

"We're divorced," Hannah says, screaming as she and her new zip-line stud careen toward the next platform.

The night before we left for Monteverde, a nineteen-year-old female volunteer named Pat, who was supposed to join us on the trip, tried joking with Hannah after dinner. Several of the under-twenty Caucasian girls have never spoken with Hispanics, Europeans, African-Americans, Muslims, Jews, or basically anyone other than their fellow Christian-American white folks. I give them credit for traveling and exposing themselves to the world, but their ignorance can be startling. A tight-faced girl from Minnesota, who looks no more than eighteen and struggles to smile, either from piety or culture shock, asks Jonathan—

"Do you have cows in England?"

He's too stunned to respond. The girl bites her lip.

"I just said something stupid, didn't I."

As for Pat, in her attempt to be funny, she nodded at Sarah, another sheltered student away from America for the first time, and said snarkily to Hannah, "Sarah has never seen a Jew before. Do you have a Star of David tattoo on your ass?"

Hannah's eyes reddened. She raced from the outdoor dining area through the kitchen and up the wood stairs to her room. James decided the weekend chemistry would now be too volatile if Pat joined us in Monteverde. So he fibbed and told her we didn't have room. And then *he* was pissed that he was the one who performed the dirty deed.

"Well," I announced to Julie, "this is going to be a fun weekend."

Ironically, I think Pat wanted to ingratiate herself to Hannah; to appeal to her tough-gal persona. And because of that tough-gal persona, I figured the sassy, in-your-face, martial arts maven Hannah would mush Pat's nose with a foot to the face. So even though Pat's comment was in poor taste—and particularly jarring in such a bastion of save-the-world political correctness—I'm surprised that

Hannah was so devastated. Her showy strength, I suspect, masks a deep vulnerability.

Hannah has told us a little about her ex-husband. "The shit-head," as she calls him. The marriage was short. He was domineering, dictating how he wanted her to dress, how she should wear her hair (one reason it's now defiantly short). Our first morning in Costa Rica, when we wrote on a whiteboard why we were volunteering, Hannah wrote that she was here because she'd turned forty.

"I've never had a sweet sixteen or Bat Mitzvah and my wedding was small—I hate parties, I think they're fucking idiotic, and I don't like being the center of attention. So I thought I would give something back instead. It was the antidote to self-pity over my old age. But I wasn't trying to find myself," she says. "I am found."

Though she no longer wears it, Hannah brought her wedding ring to Costa Rica. Late that evening, after a guided nighttime hike in the cloud forest and dinner at a local café, we all return to our cottages. But Hannah eventually goes outside. She takes a few steps in the darkness. And with the strength built from months of postmarriage, postdivorce tae kwon do, she hurls her wedding ring into the dark woods and the cloud forest fog.

On Monday, back at the school, I'm suffering a Monteverde hangover. Not from alcohol—though it was nice to down a few cold Imperials, the Budweiser of Costa Rica—but from a kick in the shin by an ill-tempered horse.

We took a guided horseback ride on Sunday along green mountain trails, passing weathered barns and lazy cattle, peering at small valley villages below. The only glitch was that James's horse hated my horse. He snorted and squealed—the horse, not James, who instead screamed "*Gaaaaaa!*"—and then James's horse, while attempting to kick my horse, kicked me instead. Hoof hitting bone, if you haven't experienced it, is like getting whacked with a baseball bat. After that, James and I tried to keep our horses apart, but we aren't exactly accomplished horsemen. So our horses still trotted close enough to neigh some pony profanity to one another, grunting and huffing and biting.

"He's bloody crazy!" cried James.

"Just keep him away from me," I said.

James's horse bristled, then took off at a trot.

"*Whooooaaa!*" hollered James, bouncing on the saddle as his horse charged ahead.

The shot to the shin was pain number one. Later that day, on the van ride back to Ciudad Quesada, I suffered a muscle strain. While sitting. Julie and I were in the back of the van, and she graciously shared her iPod earbuds: she used the left bud, I used the right. We listened to a podcast of NPR's *Car Talk*. I turned to grab a water bottle and—*pop!*—my back, right between my shoulder blades, erupted in pain that stretched to my neck. Julie thought it was a muscle spasm, though it felt like a pinched nerve. Either way, I'm clearly getting old: I'm hurting myself in the midst of inactivity.

The next morning I asked Julie for assistance from the bottom bunk.

"Can you help me?" I wheezed.

"With what?"

"With getting up."

"Seriously?"

"I can't do it on my own."

At the school, the kids view me as a human jungle gym during breaks, grabbing my arms, climbing on my back, taking turns as I swing them in circles. Given my limited Spanish, saying "Sorry— teacher popped a back muscle listening to NPR" isn't feasible, and I forgot to ask Hannah for a simple "I'm in pain" translation. So I endure the onslaught of exuberant little uniformed bodies, though it's likely the children learn a few colorful new English words, the kind you won't see on flash cards.

In our muggy classroom, we're working with three new groups of kids, and our first two classes are impressive: the students are serious, smart, motivated. Two girls in class number one—Rachel and Roxana, best friends, both fourth graders—know enough English to translate our instructions. Rachel is a chubby, thoughtful, very bright girl who could whup some serious ass if provoked. When a few boys get loud during class, Rachel yells, "*Silencio!*" The boys are silent.

The second class, fifth graders, is even better. They enjoy using letter cards we'd found at the CCS house (like flash cards, with a different letter of the alphabet on each card). They spread the cards on the desk and spell words and phrases we suggest: animals, fruits, machines—anything we can think of. We adapt our lesson to their enthusiasm. Flexibility, we've learned, is essential.

Two classes, two gems! It's like an educational Eden.

And then the first graders arrive. They run around the room, jump on the beat-up old couch, yell, hit each other—and it's the boys more than the girls, of course, testosterone transforming males under six into spastic imps when in groups of three or more. They're not bad kids, especially one on one. Timmy, one of our biggest couch bouncers, frequently shares his snacks with me and Julie, and escorts me by hand during a break one day to play foosball at a corner market. They're just high energy and rambunctious. *So* rambunctious that by the middle of the week I scream in the classroom.

It's a calculated scream, the result of strained patience. First off, I'm getting annoyed by the students' blobs: sticky wads of goo that come as a prize in bags of chips. When you throw 'em, they stick to various surfaces. Typically before and after class, a blob will hit the chalkboard—*bloop*! And then a window—*bloop*! The older kids restrain themselves while we're teaching, but with the first graders I hear the occasional *bloop* as the boys—always the boys—run, shriek, and pant.

Also, at least once a day, a soccer ball will bounce into the room, careening off the walls. We ask Hannah to translate this critical phrase for us: *Tomen la pelota afuera* (Take the ball outside). So I say *Tomen la pelota afuera*, but reading it in a stiff voice from a notepad wimpifies its impact. And even the first graders know I'm a short-timer, the equivalent of an international substitute teacher, and really, is there anybody with less authority in the world than a substitute teacher?

As Timmy and Luis, another high-energy boy, jump on the couch, I remember: during our first-day CCS orientation, Juan said that Costa Rica is a macho-male society. Indeed, the school's principal, Señor Blanco, looks more like a rancher than an educator: short-sleeve plaid shirt tucked in jeans, tan skin, firm forearms that come from work rather than workouts. He has a gold tooth, for cryin' out loud. So I decide:

I am bigger than these kids. I am stronger. They are used to a male-chauvinist, male-dominant society.

I will DOMINATE them with my manliness.

And then I use my deepest, meanest, nastiest, surliest, most pissed-off, ticked-off, bad-ass, Darth-Vader-in-a-shitty-mood voice, and I bellow—

HEY!

It's like a verbal whip crack. They stop jumping. They look up at me, surprised. I pull them off the couch. I don't hear any *bloops*. And within five to ten seconds of my ultramasculine, hairy-chested yell—I am a Costa Rican BRUTE—the boys are back on the couch, running and jumping.

But Consuela heard me yell. She is a tall, thick, imposing woman with gold hoop earrings and a demeanor that says, *I am a good person but you do not want to mess with me.* Her primary duties seem custodial—she kindly brings us *bananitas* during breaks—

but she's also the school's mother-in-chief. Señor Blanco may be the principal, but Consuela is the boss. Now she looms in the doorway and snaps at Timmy and Luis, a torrent of unyielding machine-gun Spanish. They freeze, then sit meekly at the nearest desk. She utters what I assume is Español for "Don't make me come back" and departs. The class is quiet.

Forget the salsa dancer. This is my new Costa Rican goddess.

Clearly Julie and I need to burn the first graders' energy; to transform their kiddie vigor in a way that helps them learn. This seems a wiser strategy than me yelling. So we unveil our musical ditties, starting with "Head, Shoulders, Knees, and Toes." As you sing you touch the body part mentioned in the song. We stand in a circle and with each chorus we speed it up, ultimately to ridiculous proportions—like calisthenics on amphetamines—which gets huge laughs. In fact, it's so hilarious it *increases* their energy levels.

Julie and I laugh, too, though we're thinking, *Do these kids ever get tired?* It's time to blow their little minds. Julie and I now debut our secret musical weapon, a tune that's totally new to Escuela Cuestillas: "The Hokey Pokey."

The kids look intrigued. They follow our lead. We put our right hands in, we take our right hands out. We put our right hands in and shake them all about. We do the Hokey Pokey and we turn ourselves around. That's what it's all about.

In addition to right hands we do feet, elbows, shoulders, chins, hips, and—the ultimate in first-grade comedy—butts! You can't go wrong with butt shaking if you've got the right crowd.

Maybe it's the volume—the singing, the laughs—maybe it's the novelty of the song, but as we're hokeying and pokeying scores of older kids line up outside the windows to watch. Some smile. Some seem to wonder if we're mental patients. But our energy-burning efforts are successful: Julie and I are exhausted.

"You know," Hannah tells me later, when I describe the hyperactive first graders, "if you're hoping to have kids, this was the last place you should have brought her."

Stray dogs lounge on the sidewalks in Ciudad Quesada, sprawling on shaded concrete in front of side-street bakeries and shops; sleeping, licking their paws, licking their balls, hoping for a handout, though never seeming to beg. Much as Julie and I love dogs, we don't approach them, partly because I don't want to acquaint myself with diseases carried by stray Central American pups, partly because we don't want them shadowing us through town. But they seem content, and they seem healthy, hanging with their doggie amigos. Lazy Costa Rican mutt doesn't seem like a bad life.

I was supposed to watch my friend Adam's two dogs the weekend Dad died. Adam and his family were on vacation. I'd let the dogs out that morning—Holly, their Lab, is a compulsive Frisbee catcher—and when I called Adam from the hospital parking lot I apologized, because dog walking was now low on the postdeath to-do list. And yet I felt bad for shirking my pooch duty. I apologized several times: *I'm sorry about the dogs . . .* Maybe it was the shock. I felt the same concern about our Father's Day dinner reservations for that night. I was semi-obsessed with calling the restaurant to cancel.

"Don't worry about the dogs," said Adam. "Jesus. I can't believe this. Are you okay?"

Yes. No. I don't know. I apologized again.

I read recently that Americans spend over $40 billion each year on their pets. Costa Rica's gross domestic product, by comparison, is roughly $20 billion. In the pet biz, pampered pooches are often called "fur babies": a much-coddled substitute for a child. Which is what childless people like Julie and I have. A fur baby.

I love our dog, Molly (a shepherd-terrier mix, we were told, though who knows what breeds are racing through her blood-stream). She's nine now, and though gray streaks her cheeks and floppy ears, she still loves a long walk in the woods or to chase a squirrel she'll never catch.

I was walking Molly one day when I met another dog walker, a woman Julie must chat with while plucking poo from the grass. "*Ohhh*," she cooed to Molly in a baby-talk voice, as the dogs sniffed each other's anuses. "Your mommy isn't with you today!"

Her *mommy*? Julie is not Molly's mommy. Molly's mommy had floppy ears and paws and upwards of eight nipples.

I have no problem with viewing your dog as a fur baby. But Molly is my pal, not my child. We hang out together, we walk together, we tolerate each other's farts. No matter how lousy my day might be, she scurries to the door when I come home and wags her tail as if nothing makes her happier. But I will not hear her first words. I won't help her with her homework. I won't cheer her when she gets an A and chastise her for an F. I won't console her when she breaks up with her first love even though I'm thrilled because the guy was a chump. I will not watch her graduate, grow, suffer, succeed. A dog is a dog. A baby is a baby. I have a dog.

Rice and beans are a staple of the Costa Rican diet, so we're served rice and beans at breakfast, lunch, and dinner. Overall the food is tasty—strips of sautéed chicken mixed with fresh tomatoes, on-ions, or peppers; fried fish with thick mashed potatoes for lunch on Fridays—but I admit it: I'm tired of rice and beans. It's the repetition. If someone scheduled an orgasm three times a day you'd eventually say: "I am *so* sick of orgasms. Can we have pizza instead of an orgasm?"

As part of our evening pre-dinner routine, Hannah asks me with a straight face—

"Do you think we'll have rice and beans tonight?"

"Hmmm—I hope so," I say. "That would be nice."

By the second week we make snack runs. I head with James and Cindy to a market up the hill on the main street, where we buy sodas and chips and cookies. Dessert is a rarity at the house—we have cake when it's someone's birthday—so one evening we walk to an ice cream shop. I'm enjoying my scoop of chocolate on a sugar cone when I spy a girl on the sidewalk who reminds me of Garfield: the girl from Bajo de Meco. I squint, look hard, and no, it's not her, but I wonder—

Has Garfield ever had ice cream? Her home has no electricity, so there's no refrigeration. Her family has little money, so ice cream would be a luxury. Garfield lives a rice-and-beans life, trapped in sameness. The monotony of poverty.

As melting chocolate ice cream streams over my fingers and down the cone, I wonder what I've been wondering since we arrived: what good are we actually doing here?

Think about the school: We're there for two weeks. It took us half that time to figure out what we were doing, and what the kids know. Whoever follows us will go through the same process. So how much English are these kids learning?

CCS maintains you make a difference simply by showing up. In poorer parts of the world, parents are more likely to send their kids to school—instead of sending them to work—because American and European volunteers give a school cachet. Parents figure it must be worthwhile if foreigners are there. And you improve the image of Americans. A lot of Costa Ricans think that Americans are lazy, Mauricio tells us. The Americans they see on TV shows never work; they drink coffee and sleep around.

One night Hannah encourages us. "If these kids learn one word of English, if they see what normal Americans look like, you've made a contribution." Maybe so. But I wonder.

Earlier that day at the school, Julie and I wrote seven fill-in-the-blank questions on the board:

What is your name?
My name is _____.

What is your favorite game?
My favorite game is _____.

What is your favorite animal?
My favorite animal is _____.

A boy named Carlos, probably about eight years old, writes "dog" in the space for animals, not surprising since he often pretends he's a pooch. Many of the poorer families are led by mothers, so Mauricio had warned that some kids may call me "papa." That never happens, though the grinning Carlos clings to me constantly. During a break after class, I talk with Principal Blanco, attempting to translate as he asks where Julie and I live and how long we're staying in Costa Rica. Carlos is behind me, arms around my stomach, jumping up and down, barking into my back.

Maybe, as Mauricio hinted, Carlos attaches himself to me—literally—because his father abandoned his family. So is my being here confusing to a kid like this? Am I just another father figure who can't be trusted?

In another of Dad's secret letters, which Mom found after he died, he wrote about his own impoverished youth. He wrote it, I'm sure, when Mom traveled back to Virginia to see me and my sister and the grandkids; sitting on the couch—still his office away from the office—writing on a legal pad in his lap.

"I'm listening to some old country music tonight that is triggering massive memories of my childhood," he wrote. "Sometimes the flashbacks are so strong I wish I could record it. If you could see them, you would probably cry in sadness where I could cry in happiness. Although the times were tough, they were good because they made me what I am. Therefore," he said, "they bring me happiness."

It's a staggering thing to say.

I am a product of my pain, and therefore my pain brings me joy.

He's thankful for a childhood without heat, without money, at times without food. For hand-me-down clothes; for throbbing toothaches, my grandmother pressing hot compresses against his jaw to ease the pain of bad teeth. The constant moving. For a time they lived above a country store—the owner would fire his shotgun at rats—in a house they called the Hole in the Wall (for obvious reasons). The store became a beer joint, an unfortunate switch since my grandparents were alcoholics, though no one used that term at the time. One night a fight broke out. Granddaddy was stabbed in the arm.

"I can still remember Ma taking us out through a back window because of the riot," Dad wrote. "I remember Daddy all bandaged up, Uncle Buddy all cut, the broken furniture, and people running everywhere when they heard sirens." My grandfather nearly bled to death, but survived. Dad was four when it happened.

And yet despite the hardships . . . no bitterness. At least none that I could detect.

"Please don't be sad when I go," Dad wrote in that same letter. "I've achieved more than I ever could have imagined. I've been the luckiest person in the world."

Dad made his luck, like the circuit boards he assembled at his earliest jobs. He earned everything. But he succeeded because colleagues, friends, bosses—they invested themselves in his talents. I hope that children like Garfield, the children of Bajo de Meco, find equally astute investors: vessels that will carry them to new shores, risk takers who will gamble on their growth. Because just as Julie and I have implanted some English in our tiny students, Bajo de Meco has planted some unforeseen seed in me. Long after we leave Costa Rica, the words will remain a kind of code. When some pettiness arises, some problem at work, some jerk in traffic, I'll think, *Bajo de Meco.* Which means that whatever nonsense I'm dealing with is truly nonsense. That the life of the shantytown could be my own. *There but for the grace of God go I.* It's a poetic way of saying that someone else's life is way more wretched than mine. And it will leave me to wonder . . . *Why?*

Why is it them and not me? Why are these families trapped in shabby, tin-quilt homes? Why was I born to a man of ambition? A man who pulled himself far from his own hole-in-the-wall roots?

Bajo de Meco will be the place I can't shake. Because I fear it's an unsolvable place. It's not like you can host a bake sale or collect quarters in cans and say we're gonna give these people electricity and running water—*Hooray!* These people are squatters. Improve this place and they'll be kicked out. And I respect CCS's stance on charity, which is basically that it doesn't believe in charity—that handing out money creates dependency. So nothing changes, or change comes slowly. But Bajo de Meco's mud puddle roads and its creaky homes—homes that look like they'd tumble with a shoulder's hard shove—they're in me, somewhere, like the tennis balls Rafael smacked into the rain forest brush; hidden, but there, concealed, and I'm trying to ignore them—and I will ignore them for almost two years—but eventually I'll search with the plastic bat, whacking the weeds, pushing deeper, deeper than I'd planned, still hunting, still hoping to solve the unsolvable woe.

On our last day, we attend a school assembly, which is held outside. Roberto and Enrique raise the Costa Rican flag as the kids stand in rows, fidgeting in the grass. They sing the national anthem and then the school song in a monotone chant. The porch near our classroom becomes a stage, and students present a science project on tadpoles. Awards are given. Principal Blanco holds a microphone and makes a speech. The morning is sunny and warm, so Julie and I stand in the shade of an orange tree. Since I only understand about a tenth of what the principal is saying, I mainly watch the children.

Before class started, we hosted a rousing game of bingo that filled the room with focused, excited kids. I shouted out numbers, Julie wrote them on the board.

"Twenty-seven!" I yelled. "Twenty-seven! Who has a twenty-seven!"

I felt like an overcaffeinated game show host, strutting before the blackboard in a Groucho-esque crouch. The room filled with noise, then grew quiet, a quiet I never thought possible. They waited for the next number, eyes big as I scanned the room, rubbing my chin, prolonging the drama.

"Fourteen! Does someone have fourteen!"

"Bingo!" screamed a boy to cheers and wails.

Now that we're leaving, I think we're finally getting the hang of this.

Julie nudges me, bringing me back to the assembly.

"I think he's talking about us," she says, apparently hearing our names.

It sounds like he's telling the students about the importance of knowing English, how English will create job opportunities later in life. He calls us up to the porch. They all applaud. A girl hands Julie a small package wrapped in pink tissue; I receive one in purple. We open them as everyone watches. It's a key chain with photos: on one side is the school, on the other a picture of me and Julie with some of the kids, which Principal Blanco took a few days earlier. They applaud again.

The principal hands us the microphone. We say thank you in English and clumsy Spanish. Julie wipes away a tear.

She brought her camera so we take pictures, which the kids love. With each photo they jostle and push to see the digital image on the back. She snaps one of Roberto, and he frowns when he sees it: kids are making rabbit ears behind his head. So I stand behind him, hands on his shoulders, and Julie shoots again. This time he's satisfied.

Principal Blanco later apologizes for the gift. He thinks it's too small. I try telling him it's one of the most touching things I've ever received.

Maybe, as Hannah noted, the kids learned one or two words from us. Maybe we helped improve the system: Julie and I were only the third group to work at the school, and moving forward, based in part on our evaluation, the English program will be a class, not a club, and volunteer teachers will stay for three-month stints, so there's more continuity. Principal Blanco can use his limited funds to invest in computers for the school, rather than hire an English teacher.

When the van arrives to pick us up, kids rush into our room, even older kids, sixth graders that we hadn't been teaching. We receive hugs, kisses, handshakes. A large group of students walks with us to the road. It is a warm, wonderful moment, yet sad, because we know we won't see them again, that we'll soon fade from their school-age minds. But maybe they'll remember a few words of English. Maybe we've implanted a verb. To think. To hope. To run. To learn.

We say goodbye to Jonathan and James—they'll work in Costa Rica for ten more weeks—and leave the CCS house in the afternoon with a group of departing volunteers, including Hannah. After unloading our bags at the Holiday Inn in San José, Hannah joins Julie and me for dinner. Parts of San José are lovely, such as the stately white, Old World–influenced National Theater, but as we search for a restaurant, the side streets smell of sour piss and exhaust.

We find a serviceable restaurant near a pedestrian mall. "Oh look," says Hannah, surveying the menu. "Rice and beans."

The discussion turns to Bajo de Meco. Our first day there, Hannah corrected a girl—maybe twelve or thirteen years old—who was pushing some kids off a swing. Hannah was later reprimanded by Maria of CCS.

"That girl was my instantaneous best friend, and then I was playing with some of the younger kids and she was really rude. I told her she was older; she should share. I mean, she should know better. Maria told me I was wrong. She said the girl had been sexually abused as a child and that's why she was so angry. But this girl was almost violent toward these little kids. I was telling her how to act appropriately and Maria was excusing it."

Before working for CCS, Maria had a job saving children from prostitution.

"It's legal in Costa Rica and kids were dumped into it by their parents," says Hannah. "So she was supersensitive to it. And you know, some of my students have tumultuous home lives, so when I find out, I give them extra slack. But Maria and I had a screaming match. Because yes, what happened to this girl was awful and unforgivable, and she should receive extra special care, but when her behavior is harming others who can't defend themselves, it's not a carte blanche situation. I have a girl in my class back home who was molested, and she's angry—she cursed out one of our football players—and I didn't write her up or call home but I did throw her out and then called the boy's mother to say she raised him well because he kept his composure—you know, to reward *him* and not castigate her.

"That girl in Bajo de Meco had good reason to hate the planet but she was bullying smaller kids and acting like a nasty fuck."

A waiter brings our drinks. I sip my soda from the bottle, not wanting to risk a tummy bug from the ice. Hannah looks serious.

"I was sexually molested as a young child, too, so I don't speak from my butt on this." She begins to tell us about her experience. As she does, a team of mariachi guitarists in matching black gaucho costumes stand before our table and play what sounds like the Mexican hat dance. We sit, silenced, as the three guitarists pluck their perky tune, Hannah's personal pain and perseverance lying somewhere on the table between our empty plates.

At Bajo de Meco I'd sneak peeks of Julie as I searched for tennis balls in the brush with Rafael, poking the weeds and tall grasses with the plastic bat. I watched her play a singsong pattycake game with some of the girls and volunteers. I watched her bowl with a little boy using a tennis ball and rock-filled Pepsi bottles. I watched her play dodgeball, scooting across the cleared dirt, laughing, almost shrieking, twisting to avoid being hit.

On that inevitable day when it's my turn, like Dad, to fall to the earth, this is the image, the sound, that will flash in my dying mind. Dodgeball. Julie giggling, the red rubber ball whizzing past; the ball as red as her cheeks. I hadn't seen her laugh like this in a long time. I could watch her laugh forever.

A few months after we return home, I dream, for the first time in a long time, about Dad. I'm standing on the sidewalk of a four-lane street not far from our house. It's dark. The woods and houses aren't visible. Everything is black except for the sidewalk.

He approaches from far away. We don't speak. He looks at me, hugs me in that heavy pat-on-the-back manner men use when they embrace. And then he walks away, down the sidewalk, then up the hill beyond. It's the last time I dream about him.

PART THREE

China

SEARCHING FOR MY "SQUARE OF CLARITY" IN XI'AN.

A BOY IS MOANING, an echoing, sorrowful wail like a lonesome seal.

Eeeeeeeeeee . . . Eeeeeeeeeee . . . Eeeeeeeeeee . . .

His fingers are twisted and locked—thumb out, pinky curled, middle fingers in odd directions, almost disjointed. A teacher kneels and speaks in a soft voice as he howls.

I'm wedged in a tiny plastic chair against the classroom's back wall, packed tight in a row of children, my knees near my chest. These are my first minutes at La La Shou—"Hand in Hand" in English—a school for special-needs children in Xi'an, and three classes are merged in one loud room: second graders, third graders, fourth graders; about thirty kids in all; most of them autistic, some with developmental disabilities; the room booming with squeals.

"Bà-*baaaaa* . . . ," yells one boy, pointing at me, looking as though he might cry. "Bà-*baaaaa* . . ."

He repeats this for many minutes.

Another boy raises his arms and shakes his hands, again and again, like an evangelist praising God. A thin girl with sunken eyes strokes a teacher's ponytail, gently; a tall boy jumps from his seat, rummages through a box, and finds a whistle—

Tweeeeeeeeeeet!

One of the teachers—they wear orange T-shirts with Motorola

logos—takes it from him and returns him to his chair, where a boy is stomping his feet. Another boy takes off his shoes and socks. Some kids get up and jump and sit back down; others say nothing, staring blankly at the floor.

Sitting next to me is Li Baojian, a third grader I'll be paired with most of my two weeks. He is a slow-moving boy, I'm told, and one of my tasks is to help him improve his motor skills, from exercising to writing. He looks at me with cloudy eyes, then lays his head on my leg.

The teachers speak. I understand *nothing*. They play kiddie music on a small stereo and lead a choreographed dance. Some of the kids follow. Most of the kids don't.

Liu Baojian sits up and claps, but not in rhythm. Am I supposed to help him clap?

A happy pudgy boy in pink sandals and a black mafia-style sweatsuit gets up, claps, then squeezes back into his row of chairs. As he shoves his way in, a boy on the end is squeezed off, falling to the floor.

I hear screams and squawks and sobs and laughs and *Chinese Chinese Chinese* and see heads bobbing, twisting, bouncing.

I am overwhelmed. *Culture shock overload*, I write later that morning.

A tall, chubby boy lumbers up to me and shakes my hand, almost as if he's running for office. He's wearing a green Snoopy T-shirt, one he will wear often in the days to come. He pumps my hand, up and down, up and down, a huge grin on his round face. As he ambles away, I see the back of his shirt has a sentence in English.

"Today is a good day."

Roughly eight million people live in metropolitan Xi'an. To cross a downtown street is not simply to evade cars, but to evade death itself. Unlike the streets in D.C., where walk signs tick the time before a light changes—where a turning Metrobus slows, and waits, until pedestrians cross the street—Xi'an is a collision of men, women, children, scooters, taxis, trucks, bikes, cars, and claustro-phobic buses roaring forward at once. Hesitancy is both useless and essential as you step into traffic. You let the bus pass. Take two more steps. Taxi. Step. Wait—*shit*—bus—step step step—*whoa*—car. Then more cars. A scooter so loaded with boxes you can't see the driver. And then you find you've scooched halfway through four lanes of firing-range traffic. But you keep moving forward, because if you don't, you stay on the sidewalk.

And that, I realize now, was my life after Costa Rica. Standing on the sidewalk, afraid to cross.

I never expected to volunteer in China. I'd done my interna-tional We Are the World gig. It was time to be normal again. And so two and a half years passed between our departure from San Carlos and my arrival in Xi'an.

After Julie and I left Escuela Cuestillas for the final time, as we rode away from waving hands in a van-churned fog of dust, I felt . . . relief. Yes, I would miss the children—the rowdy, sweaty soccer games; Tabitha's giggle between classes; those satisfying mo-ments when our amateur teaching techniques actually worked. I would miss the lush, wet, sticky, steamy green country. But I never quite got over that feeling of *oh my God, how are we going to teach these kids*, which slammed us so hard that first day.

A week or so after we got home, I met my best buddies—Julie's brother Tom, my old college friends Adam and Terry—at Fat Tues-day's, a strip mall bar we like because it's so unlike a strip mall bar. The cigarette smoke soaks into your clothes (or it did until the smoking laws changed), the floor is covered in peanut shells. We drank happy hour beers, and the more I told them about Roberto and Tabitha and how Julie and I scrambled to develop lesson plans, the more I appreciated the experience. I had never immersed myself that deeply in another country or another job. I'd always been a tourist. At Escuela Cuestillas I was a teacher, a playmate, a friend.

A few weeks after we came home, I exchanged e-mails with Jonathan, who was still in San Carlos with James. Jonathan filled me in on the latest gossip from the CCS house. Rumor had it a Canadian volunteer had hooked up with the guy who drove us to Monteverde. ("Talk about immersing yourself in the culture," I wrote back.) Jonathan and James had traveled on weekends to Puerto Viejo and Manuel Antonio National Park on Costa Rica's Pacific and Caribbean coasts. On a snorkeling trip, James gashed his head on a propeller and sat in a bloody daze, the boat rocking in the sun, while everyone else continued swimming and frolicking with tropical fish.

Later, I asked Jonathan why he was volunteering for three months, leaving his partner in Birmingham, something we hadn't discussed in San Carlos. "It probably started at a subconscious level about ten years ago, just before I was approaching my 40th birthday," he wrote back. "I started to take stock of what I'd achieved in my life and, more importantly, what I'd like to achieve in the time ahead. I attended a year-long course to improve my management skills and it forced me to confront myself about what mattered in life. It enabled me to see that you only really know about yourself when you face the unknown—when you're outside your comfort zone. This brought the idea of helping out in other communities from the subconscious to the conscious level. When the chance of severance came along I knew it was my time to face the unknown and take a leap of faith."

I'd had similar thoughts before I traveled to New Orleans and Costa Rica, thoughts that never faded. And two years later I was still pondering my purpose, still feeling irrelevant, when something unusual happened.

I read a book.

I say this is unusual because it was a spiritual self-help book, and

I am not a spiritual self-help book kind of guy. It was on a giveaway cart at work—*Ruling Your World,* by an incarnate lama from Tibet named Sakyong Mipham—and I grabbed it without thinking, the way I might grab a cookie from a tray; as if I routinely pick up books by incarnate lamas. Some concepts, such as *drip* (contamination stemming from negativity and selfishness) were easier for me to grasp than *windhorse* (I still have no clue). But the writing resonated.

"Getting off the 'me' plan is the cause of happiness," Mipham wrote.

> Caring for others is the basis of worldly success. This is the secret that we don't learn in school. . . . We usually don't pay attention to these truths until our expectations about life are interrupted by aches in our body or lines on our face, an accident, or the illness or death of somebody close to us. Then we experience a moment of panic that temporarily cuts through drip, our web of habitual assumptions. . . . We don't think, "Life is precious. I'd better start helping others." We just go back to pursuing pleasure or not rocking the boat. Thinking we have all the time in the world, we waste it.

I didn't tell anyone I was reading this. It sounds so damn pretentious: if someone says, "Hey—how's it going," I don't say, "Good—I'm reading a book by an incarnate lama named Sakyong Mipham." But I read that book with Sakyong's fuzzy shaved head on the shiny cover, read it on the commuter train to and from work, read it as the train crossed the Potomac: as Alexandria apartments became Fairfax parks. I hunched over the slim paperback, highlighting passages, before zipping it in my shoulder bag—hiding it—getting off at my station and driving home.

And then Terry told me a story about how he got racked.

Each March, I drive two hours south to Richmond with Terry, Adam, and Tom to root for our alma mater, George Mason University, in a college basketball tournament. Tom got his bachelor's degree in aeronautic engineering from Virginia Tech, and then his master's in structural engineering at the University of Virginia, but he feels little connection to those schools. So we've made him an honorary Mason grad.

The four of us have season tickets for men's hoops, and this is the grand finale: the school that wins the tourney gets an automatic bid for March Madness. For us, the trip is a two-to-three-day binge of booze, beer, basketball, bad jokes, bad gas, insults, cigarettes, the occasional political rant, and talk of life's joys and disappointments, all topped by morning hangover coffee and greasy sausage-and-hash-brown breakfasts. We hit our favorite spots: the Penny Lane Pub, run by a native Liverpudlian, the late-night by-the-slice pizza joint catering to inebriated barhoppers in lively yet sketchy Shockoe Bottom. We have our favorite stories: the night I fell asleep in the Penny Lane bathroom; the morning a guy tried to steal the cash we left for breakfast at a diner (the cook threatened him with a meat cleaver).

Terry told his story after a late morning walk by the James River. We stopped for coffee at a café in Shockoe Slip—a brick-sidewalk area of restaurants and bars—sitting outside, enjoying the sun and the unseasonably warm weather, trying to ignore the creepy guy behind us engaged in an argument with himself.

Adam took a call from his wife.

"How's the home front?" I said when he was done.

"Good. Erik and Amber both have soccer games."

"I miss my boys," said Terry of his two infant sons. "But I need this weekend. It scares me how much I look forward to this weekend."

Terry and Adam are great fathers. They're not remote control dads who dump the dirty work on their wives. But Adam talked about the stress of raising kids.

"Every night's an ordeal. They get so much homework. It's crazy how much homework they get. And then it's a pain getting them to do it. And then getting them to bed, packing lunches, telling them *again* to go to bed."

"Yeah, but they give so much love," said Terry.

Terry and I were roommates at Mason. I was already living in our on-campus apartment when he moved in. I peeked in his just-unpacked room and saw a God poster on the wall, a black leather Bible on his bed, his shoes perfectly aligned on the floor, as if he'd straightened them with a laser. Great, I thought: he's an anal retentive religious fanatic. A pious Felix Unger. (Terry had his own concerns. He saw three half-gallons of vodka on my desk, and found me asleep one morning on the bathroom floor, and assumed I was an alcoholic.)

We both learned we were way off. Terry became a minister and one of my best friends. What I like about Terry is that he never self-righteously shoves his Baptist beliefs down your throat. He lives his life (happily), he helps others, he cares about people, which says more about his relationship with God than any holier-than-thou pronouncements.

At the café in Richmond, he told a story about his sons, Clarence and Ray. "I was lying down on the bed. I had the flu—a fever, upset stomach—and Mary kept the boys out of the room. I felt awful. And then Clarence kind of slipped past the door, and he climbed on the bed, and he sat next to me, and he didn't say anything, but he just really gently rubbed my stomach. It's the same thing I do when he's not feeling good."

Major *awwwww* moment.

"That's nice," said Adam.

"Yeah," said Terry. "And then Ray got up on the bed and stepped on my balls."

We laughed, but it struck me as soon as he said it: that's what I'm missing by not being a parent. Those precious, life-affirming, unspeakably touching moments punctuated by the occasional shot to the balls.

The sun warmed our winter-pale skin, and the creepy guy behind us insisted to no one that his brother-in-law was a fool for buying a Cadillac, and I drank my coffee, quiet as Terry, Tom, and Adam talked a bit louder to drown out his voice.

Not long after the Richmond trip, late one night after Julie went to bed, I brewed a cup of tea, went upstairs past our darkened bedroom, and pulled a folder labeled "Dad" from my desk. This room, which would be a child's bedroom, is my office. I started the folder after Dad's death to store the letters we received from family and friends. Here I keep my eulogy, my sister's eulogy, the funeral program; photocopies of the letters Dad wrote, which Mom found after his death.

I pulled out the worn photocopy of his China journal. Dad was insecure about his writing—he'd labor into the night before giving a presentation at work—but I've always found his work to be honest and vivid, like this passage about his Chinese road trip:

> *We drove for ten hours with the horn blowing constantly, swerving around cars, carts, people, large pot holes and once a pig. My bottom became numb.*
>
> *I was surprised at the poverty and the junk and garbage everywhere. For all ten hours there was an endless stream of people and buses (totally full).*
>
> *We finally stopped around 1:00 p.m. for lunch. The dishes were so dirty we had to wash them with hot tea and wipe them with napkins. Food was good, but I tried not to visualize the kitchen!*

A few days after reading this, I visited the cemetery, a place I rarely go. Mom believes you should go out of respect. But after Dad died, Terry gave me a copy of *A Grief Observed*, C. S. Lewis's angry and often self-pitying pontification on life, death, and God following the loss of his wife. In it, Lewis writes of ballads and tales he's read "in which the dead tell us that our mourning does them some kind of wrong. They beg us to stop it. . . . It made the dead far more dead." My own interpretation is that the dead want us living, doing, being. Groovin' rather than grieving. Not hanging out in cemeteries.

I don't really believe that Dad's here. If a spirit or soul lives within us, or beyond us, his is far from this cemetery, and far beyond his grave, which rests on a hill, looking down on a bank of trees, yellow leaves falling to hard autumn earth. In summer, fireflies blink in clumps. Many Koreans and Vietnamese are buried here—behind Dad are the names Chu and Tse, below him Choi and Lim—and their families hang wind chimes, which tinkle and sing as breezes tap branches. Asian families often picnic here, sitting on blankets and eating by their loved one's grave.

I brushed away leaves from the brownish bronze stone. Sometimes when I'm here, I'll talk to Dad. But on this day I just watched the trees. I remembered one of those Dad-isms he said my entire life.

If you're going to do something, Budo, always do it right.

Yeah, I know.

It's like . . .

Running. Sometimes we run around the block and think we've run a marathon.

That's me, I realize now. New Orleans and Costa Rica were the start of the journey. Not the journey itself.

I need to do more. Like Jonathan said: Face the unknown. Be selfless instead of selfish. But wait—

Normal people don't do this.

Right?

Normal people with a wife and a job and a mortgage who commute to a tidy office five days a week don't jet around the world paying good money to work for free and perspire in developing countries for two-week intervals.

Not usually, no.

But if I'm doomed to a life without children, isn't this one of the peculiar benefits? The time not spent in Cub Scout meetings and parent-teacher conferences? The money not spent at Chuck E. Cheese or squirreled away for college?

If you're gonna do something, Budo, always do it right.

A breeze blows. I stand and I think, and dream, and wonder, and scheme, and I listen to the Asian wind chimes tinkling across the acres like the tiptoes of ghosts.

So here's the plan, not expressed to a soul, not even in the silence of the cemetery, formulated largely on my twice-a-weekday walks from the train station to the office, past government workers playing Frisbee golf on the National Mall before work.

I would fling myself around the globe. I would volunteer like I did in Costa Rica. I would rip myself from my comfort zone, scrape away the layers of myself and discover what's underneath; scrape like I scraped that stubborn shed in New Orleans, peeling off what's dry and chipped and dead.

I would take the old me and make a better me. A kind of basic training, for—

Something. I'm not sure. I won't know until it's over. But I will be trained in patience and compassion. I will think differently, eat differently. Push myself—emotionally, physically, spiritually. Meet people with real problems and different perspectives. Meet people who matter. Meet people who don't matter. See if there is power in kindness.

Asia. South America. The Middle East. Africa.

Soon.

Four trips, nine months. Trip one would replicate the Richmond trip. Because for all its beer-battered testosterone charms, I always learn something about me and my friends. Adam and Terry can't go: they're parents. It'd require too much time and money. But Tom can do it. I'll convince him.

The next two trips I would do alone. If I'm determined to break out of my comfort zone, I can't jaunt around the globe with the person I'm most comfortable with—Julie—the person I most enjoy traveling with, the person I most enjoy being with. I need separation, space, a jarring jolt of distance from my everyday life.

The last trip, Julie and I will go together.

I'll write about these trips. To pay for them. The book advance won't cover my expenses, but it'll help. And I'll use this book as a crutch, because I of course won't sit with Julie, as she deserves, and explain any of this. I won't tell her: "I was reading about *windhorse* and then Ray stepped on Terry's balls and I'm volunteering in China and Ecuador and Palestine and I'm traveling by myself because I'm not satisfied with who I am and I'm still searching and I want to create a new and better me even though the old me is the me you fell in love with and oh yes, I hope you'll join me in Kenya in nine months to work in an orphanage."

What I tell her is, I have to go alone for this book project. And because of that, I don't think she understands why I need to do this. How could she?

So, Tom—

Want to go to China?

Tom and I were friends long before Julie and I started dating. As kids we rode bikes together, swam together, blew up model airplanes with fireworks—the usual stuff. When Julie started dating Dave, the McDonald's manager, Tom bolstered my spirits as I sulked. Not long after Dave and Julie hooked up, Dave gave her a rubber-tree plant, and told her that unlike flowers, the rubber plant would never die.

Tom injected it with Windex.

Twenty-five years later, he remains my friend—a mild-mannered eccentric, analytical yet artistic; a talented weekend painter who does trigonometry for fun. And because he thinks logically—*really* logically—Tom rarely worries if his decisions seem . . .

How do I put this.

Unconventional.

Take his tactical measures to prevent sunburns. Tom is fair-skinned. A few years ago he and his wife, Teresa, traveled to the Caribbean. They walked along a white sand beach, Teresa wearing a bikini, Tom wearing long pants, hiking boots, a long-sleeve shirt, a wide-rimmed floppy sun hat, and—my favorite part—gloves.

There was also the period when he decided soap was unnecessary.

"I was curious about whether you could get clean with just water," he said.

After about two weeks, Teresa convinced him this wasn't working.

"I wasn't sure you actually needed soap," he explained one night at his parents' house for Sunday dinner. "Turns out you do."

"You stunk," Teresa said.

"I didn't really smell bad, I just smelled stale."

"You stunk."

"No—it was more stale. Kind of like a homeless guy."

"Homeless guys don't usually smell good."

Like Julie, Tom is wonderful with children, yet childless by choice. Teresa insists she doesn't want kids, then becomes a hormone-stirred *look-at-the-baybee* maniac whenever she's near an infant, so I've wondered if she doesn't want kids because *he* doesn't want kids. I think Tom is content with his life as it is: to have the free time to read, to hike, to paint, to ride his motorcycle. But this I know about Tom, and about Adam and Terry as well: He's a great friend. He'd walk off a cliff for me, just as I would for him. He makes me laugh. He makes me think. When I asked him to come to China, I wasn't sure he'd be willing to travel so far, to be away from Teresa, to spend his free time working. I sent a string of e-mails to sway him. "This will be one of the most memorable experiences of your life," I wrote. "It's unique! You'll never be at a party and hear, 'Oh, really? I worked at a special-needs school in China, too.'" But he agreed, of course, for the simple reason that I asked him. And because he knew, I think, that I needed him to come.

And so on a sunny May morning, Tom pulled up in front of our townhouse in his ancient Honda Civic. I tossed my bag in the backseat. Julie hugged me. We kissed. We said we love each other and embraced again. She hugged Tom, and then we got in the car, waving as I left her at home, alone.

My renewed quest to be a better person began with my being a selfish jerk.

It took us twenty-four hours to reach Xi'an. I already wonder if Tom regrets coming.

Our flight left Virginia on a Thursday at noon. We arrived at our hotel around two in the morning Saturday. "What the hell happened to Friday?" I said as we dropped our bags in the room.

Here's what happened to Friday: Fourteen-hour flight to Beijing. Twelve-hour time difference. Four-hour delay from Beijing to Xi'an.

We had boarded the plane in Beijing. Then we taxied for forty-five minutes before returning to the terminal, where we waited some more. Passengers revolted: angry white-shirted businessmen berating some poor Air China ticket agent struggling to explain the situation.

A college-age kid in white sneakers and jeans and a white Hollister T-shirt translated their shouts for me and Tom.

"They're asking, 'Are you putting us up in a hotel? Are we flying to Xi'an?' You know—they want answers."

"And what's he telling them?"

"He's telling them he doesn't know shit."

It rained our first day. It rained most of the first week. Someone later told us it was the most rain the city had seen in over fifty years. With damp shoes and dripping umbrellas, we sloshed through the city on Saturday, avoiding the spray of buses; inhaling a rainy stew of car exhaust and tangy spices, the occasional whiff of sewage; noting the shop signs in Chinese characters, the occasional awkward English ("The China Association of Nail Embellishment," which appeared to be a nail salon).

Most of Sunday is spent in the Xi'an Empress Hotel for a four-hour orientation, which is periodically interrupted by fireworks outside.

"It's either a wedding or a coup," says Ralph, a fifty-year-old architect from Brooklyn (or *awk*-itect, as he puts it).

Afterward, Tom feels nauseous. He decides to skip a late afternoon meeting with folks from the various schools where volunteers will be working, a meeting we are most definitely expected to attend. When I leave our room he's on his bed with cramps, face pale, clutching his stomach, trying to sleep. I close the door quietly and think . . . *I hope we're still friends when this is over.*

"Where is Tom?" asks Wang Meilin, the twentysomething team leader for Global Volunteers, our host organization here in China. We're in a hotel conference room. She looks somewhat concerned, somewhat annoyed.

"He's back in the room," I say.

"Is he okay?"

"He's in the fetal position with intestinal cramps."

"Ohhh," she says, now just looking concerned.

Despite the warnings about street food—a welcome-to-China note from Meilin asked us not to eat it—we gave in to the smells, buying a doughy, pita-like spinach bread from a woman who cooked on a griddle in a narrow alleyway (though we resisted the grilled squid-on-a-stick we saw in a park). I can't imagine that the bread made him sick, since I'm not sick—and it's just bread—though thinking about whether it made him sick is now making me feel kind of sick.

We sit, ten volunteers and the short, stylish Meilin, plus roughly fifteen Chinese teachers and high school students, facing one another at a large open-center table complete with conference room comforts: tall potted plants, red Oriental-themed carpet, kettles of steaming green tea. Most of the volunteers here—seven are over the age of sixty-five—will help teach English, a beneficial service. The students know the language; they just need practice speaking it.

After speeches and introductions from each of the host institutions, the meeting becomes a Chinese variety show. One by one, the female students rise, singing like Broadway sirens. A teenage boy in a faux tan camouflage army uniform performs kung fu as the students sing. He kicks, thrusts his arms, falls to the floor facedown, his longish hair flopping, then rolls onto his back, forming the bridge position. A girl joins him and they do tai chi, in sync, arms gliding.

Performing, apparently, is as common as handshakes here.

"You have to be ready to sing at all times," Meilin tells us.

The students read speeches.

"My dream is to be a successful person—and I need your help," reads one girl.

"This is the first time I meet so many foreigners," says a guy.

"Xi'an is better in the summer," the kung fu kid says, reading from a sheet of paper. "Summer is very beautiful. The people be proud of the Yellow River. Um . . . *mmmm* . . . I am very sorry. I am very nervous."

Everyone is a little nervous, though I mainly feel intimidated. At the orientation, Meilin told us about Zhang Tao, the woman who founded La La Shou with her fellow "desperate mothers" in 2002. A year after her son was born, she knew he was different. He never cried, never spoke. "He seemed not to recognize me as his mom," Zhang Tao later wrote for the Global Volunteers website. The boy—the same big eleven-year-old boy who will greet me with a vigorous handshake in his "Today is a good day" Snoopy shirt—was diagnosed with autism.

Zhang Tao denied his condition. She would cure him, fix him, make him normal. By the time he was three, she had quit her job, traveling from Xi'an to Beijing to meet with experts at medical centers. She had little money, and some nights she slept on the streets. "Six months later, I realized that I was so wrong and self-ish. He will be like that in his whole life. I should respect him just the way he is."

She formed a support group with other mothers. Over time, they went from commiserating about their plight to committing themselves to the children, and ensuring that the kids weren't insti-tutionalized or bullied. Using their limited resources—scraping up books and desks and toys—they formed La La Shou in 2002. Most of the children are autistic; the rest have developmental issues such as Down syndrome and cerebral palsy. The school is now at its third location, with roughly eighty students and twenty-seven teachers. Although attitudes are changing, the traditional Chinese view is that special-needs children should be kept at home, hidden from view. As for the Global Volunteers program here at La La Shou, it's still relatively new: "We're still trying to figure out the best way to help," says Meilin. Tom and I are not the first volunteers, though few have come before us. Any and all support is welcome, however, even from doofuses like us. The school obtains about 60 percent of its funding through tuition (the rest comes from private donations) and continually operates in the red, says Meilin. Always struggling to survive.

I huddle in a corner with two La La Shou teachers: Wang Xiaoqing, who works with the teenage students, and Zhang Lin, a young second-grade teacher. Meilin translates. I'll be working with a third-grade class, she says, and Tom will be with Wang Xiaoqing's fifteen-year-olds.

Meilin hands me a list of my class's students, with descriptions in English and Chinese. There's a longer description of the eleven-year-old boy I'll be working with, Liu Baojian. "Likes singing, listening music, chatting with people," it says. "Behave well; seldom cry or make troubles; often volunteer answering questions by the teacher in classes. The only thing he needs to improve is his slow movement. He is slower than other students, and needs a lot of encouragement from teachers."

Meilin asks if I have any questions, thus beginning the pattern of our meeting: I ask something straightforward, and they talk at length in Chinese, which leads to a surprisingly short answer.

"Does anyone at the school speak English?" I ask.

They chat. Finally: "No one at the school speaks English."

"Well," I say, "Tom and I don't speak any Chinese, so it should all even out."

I laugh. They don't.

We talk about Liu Baojian. Is my job to watch him? Does he know I'm coming?

Long discussion in Chinese.

"He knows you are coming."

Wang Xiaoqing speaks with Meilin.

"She says you will need to help him in the bathroom to wash his hands and brush his teeth."

"Okay. But what if we're in there and he has to pee? Does he need help?"

More Chinese chatting.

"I'm not sure how to say," says Meilin, looking embarrassed. "He needs help standing up."

"Standing up?"

"In front of toilet."

"Oh. Right. But what if he doesn't have to just pee? What if he has to—you know—do something more serious?" I scrunch my face and raise my eyebrows, which I hope is a universal signal for turd. "And if he does have to do something more serious"—I add a sheepish smile to my scrunchy raised-eyebrow turd face—"will I need to clean him?"

This causes a *really* long discussion in Chinese.

"You will need to clean him," Meilin finally says.

Lovely.

"Does he know when he needs to go?"

They talk.

"He will say he has to go."

"And then he'll say, 'Why is this strange man following me?'"

They chat again. I'd kill for subtitles. As if sensing my cluelessness, Meilin smiles. I smile back, though I hope everything seems this pleasant once we start working. Earlier in the day, Meilin had warned me and Tom that working at La La Shou can be "emotionally overwhelming." Tim, a sixtysomething volunteer from California who'll be teaching English, told me how impressed he was that we're working at the school, saying it in the sober way you'd commend an organ donor for sacrificing a kidney.

"I have a friend whose wife taught special education," he said in his deep, radio-announcer-like voice. "She finally had to quit because it was destroying her."

Despite Meilin's smile I keep thinking of that little morale booster from Tim. The three of them are still talking.

"They are asking questions about you, and I am answering," Meilin says.

"Great. Are they changing their minds?"

"No," she says. "They are afraid you will change *your* mind."

Meilin was right. My first day at the school, I am emotionally over-whelmed. First comes the shrieking/sobbing/Bà-*baaaaa!*/holy-shit/what-am-I-doing-here group session between the third-, fourth-, and fifth-grade classes, where the language difference alone is a shock. I can fake my way through Spanish, but *Chinese*?

After the group class—a practice session for a Special Olympics performance later in the month—we return to the third-grade class-room. A poster shows the day's schedule. I can't read the Chinese characters, but the pictures at least show lunchtime, nap time, wash time. Desks are pushed against the wall—we sit in small chairs in a circle. The teachers play songs on a small stereo that we will hear several times a day, every day. The first has a catchy "Loo-la-loo" chorus: the teachers perform a series of hand gestures, clapping, and twirling their hands like a football ref signaling illegal motion.

Liu Baojian sits next to me, his expression glazed. The song is happily loo-la-looing when Happy Bear grabs a clump of my hair and screams. I'm calling him Happy Bear because of the "I'm a happy bear!" patches on his shirt. Assigning names to the eleven students (since I can't pronounce their Chinese names) brings order to my rattled brain. The class's two girls become Haley and Jenna, after my nieces. Jenna is a happy short-haired little girl, who every day wears a red sweatshirt that says "Britain." (English on clothes is popular here, regardless of how it's spelled: one boy's sweatpants say "Sprots" instead of "Sports.") Haley has a long braided ponytail, and her left arm rests in a narrow sling, for reasons I never learn. Most of the kids are autistic, but Haley, like Liu Baojian, seems closer to mild mental retardation. Her head is usually tilted a bit to the side, her mouth open, her yellow polo shirt tight against her big belly.

I keep naming. A skinny, mischievous boy becomes Sleeves, because he likes to roll your shirt sleeves up and press his scrunched face against your arm. Giggles is a boy who always giggles: it's a constant tic. And then there's the Dancer—the same thin boy who pointed at me and yelled "Bà-*baaaaa.*" He enjoys dancing, specializing in a spasmodic disco/kung fu/tai chi mix that's more jerky than funky. His legs kick, arms shoot out, hips poke from side to side. He dances in front of me, then takes my hands, and we swing them side to side. Maybe it's his penetrating stare, but I feel a kinship with this kid. We're dance partners.

One of the teachers speaks to him, firmly, and returns him to his seat. I name this woman after my second-grade teacher, Ms. Brown, or Ms. B for short. The other two become Ms. L and Ms. H after other past teachers. All three appear to be in their early twenties, and though the trio runs the class by committee—the matching orange Motorola T-shirts only add to that impression—Ms. B seems to outrank Ms. L and Ms. H. She's also the only one who knows any English, though her grasp of the language is minimal.

"Toilet," she tells me after lunch, pointing at Liu Baojian and then at the door. I guide Liu Baojian down a short hall to the bathroom. He walks at the slow, deliberate pace of a small old man, rocking from side to side, his hands clasped behind his back, like a leader contemplating some dark decision.

The school is clean. This bathroom is not. I'm sure it's clean each morning before the children arrive, but now the floor is wet, a murky puddle around the drain. Behind the stall door is a stand-as-you-go toilet (meaning there's nowhere to sit, just a big hole and two spots for your feet). I'll spare you the details, but some of the kids have aiming issues.

Liu Baojian shuffles to the urinal. His pants flop to his knees. We have just violated rule number five from yesterday's orientation: volunteers cannot be left alone with anyone under the age of eighteen, let alone in a stinky bathroom where said child is draining the ol' firehose.

"I'm right here," I say, taking a few steps back to give him his privacy.

My words are gibberish, which is frustrating, though that afternoon, two local university students—one male, one female—arrive to volunteer. I'm thrilled to learn they speak English, though they apologize for its quality.

"No, no! Your English is very good," I say, eager to squelch their anxieties.

The girl's tan pants are baggy, loose around her waist; her green baseball cap has a flat rim. Asian hip-hop. The guy is tall with a long nose and short buzzed hair and Elvis Costello glasses. On his white T-shirt is an army helmet that says "Music is my weapon."

The university students are pleasant and polite, so polite that neither one asks why my shirt is so wet. After the children take their nap, one of my daily jobs, I learn, is to escort them one by one to the bathroom to brush their teeth and wash their faces. Each child has a wide plastic bowl, almost like a cooking bowl, that holds a toothbrush, toothpaste, washcloth, and cup. Ms. B says something—*Chinese Chinese Chinese*—and Lightswitch rises and strolls to the corner bookshelf where the bowls are stored.

I call him Lightswitch because throughout the day, with great purpose, he'll turn off the lights in the room. And when the lights are inevitably turned back on, he'll scan the ceiling, perplexed, like he's thinking: "What the . . . c'mon people—I just turned off these lights two minutes ago!"

We enter the bathroom. Lightswitch has powdered toothpaste in what looks like a plastic aspirin bottle. He brushes his teeth—rather efficiently, in fact—then turns on the water *full blast*, trying to fill the bottle. It sprays me, it sprays him, it sprays the wall (which may explain the puddles around the drain).

"Whoa—let's not do that," I say, turning off the faucet. He turns it back on. Off, on. Off, on. I try to interest him in the washcloth. No. He fills the bottle, pours it out, fills the bottle, pours it out.

This isn't a game. Lightswitch is as serious about filling his aspirin bottle as he is about turning off lights. I finally take the bottle and put it by the window, then hand him his washcloth.

"Okay—wet it," I say.

I do it by pantomime, pretending to turn on the faucet, pretending to stick the cloth underneath the pretend water, pretending to wipe my arms and my face.

He turns the water on full blast.

When it's the Dancer's turn, he carries his bowl with a bland disregard, until he sees himself in the mirror, which causes him to jump up and down, laughing and screeching and squealing, his arms flailing.

"Hey—jeez—let's settle down," I say, though for all I know this sounds like Chinese for "Hooray—let's get crazier!"

My words have zero effect. He acts chimp-like: arms over his head, face close to the mirror, leaping, lips pursed. Somehow he finishes brushing, then blasts the water into his cup and dumps it in the sink. And then he does it again—*splash*—and again.

Clearly I need to be affectionately forceful. I put one arm around him, pressing him against me, and wash his hands and face with my free hand. Then I push up the sleeves of his sweatsuit jacket and scrub his arms. (Eventually I realize: the wetter I am, the more convinced the teachers are that I've done a good job.)

"See?" I tell him. "That wasn't so bad." He laughs and tries to run away as we head back to the class; I grab the back of his jacket and drag him to the room.

"Bà-*baaaaaa*," the now-clean Dancer says, spotting the male "Music is my weapon" college student.

Ms. B addresses the class. The college student translates: each child will draw a large strawberry on a piece of paper, a tie-in to a vocabulary lesson from earlier in the morning. Some kids, I've noticed, seem weak verbally—they rarely speak, or they say one word over and over—but fine physically. Others are the opposite.

The Dancer can dance, but when he writes Chinese characters—or draws a strawberry—he needs someone to guide his hand.

Liu Baojian is the same way. I hover over him, my hand on his, as we draw the worst-looking strawberry in the history of crayon-drawn fruit. Unlike the smooth strokes I see elsewhere, our strawberry has crude bloated edges, like the path of a snake on a drinking binge. The sloppy green leaves on top are a pudding-esque lump.

I can't help but wonder if this mutant strawberry is symbolic of the troubles I'll be facing here. As Ms. H tapes the drawings to the wall, the other strawberries look like . . . strawberries. Poor Liu Baojian, who's stuck with me, Mr. Can't Speak the Language, has a sickly berry that looks like it crawled out of a traffic accident. My expectation was that the school would be so desperate for help, and so desperate for bodies, that anyone, even a clueless foreigner, would be a godsend. But I may be just one more complication in their already hectic days. I feel humbled. And stupid.

Liu Baojian sits at the table, his head resting limply against his shoulder. He talks to the university student. I envy their slow-yet-easy conversation. When Liu Baojian speaks to me, I can never tell if he's saying something or just making noise, as some of the kids do.

He says something to the university student, who then taps me on the arm, translating with a nod.

"He like you," says the student. "He tell me you his brother."

As the days pass, Tom and I grow accustomed to stares. Walking through Xi'an, a city of ancient pagodas and yellow construction cranes, we are pale-skinned spectacles; long-legged oddities on streets void of Westerners. We feel the weight of Chinese eyes as we stroll—from men, women, young, old; from commuters on rusty bicycles and dented scooters; from street chefs sizzling vegetables on sidewalk woks. Some folks say "Hello!" showing off their only

English. Some ask us to pose for photos. Others watch, warily. We are rock stars or extraterrestrials, I'm never sure which.

On our daily walk to the school we pass storefronts that house prostitutes. The storefronts are always the same: sliding patio glass doors, frosted white from top to bottom, except for a clear horizontal strip across the middle. The women stare through the strip, tapping the glass as we pass. Occasionally they slide open the door and laugh and wave and say something in Chinese, an invitation, I assume, for the world's oldest form of entertainment at a reasonable price.

These frosted-glass brothels are scattered along a busy street, squeezed between more legitimate businesses: small restaurants, a shop that sells copper tubing and hardware odds and ends, what appears to be an accountant's office. Next to one brothel is a family photo studio with pictures on the window of happy mommies and daddies and kiddies in red jackets and bow ties. And yet because of the white glass the brothels almost look clean. Like medical offices.

On one rainy morning walk to the school, Tom declares that the street reminds him of Paris.

"*Paris*," I say. "Are you kidding me?"

"It's the sycamore trees," says Tom.

The trees are leafy and full, in robust green lines on both sides of the street. But really . . . Paris?

The prostitutes tap the windows as we pass, as if to emphasize that Shiyuan Street is not the Chinese Champs-Elysées.

"I've noticed they knock on the window more for us than for locals," says Tom.

"They probably figure we're more likely to overpay."

"We probably *would* overpay."

"Actually, as many times as we walk back and forth, they must wonder why we never stop."

"Maybe they think we're gay."

"If they thought we were gay they wouldn't keep tapping the window."

"Maybe they need a more targeted marketing strategy."

"Well, it's not like they're doing a whole lot to entice us. A little window tapping, a few smiles—we don't even know what they're offering."

"Would you like a brochure?"

"That would help. I'm sure they don't want to put up any tacky sales signs, this being so much like Paris."

"It's the sycamore trees," he repeats.

"I'm a little offended they even think we look like the kind of guys who would use prostitutes."

"What do guys who use prostitutes look like?"

"I dunno. Less clean. Guts. Beards, maybe."

"So men with beards use Chinese prostitutes."

"I'm just saying that you don't look at us and think, 'Wow, those two guys look like they flew here to hook up with Chinese prostitutes.' You look at us and you think . . ."

"Dweebs."

"Yes. Dweebs."

"Dweebs need prostitutes, too."

"Dweebs with beards."

We make jokes, but the more we pass the prostitutes, the more they depress me: trapped in their glass cages, seeing life without living it. And on a wet, showery day like this, I find I tilt my umbrella: a rainy day blinder to block them from view.

Ms. B hunches over a bookshelf, scribbling on the back of used notepaper. She has a new communication strategy: she's writing me notes in English. It's morning break time. The "Loo-la-loo" song bebops at high volume. Ms. L brushes Haley's hair, Lightswitch turns off the light switch, and Ms. H turns it back on, while the Dancer studies a wooden block, which he will soon attempt to eat. A boy I've named Michael Jordan—he frequently wears a shirt with the number 23—twitches his hands in front of his face. It's a constant tic; he talks to himself when he does it.

Ms. B hands me the note: *Go in row five floor. With happy nurses day.*

I must look puzzled, because Ms. B giggles. She says something to Ms. H and Ms. L and they laugh, too. Ms. B points at each word with her finger.

"Go . . . in . . . row . . . five . . . floor. With happy nurses day."

"Ahhhh," I say, having no clue what it means.

Ms. B issues a command with Mao-like authority, and Ms. H and Ms. L organize the students in a single-file row. I take Liu Baojian's hand, and we walk two flights down shadowy steps to the fifth floor, past the school's offices to a makeshift gym. The floors are covered with thick rubber mats that fit like puzzle pieces. Basketballs and balance beams are shoved to the side, and chairs fill the outside square of the room, leaving an open square within. Students are led in. Milling about are the school's founder—Zhang Tao—and some school administrators, along with nurses in traditional garb: white hats and white dresses and white stockings.

A school assembly of some sort? Zhang Tao speaks, though it's hard to hear over the students' shouts, not that I can understand what she's saying. One of the teenagers in Tom's class, a thick kid built like a bouncer, yells his usual yell—"*Cheema Cheema!*"—while lifting his shirt and slapping his chest and making puckered-up smooching sounds. Another of the older students, tall and thin, smiles and yells "*Tweeeeee!*"

When Zhang Tao stops speaking the orange-shirt teachers applaud and the nurses grin and wave and nod their heads. I finally get it.

"With happy nurses day" is "Wish 'Happy Nurses Day.'"

We form three circles, students and teachers alike, holding hands. The first group jumps up and down and shouts a Chinese chant. It's the same rhythm as "We're Num-ber One!" but to my English-language ears it sounds like—

See Pa-pa John!
See Pa-pa John!
See Pa-pa John!

The first group quiets, and the second group—Tom's group—jumps and chants. The student Tom is primarily working with, Wu Feng, beams as they shout. Now it's our class's turn: the kids leap and laugh. Liu Baojian can't get off the ground, but he yells—

UhhhhhUhhhhUhhhhhh

We do this for a few minutes, alternating between groups. *Why* we're doing this, I have no idea. Maybe it's some sort of tribute for the nurses. Maybe it's a tribute to ultimate victory of communism over democracy. Who knows? I never know what's happening until it happens, and even then I'm not sure. Later, before lunch, Ms. B looks at me, rubs her hands together, and nods her head toward the bathroom—meaning, I assume, "wash your hands." So I go to the bathroom, squirt some Purell—I'd rather not use the sink—and gaze out the window at the gray buildings as I wash.

I dry my hands on my jeans as I walk back to class. Liu Baojian stands outside the room, a bit forlorn, waiting.

Oh. I was supposed to wash *his* hands.

"With Happy Nurses Day" is the first time I notice Buddha Boy. He's probably five years old. Maybe six. He smiles as if incapable of sadness, as if he doesn't know what sadness *is*; his grin so bright he makes the street vendors' Buddha statues seem melancholic. It's a smile that could sell cereal or toys on television.

A man is with him. I'm guessing it's his grandfather, though the man's hair is black. He reminds me a bit of Dad, actually—the slight belly, the tan sweater and black jeans, the hair that's thinning yet thick.

The boy has cerebral palsy. He can't walk without help. He

raises his hands above his head, and the grandfather grips them, guiding the boy, his frail legs wobbling, noodlelike, with each step. If the man let go, the boy would fall. But of course he does not let go.

I see them at the health screening that's part of the nurses' visit. Most of the third graders cry or resist the tests: Liu Baojian winces and cowers when his eye is covered for a vision exam. The Dancer weeps as the blood pressure strap inflates around his arm. But not the Buddha Boy, who is younger than them all. He keeps smiling. Like he knows his smile will sustain the nurses through a stressful day.

I watch the grandfather; the subtle grin that hints at his affection for the boy. I will never see one without the other. I can't fathom one without the other. They don't seem to talk—maybe the boy *can't* talk—though sometimes the grandfather, while holding the boy's raised hands, will lean down and whisper in his ear. I wonder what he tells him. I wonder what secrets they share.

That afternoon we saunter into sunshine for a class outing, walking to Ren Ren Le, the department store/supermarket hybrid near the east gate of Xi'an's 640-year-old wall. The Ren Ren Le is crammed between a ground-floor KFC and the Agricultural Bank of China, with floors of offices above. It's like the Super Target of China: clothes, furniture, electronics, toys, appliances, plus a large bottom-floor grocery, complete with a butcher, bakery, fresh produce, and seafood. (Near the Bell Tower, one of the city's signature fourteenth-century landmarks, is a new Wal-Mart. As Tom notes, since everything at Wal-Mart is made in China, the stuff at this Wal-Mart must be *really* cheap.)

We're at Ren Ren Le as part of a class project, buying fruit to support our continuing produce-based vocabulary lessons. We're also here to support the school's larger mission: to expose the world to the children, and expose the children to the world. During our orientation, Meilin told us that attitudes about special-needs kids are changing, but prejudices remain. Other kids taunt special-needs children at parks. Parents sneer at mothers, telling them to keep their kids at home. So while attitudes may be improving, we are still an unusual sight: ten special-needs kids, three teachers, one lanky foreigner. Shoppers discreetly and not so discreetly watch as we wander past the shoe department and women's underwear, past refrigerators about half the width of the ones back home; as we ride the escalator down to the grocery. We all hold hands, shuffling through the market like a grade-school chain gang. I tower Lurch-like over the students, a foot taller than even the teachers, the only Westerner in the store. One slightly bent-over, white-haired old woman walks to our group near the checkout lanes, hands clasped behind her back, studying us like we're an art exhibit she finds distasteful.

The kids are quieter here than at the school, though their occasional twitches and squeals—Haley's tilted head and open mouth—signal their conditions as we file past bins of pigs' ears, peanuts, and shrink-wrapped cookie boxes. Sleeves attempts to grab a man's cane. Each of the kids has a notepad-sized piece of paper: on it, the teachers have drawn a piece of fruit. Liu Baojian has a strawberry. We identify it in the bins, but don't buy: strawberries are too expensive. Ms. B fills a basket with plum tomatoes and crackers and cookies instead.

Our hand-holding posse shuffles outside while Ms. H pays the bill. We wait, conspicuously, on the bright, busy sidewalk. As I watch the passing buses and taxis—the cell phone pedestrians talking and walking, glancing at our little group—I turn to see that Happy Bear has lowered his sweatpants and underpants to his knees, his pecker dangling in the breeze. Since I don't know the Chinese word for "pecker," I'm not sure how to communicate this unexpected event to the teachers. I'm about to simply yell "Yo!" to Ms. L—I'm holding hands with Liu Baojian, which means I'm tethered to a three-and-a-half-foot anchor—when I hear above the voices and cars and honks a sound curiously like a splattering stream.

Happy Bear is peeing amid the passing pedestrians on the sidewalk.

By the time Ms. L notices, he's finished relieving himself. She lifts up his drawers and snaps at him, telling him, presumably, "Listen—it's okay to pee on side streets"—we've seen men pee against walls—"but you *do not* do it in the middle of the sidewalk!"

Walkers pass by with even more befuddled faces, and I feel myself tensing up. Not because Happy Bear was peeing. Because I'm wondering about the response his puddle will get from passersby. I'm a mellow guy—I'm the kind of guy you occasionally need to check for a pulse—but if anyone confronts one of these teachers, if anyone dares to say anything about these kids, he will have one very angry foreigner in his face.

Being in Xi'an reminds me not so much of Dad's trip to China as of his periodic business trips to Japan. He was forever smitten by Tokyo, marveling at the city's mobbed yet clean, safe streets; reminiscing about the nights he ate *kodako* (baby octopus), *unagi* (freshwater eel), *odori ebi* (raw prawns, their antennae waving). The night at a bathhouse when he climbed out of the tub and slipped on the wet floor, knocking him unconscious. When he opened his eyes, his naked Japanese friends were huddled over him, dripping, saying, "Bob-san! Bob-san!"

"I felt such spirit of modesty [*seijitu*] and sincerity [*majime*] when I first met Bob," his boss and close friend, Mr. Tanaka, told me by e-mail. "I can believe it is a real reason why Bob made so many Japanese friends."

In the months after I returned from China, I contacted Mr. Tanaka and some of Dad's old colleagues. In some ways, they knew him better than I did. Parts of Dad remain elusive to me, as unde-cipherable as the classroom banter at La La Shou. His satisfactions, his disappointments, his affections—he expressed them mainly on paper, in letters he never mentioned. He internalized, as I do.

When Dad worked at the MRI facility in South San Francisco, he decided who stayed and who lost their jobs during layoffs. It weighed on him, because he'd seen his father desperate to find work, and he'd experienced joblessness himself. For a man defined by his work ethic, applying for unemployment was a low point in his life, though I never heard him discuss it. I know it pained him to put good people in that same frightening, humiliating position.

"It seemed like there was always a financial crisis," said Kevin, the manager I'd spoken with at Dad's retirement party. "It was cut back, cut back—do more—cut back—do more, cut back. Bob was a calming influence. He always stepped back, looked at every angle. And no matter how difficult things got, he never showed his anger."

I e-mailed Dad's friend Will, who worked in HR.

"Bob exhorted me to fight for the best exit packages possible. He told me, on multiple occasions, 'Will, no company has ever gone broke from treating its employees too well. It's the organiza-tion that ruthlessly economizes at the expense of its workers that ends up broken.'"

Will refers to that time as "repetitive downsizing."

"We experienced plenty of going-away parties—more like wakes, really. And Bob would inevitably say a few good words about the persons being honored, and his eyes would get misty, and he'd close by saying, 'I better quit talking before I get too choked up.' Bob had a strong bond with nearly everyone he worked with. It broke his heart every time he needed to show someone out the door—he cared so much about the plight of others. He had a knack for recognizing employees who knew their time was going to end with a layoff—and who didn't want to be 'paraded' through the HR process. Bob would conspire with me so that the individual could resign preemptively. Then we'd collaborate to get the same benefits that person would have received if he or she had stuck around long enough to be formally laid off. Because of Bob, we were able to secure much better severance packages, and keep the remaining workforce relatively stable."

Mr. Tanaka remembers one particularly difficult layoff: close to thirty employees lost their jobs during the recession in 1991.

"It was very difficult and painful for your father to decide who to keep and who to lay off," he says. And then he adds, quite simply, "We cried together."

Each day at La La Shou I sit in a language class that's a mix of third and fourth graders. It's a small room, probably an office from the building's tea distributor days, with a lone discarded teacher's desk, a clock on the chipped gray wall. We drag in wooden chairs. I'm here to help Liu Baojian and the Dancer write Chinese characters—they need someone to help guide their pencils—and to drag students back to their seats when they walk to the window or whack another kid. The words are presented in such a clear, enunciated way that I learn a few. I manage to say "yellow" (*huáng sè de*). One day I tap Ms. H on the arm, point at the numbers on the clock, and count from one to six. She smiles and cheers. A bespectacled fourth-grade teacher applauds.

They ask me the English words for the same objects: strawberry, red, yellow, pineapple. After one of the classes, a student teacher approaches me. She wears a red Motorola shirt instead of orange—red seems to be the color for student teachers—she's here for the week, and she speaks pretty good English.

"Parable," she says to me.

"Excuse me?"

"Parable."

"Parable?"

"Yes—parable."

I look at her with the dumb expression that has become my hallmark.

"I'm sorry—"

"That not right?"

"Well, 'parable' is a word . . ."

"You say this morning for fruit."

She thinks she's saying *pineapple*.

I can empathize with this woman, who in my mental names roster is now Ms. Parable. Aside from my recent success with "yellow" and the numbers one to six, I'm struggling big-time with Chinese. I'm usually decent about picking up words when I travel, but not here. Tom has told me the word for beer multiple times now—*pí jiŭ*—and if you're going to learn a word, this is a good one to know. But I still mispronounce it.

"I always have a hard time saying the 'r' sound at the beginning of Chinese words," says Brenda, a volunteer from North Carolina who's working at a center for abused children, and who speaks a little Chinese. "Their 'r' sounds the same as ours in the middle or at the end of words, but not if 'r' is the first letter. They also don't tend to have clusters of consonants, like 'str.' I remember the translation of Michael Jackson's name sounded like: 'Mi-kul Jak-uh-sun.' I don't think they can make the 's' sound of *son* right after the 'k' sound of *Jack*."

Chinese words can also have entirely different meanings depending on the emphasis and inflection. "The inflection has everything to do with the meaning," says Brenda. "Mandarin has four tones. That means that the same set of letters, such as 'ma,' could have four different meanings. Sometimes I've said a word over and over—such as *ma*—and a Chinese person will struggle to understand and then finally say: 'Oh, you mean *ma*.'"

So you can see why I'm mangling the language. One day I ask the teachers to write their names for me on a piece of paper. I point at Ms. H's name and she pronounces it: Huang Hua.

I nod and say it with confidence. *Huang Hua.*

She explodes with laughter. She's laughing so hard she can barely keep her tiny Huang Hua frame upright, holding on to a chair for support. Ms. B and Ms. L laugh as well. To my ears I said exactly what she said, but I've clearly just called Huang Hua a cattle prod or a potted plant.

My main language legacy is that some of the teachers, thanks to an English-language phrase book I brought, are learning profanities. Tom observes this: I've let him carry the book in his pocket, since he's more frustrated by the language barriers.

"To fuck," says one of the orange-shirt teachers, looking at the phrase book.

"To fuck," repeats her colleague.

They must know what they're saying, because beneath "to fuck" in the book is Chinese characters. They also sample the word *ass*, but they particularly like *jerk*.

"You jerk," says one teacher to the other.

"No—you jerk."

And then they laugh.

Now that the rains have stopped, Tom and I walk through Xing Qing Park most evenings on our way back to the hotel. Xing Qing is the Central Park of Xi'an: more than one 120 acres of greenery, with a lake, Ferris wheel, walking paths, tulips, and the city's rapidly blooming skyscrapers above the trees. Once the site of an eighth-century Tang Dynasty palace, it's a popular spot for morning tai chi, wedding photos, badminton, and casual strolls with your government-mandated one child; a bucolic respite for anyone, like us, who craves a break from people and cars.

"Listen," says Tom, stopping as we walk. "You can actually hear birds."

We wander toward a small *dian*—like a one-story pagoda—

with red doors and columns, decorative blue borders separating layered green roofs. It sits on a concrete pavilion, and we walk up wide stairs to reach it, looking out over trees and paddleboaters churning across the lake. It's a lovely spot, except for the perky pop music drowning out the birds with the unexpected sounds of:

Oh Mickey you're so fine, you're so fine you blow my mind
Hey Mickey! [Clap clap-clap] *Hey Mickey!*

We lean against a concrete rail, watching the rippling reflections of the trees.

"I wonder if you'd go insane if you worked for a long time in an insane asylum," Tom says.

"Is this something you think about often?"

"It just occurred to me today."

Tom is struggling at the school. While I find the language barrier frustrating, Tom finds it maddening, because he can't be clear with the teachers about what they need or expect. I've tried telling him to think big picture. That was a lesson from Costa Rica. Yes, we could contribute more if we spoke the language, but we're a welcome diversion for the teachers. If we do a few things that simplify their lives—each day I haul a heavy pot of rice up two flights of steps—well, that's something, right?

The bigger problem for Tom is a sense of futility. Part of Tom's job is to guide Wu Feng through a variety of mind-numbing school assignments, such as writing the same number fifty times—a slow task given his microsecond attention span.

"It's torture," Tom says, looking out at the lake.

He shares his difficulties in a journal entry. Each member of Global Volunteers team 173 has to write an entry in a spiral notebook. We're asked to include a quote—a thought of the day—and read the entry aloud in the morning as we eat breakfast. Tom's turn comes at the end of week one. He reads it as we drink our coffee and tea and eat our Western-style buffet breakfast (French toast) with its Eastern-style touches (noodles):

May 14

    <u>*Thought for the day*</u>:

      "I know of no more encouraging fact than the unquestioned ability of a man to elevate his life by conscious endeavor."

            —HENRY DAVID THOREAU

    The student slid two chairs to the table at the apartment's large window, which overlooked the building's courtyard. It was raining outside and cool fresh air poured across the tabletop. I sat down and opened the practice book. I was familiar with the exercise.

    "Oh, seven today," I said. The teacher had drawn a grid— six rows, nine columns. In the left-hand column were six neatly drawn sevens. The student was to copy the example into each of the boxes of the grid.

    "Right here," I said, tapping my finger on the first blank box to try and draw his attention.

    "Bah."

    He half shouted this and thrust his hand up to point to something outside the window. He turned to me, smiling broadly.

    I tapped my finger a few more times and looked down at the sheet.

    He reached for his pencil box, opened one side, pulled out one of the pencils and examined the tip.

    A few more finger taps.

    He held the paper flat with his left hand and drew a seven with the right. He drew a second. He began a third but then, dissatisfied, he reached for his pencil box and retrieved his eraser.

He closed the box and paused to look at one of the stickers
on it.
I tapped my finger on the page a few more times.
He turned to look out the window.

And so the exercise goes, for over an hour. A few sevens that start to look like ones. Stopping at the sounds of other students, stopping to pull a new pencil from his pencil box, stopping to sharpen his new pencil. The pencil tip breaking. Tom handing him the original pencil and refocusing him on the assignment, followed by more distractions.

"I tapped my finger," Tom wrote. "He looked down, drew another seven, then flipped forward to the next page in the practice book. Another page of sevens was waiting. He flipped again. More sevens. He flipped again. There were the eights."

My days are less tedious than Tom's, though I share his sense of uselessness. One of my more effective duties is to take Liu Baojian each day to an apartment across the street for his nap. The nap follows lunch. The kids eat in the classroom; Tom and I eat together near the offices, in front of the trampoline, on the fifth floor. Before the week began, Meilin told us we'd eat lunch at the school, which I found about as enticing as undergoing surgery at the school. I expected the Chinese equivalent of the food from my high school— wrinkled green soybean hot dogs on soggy buns. But eat it we must, I decided, as a courtesy, though Meilin suggested we be honest if we dislike the choices.

"Tell them, I don't like spicy food, I don't like pig organs," she said.

The orange-shirted teachers dished it up. We received a small bowl of lo mein–style noodles, and a bowl of rice with chicken, tofu, sprouts, peas, and stewed tomatoes.

It's spectacular. The school food is the best food we eat in China. We rave about it to Meilin, who looks at us like, yeah, okay, it's fine, but it's *school food*. The ingredients are fresh, probably bought that morning. The cook does her steaming and stirring magic in the school kitchen right before the meal is served.

Our dinners are almost exclusively in the hotel. The food is fine—our group sits in a private room with Meilin, sharing food from a lazy Susan the size of a satellite dish—but it seems a shame to travel eighteen hours to Xi'an and eat in a hotel each night. Tom and I consider playing mealtime hooky, but dinners tend to include a discussion of volunteer-related business. Ralph later finds a more exotic menu that includes a variety of penis dishes. I'd be willing to try the assorted phallic entrées, but as part of her arrangement with the hotel, Meilin must order our meals off the nonpenis menu.

One theory for our dinnertime quarantine is that Global Volunteers doesn't want us to catch the H1N1 virus, which seems silly since Tom and I are immersed in germs at the school. Kids cough without covering their mouths. Kids sneeze. Kids go to the bathroom and never wash their hands. One afternoon, during a classroom tea party (minus the tea), Jenna sticks her hands down her pants, then hands me a cookie. I thank her and discreetly slip it in my back pocket, a strategy I've used on several occasions: my back pocket has been filled with everything from plum tomatoes to an oddly spiced cracker from Liu Baojian's wet hand. Despite my caution, I'm having some "D" issues, if you know what I mean. Nothing severe, though one day I felt gross enough that I skipped lunch and walked to Ren Ren Le for the blandest-looking bread I could find. This leads to the misconception that I won't eat spicy foods.

Ralph, bless him, shares some Pepto tablets he brought. He's teaching English at the Xi'an Biomedical Technical College. The goal is to chat with the students—they need practice speaking—though Ralph employs a clever tactic he used on a Global Volunteers trip in Vietnam. "The first time I went to Hanoi I asked the students what they wanted to learn about the U.S.A. One student wanted to learn about baseball. So on my second trip I brought ten baseball gloves, three bats, twelve balls, and a hitting tee, and I taught a baseball clinic. It was pandemonium. There were twenty-four hundred kids in the school and I think I played with two thousand over two weeks."

He brought baseball gear to Xi'an as well. "I see it as another way to initiate a conversation—and get us out of the classroom," he says, laughing his boisterous *heh-heh-heh* laugh. I wonder if his students will develop his Brooklyn accent. Park is *pawk*. March is *mawch*. Large is *lawge*.

After Tom and I finish the day's delicious lunch, I walk back up to my own classroom, the floor now covered with noodles and rice. Ms. B and Ms. H take the other students for their nap at a building across the street, while Ms. L cleans up. We're joined by an older woman who speaks to a few children and leads them to the stairs. As far as I can tell, this is her part-time job: nap coordinator.

Since Liu Baojian moves more slowly than the other kids, he needs his own individual walk-mate. I take his hand. We walk down the seven flights of stairs. He does the both-feet-per-step method. Right foot down, left foot down. Stand. Right foot down, left foot down. Stand. I'm tempted to pick him up, but he needs to do this himself.

Ms. H and Ms. B are chugging down the stairs with three children each.

Right foot down, left foot down. Stand . . .

Once outside we cross the street—all gray apartments, no shops, still prone to speeding scooters and too-fast cars—and stroll about twenty yards on the sidewalk to the nap building. I push open the dented metal door. We walk through a narrow covered alley. It's dark—shadowy—quiet except for mysterious drips hitting pavement and a television's tinny talk show conversations.

I steer Liu Baojian around puddles. We climb up another three flights of steps. We're still holding hands. Mine is warm. His must be, too. A motion sensor provides a feeble light on the stairs, but we're so slow it turns off before we finish the first flight. The darkness further diminishes our speed.

We reach a stale-smelling apartment that's loaded with bunk beds. The nap coordinator lets me in. She smiles, bows slightly a few times, motions at me to enter. I take Liu Baojian to his bed in the back corner. He takes off his shoes. I'm not sure where he's supposed to go. Upper bunk? Lower bunk? Must be the lower bunk, because that's where he goes. He pulls my arm. He wants me to stay and sleep. "I have to go, buddy," I say. The nap coordinator says something and he lets go. I wave and head out. They will all sleep, teachers and children, for almost two hours.

As I leave, I see Sleeves crawl into a lower bed with Ms. H for their nap, and I remember when I was little, when a nightmare would stir me awake in the night. It didn't happen often, but I would cower under the covers before building up the courage to yell, "*Daaddddd-eeeee . . .*"

After another holler or two, his shadowy figure would trudge into the room.

"I had a bad dream," I'd say.

He'd crawl into bed with me. One time I told him I was sorry.

"That's okay," he told me. "Someday you'll have a son of your own."

I never felt as guilty about calling him after that.

While the kids sleep, I walk back to the Empress Hotel and e-mail Julie. Tom is still at the school: his students are teenagers, so they aren't napping. Which means I get a break and Tom doesn't. Did I mention my concern that this trip might destroy the friendship?

"Nah, nah," he says one night when I broach the subject. "It's not that bad."

If Tom and I are an unusual, aliens-have-landed sight, me solo is even stranger. The expressions seem more intense: the wary gaze of merchants as I stroll up a shop-filled street; idle hairdressers peering over magazines at small salons; customers whispering at dumpy takeout restaurants, clouds of steam and grease rising above the sidewalk. The word for foreigner is *wàiguórén*—*wàiguó* means "outside land," *rén* means "person"—though the slang is *lǎowài*. I've heard conflicting views on whether it's negative, though I believe it depends on the context. Meaning, you might say *lǎowài* because it's so danged unexpected. Like seeing Santa Claus in June.

Some schoolkids run down the sidewalk. Whenever I see children here, running or yelling or playing, I assume they're autistic. Because all the kids sound exactly the same to me. In my head, I hear the Dancer say "Bà-*baaaa . . .*"

I'm sweating when I arrive at the Empress. The hotel computer isn't speedy, but it works. I sit in a small glass office that's also used to book tours. A woman in a blue jacket and blue skirt sits at a desk, full ashtray on top, spacing out. It's quiet enough that I can hear the bubbling of the fish tank near the office's open glass doors.

I tell Julie about Liu Baojian and the other children. I tell her about the wounds I'm collecting from the unpredictability of the children's conditions. Liu Baojian has bitten me twice on the arm while slumped against me. Not hard, not painful, but enough to leave marks. "I've got a bite mark on my left hand, scratch marks on my right arm," I write. "I've had my hair pulled, ear pulled, nose pulled, and I've been pinched more times than I can remember."

But the same day I was bit, I tell her, a boy ran into the class, sat on my lap, hugged me, and kissed me on the cheek, as the teachers laughed. "The work is intense, and the language barrier is difficult, but I like the kids a lot, and in some ways it's easier than Costa Rica because we don't have to plan. Just show up. And the teachers are amazing. They're in their early twenties—enthusiastic, energetic, incredibly patient women."

"Excellent—no planning!" she writes back. "You are right about the teachers of disabled and handicapped kids having the patience of Job. There's a reason that is not my chosen profession."

"It sounds cornball," I write, "but there's a lot of love in this school. And it's not easy love. It's the kind of love that tests your patience; the kind of love that tests your limits."

It's so strange to travel without her. Ten years earlier, Julie and I took a road trip in Arizona, from Flagstaff to Phoenix, including three days at the Grand Canyon. We mainly hiked, but one morning we toured the south rim by helicopter. Julie rode in front with the pilot; I sat in back with an elderly couple who looked like they'd posed for *American Gothic*.

We wore headphones. "How's everyone doing?" the pilot said. "I know you're really going to enjoy this—you'll see the canyon in a totally different way."

The propellers whirred. As soon as we took off, the woman in back with me started sweating. We sped toward the canyon, flying low over the trees. Music boomed through the headphones: Wagner's "The Ride of the Valkyries"—like the famous helicopter scene from *Apocalypse Now*. The orchestra hits its peak as the earth opened up before us, the canyon infinite in jagged reds below.

The woman reached for an airsick bag.

"How about *that*," said the pilot through the headphones. Wagner thundered—

Dum dum-dum-dum-dum, DUM dum-dum-dum-dum, DUM dum-dum DUM!, dum-dum dum-dum-dum DUMMMM . . .

The woman barfed.

Up front the pilot pointed out some noteworthy scenery to Julie, who wore a big isn't-this-amazing smile on her face.

The man reached for a barf bag. Then *he* started barfing.

The woman's glasses fogged up. The helicopter began to smell like sausage.

Twenty-five minutes later, when we finally landed, the couple wobbled off the helicopter across the hot pavement, weak-kneed, hair damp. I wasn't feeling so great myself. Julie, meanwhile, trotted from the copter wearing her jaunty tourist smile.

"Do you have any idea what was going on back there?" I said.

"No—why?"

"They were throwing up! She started throwing up as soon as we took off!"

"Really?"

"You didn't smell it?"

"No—I had no idea."

That's how I feel now. I'm experiencing things she'll never know.

A boy I've named Robby is sobbing, stomping his feet, and bouncing up and down on a wooden chair. As his butt lands the chair rocks against the floor—

Bonk! Bonk! Bonk! Bonk!

Robby wants bread. Happy Bear's bread. Each morning, Happy Bear arrives late, shuffling into the room with a plastic bag of store-bought rolls. Once Happy Bear starts eating, Robby pouts and cries and bonks.

A few days ago, Robby snatched one of Happy Bear's rolls, then fled to the window, eating the pilfered bread, wiping his tears with the curtain. It was a daring theft. Robby is a big kid—I named him after Roberto at Escuela Cuestillas—but he's soft: round baby cheeks and a plump tummy under a yellow Winnie the Pooh shirt. Happy Bear is more like a bouncer: big, solid, strong. One afternoon Happy Bear freaked out—he wanted a glass of water and became hysterical when Ms. B stopped him to tie his shoelaces—and it took three of us to restrain him as he screamed and fought, struggling to march from the room.

On this morning, Robby won't be stealing bread: Ms. B speaks to him, saying, I assume—"Sorry, pal, but that ain't your food."

When Robby ignores her, rushing from his chair to repeat his theft, Ms. L grabs him and guides him back to his seat, lecturing him along the way. Now the sobbing is more intense, as is the violent bouncing in his chair.

BONK! BONK! BONK! BONK!

Robby eventually crawls under Happy Bear's chair, still whimpering, picking up crumbs from the floor, eating them one by one.

Perhaps thinking some entertainment will ease the tension, Ms. B shows me the dictionary and points to the word "performance." She motions for me to stand in front of the class.

"You sing song," Ms. Parable tells me since I looked confused.

I'm surprised I haven't sung sooner: Tom has been a human jukebox for his class. As a Frank Zappa fan, he thought about singing "Galoot Up-Date" from *Thing-Fish*, but instead dredged up memories of simple children's songs: "This Old Man," "Row, Row, Row Your Boat." By the end of our stint he's like a lounge act, performing two or three times a day, often making up the words as he goes: "I haven't sung these in thirty years," he says.

I choose a kiddie song, though I regret not singing some Elvis. I was surprised, when talking with Meilin one day, to learn she'd never heard of Elvis, who I assumed was among America's best-known dead Caucasians. But instead of "Mystery Train" I go with "Old McDonald." Seems safe: oinks, moos, meows—real crowd-pleasin' stuff. When I'm done mooing, Ms. B says *Chinese Chinese Chinese* to Ms. Parable, and amid the indecipherable dialogue I pick up two familiar words, which transport me back to Costa Rica, back to San Carlos, back to Escuela Cuestillas.

"You know Hokey Pokey?" asks Ms. Parable.

Do I know Hokey Pokey? *Do I know Hokey Pokey?* Are you kidding? Does China know chopsticks? Hell yes I know Hokey Pokey. I hokey-pokeyed to rave reviews among five-year-olds in Central America.

I organize a small circle: Ms. B, Ms. H, Jenna, Lightswitch, and me. We put our right hand in and take our right hand out. We shake them all about. Huge success.

Ms. B digs out a sheet with some of the words in English. "Hokey Pokey," she says, pointing at the paper. It's like we've just solved the riddle of some ancient, confounding text.

My most memorable performance comes later in the week when I spin a volleyball on my finger. The teachers are amazed. Ms. B makes me stand before the class and perform. She and Ms. L both try it, without success, the ball bouncing against desks and shelves. I hold the volleyball on Jenna's finger and rotate it, and she giggles, a giggle so genuine and sweet it makes me giggle, too.

Later that morning, Ms. B asks me a question.

Uncle or brother?

She's asking what the children should call me. I'm tempted to go with brother, but I tell her uncle, which seems more realistic.

"*Shūshu*," she says, translating.

It sounds like "shoo shoo," and it's more helpful for me than for the students. Now when I hear *shūshu* amid the unintelligible Chinese, I know I'm being discussed. And now that I'm an uncle, I feel just a wee bit like part of the family.

I'm holding another man's underpants. I tell Tom this when we return to our hotel room.

"That blue pair isn't mine," I say, peering at a shrink-wrapped bag of recently returned laundry. "Neither is the black pair."

The hotel laundry service is simple: leave your dirty clothes in burlap sacks on the beds and check off a form showing the number and types of items. The next day, your clothes are returned. Or, in this case, someone else's clothes are returned.

My first clue that something's amiss is that the shrink-wrapped underpants look so nice and new. No rips! No holes! And the elastic is attached! Wow! My own boxers and briefs are a bit . . . tattered. Still functional, which is why I continue to wear them, but threadbare. The kind of underwear Lee's army wore by the time of Appomattox.

Tom is now in the bathroom brushing his teeth, which is—no exaggeration—a twenty-five-minute exercise. Precision brushing, meticulous flossing, Waterpik. He has perfect teeth, but he loses, by my calculations, six days a year to oral care.

He walks by my bed, still brushing, as I rip open the shrink-wrapped package and inspect the unidentified underwear. I consider going to the front desk and pointing out the error, but usually only one of the blue-suited staffers speaks English, and that English is severely limited. So showing up in the lobby and saying "I have another man's underpants" may create more confusion than solutions.

Then it occurs to me: why not *wear* these mystery underpants? Seems logical enough. They're clean. They're in better shape than the undies I'm now missing. And they're black and blue, so they have this pristine, never-been-touched quality (meaning, you know . . . any stains won't be visible).

I tell Tom my plan. He's now boiling water, his toothbrush hanging from his mouth like a cigar (all the rooms include a Mr. Coffee–type machine for boiling water—even the locals don't drink from the tap). I thought he'd back me up on the underpants decision given his gloves-at-the-beach practicality, but he seems grossed out.

"I don't know," he says. "You're wearing a stranger's underwear."

"Yeah, but they're clean."

"Okay, you're wearing a stranger's clean underwear. You don't know where that underwear has been."

I mention this to Julie in one of our e-mail exchanges.

"That has so many *eewww* possibilities that I don't know where to start," she says.

I wear them the next morning. They fit nicely. And I'll keep wearing them when I return home. It occurs to me there are two kinds of people in the world: those who will wear freshly laundered mystery Chinese underpants, and those who won't. Though I do feel bad that somewhere in the hotel, some bewildered guest is saying, "Why did I receive these hole-filled undies?"

The grandfather carries Buddha Boy on his back up the stairs. The boy's butt rests on the grandfather's clasped hands, which also hold his backpack. The boy is smiling, of course, his arms around his grandfather's neck.

By the time they reach the fifth floor the grandfather is breathing hard. He probably smokes, as do roughly 60 percent of men in China (most women do not). Between the cigarettes and the polluted air—the city of Benxi once disappeared from satellite images because the pollution was so thick—and the sands that drift from the Gobi Desert, a male emphysema epidemic seems inevitable.

It's hard to imagine what would happen to Buddha Boy if the grandfather gets sick. Does the boy have other family? Could anyone else give him constant care?

I don't see the grandfather every day, and when I do it's for seconds at a time. And yet I admire him. I admire his devotion. I envy it. I envy his dedication, his commitment; his determined, unyielding love.

I wonder about Julie and me—if we'll feel empty when we're older. I wonder how my mom would have survived Dad's death without me and my sister, without Julie and my brother-in-law, my nephew and nieces—a support network that we won't have. Who will care for us if our minds deteriorate? Who will be there for Julie when I'm dead and she's alone in a nursing home? Who will want Julie's photographs when we're gone? Who's gonna give a shit?

The grandfather stops, catches his breath. Buddha Boy smiles from his back. And then the grandfather exhales and continues climbing the steps.

Ms. B is laboring over another note, consulting a Chinese-English dictionary as she writes. I'm guessing she bought the paperback book, because it looks brand-new. I'm not sure if I should feel flattered or guilty.

She checks words with her finger. Ms. L and Ms. H occasionally peek over her shoulder and comment and check the dictionary as well. They seem to enjoy it. Ms. B hands me the note:

> *have lunch eat flax feed and steamed bun. all of us make of flour. are you American eat?*

She's asking if my American taste buds will enjoy lunch: a quasi-hamburger bun you fill with *là jiāo jiàng*, a chili sauce from a jar. Her notes help me learn more about the day's activities and the students themselves, such as the chubby Robby, who has plopped himself in my lap. Given that I'm sitting on a less-than-comfortable wood chair, his weight is a bit hard on the butt. But how can I boot him off? He's rubbing his head against my arm like a cat.

Ms. B grins her happy grin, points at him, and says, "America."

I'm not sure what this means. She pokes through her dictionary, grabs her pen, and hands me another note.

Mix blood, it says.

"So you must have an American daddy," I tell Robby. "Or an American mommy."

Robby holds my hand, rests his head on my shoulder. The Dancer approaches, awkwardly dancing. He stops, abruptly, and stares into my eyes, as he frequently does, his face without expression.

"He mother father not married—like men," Ms. B tells me.

That afternoon we move to the big room so the kids can stare instead at cartoons, combining classes with the fourth graders. This is the first time we've plopped the kids in front of a TV, so I assume it's a Friday afternoon treat: a chance for the teachers to unwind at the end of another exhausting week—though from their laughter they seem more perky than pooped—and a chance to grill Mr. Big American Foreigner with questions. They write queries with the help of Ms. Parable, and I write answers, since that seems easier for us all to decipher. They want to know what I do for a living. Do I have wife. Do I have children. "Photo about environment," a teacher writes, which I assume means do I have pictures of my home.

I'm sitting on a tiny blue plastic chair, which is too small for some of the children, let alone a six-foot-two, two-hundred-pound man, and as I ponder my answers, the legs bend and the chair collapses: it shoots out behind me. The kids are oblivious to the thud of my butt on the tile, but the teachers laugh, almost like children themselves. A fourth-grade teacher races to bring me a bigger chair.

"Who sent to Xi'an," writes Ms. Parable, as if I hadn't just crashed to the floor.

I show them my Global Volunteers name tag, but that's not what they mean.

"No—who sent."

"Me. I decide to come here."

She circles "who" on the paper.

"*Who* send," she asks.

"No one send me here. I send me here."

"You send?"

"I send," I say, pointing at my chest.

It takes about ten minutes to convince them I wasn't sent to Xi'an by the United States government. Volunteerism, from what Meilin told us at the orientation, is not yet a huge concept in China, though benevolence is a guiding principle of Confucianism. "For many years in the ancient times, due to the feudal system, people were exploited and very poor, they did not have enough to share," Meilin said. In modern times, Mao's brutal Cultural Revolution didn't exactly create a groovy let's-help-our-neighbors vibe, though the 2008 Olympics and the Sichuan earthquake helped spur a greater spirit of service throughout the country.

"You like Xi'an?" asks Ms. Parable.

"I like Xi'an very much."

"Xi'an good food?"

"Yes—food very good."

"You come back?"

"Yes—I like to come back."

"When?"

Ms. Parable clasps her hands and sets them in her lap. I think she's waiting for me to flip through a calendar and pinpoint a date.

"Don't know when," I say. "I'm still *here*."

One of the teachers, through Ms. Parable, asks: "Your wife beautiful?"

"Oh yes," I say. And then, because I'm a *báichī*, which is roughly the Chinese word for dunderhead, I add: "But really—what answer could I possibly give?"

When there's a significant language barrier, one should never make a joke. Because this innocent-yet-misguided aside leads to roughly fifteen minutes of my explaining that the only way to answer the question "Your wife beautiful?" is with a "yes," because to say "no" would make me an insensitive creep. Though from the puzzled expressions it's like I've said my wife has a mustache and floppy beagle ears.

"Your wife not beautiful?" says Ms. Parable.

"No, no—wife beautiful. But can't say no. Must say yes."

Blank stares. I write it: "I can't say no. Must say yes!"

"Why wife not beautiful?"

"Wife *is* beautiful. I make joke. Be funny. You know: *ha ha.*"

This leads to a discussion about the word *funny*, and what *funny* means, and what funny is, and how one defines funny. And there's nothing less funny, of course, than describing why something is funny, particularly when describing it to people who have only a minimal grasp of the language (which, actually, is kind of funny).

"Funny is joke," she says.

"Joke—yes. But also physical."

"I sorry—not understand."

"Okay . . . someone fall. Me! I fall in chair. Remember? That's funny!"

I grab the tiny blue chair and re-create my fall.

"Remember? Everyone laugh?"

"Ahhh . . . ," says Ms. Parable with a nod. "Wife funny."

"No, no—wife beautiful."

"Wife beautiful?"

"Right. But if I say 'no,' wife *not* beautiful, I get in trouble."

Ms. Parable looks at me. Her face becomes sad. She cocks her head, slightly.

"Your wife troubled?" she says.

I wave my hands and shake my head.

"My wife beautiful," I say. "My wife very beautiful."

For Friday, Meilin has arranged an optional evening of dumplings and a Tang Dynasty costumed theater show that, she says, "is something tourists like." I'm all for dumplings. *Love* dumplings. But that "something tourists like" theater line concerns me. After an intense week at the school, I figured Tom and I would join the gorging-on-dumplings part of the proceedings, skip the show, and down a much-needed beer. So I was surprised to hear Tom say, "Yeah, sure," when Meilin asked during breakfast who'd like to attend the show.

Not my first choice. But given that Tom's had a lousy first week, and that I'm the one who convinced him to come, I'd have donned bright silk Tang robes and performed the show myself if I thought it'd make him happy.

The next morning, when more Friday night arrangements are discussed over breakfast, Tom leans to me and says, "Maybe we should just have a beer that night."

Now *that's* the mind-reading Tom I know and love.

The dumplings and show are at a local dinner theater. After surviving the ten-minute cab ride—I counted eight white-knuckle instances when we nearly collided with cars, bikes, buses, pedestrians, or dogs—we arrive to find the tables packed with Germans, Russians, Swedes, Americans, Brits. All the tour bus Westerners we haven't seen until now.

Tom and I revel in the dumplings and the multitude of fillings—vegetables, beef, fish (which are shaped like fish with peas for eyes)—and once the lights dim, we escape the theater. We head to the Xi'an City Wall, the ancient, nearly forty-foot-high square wall built in 1370 to protect the city. It's about nine miles in circumference, and the outer portion is now surrounded by paved walking trails, part of a narrow park lined with trees and occasional diversions, from a small roller skating rink to public bathrooms. You can buy tickets to walk or bike on top of the wall; the "Notice to Visitors" includes such warnings as "Prohibit from carrying inflammable and explosive dangerous good into scenic spot."

A large group of singers stands in a boomerang-shaped row. I count roughly sixty of them, men and women in a dark sidewalk plaza thick with trees. Four musicians accompany them on traditional stringed instruments: the twanging *èrhú* and *bǎnhú*. The song is beautiful yet mournful, a melodic chant, the kind of song laborers might sing to pass time. I learn later it's *qíngqiāng*, the local opera of Shanxi Province; the singers are retirees who were sent for reeducation during the Cultural Revolution. "That is when they worked hard during the day and sing to let go the inside pain," explains Hu Hongxia, who oversees Global

Volunteers' China program and joins us one night for our group dinner.

"Older people don't really talk about the Cultural Revolution, unless it is brought up or reminded by something shown on TV or as an education course to their grandchildren," says Hu Hongxia. "When people talk about the Cultural Revolution—even those who suffered from it—they are very calm. It almost looks like they are telling someone else's story. Even my grandfather does that, although two of his good friends died during the persecution. He always tells it with a slight smile and with a tone saying, 'It's all history. Who doesn't make mistakes?' But it also reflects how passive and obedient Chinese people are, compared to Americans."

We walk further and stop at a smaller performance: six women singing, operatically, beneath an arch in the wall, accompanied by an accordion player on a folding chair. A smaller crowd watches—maybe fifteen people.

A chipper middle-aged gentleman approaches and chats with Tom in very good English. They cover a variety of topics: the man asks why Americans aren't more concerned about the H1N1 virus. He asks if it's true that street musicians in the United States expect money, and is shocked to learn the answer is yes. They talk for a while, and then he asks Tom if he plays a musical instrument.

"I took piano lessons as a kid," says Tom.

The gentleman nods, then talks with the accordion player, who gets up and lifts the instrument over his head, the strap slipping off his shoulder.

"You play," the gentleman says to Tom, pointing at the seat.

Tom hesitates—he has never played the accordion (and I've heard his clunky piano skills)—then gets that look that says, "Eh, why the hell not."

He sits. The bulky instrument rests on his lap. Tom carefully sets his fingers on the keys and plays one chord, then another.

Bwwwaaannkkk.

Brrrrreeeeennkkk.

It sounds like the accordion has a sinus infection. Tom's new friend tries to help. He sings "Jingle Bells," clapping his hands and tapping his foot—"*Da-da-da, da-da-da, da-DAH-da-da-da* . . ." As if Tom will hear the melody and go "Ohhhh . . ." and instantly master the accordion.

Bwwwaaannkkk.

Brrrrreeeeennkkk.

Tom laughs. The crowd laughs. People travel for many reasons, but no matter where or why you go, you hope for something like this. A serendipitous moment. A one-of-a-kind story you'll tell the rest of your life at work, at parties, at bars. As Tom mangles each off-kilter chord, as the crowd's jolly spirit grows, it confirms my personal rule of travel: always choose the streets over tourist shows.

After the China trip, I call Dad's friend Kevin one day at work during my lunch hour. Kevin and Dad were more than just work buddies. "I really thought of him as my older brother," says Kevin. Not long after Dad retired and my folks moved back to Virginia, Kevin's younger brother died.

"I didn't know how to handle it," he said. "And Bob could obviously tell on the phone, because I'm all upset. And he just said, 'You know what—I'll be there tomorrow.' And boom—he was there. He stayed for a few days. He came to the service. And before he left, he looked me in the eye, and he said, 'You ever need anything, I'm there for you. I'm just a phone call away.' And it meant so darned much to me. I can't say how much it meant to me."

"Was that the last time you saw him?" I ask.

"That was the last time I saw him. We talked every week, but that was the last time I saw him. I go to the cemetery, and there's a little corner there where Bob stood during the service. So every time I'm there, I look over at that spot."

I remind Kevin that the five-year anniversary of Dad's death is rapidly approaching. "I think it's the thing that we'll never get over in our lifetimes," he says.

The weekend is free time, and Tom and I walk to a cash machine near the hotel for Chinese yuans. I like foreign money: red bills, blue bills, yellow bills—it's like paper candy. And in China, the higher the denomination, the bigger the bill, which means the bigger the image of a somewhat-smirking Mao. I expected to see ubiquitous Mao images across the city, but I see him only twice, in paintings hanging in restaurant lobbies. His portrait is more common in rural homes, I'm told, and some taxi drivers hang a mini-Mao on their rearview mirror for good luck and safety (which they need, given their driving skills). The main place we see the Communist dictator, however, is on the capitalist cash.

It's reasonably sunny out for Xi'an, and Tom wears what I affectionately call his safari outfit: sun hat, wide sunglasses, long-sleeved button-up shirt, hiking pants, and hiking boots. What little skin that shows is slathered with sunscreen; he also carries a tube in his big blue backpack. As we leave the ATM, we walk down the sidewalk, cars and bikes and scooters racing past. A father lifts up a little boy, probably age three or four. The boy points at us and says something to the dad.

"Even four-year-olds know we're foreigners," I say to Tom.

"Well, c'mon," he says. "Could I stand out any more? I've got a hat, backpack, hiking boots . . . The only thing I'm missing is clown makeup."

"People probably think this is the hot new fashion in America. A year from now everyone'll be dressed like you."

"At least they won't get sunburned."

We take a cab to the Dayan Ta, known in English as the Great Goose Pagoda. Tom sits up front with the driver. When he reaches for his seat belt, the driver says "No, no," shaking his head and waving his hand. We're not clear if he's saying dude, relax, you're not required to wear a seat belt, or if wearing a safety restraint is an insult to his driving skills, which are in fine display as he makes a screeching U-turn in two lanes of oncoming traffic. Tom wisely ignores him. I have no choice: the backseat is seat belt–free. Fortunately, the metal bars that separate front seat from back will absorb the impact of my face if we crash.

The pagoda area is a mix of ancient yin and modern yang. Built in 652 A.D. to house Buddhist scriptures, the pagoda looms over a recently built square, where a series of massive fountains offer Asia's biggest water show. Along both sides of the square are strip mall-ish food joints, including McDonald's, Baskin-Robbins, and KFC (by far the most prominent U.S. fast food chain in Xi'an). Day or night, the area is packed with locals, perhaps because open space is such a rarity. But once you leave the square and enter the pagoda's walled grounds, the scene is far more serene. Tom and I wander through gardens, past a main hall with three statues of the Buddha. Monks light candles in a quiet courtyard. Away from the throngs and cabs and cars, the tranquility here is magnified. As we walk, Tom says something that surprises me.

"I never knew you wanted kids until I read your article about Costa Rica."

I had written, quite unexpectedly, about the Costa Rica trip. I know I can tell Tom anything, and I hope he feels the same about me, though we rarely talk with any deep honesty about our lives. As soon as he says this I feel like an ass: one of my best friends learned about one of my darkest issues by reading it in a magazine.

"Yeah, well, it's hard," I say.

"Do you and Julie ever talk about it?"

"Not really. I mean, you know how we are."

"That's not healthy."

"I know."

I tell him how angry I got when our nephew was born. How I haven't come to terms with the finality of it, the sense of loss. If I *had* come to terms with it, Tom and I wouldn't be discussing it in the gardens of a Buddhist temple fourteen thousand miles from home.

Tom had mentioned to Ralph one night that of his two sisters and three cousins, only Sarah, his younger sister, had wanted, or had, a child.

"I've never entirely understood that—you and Julie are both so good with kids," I say.

"I like being with kids. I like playing with them. I like the way they think. But . . . I want to be able to paint when I want. Or go hiking."

"I always thought Teresa really wanted a baby. That if you had said, 'Hey, I want kids,' she'd be like, 'Okay!' "

"I don't think so. We both feel the same way."

"Well, it takes Julie and me forever to do anything, so who knows: maybe by the time we're sixty we'll adopt. But I just don't get it, you know? She's my soul mate, or whatever you want to call it. Clearly we're supposed to be together. So why this void? Why did this never happen? I just . . . I don't get it."

The next day, for the weekend's main event, we hop in a van with a guide and three other volunteers to see the famous terracotta warriors. The thousands of carved figures—chariots, horses, archers, soldiers—were the afterlife army of Qin Shihuangdi, China's first emperor. Qin brutalized hundreds of thousands of laborers to create the warriors, a project that began in 246 B.C. when he was thirteen, thus proving it's never too early to obsess about death.

What's most striking about the warriors isn't the statues themselves—and they're impressive, each soldier with his own unique face—but the scale of the collection: three massive pits the size of football fields, covered by arched ceilings, the buildings wide and open like hangars. We loop around each pit, peering down at the figures, the crowd's murmur bouncing loudly through the massive chamber. The warriors we see today were carefully reconstructed, their paint long faded. Archaeologists suspect that still more pits lie in surrounding fields.

Tom and I go to dinner that evening with Brenda. At thirty-five, she's the youngest volunteer on the trip. Blessed with a soft North Carolina accent and a runner's trim build, she lives with her husband in the Bay Area, where she graduated from Stanford with a doctorate in psychology and treats substance-abusing vets. This is her third trip to China: she taught English the previous two times. Now she's volunteering at a child abuse prevention center. The assignment was created just for her, so she's grateful, but frustrated: the center's staff has little or no background in social work or psychology. When they visited a seven-year-old rape victim in a hospital, one of the center's staff workers said the girl was too young to be traumatized by her experience. The center cannot take children from abusive families and place them in foster care unless the families agree. Brenda made clear before the trip that she wasn't an expert in child abuse; once she arrived, the staff asked her to give expert lectures. "I pretty much pulled information off the Internet," she tells us. "I have the sense no one knows what to do with me. Maybe I should have stuck to teaching English."

We go to a restaurant near the city wall: the Laosunjia Restaurant of Sliced Pancake in Mutton Soup. Ms. B recommended it while looking at my map. We tink our beer glasses and Brenda teaches us one of the few Chinese words I easily remember: *gānbēi!*—"Bottoms up!" Her language skills come in handy when ordering our meal, because there's a procedure to eating sliced pancake in mutton soup. You take the pancake, which is a hard, saucer-sized biscuit—a collection sit in a basket on the table—and you rip it into pieces, which you drop in your bowl. The waiters take the bowl to the kitchen and pour the soup over the torn-up pancakes, which softens them. The soup is hot and hearty and salty, a nice complement to the Tsingtao beer.

Afterward, we walk along the city wall, and she asks about La La Shou. I tell her about my class. I tell her about the Dancer, and how his parents are divorced; how he gravitates toward men.

"Hey, you speak Chinese," I say. "He says *bàba* a lot. Any idea what that means?"

We stop on a street corner, waiting for the lights to change.

Bàba, she says, means "father."

I don't look at the Dancer the same way after that. I'd always felt some connection with him—the way he stares with those sad, penetrating eyes—but it was something I couldn't define. Now I see we are kindred spirits. The boy who longs for his father. The man who longed to be a dad. Each of us lucky to have amazing women in our lives. I will never meet the Dancer's mother, but she's a single mom raising an autistic child, who has managed to send her son to a school that best serves his need.

I'd like to find the father. I'd like to hurt the father. This isn't like me, but I feel anger. Aggressive anger. Outrage that some self-centered prick would leave his son; would abandon this sweet, bright, sensitive kid. Okay, I don't know for certain that the Dancer's autism led his parents to divorce. But I've heard multiple stories of fathers who walked out on their families after learning a child was not "normal."

I watch the Dancer when we're back on Monday morning. He sits with his legs crossed. Quiet. Like he's in deep thought. And I think—

Who the hell am I to judge. In four more days, I'll be just another man who has entered the Dancer's life and left him behind.

And then there's little Liu Baojian, who's pissing me off.

On Tuesday, like every afternoon, I pick him up at the apartment after his nap. The kids are usually a little groggy, though Jenna smiles from the top bunk and says "Good morning!" in English. I help her climb down the ladder since her socks look slippery. Ms. B is in the bottom bunk with Giggles, the two of them still asleep.

I wait for Liu Baojian. Sometimes he wakes up early, but waits for me to arrive. Our routine is to repeat what each other says.

"*Nǐhǎo*," he says—"Hello," pronounced "Nee how," as we clamber down the dark stairwell.

"*Nǐhǎo*," I reply.

"*Nǐhǎo*."

"*Nǐhǎo*."

We do the same with "good morning," which the teachers now say at the start of each class, and we take turns laughing. I laugh, he laughs, I laugh, he laughs . . .

The week before, he scratched my right forearm. Not intentionally—I think he was pinching me—but it broke the skin, and I have a nice collection of scabs below my wrist. Now, as we walk hand in hand down the dank apartment building steps, he does it again. His nails need clipping, so it hurts, like being scratched by a cat.

"*Búshì*," I tell him. No. We trudge down the stairs. Again his nails dig into my arms. I stop at the end of the first flight of steps.

"Hey," I say, leaning down and looking into his hazy eyes. "No. Uh-uh. *Búshì*."

We walk down the steps. He digs into my skin again.

"*Shit*," I say, stopping a second time. "Listen. That hurts. You gotta stop doing that." Of course, I might as well be speaking Klingon since he doesn't speak English.

Later, in class, he takes a slight, clumsy swing at my face. Wang Xue, a college student who'll spend most of week two with us, corrects him, and Ms. B orders him to stand outside the class. She walks by the chair, then stops hard when she sees my arm—or, more specifically, my Liu Baojian–related scratches and scabs. He broke the skin in several places, and my arm is redder and more gouged than I'd realized. She asks through Wang Xue if Liu Baojian did this.

"It's not a big deal," I say.

Ms. B scurries to where Liu Baojian stands outside the class. I hear a long and pointed lecture: "*Chinese Chinese Chinese! Chinese Shoo Shoo Chinese Chinese!*"

Ms. B marches back in and chatters to Ms. H and Ms. L. I don't need a translator: she's mortified. "Really—it's not a problem," I say to Wang Xue. But it *is* a big deal to the teachers, because part of their mission is to show these children what's acceptable behavior and what's not.

Liu Baojian cries outside the door. Ms. B finally talks to him again while I play blocks with Jenna, and Haley pushes buttons on my digital watch to make it beep, and Sleeves pushes up my sleeves.

The lecture continues. Finally Liu Baojian shuffles back into the room, whimpering, chin against his chest. He stands behind me and pets me on the shoulder.

"He say sorry," says Ms. B.

I put my hand on his. "It's all right," I say. "We're still buddies."

He keeps petting me, sniffling, tears drying on his cheeks. Ms. B rifles through a desk drawer and pulls out a pair of scissors, then straddles Liu Baojian and clips his nails. As would be expected of a kid who doesn't like having his face washed, he clearly dislikes having his nails clipped, but his whines and squirms are minimal. He knows he's in trouble: the teachers send home a daily report to parents. When she's done, Liu Baojian returns, petting my shoulder with his newly sheared fingers, and Ms. B inspects every nail on every child. At least half the class gets a trim. Michael Jordan is so twitchy and uncooperative that Ms. L practically sits on him while Ms. B snips.

At end of the day, Ms. B apologizes. When I meet Tom at the lockers where we store our stuff, two female administrators apologize through Wang Xue. "She say they are sorry. They hope you understand the children sometime have emotional issues."

"It's fine," I insist with a smile.

I'll receive apologies the rest of the week. A few days later Ms. B will see a birthmark on my arm and think I've been mauled.

"You know," I tell Tom as we leave the building, "I should come in tomorrow with my arm all bandaged up. Just as a joke." Though something tells me it would get lost in translation.

Wang Xue speaks excellent English, which makes her indispensable. She's on summer break from a university in Xi'an, where she's studying to be a packaging engineer. I had no idea that packaging engineer was a profession, but given the colossal growth of manufacturing in China over the past twenty years, experts on consumer goods are surely in demand. Xi'an itself produces a slew of engineers—the city has more than twenty public universities—though Wang Xue, a native of Linfen, about 235 miles northeast of Xi'an, is not terribly fond of her adopted home.

"I have been stolen three times in Xi'an," she says—twice by pickpockets, once by a girl in her dorm selling phony beauty products. "One time was on my birthday, which hurt me a lot. I was supposed to buy some medicine for my aunt with the money."

With her above-average English skills, Wang Xue provides insights I missed the week before. When Jenna says something to me in Chinese, and everyone laughs an embarrassed laugh, Wang Xue fills me in. "She call you 'foreigner.' They all say, 'No, no! Uncle!'"

"I've heard worse," I tell Wang Xue.

Meilin joined us one morning last week and I realized then how much I'm missing; the daily dramas and comedy. When Happy Bear arrived late, sauntering in with his bag of rolls, Ms. B spoke to the students as he ate. Meilin translated: "She says, since you all stare at his food, maybe we should get some."

Ms. B pulled out a bag of candy from the previous day's tea party. The Dancer started bawling. "He wants candy," said Meilin.

Ms. B used it as a reward. Liu Baojian got candy for correctly pointing at the day's date on the schedule. He did such a good job that he got what I call the Pesto-Shah cheer. The three teachers do it, clapping and chanting. It sounds like:

Pesto Pesto Shah!
Pesto Pesto Shah!
Pesto Pesto Shah!

And then they raise their hands and wiggle their fingers and yell *WOOOOO!*

"Their fingers are fireworks," said Meilin.

The students prepped for their march at the opening ceremonies of next month's Special Olympics. Ms. B led the group in a single-file line with red and green flags; martial music blared from the stereo. They paraded around the room in a messy circle.

"You are all athletes and we are marching into the stadium!" Ms. B declared.

She pointed at Happy Bear, who was in his customary position: tipped back in a chair, leaning against the wall.

"There's a general!" she said, saluting.

Lightswitch turned off the lights.

"It's cloudy!" said Jenna.

Afterward, Meilin left the room with Ms. B, which was kind of like your mother talking with your teacher: you know they're discussing you, and you hope it's good, but you suspect it's bad, and you're preparing excuses. I had expressed concerns to Meilin that perhaps I was a burden. Ms. B came back, and then Meilin signaled me to join her outside the room. The language difference makes subtlety difficult. "She say the first day you have no clue," said Meilin. "But since then you do much better."

. . .

It's not quite 11 p.m. when Tom turns off his light and rolls on his stomach, his blankets shoved to the side of his bed. He covers his face with a red T-shirt. I tend to stay up later than him, reading, so each night he uses the shirt to block my light.

"You sure that isn't bothering you?" I ask.

"It's fine."

It's weird talking to a headless, motionless man in boxer shorts sprawled chest-down on a hotel bed. He looks like a just-discovered corpse on *CSI*.

"That T-shirt isn't distracting?"

"Having soft cotton across your head is not that distracting."

Lately I've found myself thinking of a *Star Trek: The Next Generation* episode called "The Inner Light," in which a probe approaches the *Enterprise* and zaps Captain Picard in the head with—to use the geek term—a nucleonic particle stream. Picard wakes up, groggy, no longer on the bridge, but in an unknown home, on an unknown planet—Kataan—gazing at an unknown woman, Eline, who says she's his wife. As the years pass, slowly convinced that his Starfleet career was an illness-induced dream, Picard settles into a long life, becoming a scientist, father, grandfather, widower; a hunched, crusty old man. "I never thought I would need children to complete my life," he says after the birth of his second child. "But now I can't imagine life without them." When the probe shuts down—it was sent by the people of Kataan, to tell their story, after their sun went nova—he learns he's been unconscious a mere twenty-five minutes.

I feel like Picard, like I'm living a long and separate life, though I've been in Xi'an for an instant. Tom and I have a routine. We eat breakfast every morning with the other volunteers. We shave and brush our teeth and walk to the school. We work. At night, we walk through the city on blinking sidewalks, the concrete orange and red from Vegas-like neon on hotels and rooftop karaoke bars.

We exercise in the hotel gym, then watch the surprisingly absorbing world badminton championships on TV, the Chinese play-by-play as much of a blur as the shuttlecock zipping over the net. We sleep, Tom with a T-shirt over his face. We start over.

I miss home, of course. I miss Julie. We e-mail almost daily. ("The dog is laying next to me kind of half snoring and letting out little stinky poots," she writes. "Don't you wish you were here?") I e-mail my sister and mom and Adam and Terry ("That would be a deal breaker," Adam writes, when I say that Tom and I have to sing). I read the *Washington Post* online. I would *love* a gooey chocolate dessert. (Brownies. I keep thinking about brownies.) But part of me would be content to stay at this school, to stay with these kids, to continue my routine that is real and yet not real. As piercing as the shouts can be, as unpredictable the behavior, as limited as I am by the language—I feel at home here. It's like finding solace in a thunderstorm. What scared you becomes familiar. The thunder becomes a comfort.

On a recent afternoon, a group of art teachers arrived to show the kids paintings from children at their schools. The paintings were mounted on black poster board and set on a row of desks along the wall. As the art teachers spoke, the Dancer pointed and shouted, repeating a word that Wang Xue believed was "That! That!" Giggles rocked and repeated gibberish, saying a word and giggling, saying a word and giggling. Happy Bear tried to pinch one of the art teachers. The teacher fended him off, but he persisted. Before that he pinched Ms. H so hard she yelped, still rubbing her arm an hour later.

The art teachers look stunned, the same look I'm sure I wore my first day. Part of me is smug, because I'm a La La Shou vet. And yet part of me is embarrassed, because I've grown terribly fond of these kids.

Late in the afternoon we watch a Chinese cartoon starring a mouse who battles a pack of marauding cats by emitting gas from his little rodent butt. (Despite the rich fart material it's a pretty boring cartoon, though I'm sure I was missing subtleties in the plot.) As we watch, Jenna nestles against me and holds my hand. She speaks and the teachers chuckle.

"She no want you go Washington," says Ms. B.

I'll miss Jenna. I'll miss the teachers: Ms. H cuddling Sleeves, Ms. L brushing Haley's hair. I'll miss watching the Buddha Boy and his grandfather. Yesterday the kids practiced a Special Olympics activity: each one stands in the center square of two intersected rectangles; like the middle of a plus sign. The child jumps in a square to the left. Then back to the center. And then to the right. The grandfather lifted Buddha Boy into each square, the boy's legs dangling. The teachers cheered.

I'll miss being close to people so committed to their work, so committed to finding joy.

"I feel like we've been here forever," I say to Tom. "In a weird way, I feel like this is my life."

On one of our after-school walks to the park, we pass a food cart selling the appropriately named stinky tofu. It smells, Tom says, "like a gym shoe filled with feces and set on fire." For Tom, week two has been far more rewarding than week one. Dry weather has meant more outside activities. On Monday his class went for a long, invigorating walk at the park. On Tuesday they shopped for groceries at Ren Ren Le, then made dumplings. Tom was amazed at how quickly the teachers scooped the filling on a spoon—celery and ground pork with ginger and garlic and red pepper—dumped it in a square of dough, squeezed it, and just like that: done. It took him a minute to do what took them seconds. "Delicious," he told me months later. "I can still taste it."

Near the end of the week, before lunch, I spied him in the small room where my group has language classes. He was sketching his students, profiling them one by one with pencil and pad. The resemblances were spot on, but he captured something more:

the vulnerability that's easy to miss beneath the seemingly brazen squawks.

The students watched him draw, mesmerized. Their teacher, Wang Xiaoqing, who I can tell has developed a friendly affection for Tom, stood behind him, a firm and glowing pride in his work. She has transformed Tom's perception of the school. Through her limited English, she told him about the thick, strong teen who slaps his chest and yells "*Cheema Cheema!*" He used to be abusive. He would strike his parents. He would strike teachers. Because of this, he was booted out of other schools. Wang Xiaoqing believed no one had ever shown him why his behavior was wrong. So the two of them went to a room. In private. He tried to strike her. She struck back. No one had ever done this before. It's unfathomable that this sort of eye-for-an-eye teaching technique could happen back home, but here, well, it somehow makes sense.

"I was amazed because overall he's a pretty gentle kid," said Tom. "I couldn't believe he'd undergone such a transformation."

Another boy in Tom's class has cerebral palsy. He's accompanied everywhere by his aunt. Before coming to La La Shou, he couldn't walk.

On our second-to-last day at the school, Tom and I are invited to the main office to talk with Zhang Tao, La La Shou's founder. We settle in at a table; Wang Xue translates. Zhang Tao's ebullient son sings a song that he appears to make up with each note. We've noticed bandages around his back and legs. Wang Xue tells us he burned himself in the school kitchen after knocking over a pot of boiling water. He was in the hospital for two months.

"Her son like foreigners," says Wang Xue. "He has more English vocabulary than she does." Zhang Tao talks about learning to accept her son's autism, how she met with other mothers; how they morphed from a support group into an action team.

"There come a time when you must do more than complain," she says through Wang Xue.

She thanks me and Tom for our work. "You may not feel like you help much, but it makes a big difference. We tell parents, 'Look—these people came all the way from America because they love your children. You need to love your children more.'"

I ask if the goal is to help the students live independently. For some it's not realistic, says Zhang Tao. Even if they're capable of working and living by themselves, finding jobs is difficult, though La La Shou tries to help.

"You know that man doing the cleaning job?" says Wang Xue.

I nod. "Tall guy, right? We've seen him around."

"He have some problems," says Wang Xue.

Tom and I thought he was a teacher. He's actually a former student. "They train him for three years," says Wang Xue. "Now he can do almost all the cleaning jobs. At first, he don't even know how to take a bath. Now he can go home by himself and come here by himself. They train him to ride on bus. They taught him how to use his salary—how much you keep for food and how much you need for other things."

He still struggles with numbers. Recently he asked a shopkeeper the price of a video. "Eight yuan," said the shopkeeper.

"I'll give you ten," our janitor countered.

Zhang Tao laughs softly, telling the story. She says nearby shopkeepers don't take advantage of him; they actually help. "There is more understanding," says Wang Xue.

For the school, raising money is a persistent problem. She shows us photographs from last year's Special Olympics: a picture of a boy and his father. The family can no longer afford to send the boy to La La Shou, and the school lacks the resources to help.

"Sometimes she feels helpless," says Wang Xue.

Zhang Tao talks in a serious voice. "The teachers here are really under burden," Wang Xue tells us. "They take care of these kids from eight thirty to four thirty and they cannot relax even for a minute because the kids must be watched always."

"It's daunting work," says Tom.

"And during the weekend sometimes the teachers will go out with the kids. Not have their free time. That is a big challenge for the teachers here. She worry that the teachers become frustrated. The teachers may teach the children that one plus one is two, several times, and the children couldn't remember. And the teacher may feel really bad. They may look for other jobs."

I nod. Tom nods. And then he says something that surprises me.

"Can you tell her," he says to Wang Xue, "that we both admire her courage and her dedication. And we think she's made a big improvement in life for a lot of people."

Wang Xue translates. Zhang Tao nods, and wipes away a tear. She says thank you. I know Tom has felt frustrated by the language barriers, I know he's felt useless, but kind words have force. As the Chinese philosopher Lao Tzu once said—

Kindness in words creates confidence.
Kindness in thinking creates profoundness.
Kindness in giving creates love.

I smile at Tom. I hope he no longer doubts that he's done something good here.

It's our last day at the school. In the morning, at Ms. H's instruction, each student shakes my hand. Robby hugs me. Ms. B talks to the children, who sit against the wall behind their desks. Wang Xue translates. They have a gift. Ms. B holds a white paper bag and removes a laminated photo. It's a group shot of me and the class, a shot we posed for a few days earlier. I sit in the center of the first row, my arm around a pensive Liu Baojian. To my left are Giggles, Sleeves, and a big-smiling Haley, who loves to be photographed. (One day Tom came in the room and snapped her picture; she practically hyperventilated until she could see it. "Am I pretty?" she asked through Wang Xue.)

Above the photo is Chinese script that says, "La La Shou, Third-Grade Class, 2009." The Dancer reaches for it. "Sorry, buddy," I say. "I've seen you mangle too many things to give you this." Indeed, a few minutes later he rips fish decals off an ocean-themed puzzle.

Now Ms. B pulls a Chinese knot from the bag. She slips the top loop over her index finger and turns the moment into a teaching exercise, asking the children to identify the colors. The top of the knot is red and gold. Below are two knit objects that look like strawberries: one is yellow with a purple bottom, the other is red with a yellow bottom.

"She tells the children, 'These are two fruits,'" says Wang Xue. "One is them, and one is you, because they love you and they will miss you." Ms. B hands it to Liu Baojian. He walks to me in his slow, measured way. I thank him.

As we wait to leave for another health screening, Ms. B and I talk through Wang Xue. Other volunteers, she says, have not seemed as comfortable with the children. "She says you have a warm heart," says Wang Xue. "If you speak Chinese, you be perfect." These are good children, Ms. B tells her. They just need more attention and care.

"She say next time you come to Xi'an, you stay in her home."

Wang Xue asks if I'd like to say anything to Mss. B, H, and L. "Yes," I say. "Please tell them that they are my heroes. It was clear my first day how much affection they have for the children. And tell them that when I think of this school, and when I think of Xi'an, I will think of their laughter."

Upon hearing the translation, an embarrassed Ms. B laughs. Once we finish our mutual admiration lovefest, I ask a question through Wang Xue.

"There's a little boy here. He's always accompanied by an older gentleman, probably in his late fifties, early sixties. The boy is small—he smiles a lot. The two of them are always together. Do you know—is that the boy's grandfather?"

Wang Xue relays my question. Ms. B has her arm around the smirking, mischievous Sleeves.

"He is the grandfather," says Wang Xue. "The father left the mother when the son was born and they see the son have problems. The mother has to work, so the grandfather take care of him."

I see Buddha Boy and his devoted grandfather one final time, on the street that afternoon. They're riding a bicycle. The grandfather pedals. They pass parked cars and smokers perusing newsstands; a group of men on small sidewalk chairs, practically squatting, playing Chinese chess on a low square table. Buddha Boy is strapped into a seat behind the grandfather. He smiles, of course.

In his book *Stumbling on Happiness*, Daniel Gilbert, a Harvard psychology professor, determined that most parents aren't happy when dealing with their kids. Mothers are happier doing almost any other task: shopping, exercising, watching TV. That's because parenting is difficult. It's work. Tiring, stressful, frequently irritating work. For most parents, happiness doesn't return to pre-kid levels until the children are grown and gone. But while parents may be less happy on a day-to-day basis, many say their most profoundly happy moments involve their kids. It's a transcendental happiness that goes way beyond the day-to-day.

For all the burdens the grandfather must suffer—the caregiver's exhaustion, the scramble for tuition funds, the worries about his grandson's future—I know he has experienced transcendental happiness. In his own mellow, mild way, he exudes it.

The grandfather pedals slowly up the street. They pull from view, the boy disappearing, blending into the grandfather's back.

•   •   •

After a lunch of noodles and red bean porridge, I walk Liu Baojian to the nap apartment for the last time. Tom and I are only working a half day: there'll be a goodbye ceremony this afternoon for all the volunteers and representatives of their various schools.

Like always, Liu Baojian and I receive curious stares as we cross the street: the tall Westerner and the small boy who's not quite like the other boys. As we tend to do, we trade laughs.

"Ah-*hahahaha*," he chuckles.

"Ah-*hahahaha*," I reply.

"Ah-*hahahaha*."

"Ah-*hahahaha*."

We plod up the steps in the apartment building. I want to tell him he's a good boy. I want to tell him he *is* my brother. That I wonder what his life will be like; what lives await all of these children. Some, like the Dancer and Sleeves, may someday live on their own. But I worry about Liu Baojian: his lack of motor skills, his small frame, the mind that seems adept at language yet works at a slower speed. I want to tell him I believe in him, but there's no one here to translate. I say it anyway.

"*Nǐhǎo*," he says.

"*Nǐhǎo*," I reply.

I let go of his hand and he walks into the apartment. The nap coordinator bends over and tells him to wave, in the exaggerated way that she does. I wave as well, and then the brown metal door clangs shut.

So here is my final memory of the Dancer. After he repeatedly runs around the room, shouting, arms flailing—knocking down books from the bookshelf—Ms. L rearranges the desks to confine him. I sit outside of his desk-cage. Making the best of his detention, the Dancer contemplates a puzzle: a simple wooden one where you fit various shapes—circle, square, star, triangle—into corresponding slots. It's the kind of puzzle my three-year-old nephew can manage in minutes, but the Dancer, a third grader, can't do it. He puts the square against the circle. The circle against the triangle. He taps the circle against the desk. Then, either aggravated or bored, he chews it.

Next we play with plastic blocks: kind of like Legos, but flatter and curved, connecting at their ends like jigsaw pieces. We connect them in a long squiggle across the desk, which the Dancer carefully lifts, grabbing it from each end. He stands up, shouting the same word, over and over.

Yaaaag! Yaaaag!

Or at least that's how it sounds to me. I have no idea what he's saying—nor does Wang Xue—but the tone and the urgency seem like—

Look at this amazing feat of engineering! Look! For the love of God—LOOK!

There's equal excitement and anguish in his face as he holds it aloft, as if overwhelmed by the beauty of our snaking plastic creation.

He sits back down. We've been connecting the puzzle pieces flat against the table, but now he connects a piece vertically. And he adds more, building up instead of out.

I'm shocked. It never occurred to me build up: your first instinct is to connect them flat. Moments ago the Dancer failed a puzzle a two-year-old could handle, but now he's thinking in an original, inventive way.

"That's excellent!" I tell him. "Really smart thinking."

I scan the room, wanting to share his accomplishment. All the teachers are busy, not that I can communicate with them anyway. Wang Xue is out of the room.

"That's great," I tell the Dancer. "That's really great."

I hope in some way that despite his blank expression he can see how happy I am, and see me applauding, and somehow understand.

• • •

Adam had asked Tom and me to bring back some Chinese cigarettes and booze. We buy a pack of smokes from a sidewalk tobacco vendor near the hotel. The stand looks like a booth for a carnival game: glass cases with shelves of cigarette boxes, just enough room behind for the seller to walk. We settle on Pride cigarettes, mainly because of the cute cartoon panda on the front. If Disney sold cigarettes, this is what they'd look like. (Disney rip-offs abound here. My favorite is a "Walt Dasney" shirt with Minnie looking like a ferret in drag.)

We buy the booze at Ren Ren Le. We want something Chinese looking, so we settle on two small flask-sized bottles of . . . well, we don't know what we've bought, but it looks like whiskey. One bottle we'll take home, one bottle is for us. We can't find shot glasses, so we buy tiny teacups.

Tom screws off the cap. This is our Friday night, end-of-our-volunteering-stint treat. We'd spent the afternoon at the final ceremony, held in the same hotel conference room as the opening ceremony two weeks earlier. All the volunteers attended, plus the students and teachers from the schools where they taught. Wang Xiaoqing again represented La La Shou, along with one of the administrators, Tom's entire class of five students, and Wang Xue. We sat around the same open square table.

As everyone from volunteers to students made earnest speeches, the La La Shou students emitted a series of uncontrollable chirps and burps and fart sounds; a few screeching parrot-like echoes of speechmakers' phrases.

Meilin held a microphone and started the speechifying.

"This experience is about making connections—"

Ooo-Ooo-Ooo-Ooo!

"—and making friendships."

Urrrrrp!

"Only by doing this—"

Fgggghhhhtttt!

"—can we achieve world peace."

A university student sang in an operatic style, her performance spiced with—

Bppplllpppphhhh!

Bah! Bah!

Cheema Cheema!

Tom and I found this hilarious. These were our buddies. We knew how happy they were to be here. But the funny part was how everyone pretended it wasn't happening: they plowed on with noble speeches as if the room weren't echoing with—

Sttweeeeee!

Thfffgggtttt!

Tom leaned over and whispered: "This is the kind of thing you dream about doing in a meeting."

The La La Shou administrator spoke, with Wang Xue as translator.

"The students do not mean to be rude," she said. "Sometimes they cannot control themselves. They are very excited."

And then it was showtime. The La La Shou students and teachers rose to perform and asked Tom and me to join them. We sang "Row, Row, Row Your Boat," which Tom had taught them. One of the students is a tall boy with a strong grip, as I discovered last week when he happily grabbed my arm and nearly caused nerve damage. He wrapped his arm around my shoulder and held my hand. We sang a traditional Chinese song with a variety of flowing hand motions, which Tom and I mimicked with minimal success.

The teachers and students performed their final tune alone. It's called "Grateful Heart," written for a Japanese TV show about a girl who succeeds despite many difficulties. The La La Shou teens were nearly as graceful as their two female teachers, arms and hands

swimming and swaying. The English-language students spontaneously rushed alongside them, joining them in song.

To close, we the volunteers performed a medley of show tunes
about America: chestnuts such as "Deep in the Heart of Texas"
and "California Here I Come," a clear sign that most of our group
was born before World War II. The highlight was Ralph singing
"New York, New York," with Brenda and the female volunteers
kicking like Rockettes, soon joined by the young Chinese students.

That evening, a handful of us go with Ralph and Brenda to see
the nighttime water show at the Great Goose Pagoda—though Tom
and I first open our bottle of Chinese hooch for a pre-departure
shot in our room.

He sniffs, then hands me the bottle.

"Kind of smells like whiskey," I say.

"Mixed with fish oil," he adds.

We pour.

"A toast," I say.

We hold up our tiny teacups.

"To China," says Tom.

"To China."

We clink cups and drink.

"Not bad," I say of the slight burn on my throat.

"I think I taste soy sauce."

We pour another.

"Thank you for coming," I say.

"My pleasure."

We clink glasses and pound number two.

"One more?" I say.

"Why not."

We raise our cups.

"Here's hoping this doesn't make us go blind," says Tom.

A worthy toast. The bottle empty, we walk to the elevator.

Brenda says our departure time has been delayed: we'll meet in the lobby in fifteen minutes.

"We can buy Adam another bottle," I say, digging in my pocket for the room key. One more shot. We hold our tiny tea-cups aloft.

"To China again," says Tom. "It's a big country."

We call it the square of clarity: a clear spot Tom and I made on the grimy glass window of our tenth-floor hotel room. I'd unlocked a small bottom panel of the window; Tom stuck his arm through, reached up, and cleaned a roughly twelve-inch-square area with wet toilet paper. Suddenly the city came into focus, the rooftops extending to the horizon.

"I really like that term 'square of clarity,'" I tell Tom as I look out. "I want a square of clarity for life."

As we drag our bags from our fourteen-day home, I don't feel clear about anything. I want to see Julie, but I hate to leave the kids. I've come to realize, more so than in Costa Rica, both the importance and the irrelevance of language. I felt close to Liu Baojian, to the Dancer—to all the kids—even though we never conversed or exchanged a meaningful word. Ms. B and I communicated on a simplistic level, and yet if I return ten years from now, twenty years from now, she'll welcome me as an old friend. At the risk of sounding like Mr. Kumbaya, our humanity runs deeper than our differences.

Tom and I catch a cab to the airport, leaving apartments and offices and crowds behind. The highway extends through untouched land that will surely be swallowed by sprawl. On the flight to Beijing, I flip through my notepad, the one where I wrote "culture shock overload," and find a draft of my entry for the group journal.

May 21

<u>*Thought for the day:*</u>
"*Outside of a dog, a book is man's best friend. Inside of a dog, it's too dark to read.*"
—GROUCHO MARX

I'm a fan of old Marx Brothers movies from the 1930s. This past week at La La Shou, I've often felt like a straight man in one of those films, swept up by the school's frenetic energy. Like silent Harpo, I communicate by pantomime. Because of the language barrier, I feel as though I'm experiencing the school in black and white, much as these children must live their lives.

But the teachers at La La Shou, through humor and patience and unflagging energy, are determined to give the kids lives that are rich in color. I work with three teachers in a class of 10 students. One teacher is 22, the other two are 25. They are caregivers, wrestlers, therapists. The room is filled with twitches and shouts, with hopping and stomping and moans. They never lose their temper. The teachers will correct kids—they will be firm. This morning, a boy I've taken to calling "Sleeves" (because he likes to lift your sleeves up to your shoulders) punched the boy sitting next to him in the back. And then he did it again—despite being corrected. After a third shot, a teacher smacked his hand, not hard, but enough to get his attention. And then she said something that sounded to me like, "Not so much fun when it happens to you, huh." And then she kissed him.

La La Shou is not a sad place. The students are usually smiling, the teachers seem always to laugh. The affection they have for the kids is obvious: the way they cup a hand around a child's cheek, the way they giggle when a child says something cute. My biggest regret is that I'm missing out on so much of the comedy, though I find myself laughing too.

I don't think I'm helping much here. The language barriers are too great. I often feel like the 11th student. But I think the teachers like having me around. I'm an English-speaking novelty; a break from their exhausting routine. So I smile, more than I ever have before, and I do whatever I can to ease their load rather than add to it. I consider it a privilege to know these strong, spirited women, who help these children to experience life outside of the dog, away from the dark.

Once I return home, Ms. B e-mails me an MP3 of the "Loo-la-loo" song. I listen and I'm instantly in the classroom again, hearing the grunts, the yelps, Sleeves yelling *Eh! Eh! Eh!* I see the Dancer dancing. I see Liu Baojian, head tilted, a blue fog in his eyes.

I'm trying to live up to my father's life while not being a father myself, and yet it's the women in China who most impressed me. Ms. B, Ms. L, Ms. H, Zhang Tao—they want only for you to love the children as much as they do. To bring a little brightness to the school. "We seem to laugh more when volunteers are here," a teacher said to Meilin after we left. These women are my new standard as I seek my square of clarity.

PART FOUR

Ecuador

A TINY CHUNK OF THE CLOUD FOREST
HAS MORE TREE SPECIES THAN THE
ENTIRE BRITISH ISLES.

I'M PACKING FOR ECUADOR, rolling T-shirts like cigars and stuffing them in my backpack, when I hear Adam's motorcycle through the open window upstairs. Normally he rides the Yamaha to work, to access HOV lanes and speed his commute, but tonight he needs the adrenaline, the speed, the rush of night air. His seventy-year-old dad, George, has cirrhosis of the liver. Adam spent most of the day at the hospital, at his father's bedside, watching him slide toward death.

I hope I'm here for the funeral, I think, meeting Adam at the door. I didn't understand the importance of funerals until Dad died; until I found such comfort from family and friends. A few years ago, when Adam's grandmother died, I felt I shouldn't attend the funeral. His grandmother was German and spoke no English. We would smile and nod on the occasions I saw her, before the Alzheimer's grew severe. Adam was close to his grandmother, and I've always regretted, in a major way, not attending the funeral.

He follows me into the living room, sinking into our comfy-yet-crummy couch. Our dog, Molly, sniffs his jeans. His padded purple motorcycle jacket and stubble give him a bit of a *Mad Max*, sci-fi look.

He brought me his headlamp. It was on the equipment list from Earthwatch, the volunteer organization for the Ecuador trip. I forgot to buy one and it seems essential. I'll be working on a global-warming research project in a remote region of the Andes Mountains, in a mountain cloud forest north of the equator, home to pumas and rare spectacled bears. The lodge is accessible only by foot, a two-hour walk from the nearest road. Supplies are delivered by mule. Electricity is limited to a generator's short stints. As a volunteer, I'll help scientists collect data as they study the effect of global warming on this diverse area, home to forty-five species of mammals, nearly four hundred tropical bird species, and thousands of species of plants.

"How's your dad?" I say, easing into my favorite chair.

"I dunno . . . I'm just—I'm stunned by how fast he's declining. Last week he stood up. His thinking was clearer."

"Julie used to see that at the hospital. People have a last stand. They can be totally out of it, the end seems near, and then boom—they're alert, they're talking . . . but it doesn't last."

He nods. Adam has a brash, sarcastic sense of humor, but tonight he's just . . . weary. Pale.

"The doctor said his kidneys aren't functioning. He's got fluid building in his brain and lungs. The drugs haven't helped and his liver has failed and he can't breathe without an oxygen mask. This afternoon we just—we decided to give up. Give him as much comfort as possible. He's getting morphine. Once his breathing stabilizes, they'll remove the oxygen mask."

"And then what?"

"Then he'll lose consciousness."

"And then how long . . ."

"I don't know."

He changes the subject, asks if I'm done packing, tells me he talked to Terry. I mention I saw Tom over the weekend, who in the course of the conversation revealed he not only doesn't wear underwear—which we knew—but he doesn't wear it when he bikes, runs, or exercises.

"I would think he'd have chafing issues," I say.

Adam smiles faintly. "He probably doesn't have any hair on his ass."

I offer a beer, but he heads out. He's tired, he knows I've got a 7 a.m. flight to Miami, then Quito. "Hang in there," I say as he leaves, knowing it's a useless thing to say, but having no wisdom to offer.

I finish packing, and watch Julie eat a bowl of raisin bran when she gets home. This is her noon-to-eight workday, which usually stretches to nine thirty. In the morning I leave a goodbye note on the stove. I drive to the train station, slug my long blue backpack over my shoulders. By 6 a.m. I'm on a commuter train, on my way to National Airport, on my way to Ecuador. I turn on my phone. Among the junk e-mail is a note from Adam.

Friends,

> *I wanted to let you know that my father passed away at about 2:15 a.m. We were by his side and he passed peacefully.*

Adam

I know this is best. I know it ends the suffering for Adam's dad, though it's only beginning for Adam's mom. But I also know I won't be here for one of my closest friends. When dirt falls upon the casket, when mourners say their goodbyes, I'll be in the Andes Mountains, cut off from the world, cut off from the people I love.

The plane descends on its valley path to Quito, mountain brawn filling the windows, the black shadows of clouds against the forest below. The city sits at roughly 9,300 feet—the second-highest capital in the world—on the eastern slopes of the Pichincha volcano.

Between the trees and scraggly peaks it's like we're approaching some South American Shangri-la; a magical cloud city, though like any city Quito is a mix of old splendors and new ills; of wealthy hillside homes and hard barrios lacking hope.

After feeling so confounded by the language in Xi'an, the bright Spanish billboards seem almost familiar on the cab ride to my hotel. A sign featuring a shapely babe with airbrushed cleavage says, *Tenemos el mejor señal*, which of course means, "We have the best—"

Okay, I don't know that last word—I'm guessing it's "sign"—but still. That's an exciting translation moment, as opposed to me staring dumbly at, oh, 茶. (That means "tea." Tom and I spent days searching for a tea shop in Xi'an, not knowing we'd passed them repeatedly.)

I even chat a bit with the taxi driver after warning him that my Spanish is *no bueno*.

"*¿Cuál es tu país?*" he asks.

"*Estados Unidos.*"

"*¿Cuantas días en Quito?*"

"*Un día,*" I say.

"*¿Un día? Ohhh—hay muchas cosas a ver en Quito.*"

The inn, La Casa Sol, is charming, painted in vibrant yet washed-out oranges and blues. Located in La Mariscal, Quito's new town, it sits in a quiet neighborhood, though nearby restaurants and bars seem full, a mix of college-age tourists and Ecuadoran yuppies. I check my e-mail on the hotel computer. I want Julie to know I'm alive before I vanish into the Andes. She's already sent me a note: "The house is too quiet. Take lots of pictures to share when you get back. Miss you, love you." I tell her I miss her and love her, too.

In the morning I take a cab to Quito's old town. It's my only day to explore before the trip to the cloud forest. My friendly driver, Byron, first drives me up El Panecillo hill, which offers a wide valley view of the old town: the white buildings with red roofs, the church domes and brownish haze, the massive Basílica del Voto Nacional with its dual Gothic spires. Behind me is Quito's winged virgin, more than one hundred feet tall, an arched halo of stars above her silver head, a chain-bound serpent at her feet.

I'd thought about walking the steep streets to see the virgin, but the guidebook notes that the route is prone to "violent muggings." Hence my ride with Byron, who drives me back down to the old town's central square. The Plaza de la Independencia dates back to 1534, walled on each side by the city's key buildings, from the Archbishop's Palace to City Hall. Statues and fountains rise between crisscrossing sidewalks; fanny-pack tourists pass an Inca woman in a green felt hat and plaid shawl, her ponytail resting next to the sleeping baby strapped against her back. Men sit on benches in sun and shade, possibly killing time, possibly out of work. One reads a newspaper. Another picks his ear. A gray-haired businessman gets a shoe shine beneath a puffy crepe myrtle. Soldiers with machine guns chat in clumps.

Quito is known for its ornate Spanish colonial churches, so I work my way to La Compañía de Jesús, the city's most lavish church, where a local college student gives me a tour. The ornate arches and pillars are painted gold; intricate carved patterns filled with touches of red. On a wall near the entrance, my student guide shows me a massive painting of a jam-packed, orange-hot hell. Lucifer stands with a snarling three-headed dog, watching over the anguished residents of his domain. Drunks. Whores. Murderers. Adulterers. Cheats.

"What's that one?" I say, pointing to a man at the bottom.

"*Registrador*," she says. "Lawyer." We look at each other and laugh.

I leave, eat lunch, and think about Adam's dad. I'd e-mailed Adam yesterday from the train; he wrote back as I ate pizza in the Miami airport: "I'm still a bit in shock over how quickly everything went," he said.

He's in my thoughts as I wander old Spanish streets with bright white spires and tiled domes, the buildings yellow and cream and blue, railed balconies lined with flowers. I wish I could do something for him. And then it hits me, quite unexpectedly: I'm in an old town loaded with historic churches. I could pray.

I don't really know how to pray, though I suppose there's no right or wrong way to do it. After much wandering, I visit the 350-year-old San Agustín church, walking to the convent: a courtyard with stout palm trees, a fountain in its center, surrounded by an arched two-level cloister. I peek in a dark rectangular room that, I learn later, is more like a meeting room for area priests. Two rows of tall-back Baroque benches line the walls, approaching an altar. I enter and stand before a cordoned-off Jesus on a green cross: St. John on his left, the Virgin Mary on his right. A church staffer sees me, walks in, and flicks a switch behind a wood door.

Let there be light.

Only the ceiling corners and altar are illuminated; the mournful, bleeding Jesus. The room is silent except for the splash of the courtyard fountain. Praying here, rather than in the lush church, isn't exactly logical; it's like visiting the Palace of Versailles and ensconcing myself in the laundry room. But this, I decide, feels right.

I lower my head before the roped-off altar and Christ's punctured plaster feet. I close my eyes, and I pray aloud for Adam's dad. And I pray for his soul, if there is a soul, or whatever the soul may be, though I realize—*damn*—I shouldn't qualify it and I shouldn't say *damn* so I pray again for his soul. And I pray for Adam, and his mom, and his family, and while I'm at it I pray for Julie, and for my mom, and my sister, and her family, and for Tom and Terry and all my friends, all the good people in my life, and then, well—how often am I going to do this—I pray for the world, and I pray for peace.

I feel embarrassed when I'm done, even though I'm alone. And I sit outside on a bench, watching the courtyard fountain; the water shooting high from the mouth of a boy, his face gazing at the sky, a lion at his feet. The spray sparkles in the sun, and I listen to rustling palm leaves, the drops of water splashing in the concrete pool. And I stay a long time. Listening, looking, thinking.

I'm not someone who minds being alone, and maybe it's because I'm in a different country, on a different continent, but that evening, sitting in my Spartan room, lying on the bed, my pillow my only companion, I think—

Wow. I am *really* bored with me right now.

I'd spent the morning by myself. I ate lunch by myself looking out on the Plaza San Francisco, watching a big-bellied woman and her son toss bread to hungry pigeons. I took a cab by myself back to the hotel. I checked my e-mail, browsed a knickknack area with local pottery for sale, snagged an Ian Rankin novel from the bookshelf—Julie is a fan—and returned to my room. Now it's evening and I've reread the same page four times when mercifully the phone rings.

"Someone is here to see you," says the female clerk from the front desk. Waiting there is Charles, a fellow Earthwatch volunteer.

I'm rescued.

Charles lives in Kent, England, the birthplace of my greatgrandfather, who brought his eight children to America in 1907. Maybe it's the accent, or the high cheekbones and jutting nose, but Charles reminds me of an old-time English army officer; the kind of military chap you see in movies patting his belly and telling jolly good stories about long-ago battles. He works in London and appears to be roughly my age. We'd exchanged a few e-mails, weeks ago, after Earthwatch sent a roster of volunteers, but I didn't have his phone number, and didn't really expect him to swing by La Casa Sol.

We walk past gated guesthouses and closed shops to Azuca, a

busy Latin bistro in Quito's new town. The place exudes sleek chic, from the thumping techno-pop tunes to the small silver tables with silver lime-cushioned seats. We sit outside under heat lamps that resemble tall metallic mushrooms and order beers. This is Charles's second Earthwatch trip. In 2007 he worked in Madagascar: a project studying lemurs. Ten years earlier, a cyclone had ravaged the lemurs' home in the Monombo rain forest, toppling up to 90 percent of the largest trees. Volunteers gathered data to determine how the lemurs were coping, and whether trees and vines were growing in the regenerating forest, to help scientists determine their long-term sustainability.

"We had pit toilets," he tells me, leaning back in his chair. "A bamboo shack with a hole in the ground. I'd go in the morning. Before the flies woke up. The shower was another shack—you'd dump cold water over your head from a small bucket with a plastic cup. It was better to wait until evening—the water would warm up a little during the day."

We down a second beer, then stroll to Mama Clorinda, a homey restaurant serving traditional Ecuadoran dishes. The outside is nondescript, but the inside is cozy: red-and-white-checkered floor, tables packed tight. We meet up with two other volunteers. Earl is an Australian in his midsixties: lean, white hair, firm handshake. An entrepreneur who once owned a racehorse and now works in shipping in Perth, Earl visited Buenos Aires and Iguazú Falls before arriving in Quito, where he narrowly evaded a robbery attempt in the Plaza de la Independencia, a common two-man scam that works like this:

Scammer #1 spills a nasty paintlike substance on your pants.
Scammer #1 apologizes in an overblown way and helps you
   de-goo yourself.
Scammer #2 swoops in while you're distracted and steals
   your wallet or bag.

Earl was touring the old town with a guide, who instantly recognized the ploy and told him to keep moving. So he escaped with his valuables, though the pants were ruined.

"Those were me best pants," complains a smirking Earl.

Wayne rounds out the group. He works for an oil company in Houston; his blond beard and friendly, confident air make him seem older than thirty. Charles and Wayne have spent two days together, traveling north to the famous market in Otavalo, buying alpaca blankets and Panama hats. Wayne also bought a whistle with a carved troll face for his goth sister. "The craftsman used cow's teeth for the teeth of the troll—always a sign of quality," says Wayne.

On the way back they were pulled over by police and Ecuadoran soldiers.

"They were probably just bored but they wanted to check all our luggage," says Charles.

"That's not all they checked," says Wayne.

"No, right—they made me spread with my hands on my boots so that they could have a quick feel between my legs."

"Welcome to Ecuador," says Wayne.

"I think it might have been part of a bet—one of the army guys was laughing."

I order roast chicken for dinner, which comes with a *llapingacho*, a crispy fried potato patty mixed with cheese. The conversation is enjoyable, even though I barely know these guys. The people who take these types of trips are rarely jerks, though there are exceptions, of course. Jonathan told us about a college-age girl who volunteered at Escuela Cuestillas after Julie and I left. She didn't like the children: they were too high-energy. She rarely worked, reading a book during classes. She was volunteering, she told Jonathan, because it would look good on her résumé.

When Julie and I left the school for the last time, the students accompanied us to the waiting van. When this girl left on her final day, she walked alone.

• • •

Two months before going to Ecuador, I traveled with Julie to spend a week in England with Jonathan and his partner, William. Hannah, our diminutive f-bomb-dropping Spanish teacher friend from New Jersey, had organized the trip the previous summer, then bowed out because of debt issues, tax issues, and the deaths of her two cats, her companions since her divorce.

I thought about canceling as well, given how much I'm already traveling, and the expense of my voluntourism trips (the one upside: most of them are tax-deductible). But I knew Julie wanted to go, and I wanted to see Jonathan, as well as James. They've both traveled to the United States: we've met them in New York City for reunions with Hannah. Besides—travel is the one area where Julie and I splurge.

We spent a few days with Jonathan and William, using their Birmingham home as a base for day trips, then the four of us rode the rails to London to visit James, who lives about twenty minutes outside the city with his girlfriend, Nancy, a fellow CCS volunteer who worked in Costa Rica after Julie and I left. James drove us to Windsor to see the castle. A student of royal and military ceremonies, he explained the intricacies and symbolism of the changing of the guard. (James kept a photo of the queen in his room in Costa Rica. When someone drew a mustache on her, he was not amused. "It is against the law to deface the queen," he declared.)

Our last night in England, hanging out in James's flat drinking tea before dinner, we reminisced about Costa Rica. James told us about Lola, one of the ladies who founded the recycling group where they worked. Before leaving San Carlos, Jonathan and James took the ladies out for a going-away thank-you dinner. As midnight approached, Lola offered to drop them off at the "gringo house" on her way home. She also wanted to show them her business. James knew nothing about their destination when they got in the car, until Jonathan casually mentioned, oh yes, we're stopping at a funeral parlor.

"So it turns out she's Costa Rica's first female funeral director," said James. "And she's quite proud of it. As well she should be. It's elevated her standing in the community, particularly among the women. So we said, great, yeah, fantastic. Let's do it. And we went to this funeral parlor. And then I thought, 'Well, this is a bit creepy.'"

"Gas lamps, candles—*total* silence—it was eerie," said Jonathan.

"She starts opening the coffins, and inviting us to feel the silk lining and the wood finish and the little window in the lid. And she's getting excited! She's like, 'Look at the quality! Look at the craftsmanship!' I thought she was gonna ask us to get in."

"She locked the door as well," said Jonathan. "We were worried she wouldn't let us out."

"Yeah—and then she gave us business cards!" said James, laughing.

"In case you die while you're in Costa Rica," I said.

"I was beginning to think maybe the gringos were gonna get whacked."

"She's a stalker preying on English recycling volunteers," I added.

Nancy had several placements in Costa Rica, and found herself one day at a new school. "For some reason all the teachers start leaving, and my teacher takes me along. And I don't speak Spanish so I have no clue what's going on. I just thought, 'Oh, okay, we're going somewhere . . .'"

"Woo hoo! Field trip!" says Julie.

"Right. And they left all the kids behind. So I get in the teacher's car and we drive up the street into a village and there's a house with all these people standing outside. We get out of the car, and we walk in this person's house, and there's a *coffin* in the middle of the room!"

"And you don't know anyone," I say.

"No! I don't know anyone! And all these people are milling

about talking to me in Spanish and I'm just standing there not knowing what to do."

"Was the coffin open?" Jonathan asks.

"I didn't look in but it definitely wasn't covered."

"Probably one of Lola's," says James.

We all laugh. I've never liked the open casket. When my grandfather died—my father's father—I asked to see him at the viewing. I was eight. He'd died in the hospital of a blood clot the day before he was due to come home. But the man in the casket wasn't the man I loved. Granddaddy was a handyman. I'd never seen him in a suit and tie. Or in a casket, for that matter. When Dad died, my mom and my sister and I decided: no open casket.

I've always joked that when I croak I want my stiff right arm sticking out of the open casket, palm up, holding a platter of candy and nuts. So people can grab a snack while they're peering at my pasty face. Adam wants to be painted with clown makeup and dressed in clown shoes that stick up through a slot at the end of the casket.

You hear that, death? We mock you. We have no choice.

Everyone in James's flat that night had lost someone close to them. Jonathan lost his mother. Nancy's stepfather died in the World Trade Center on 9/11. For we the survivors, our mission—our obligation—is to live and to laugh and to learn, and to pry joy from life, and to bring joy to others, and to strive, as I know Dad strived, to help more people than we hurt.

That evening, we walked to an Italian restaurant near James's flat. We drank wine, and Jonathan ordered champagne, and we told stories, and we laughed, and though no one ever said it, we felt grateful for our enduring friendship.

Our Earthwatch group meets in the morning at a hotel about two short blocks from La Casa Sol. We introduce ourselves, shake hands—we're a mix of five Americans, three Brits, two Canadians, and Earl the Australian—then load the belly of the bus with backpacks. A sad-faced boy, kindergarten age, tries to sell us gum. He walks from person to person, holding out his spearmint wares, unsuccessful, before plodding down the street.

We see indigenous candy sellers as our bus rolls through Quito, mothers and children on narrow concrete islands between streets, stooped over boxes of gum and mints. About fifteen miles north of the city we cross the equator, passing the *Mitad del Mundo* monument: a hundred-foot-high pyramid, a globe upon its flat top, like an erect equatorial nipple. GPS systems now indicate the equator is actually about eight hundred feet to the nipple's north.

After stopping in a nowhere town called Nanegalito, our last chance for a bathroom and a bite to eat, we wind through green mountains, finally leaving pavement for a gravel road. A scruffy dog barks at our bus from a one-level house; a boy and his mother wave. We bump-bump-bump to a small, rustic lodge that is literally the end of the road. From here we'll walk. Mules will carry our backpacks. Mules carry all supplies—primarily food and beer—because other than walking, or perhaps parachuting, there's no way to reach the Santa Lucía lodge. We're assured the mules live a luxurious life by mule standards, spending more time eating grass than hauling beer.

A welcome sign gives the distances. It's about a two-mile walk, but a nearly two-thousand-foot climb. We ascend a dusty dirt road still being cleared by bulldozers, part one of our trek. This close to the equator, the sun is intense, despite the hazy sky. I've smeared on sunscreen in Tom-like quantities, but perspiration surely flushes it to my feet. My lungs are laboring, and we're still forty minutes away from the mountain forest that looms before us.

Earthwatch rates this trip as strenuous, the most severe of its ratings, with promises of "hiking up to 15 miles/day, possibly back-country and/or uphill; carrying equipment weighing up to 40 lbs." Fortunately I'm lighter than I was a few months ago. I lost eight pounds in China, I assume from a calorie-busting combo of fresh food, no desserts, no sodas, and lots of walking.

"So if this is a song is it 'Stairway to Heaven' or 'Highway to Hell'?" asks a wheezing Wayne.

"Think of it as the aperitif," says Natalie, wiping her face with her arm, brown hair in a ponytail. Natalie is married to Nick, one of four British researchers for the climate-change project. They can't be older than thirty. She decided that staying home in London wasn't nearly as exciting as joining her husband in South America. She's been here for a few weeks.

"This is the hottest day yet," says Natalie. "But from here on it'll be cooler."

"And steeper," adds Nick.

After a brief rest, we walk again, passing lumpy piles of mule doo as we enter the woods.

"Just follow the nutrition and you're probably on the right track," says Charles, his tan shirt dark with sweat.

"All poo leads to home," says Wayne.

"That sounds like the title of a bad kids' book," I tell him.

The walk is a series of sharp, steep switchbacks. We stop for periodic, much-needed breaks. I rest my hand on the moss-covered stub of a fallen tree, gasping, looking through a gap in the trees at the valley below. Leaves clack in the wind like faint applause. Birds and bugs chatter. I'd arrived in Quito a day early to acclimate to the altitude, but it didn't work. For all the rain forest's aural charms, the most prominent noise, it seems, is my panting.

"It's like I'm chain-smoking Marlboros," I tell Wayne. The pattern of the hike will continue for an hour and a half: climb, stop, pant. Sweat, sweat, sweat.

"The only good thing," says Charles, huffing between sips from his CamelBak, "is that the more water I drink, the lighter my pack gets."

The trail remains steep as we approach the lodge. When we

finally exit the forest, transitioning from near-vertical path to flat grass, I laugh. A staff woman, Sofi, hands me a glass of lemonade. The lodge is a two-story wood building, a log-railing porch lined by bright orange flowers, covered by a green tin awning. Above that it's largely glass, a mix of square and rectangular windows, rising in a peak to the sloped top-floor roof. For the next eleven days, this is home.

At almost the same hour I was trudging up trails to the Santa Lucía lodge, Adam walked to a podium at the Lord of Life Lutheran Church near our homes. Unlike the last night I saw him, Adam was clean shaven, wearing a suit and tie. Setting papers before him, he read his eulogy, nervous, yet finding strength, speaking naturally as if to a circle of friends—like speaking to us over beers at Fat's. He told stories: his dad enjoyed hunting, and as a teenager Adam reluctantly helped his father butcher deer in the garage. "When it came time, he would come get me and say, 'I need your help—put on an old shirt.' I would hug the deer carcass to keep it from swaying while my dad sawed and carved. He would remind me to breathe though my mouth so I'd stop dry heaving."

I look out over the Andes, my own gasping starting to slow. I am conscious that, in my own way, I too am hugging the carcass: still comparing myself to my father, dead now three years; knowing that I won't be a parent, yet unwilling to let go.

When I was in China, my nephew graduated from college. Julie rode with my sister and brother-in-law and nieces to the convocation ceremony at McDaniel University in western Maryland, made the two-hour drive up and the two-hour drive back. Now she's attending the funeral for Adam's dad, without me. She hasn't complained about my travels, hasn't told me I'm a self-centered prick. Yet.

I'm rooming with Wayne and Charles in cabana five, the last cabana at the end of a dirt path. We cross a bridge, about eight feet long, to reach the cabin door, crossing a gully that becomes a stream in the rainy season. The green-tin-roof cabins sit along the side of a ridge. The cabanas are spacious, with room for two bunk beds and a single bed, plus a two-seat wicker couch. Tall windows line the back wall, providing a view of descending forest. There's no electricity, but the bathroom has running water (though go easy on the *agua*, we're told). Folks in the lodge use an outdoor bathroom that reminds me of a horse stable, long and wood and open, with two sinks, two urinals, and two composting toilets with a view that is staggering for a lavatory: a panorama of the Andes, the mountains in layers of fading silhouettes. To the left, the clouds creep in, as they do almost every afternoon, obscuring the peaks, creating the damp environment that allows mosses, ferns, and orchids to thrive. Nick later points out the deforestation of one distant ridge. "That's the kind that mucks up the watershed," he says.

Our cabana is supplied with candles and two candleholders. I'm glad I borrowed Adam's headlamp: at night, the path becomes utterly, impossibly black. The more immediate issue, however, is horseflies. As we unpack—Wayne plays The Cure on an iPod he connects to a battery-operated speaker system—the horseflies buzz like long-term occupants annoyed by new guests. Horseflies are actually new to the area, says Nick, and they're unfazed by bug spray. Wayne was stung as he relaxed postclimb in one of the lodge's two porch-side hammocks, the stinger poking *through* the fabric to pierce his butt.

Charles kills a horsefly with a sandal—*wham!*

"You won't be listening to The Cure again, ya bastard," he says.

Later that evening I kill one with a book. The window is spotted with blood; the mangled body lies on its back. It looks like a mafia hit.

"Maybe we should leave it—to send a message to the other horseflies," I say.

Wayne nods approvingly and looks at the assorted fly carcasses on the windowsills.

"The killing grounds," he says.

A British volunteer, Edward, captures horseflies in a glass and releases them out the window. The next day, when we're in the woods for an orientation, Wayne discusses the ethics of horsefly murder with Anita Diaz, a botanist who's part of the research staff.

"Is it morally wrong to kill horseflies?" he asks.

"Oh no, no," she says. "Kill the little buggers."

We assemble that afternoon in the main level of the cabin-like lodge, where one of the researchers, Tim Cane, a geography specialist from the University of Sussex, outlines Santa Lucía's risks and hazards—all the things that can bite us, blind us, sting us, spray us, kill us, give us a rash, or transform every solid in our intestinal system to liquid.

We sit on picnic-style wood benches. The upper floor is mainly bedrooms; this first floor is an open area that serves as dining room, meeting room, research facility, and gathering spot. Tim looks to be in his thirties, black hair buzzed to almost flattop length, though it's gone above the forehead. A two-day beard—seemingly obligatory for the men here—darkens his round face.

"For a rain forest, this is a fairly benign environment," he says, beginning his list of perils. "It's extra dry at the moment, so hiking boots are okay—you probably won't need Wellies. The trails are good—they're wide—but you've got all the normal hazards: roots, sticks, rocks. Go slow. Some of our activities will be off the trail. It can be slick, lots of holes, and the ground can be unstable. You don't want a broken leg or a sprained ankle. The bamboo is strong, it's good for pulling yourself up a hill, but watch for thorns. The moss here has needles—watch for that as well. There's a type of poison ivy that stings for two minutes. And snakes—watch for snakes—they can be poisonous—though no volunteers have been bitten here. They're slow and a little sluggish at this altitude."

I assume he means the snakes and not the volunteers.

"Watch for little scorpions. And centipedes. They can have a painful bite. And the caterpillars—they fall from the trees—that can be a *really* painful bite. The locals are careful to avoid them. Ants and spiders have an uncomfortable little nip. The wasps and bees—run away if you break open a wasp nest. Multiple stings can be quite fatal. Don't eat berries, obviously. Many of the plants here are poisonous.

"Okay—large mammals. If you see one, you're lucky. If you see bears, they'll run. Pigs can be aggressive. If a pig comes after you, all you can do is kick him and try to run up a tree. Mites: They have intense bites. They go for your ankles. The bites will itch for a couple of days. As far as machete work, leave that to the pros. Even they struggle with it. We've had two guys hit themselves in the knee. So give them distance. The last thing you want is a machete to the jugular.

"If you use the laser equipment, don't shine it in anyone's eyes. Oh—and the sun is really strong at this altitude. Stay covered. You can dehydrate easily: bring plenty of water. And bring a first-aid kit. Your team leaders will have one as well. This is a humid area, so there's a slightly greater risk of infection. And watch for tarantulas, though you'll be lucky to see one."

I think he's done.

"Okay—diarrhea."

He's not done.

"We all get the squits at some point."

The squits?

"I was laid up for two days last year," says Nick. "It was bad."

Bad squits.

"If it happens, you'll just have to ride it out," says Tim. "And stay hydrated."

Finally, he's finished. The only condition he doesn't cover is the massive paranoia now permeating the room.

• • •

A few months before I learned about the squits, on a spring night in D.C., a perky volunteer for an environmental group bounded toward me on the sidewalk with a clipboard.

"Hey—how about giving me a high-five for our favorite planet!" he chirped.

I was racing down Seventh Street toward Pennsylvania Avenue at my usual damn-I'm-*this*-close-to-missing-my-train pace, weaving around tourists and red-jersey hockey fans on their way to a Caps game, past the Temperance Fountain: an 1882 gift to the city from a dentist who believed that if folks drank from its dolphin-shaped water fountain—which sits in a four-columned gazebo and hasn't worked for years—they wouldn't drink, say, gin.

Just as the Temperance Fountain makes me want to guzzle mai tais through a beer bong, this high-five request is an eco-turnoff. I've seen these well-meaning volunteers manning downtown D.C.'s sidewalks, wanting you to sign something, implying through their giddiness—or their dismay as you skip their clipboard spiel—that if you were smarter you'd love the planet or whatever cause they're promoting almost as much as they do. But I also understand why my perky Seventh Street volunteer must be appalled by the disregard he encounters while trying to high-five pedestrians on behalf of the Earth. Because none of us seem bothered by breathing polluted air, eating food grown with polluted rainfall, and drinking water from polluted rivers and reservoirs. Factory soot, car exhaust, livestock poop, lawn chemicals—they're all streaming into our atmosphere and water supplies and swishing around in our lungs and our blood. Studies have found toxins in breast milk. But unless you're a fisherman who can't fish because of an oil spill, or a homeowner with nuclear waste glowing beneath your daffodils, or you're the victim of any colossal unnatural disaster, environmental issues don't seem to affect you on a day-to-day basis.

That's the problem with global warming. It's hard to freak out about monstrous levels of carbon dioxide in the atmosphere and small rises in temperatures when everything seems pretty much the same today as it did yesterday. Your kid is still struggling with algebra, your bills are due, and there's not a damn thing for dinner. And then there's the task of wrenching ourselves from a global economic system based around massive consumption of fossil fuels. Not easy.

But someday we'll be judged by the poisoned planet and carbon-drenched atmosphere we're leaving behind. Someday, future generations will say, "You knew what was happening—and you did *nothing.*" And that's why I'm here. If I were a parent, I'd be worried—*really* worried—about the planet we're leaving our children.

In the Andes, rising temperatures are already damaging one of the Earth's most vibrant ecosystems. "Ecuador is a top-ten biodiversity hot spot," says Mika Peck, leader of the research work in Santa Lucía. "A patch of ground here—meaning a one-hundred-by-one-hundred-meter area—has more tree species than the entire British Isles."

Mika is an athletic forty-year-old University of Sussex professor who looks like he'd be more comfortable in a pub than a lecture hall. Our first night, he gives a PowerPoint climate change presentation on his laptop. Seventy percent of Ecuador's rain forests, home to one of the world's largest arrays of plants and animals—and an important force for capturing carbon—has been destroyed. Tree by chopped tree, miners, loggers, and ranchers are clearing forests (cattle pastures are a particularly ineffective use of the land given the poor soil, which leads to more clearing). The forests' winged and four-legged residents are not only losing their habitats, but their numbers are diminishing from animal trafficking and hunting (a jaguar was recently shot nearby, Mika says, because it attacked a herd of cattle).

Here in the higher altitudes, climate change is the top threat. Increased temperatures mean more condensation in the damp rain forests. That causes the cloud base to rise: one meter every year, says

Mika. Without the clouds, plants that thrive in the misty environment are exposed to direct sunlight, which could eventually annihilate them. Rising clouds also mean more rain: Mika has noted an increase in landslides. All of this affects where plant species live, or can't live, which in turns affects the animals who feed on them.

Santa Lucía has already seen the potential catastrophes associated with rising temperatures. Mika mentions the Jambato toad, last seen here in 1987—a hot year. The toad likely perished from a chytrid fungus, which can't survive in temperatures less than 17 degrees Celsius. Now, as in '87, temperatures aren't cold enough to kill the fungus, which means it could once again wipe out whole species. "And extinction," Mika reminds us, "is forever."

At 6:42 a.m. the sun creeps over the Andes and into my face: nature's wake-up call. Birds squawk from nearby trees as I pull the covers to my neck and squint at the wide window view. Waxy green leaves rustle in the foreground, mountains with broccoli-like trees stand behind. Since Wayne and Charles are on the shady side of the room, I wake first, and I'm already at the lodge eating breakfast—coffee, porridge, *buñuelos* (doughnut-like fried balls)—when Charles arrives.

"Are you not at work yet, you lazy bugger?" he jokes.

I'm enjoying my coffee. The beans are grown and roasted about an hour's walk down one of the trails. Since there's no electricity, I helped grind the beans by hand, turning the crank as Natalie dropped beans through the metal funnel, brown powder spilling into a pan. It's a hearty workout. Gyms everywhere should replace Nautilus machines with manual coffee grinders.

The night before, we each signed up for one of five research projects, from camera traps to bird tracking. These first two days I'll assist Anita's group with habitat assessment. The goal is to study how vegetation differs between primary and secondary forests, and how this affects plants, bird populations, and mammals (what they're eating, is there enough of it). To do this, we'll create plots in areas where Mika and his team have shot aerial images, and make a series of estimates: For example, what percentage of the ground cover is deadwood, what percentage is mosses and lichens, what percentage is liverworts and ferns, and so on. We'll make similar estimates of what we see in the canopy. Roughly forty questions in all.

"So it's like a game show," I say as we begin our hike to the work site.

"Only no prizes," adds Ellen.

Ellen is one of the six British students who accompanied Anita from the University of Bournemouth. At age forty-two, she's about twenty years older than her companions, and she's romping through the rain forest because a Bill Bryson book changed her life.

"I was working as an office manager for a company involved in maintenance for Ministry of Defence properties," she tells me as we hike. "I had to attend meetings and produce minutes, provide spreadsheets, organize contractors, invoicing—none of it terribly interesting." Then she read Bryson's *A Short History of Nearly Everything*, his book on the origins of the universe and man. On page two of the introduction, he writes that even a long human life lasts only about 650,000 hours.

"I remember reading that sentence, and attending a meeting at work, and thinking, 'Why am I giving you lot one of my hours?'"

A floppy tan sun hat covers her short auburn hair; a red handkerchief covers her neck, matching her red backpack. She's been in Ecuador for almost a month, leaving her husband at home, working in three different reserves before arriving in Santa Lucía. Her walking stick is wrapped at the top with silver electrical tape: it was splitting from overuse.

"I remember reading the e-mail from Anita about this project and thinking that come what may, I wanted to be involved," she says. She's studying ecology, conservation, and wildlife at the university while working for a consulting firm that conducts ecological studies for developers.

We hike about an hour to the site, along trails hacked by Ecuadorans almost fifty years before. Pioneer farmers cleared areas along the ridge, hoping to grow crops, moving on once the soil was depleted. I'm winded when we arrive. Anita rambles off the trail to confirm the location, disappearing through steep brush to match numbers on her map to tree tags.

"She's like a goat," marvels Ellen.

The cloud forest, for Anita, is a source of giddy wonder. She notes the differences between various epiphytes, jumping and laughing when excited. "Brilliant! Cheers!" she shouts upon spotting some rare plant. She'll squat in front of a bug, her thin butt almost in the dirt, camera in an insect's face. I'm convinced she sleeps with a bromeliad under her pillow.

Anita climbs back up, issues directions, and we all go off the trail—down about a thirty-degree slope—breaking into groups to set up measurement areas. To do this, you pound a pole in the ground, then use string to create four distinct sections—north, south, east, west. One of us will stand in each quadrant. Ellen will bark out questions, and we'll shout back answers, which she'll jot on her clipboard.

The rain forest is not for the claustrophobic. I'm encircled by vines, trees, ferns; by palm leaves the size of car doors, by fuzzy, frilly branches that brush my neck and back; by heart-shaped aroid leaves slapping my face. It's like rush hour on a cramped botanical subway.

The ground looks solid as we descend—it's dense with foliage and rotting wood—but it's slick and easily gives way. A rotting log crumbles beneath my boot. I duck my head, descending carefully, like Liu Baojian walking down steps. Flecks of seeds cling to my shirt. The thump of a hummingbird pulses by my ear, but as soon as I turn it's gone.

I volunteer to shove the pole in the ground. Ellen points out the spot and I climb, carefully, stooping below branches and vines and platter-sized leaves.

Which is when I slip.

Months earlier, we all received an equipment list, which included work gloves. My gloves, at the moment, are on my bed in the cabana. As I fall, I reach for a tree, and a chunk of brown bark slices behind the thumbnail on my left hand. It's throbbing—instantly. I pull out a clump—it's poking above the nail—but most of it is trapped *behind* the nail, as if inserted by interrogators to induce a confession. For now, there's nothing I can do. We haven't started our work. Only after an hour and a half of recording data, of guessing what percentage of the ground is sticks versus dead logs, after an hour-long hike back to the lodge for lunch, can I finally confront the thick green and brown foreign object wedged behind my nail.

Bridget, one of the students, loans me her tweezers. Ellen hands me her clippers. "That's really in deep," she says. "You should soak it in hot water. With salt." I fill a coffee cup with steaming water, tap a salt shaker, then go to the outdoor bathroom with the amazing mountain view. It's tedious work: I soak, dig, tap slivers of bark into the sink. And then I soak it again. But I soon realize that scooping and gouging isn't sufficient. This requires something more serious.

This requires self-surgery. Meaning I'll have to cut the nail low. Uncomfortably low.

I stare at my pounding thumb. And then I clip at about the midpoint of the nail, cutting down at a sharp angle. As I cut, I think of Julie: normally she would be treating my wound. I extract nearly all of the bark. Helen, a sexagenarian volunteer from Canada, brings me some hard-core extra-sticky bandages. I wash my sore, wounded thumb in the sink, cover it with ointment, then wrap it with the bandage.

Everyone has finished lunch by the time I enter the lodge. I quickly down some *locro*—a soup made from potato, cheese, avocado, and corn kernels—and then beans and rice, a lunchtime staple, along with baked plantains. We remove our shoes before entering the lodge, and when I'm done with lunch I struggle to tie my boot laces.

Like so many things in life, I've taken my thumb for granted.

When I was a kid, my mother hosted a garden club party, which I found odd since we didn't have a garden. Garden club, I assume now, was code for a mommies' cocktail hour, although my mom is a notorious nondrinker, which is probably good because she has an addictive personality. She'll get hooked on a type of candy—once it was caramel creams—or a song: we'd listen to Gladys Knight and the Pips' "Midnight Train to Georgia" again and again in the car when I was a kid, my sister and I performing the Pip parts. Dad once asked Mom's cousin, Lee, who's had a forty-year love affair with marijuana, to never give my uptight mother a joint.

Lee grudgingly agreed. "Really, it'd be the best thing for her," he said. "It'd help her relax."

The night of the garden club shindig, Dad and I were banished from the house. Dad was taking me to dinner and then bowling, but first we drove to Arlington to see Granddaddy. He was home alone that night. My grandmother was probably playing bingo, one of her passions. I went with her once: she played six cards at a time, cigarette hanging from her mouth, studying the cards like an astronomer eyeing stars.

We took Granddaddy to Gino's, a now-defunct chicken chain. Granddaddy was in a chatty mood, telling a story, one my sister and I loved, about how he set down his hat at a Kmart, forgot it, went back the next day, found a price tag on it, and wound up re-buying his own hat.

By the time we took Granddaddy home, it was too late to go bowling. Dad apologized, but I said it was fine. Even that young,

I knew that something cool had transpired. Just the three of us, together. The kind of moment you'd do anything to re-create.

We got home about fifteen minutes early, so Dad kept driving, past our house toward the river town of Occoquan, down Route 123. Now it's a four-lane highway, then it was a two-lane road through low-hanging woods. The car's high beams were the only light.

"I had an old car in high school," Dad said, referring to his car with the wheel that fell off. "Sometimes the lights wouldn't work. When they'd flick off it'd look just like this—"

He flipped off the lights. We cruised at 50 miles per hour in absolute darkness.

I screamed in shock and delight, and Dad laughed—hard. It wasn't easy to make him laugh, but when he did, it was full body. He turned the headlights back on. I'm sure they were off two, maybe three seconds, but it felt like we were roaring through deep space; an Oldsmobile in a black hole. I practically hyperventilated with giggles.

"Don't tell your mother about this," he said, still smiling.

Now, on my first night in the Andes, I leave the lodge and walk the trail to the cabana, using Adam's headlamp to see. And then I turn it off, and I take a few quick steps in absolute darkness.

Feeling stupid is good. It keeps you humble. Makes you learn. I felt stupid working in New Orleans, and Costa Rica, and China, and I feel stupid doing these vegetation surveys.

Ellen holds the clipboard, shouting questions in her "school-ma'am-ish voice," as she calls it, recording answers on a worksheet. The rest of us stand in our leafy quadrants. In the interest of speed, she abbreviates the questions, such as "What percentage of the ground cover is leaf litter," to a quicker shorthand.

Ellen: "Okay, ground cover. Percentage leaf litter—Ken."

"Ten."

"Bridget?"

"Ten."

"Phillip?"

"Five."

"Janet?"

"Five."

"Percentage twigs—Ken?"

"Twigs?"

"Twigs."

"Er—about thirty."

"Thirty or thirteen?"

"Thirty."

"Bridget?"

"Twenty-five."

"Phillip?"

"Twenty-five."

"Janet?" . . .

After close to an hour of this, we move to another site. It takes some getting used to. I struggle to remember which plants are which when Ellen calls them out. "Total percentage bromeliads on trunk," she says, and I think—

Shit—what's a bromeliad?

Oh yeah—the thing that looks like a pineapple.

On another occasion—*really* stupid—I record the circumference of a tree rather than the diameter with our handmade yellow tape measure.

Ellen assures me our readings are pretty much in line with everyone else's. The university students still struggle to identify orchids, she says. By day two—the most taxing day of the trip—I'm more comfortable. We head to the bird tower: a wooden tower for bird-watching, about 3.75 miles away, at an altitude of eight thousand feet. We won't return to the lodge for lunchtime beans and rice; instead, we each receive a brown bag to stuff in our packs (and yes, I packed my gloves).

Initially we make good time, arriving at Nathaniel's farm—a key landmark on the main trail from the lodge—in thirty minutes. Nathaniel runs the lodge where we're staying. It's an attempt at eco-tourism; Earthwatch's involvement helps make it a sustainable venture. His former farm—a house and a rickety open stable—is a frequent stopping point for breaks and toilet trips. Directions often begin with, "You go past Nathaniel's farm, and then . . ."

We walk a bit farther, and then our same group as yesterday—Ellen, Bridget, Chloe, Helen, me—surveys site FP30. We descend off the trail, moving gingerly down the dense forest slope. A hummingbird feeds on bell-like flowers. I wind up in a patch of aroids, their leaves brushing my face. We've finished the ground and deadwood surveys when Mateo, a botanist from Quito, announces—oops—we're in the wrong area.

"I'm a bit cheesed off," says Ellen as we climb back up, since she'd asked more than once if FP30 was correct. We assist the other team, even though they don't need assistance, then gather on the trail for an energy bar break.

And then Chloe shrieks.

The pea-green snake is coiled around a palm stem, its head and upper body frozen along a large leaf at about the height of my chest. Uniform black patterns, the kind you'd find on a woven straw basket, are stamped in scaly X's along its back. Because it's thin, it doesn't look overly threatening, though we all know better. Its body is compact, close to the stem, a defensive posture, perhaps. Or a pre-strike position.

"Don't get too close—I think it's poisonous," says Chloe.

We get too close, holding cameras within a foot of its eyes.

Anita arrives.

"Ahhh—an eyelash viper! Brilliant!"

She takes photos as well, pointing out the viper's triangular head and noting that yes, these vipers are quite poisonous, and can strike up to a meter away, and then someone remembers a story about a woman whose right foot was amputated after getting bitten on a trail by a viper not all that different from this scaly specimen.

We all nod and say, "Huh—interesting . . . ," as we quickly step back.

"I'd rather not go home with my right foot in my backpack," I tell Ellen.

"Oh, don't worry—your wife is a nurse."

"Yeah—that'll work. 'Honey, I'm back—can you reattach my foot?'"

We walk again. Up. I ask Ellen if she's enjoyed her weeks of work, but the higher we go, the harder we breathe, and the harder it is to talk.

"I . . . love it . . . ," she huffs.

She enjoys the hikes, the isolation, calling out the survey questions, managing the forms.

"If you haven't noticed . . . I'm a bit bossy," she says.

For her dissertation she's studying the effect of wind turbines on bats. "Suffice it to say . . . for the bats . . . these turbines . . . are not the environmental solution . . . to energy problems."

Mateo stops and points through a gap in the trees. Far in the distance, on the edge of a sprawling ridge, is a whitish dot. "The lodge," he says. Three other group members—Helen, Chloe, and Hailey—are lagging behind, so we wait for them and enjoy the view. Helen is in her sixties, and seems fit, but she's struggling with the altitude and steep trail. Hailey is a little out of shape; Chloe smokes.

Anita crouches on the rising trail. She's barely sweating. Same with Mateo, who has the nonchalant look of a man on a morning stroll.

"We may not reach the tower at this pace—we won't have time to do the surveys," says Anita. "We can't make so many stops."

And so we split: a group of four will do surveys here, the rest of us will move on. Our pace quickens. A drizzly fog slithers through the trees. I've hiked at higher elevations with Julie, but this is draining, partly because of the humidity, partly because of the climb.

"Well . . . my heart works," I say to Ellen.

Sweat drips from my chin to my pants. Ellen asks Mateo how much farther.

"Twenty minutes," he says.

Thirty minutes later she asks him again.

"Fifteen minutes," he says.

We're probably slowing him down. The guy *still* isn't even sweating.

We hike up, up, up—and then a few short, steep downs—and then up, up, up.

"Oh my . . . goodness . . . ," says Ellen as we turn a corner, realizing we have more to scale.

At a small, flat clearing, we stand behind thigh-high West African grass, the trees parting. Clouds consume the mountains, the trees disappearing under a blanket of gray; like God is dissatisfied, erasing His work. The grass flutters in the wind, and it looks lovely until you realize: it's a nonnative species. It shouldn't be in Ecuador.

Another twenty minutes of hiking and finally, mercifully, we see it. The tower. After a few wheezing cheers, we unload our bags and take turns climbing up. It's three stories, rickety, built on top of a metal-roof shack. I go first. It's wobbly. Really wobbly. With each step it jiggers and jerks, yanked by the swirling wind, which chills my sweaty shirt. At the top, three flights in all, is a bare-bones wood platform. Forget the view: the fog is so thick that not only has the forest vanished, but even the roof below seems dim. Between the mist and the seclusion and the tower's swaying shipwreck design, standing alone up top is . . . spooky. Like the place is haunted by dead ornithologists.

I climb down for lunch in the wall-less cabin. Each lunch bag contains a juice box, a Nestlé Crunch bar, and two foil packages: one with rice, the other with potato salad. No forks. Ellen makes a spoonlike scoop out of foil, but it's only semisuccessful. I go with the trough method, dumping the potato salad into the rice, cupping the foil in both hands, and plunging my face in. Much more effective, and more satisfying in a primal, me-hungry kind of way.

The postlunch plan is to do two surveys, but the fog is so thick—and visibility so poor—it's impossible to see the canopy. I can't even see Ellen beyond the ferns and vines and wide leaves; I hear only voices, a bird swooping and calling, the flap of its wings echoing off the trees. I stand on a fallen tree, awkwardly, holding on to another thin tree for support. If I lower my left foot, the ground gives out.

Anita halts the survey. It's pointless. She and Mateo stay to wrap up some additional work, and the rest of us begin the three-hour hike to the lodge. I'm the only American with four Brits, and they ask me about U.S. national parks. I tell them about various parks I've visited—Grand Canyon, Crater Lake, Great Smoky Mountains—though given the thick clouds and impending darkness, I'm reminded most of a trip Julie and I took to Yellowstone and the Grand Tetons with Teresa and Tom.

Teresa and Tom and I tended to pull ahead of Julie on the trails, partly because she's pokey, partly because she'd stop to shoot photos of wildflowers. We'd wait for her, since separating is high on the list of dumb things to do while hiking (on one hike the four of us walked waaay around a bison that blocked a trail). We were trekking up the Amphitheater Lake Trail, about a 9.5-mile round-trip hike and a three-thousand-foot climb in the Tetons, the payoff being two lakes at about ten thousand feet. But as we approached the aptly named Disappointment Peak, we again became separated from Julie.

Storms arrive fast in the mountains. The temperature dropped about twenty degrees. Black clouds, grim and muscular, rolled over the mountains. Showers and thunder shook the trees.

We walked back down the trail, calling for Julie, yelling over the rain and wind.

Juuuuuuu-lieeeee!

The rain became hail. We scurried near the lake, seeking shelter beneath the trees.

We called her name again.

The three of us huddled, freezing from the rain and the suddenly frigid temperatures, hail bouncing off our packs.

"She could be anywhere!" I yelled.

"Maybe we should just go back down and meet her at the trailhead!" Tom yelled back.

No way. I wasn't leaving until we found her. For all we knew she'd sprained an ankle, been mauled by a bear. No. We were staying here. I imagined myself telling her parents, "Well, we didn't know where she was, so we left."

I checked a few side trails. Tom and Teresa stayed put. We didn't want *all* of us splitting up. I splashed up a trail that led to a campsite, yelling her name, competing against the rain and the wind, the trail like a stream.

I walked farther through the woods. A few more minutes, I told myself. I shouldn't go too far. The hail had stopped, but the rain was loud, like static.

When I turned a corner, she was walking toward me, drenched.

I've never felt relief that strong.

I didn't run through the puddles to embrace her. I didn't lecture her on the need to stick with the group. She didn't lecture me for leaving her behind.

I smiled faintly from under my dripping hood. She smiled back.

"It's good to see you!" I shouted above the rain.

"Where is the bucket of tarantulas?" asks Zachary. He's a British college student, a mix of erudite book smarts and daring nature-boy physique, topped by a Thor-like mane of blond hair. He needs the tarantulas so they can be photographed and ID'd. It would be easy to dislike him, given that he's a tall, brainiac young stud who tends to walk around shirtless with his bucket of tarantulas and a machete (that's right, *he* gets to carry a machete), but I've reached a point in life where I'm beyond being jealous of eighteen-year-old wunderkinds. Besides—he's such a nice kid he's impossible to dislike. The bastard.

While Zachary searches for his tarantula bucket, I'm engaged in my newest activity to boost mankind's knowledge of the cloud forest: picking through muck to search for grubs, slugs, leeches, cockroaches, and whatever critters might be living inside a bromeliad.

Investigating the muck, we're told, will help scientists understand how much these slimy, wiggly creatures depend on plants threatened by global warming. The project works like this: Mika shoots a weighted rope around the base of a branch with a slingshot-like device, then, when it's tight, uses a foot system to pull himself up. Once there, he whacks off a bromeliad with his machete, climbing as high as sixty feet (he's the only who can do it because he's the only one *insured* to do it). Apparently some of the Ecuadorans—expert climbers who can scale trees quickly with their hands and feet—find the heavy apparatus amusing. Gabriel, a staff member and ornithologist, climbed about fifty feet to set up a tree swing (which we're forbidden to use, since a drunk volunteer once leapt off the swing and broke his leg). When Mika hooks up his ropes, says Natalie, the Ecuadorans look like they're thinking—

We could shimmy up that tree in a few minutes.

"They probably think we're right wussies," she says.

Wayne chops off the leaves from one of Mika's bromeliads and rinses them with a watering can over a net, which collects the mud and debris for inspection. Chunks of mud are put in a bowl, along with the bromeliad's core, and brought to one of the tables inside, where Phillip, Natalie, and I sort through it to find anything that's living.

I hit instant biological jackpot: scorpion.

Phillip and Natalie serenade me with *ooh*s as I hold up the two-inch-long scorpion with tweezers. Many species here are unidentified—Natalie says I should campaign to have the scorpion classified in my name (*Scorpicanus buddus*)—which surprises me: I thought mankind had pretty much discovered all the creatures that are crawling, flying, or running around the Earth. Our focus, I assumed, had shifted from discovering species to exterminating them. Yet here in the Andes, unidentified species, particularly plants, lurk everywhere. We occasionally pass a red flower that looks like a fat, bloated, prickly hot dog, which Anita and the other researchers had never seen before. She nicknamed it the "Diseased Willie," for obvious reasons, a name the women find more amusing than the men. (Adam and I recently accompanied our wives to a fortieth birthday party for a mutual friend. The birthday girl received a book called *Sex After 40*, which contained nothing but blank pages. The women found this losing-their-breath funny. Adam nudged me: "You notice none of the dudes are laughing," he said.)

I study my scorpion. He's already dead, which means I don't have to watch him drown in a beaker of alcohol. The researchers will send any creatures we find to a university in Quito for identification.

The work is tedious. We sift through small piles of dirt in rectangular petri dishes, studying them with magnifying glasses. Phillip finds a thick slug and unwittingly slices it with his tweezers; its midsection oozes purple goo. I mainly find tiny white larvae, which can't be more than a millimeter or two in length, presumably the offspring of caterpillars or worms. They squirm as they plummet to the bottom of the alcohol-filled beaker. In one clump of mud—which smells like pond scum—I pluck out ninety-seven mosquito larvae.

We talk to pass time as we sift. Natalie chats about her and Nick. Before earning his degree in environmental science, he was an expert carpenter who specialized in cabinets, but he grew weary of his upscale clients. "He got tired of taking out a posh kitchen and replacing it with another posh kitchen," says Natalie.

She wants to have kids. She mentions a single friend who got inseminated. "I think she should have adopted," Natalie says, dropping some sort of mitelike creature into the alcohol. "So many children need homes."

I once considered being a sperm donor. I even filled out an online application for a nearby fertility clinic, not to ensure the Budd seed got planted in some lucky egg, or because I thought I'd take my mystery child to baseball games and amusement parks. I just thought that maybe, assuming my sperm were up to snuff, I could help some couple that couldn't have kids. And no, I didn't tell Julie about this.

I then received an e-mail from the clinic:

> *Thank you for your interest in our donor program. Your application lists a birth date of 1966, which unfortunately will not allow you to complete the six-month contract period before turning 40. At this time we will not be able to accept you as a donor. However, you have the option to earn significant rewards as a donor RECRUITER: an average of $500–$1,000 for every prospect you recruit who successfully enters our donor program. We will gladly provide marketing information and tools to assist you in this effort.*

So they don't want my sperm, though they'd love a donation from someone like Zachary.

My sister has three children, so the genes of my parents will live on. But the Budd name, as it extends through my father and grandfather, ends with me. And that ends one helluva long string of creation. Think about it: It took two people to create you. Four people to create your parents. Eight people to create your grandparents. It's astounding, really, when you ponder how many *Homo sapiens* pairings occurred over the last two hundred thousand years so that someone could give birth to you, to me, to all of us.

I sit at the long wood table in the lodge, and I spend the morning plucking more larvae from smelly mud, and I drop them with tweezers into the beaker of alcohol. Their tiny white ridged bodies curl as they descend, until they die upon the bottom of the glass.

Rather than spend the entire day picking through bromeliad gunk—"It's like factory work," says Natalie—she takes Phillip and me for a postlunch hike down roller-coaster trails, searching for more high-in-the-canopy bromeliads. We pass two tall, heavenly waterfalls, the second forty-five to fifty feet high, the mountain wall thick with mosses and ferns.

Once we identify a worthy bromeliad candidate, Phillip and I wrap a red string around the damp trunk, and loop a numbered round metal marker—like a dog tag—before tying it. Natalie records the tree's position with a GPS. Eventually Mika will climb it and chop down the bromeliad so its insides can be investigated, its residents plopped into more alcohol-filled beakers.

The trek back up is arduous, but we move at a decent clip. When we return, sweating, reaching the back side of the lodge, I stop.

"Tarantula," I say, pointing to the ground.

We huddle around it. The tarantula isn't moving. Natalie calls young Zachary, the resident bug expert.

"It's paralyzed," he says, crouching down. "See?"

He lifts one of the tarantula's hairy back legs. Lifting a tarantula's leg to test for paralysis is probably on the list of frowned-upon activities for students and volunteers.

A wasp creeps through the grass toward the tarantula. As Zachary explains it, a sting from the wasp—called a tarantula hawk—is what caused the spider's paralysis. Now the wasp drags the tarantula to a burrow, where it'll stuff the still-alive-but-paralyzed tarantula inside. There, the wasp will lay an egg in the hapless spider, which will slowly die in the burrow. Eventually the egg will hatch, Zachary says, and the little wasp baby will eat its way out of the tarantula's body to start a new life.

Ah, the glories of nature. Eat food, become food. Return to the soil and enrich the earth. Ashes to ashes, dust to dust. Have your insides eaten out by a burrowed wasp baby.

Death is one of God's shrewder, if less popular, creations. Our participation fee for this brief, uncommon opportunity to experience life. And what would life be without death?

Roughly a year before I arrived in Ecuador, my grandmother went to Fairfax Hospital with pneumonia. She was eighty-eight. The clouds of Alzheimer's were consuming more of her mind.

"If you want to see her," Mom told me, "you better do it soon."

My sister and I called my grandmother "Daa," a name thrust upon us for reasons we never understood. Daa had six brothers and sisters and they all had Smurf-like nicknames—Humpet, Sommer, Honey—so I suppose this was the continuation of some unfortunate family tradition. Most of Daa's siblings called her Kinky because of the kinkiness of her hair, clearly oblivious to the word's leather-whips-and-candle-wax connotations.

When my sister went to the hospital, a day before I did, Daa was drifting in and out of consciousness, talking to her deceased sister Elizabeth and my father. "Don't sit there," she told my sister, pointing at the empty end of the bed. "Bob is sitting there."

Who knows, my sister said later—maybe Dad really *was* sitting there.

I went to the hospital the next morning. It was worse than I expected. Until then, she'd been forgetful, and she occasionally said peculiar things, but now she seemed more frail, more distant—her consciousness altered. She reached for invisible objects on the blanket with withered, blue-veined hands. She put the invisible objects to her mouth. Sometimes she'd mumble or say random words in a weak voice. My mother's name. Family. Bob. And then she'd say something lucid—"This isn't a fun way for you to start your day"—followed by something not so lucid: "I'm just trying to straighten the table."

Sometimes she'd look at me, squinting, as if trying to make me out.

When Terry's father, Howard, approached death after successive heart attacks, he began hallucinating. Terry was alone with him in the hospital. Howard stared at a bare white wall.

"What are you looking at?" Terry asked, sitting next to the bed.

"I'm watching a movie," said Howard. "*Lonesome Dove.*"

So Terry stared at the blank wall with him, watching the movie that wasn't there.

Now Daa licked her lips, breathed heavy, dozed, then lifted her head, squinting.

"You look like you're up to something," she murmured.

The room was dark, the medical machinery humming. Remarkably, a few days later, she would return home, looking vibrant despite never leaving bed, and seeming, for that first weekend at least, alert. Unlike Adam's dad, her last stand would endure a few months. She would live past her eighty-ninth birthday, lingering in hospice care. But it was clear that day, as she plucked unseen items from the bed, that death was near. And I looked at her, asleep despite the tubes and the screens and the beeping devices, and then I looked up at the TV: while my grandmother approached death, an in-hospital service called the Newborn Channel showed a new mother breastfeeding her baby. The circle of life in a strange electronic way.

When it's me on this bed with tubes and machines, when it's my heart wrenching to a halt like Dad's—when I'm the tarantula trapped in the burrow—I don't want any regrets. I don't want to be defined by disappointments.

• • •

For all the brilliant scientists here, Wayne is the true genius. He brought Scotch.

"I decided if I'm literally in the middle of nowhere and I have a zero-luxury lifestyle, maybe I can make it just a little more comfortable," he says.

Genius.

I was planning to scrub a few clothes after walking back from the waterfalls, but as soon as he offers Scotch, I toss the stinky shirts on my backpack.

Wayne holds up a shiny silver flask shaped like a small bowling pin. "It's Oban," he says, opening it. "Fourteen years old." He pours about an inch in my glass, then his, adding a little water from a pitcher covered with tin foil to keep out bugs.

"Scotch aficionados say the water brings out the flavor. It's a chemical thing. You don't want ice. If Scotch is cold, you taste the alcohol and not the nuances. Drink it straight and it burns the hell out of your nose. But a little water dilutes it just enough to get rid of the burn, but doesn't cool it down to where you can't really taste it. I know—it's weird. But it works."

"You're like a whiskey chemist," I say.

I sit on my bed, Wayne sits on the wicker couch. I sip.

"Damn," I say. "This is really nice."

As we drink we hear shouts from a cleared-out dirt field below and behind our cabana, where a soccer game rages: the gringos versus the Ecuadorans (though all the gringos are Brits). The Ecuadorans usually win, as well they should: they have home-field advantage.

Wayne wipes a dribble of Scotch from his mustache.

"Have you always had the beard?" I ask.

"Nah. I grew it for the trip. I didn't want to shave. I figured I'm going into the mountains, I should have a beard. It's appropriate. How 'bout you—ever grow one?"

"I had a mustache for about seven years. I looked like a lounge singer."

"Like Ron Burgundy?"

"Pretty much."

"Ever thought about going for the full beard?"

"Well, the problem is that it comes in half gray."

"That's the distinguished beard!" he says. "That's the look."

I laugh. "I once let it go unshaven for about a week. And then I got up one morning, looked in the mirror—my hair was messed up, I had this nasty brown and gray stubble—and I thought, 'I look like an old alcoholic.' That was the last time I tried to grow a beard."

When I came back to the cabana, before we poured the Scotch, Wayne lay in his top bunk, talking on his phone to his wife. Somehow, despite our remote location, despite our distance from civilization—despite my understanding that we might as well be on Mars—Wayne was *getting a cell phone signal*. It was only one bar, and it was inconsistent, but it worked. Charles, it turns out, is also getting a signal.

"I spent the morning answering e-mails from the office," he says.

I question Nick about this after dinner.

"We're nowhere near a tower—the signal somehow bounces over the mountain," he says.

I'm deeply disappointed by this. I like our isolation. And yet as Wayne spoke with his wife, I pulled my phone from my pack. I held it. I pondered turning it on, though now, as we drink Scotch, it's still off, sitting on the bed next to me.

A sweaty Charles enters the cabana from the soccer game, jubilant.

"England won—three to two!" he proclaims. "Mike had two goals. Zachary had the game winner. Mika stopped close to thirty shots."

"That's great," says Wayne. "We'll probably get smaller portions at dinner now."

He rises from the couch and pours Scotch for Charles, who wipes his face with a towel and pulls a few bags of banana chips from his suitcase. "I didn't know you have a stash," I say, practically pouncing as he rips them open. (I got hooked after buying some in Nanegalito.)

It's like being in a college dorm. We're drinking, listening to music, doing dumb stuff—Wayne tries out his snakebite kit on his forearm and yelps in pain from the suction—we're grubby, eating chips . . . it's an unexpected benefit to the trip.

We take turns showering before dinner. I go first, running the water only twice: to get wet and then to rinse off the soap and shampoo. The water goes from freezing to scalding then back to freezing as I adjust the knob, with ten-second, just-right *ahhhh* periods in between. There's no mirror, so I shave blindly with my electric razor, wondering if I'm missing spots.

I get dressed and sit on my bed. My phone is next to me. I think about turning it on. Maybe I'll get a signal, maybe I won't. If I do, I'll think about calling Julie. And I'll answer e-mails from work. And I'll check headlines. But I keep thinking of that old line of Jonathan's that is still with me three years later: *You only really learn about yourself when you're out of your comfort zone.* And so I never turn it on. And I put it back in my pack.

In the evenings, before dinner, the lodge's front porch becomes happy-hour central. The kitchen sells Pilsener beer and Chilean wine, hauled to the lodge on the strong backs of mules, as Wayne and Jade know too well. Jade is an Atlanta native turned Brooklynite who's here through her company. The day before, as they walked back to the lodge from a work site, they heard a speeding *clip-clop* behind them. They turned and saw two mules, loaded with beer and supplies, approaching at a dead gallop. Wayne and Jade leapt off the trail into the brush.

"They just missed us," said Wayne.

Nathaniel walked nonchalantly behind, they said, and kind of smirked as he passed.

"You could almost hear him saying 'silly gringos,'" said Jade. "Scared the crap out of us. Can you imagine? Death by beer donkey."

Volunteers and Bournemouth students sit on porch benches and pull chairs from the tables inside; I lean against the rails, facing the clutter of Wellies and buckets and stray walking sticks. Earl, the pleasant gray-and-white-haired Australian, pours his beer into a glass.

"This beer is Kimberley cool," says Earl.

"Kimberley?"

"Kimberley is the hottest place in Australia," he says with a wink.

Earl's blue fleece jacket is zipped high. The evenings are cool. I walk with my beer from the porch across the grass. The panorama view never fails to provoke awe. On a night like this, when the clouds complement rather than gobble the sky, the sunset is a slide show of fire, yellow beams streaming through dark clouds, a spotlight on valley trees. As the sun drops, the sky turns pink, the mountains layered like torn paper; the clouds like smoke in battle. The sun burns, alive, then fades, fades, fades.

We enter the lodge for dinner, usually a small amount of meat, some veggies, a colossal mound of mashed potatoes. The potatoes frequently take up half the plate. Tonight we have meatballs. Given that beef is expensive, I wonder if any of the mules are missing.

After dinner, a group of us sit inside, finishing beers and talking. That afternoon in the woods, Charles had found a nutmeg: smaller than a golf ball, almost perfectly round except for a slight nub at the top. He's flicking it into a glass he'd laid on its side. Over time, it evolves into a game: to see who can flick the nutmeg closest to the edge of the table without its rolling off. We mark the leader's spot with a strip of yellow tape tied in a bow. Because the table is uneven and not terribly smooth, the ball teeters near the edge, tugged by gravity, maybe staying, maybe falling, leading to cries of triumph—*Oh Oh Oh Oh YEAAAHHHH!*—and despair: *go go go STOP! Awwwwwww . . .*

We first call our new game Flickball, but it then becomes Flicknut.

It's Jade's turn. She drinks her beer, then steadies her right hand behind the nut.

"In a few days we'll be gambling on this," I say.

"Try a few minutes," says Wayne.

"Please," says Jade. "I need quiet."

The light is dim; a few feeble fluorescent lights powered by the generator. Jade flicks the nut with too much *oomph*: it rolls off the table toward Wayne, who catches it.

"Be gentle with the nut," says Wayne.

Flicknut devolves, naturally, into a series of nut jokes. Holding your nut, handling your nut, stroking your nut, warming your nut. Charles has the best shot so far, about an inch and a half from the edge. Jade then surpasses him with a curving shot reminiscent of a golf putt.

About eight flicks later, Charles lands another shot near the edge. Wayne kneels at the end of the table and examines the nut's placement. He nods, then marks it with the yellow tape.

"Another victory for England," says Charles, arms raised to the air.

New theories develop: spinning the shot, banking it off a beer glass. And new obstacles: a corner beer trap where Jade and Jean, a Canadian volunteer, have placed their glasses.

"Be the nut," says Wayne, as Jean prepares a shot.

On a second Flicknut night, after Mika showed some folks a

documentary about mining companies on his laptop, people actually huddled around us, watching.

"What's this?" says Nick.

"Flicknut," says Wayne, concentrating, now wearing a striped knit glove he bought in Otavalo to give his flick a softer touch.

The night ends when the generator is turned off. We walk back to the cabana, Charles and Wayne and I, the light from our headlamps bouncing along the trail and the aroid leaves.

"Flicknut is a good example of how people adapt when they don't have electricity," I say as we carefully walk in a row.

"And yet it's strangely satisfying," says Wayne from the front.

"Think it'll take off in the States?" asks Charles.

"People will watch anything," I say.

"We'll contact ESPN," adds Wayne.

"Good idea," I say. "*Monday Night Flicknut.*"

Flicknut, I decide, is a good metaphor for life: enjoy what you have instead of lamenting what you lack.

Our rice-and-beans lunch is still a half-hour away, so I watch hummingbirds dart around feeders at the side of the lodge. A cheap out-of-tune guitar twangs from inside. Two teenage Ecuadorans, Jason and Julia, are here to assist with research. They live in Nanegal, a village at the bottom of the mountain, and they're here as a reward: the two led an environmental initiative at their school. Jason is tall, athletic, frequently wears a wool cap during the day despite the humidity. He's teaching himself guitar, using one the lodge keeps for guests. I admire his persistence, though as he repeats the same four awkward out-of-tune chords, I'm reminded of Tom's attempt to play the accordion in Xi'an. Except Jason has been "playing" for twenty minutes.

We're back early from our newest assignment: checking camera traps. The traps are set to photograph spectacled bears and pumas, to help researchers determine their population size. The camera takes three pictures when triggered by motion sensors. To attract their furry subjects, we spray the traps with puma urine and bear urine. Unlike the pee smell of, say, a New York City subway station, puma urine smells like a rather old shoe, while the bear urine has the surprisingly pleasing scent of vanilla extract.

We walk to the trap sites—me, Wayne, Jade, and three other volunteers—with Javier, who seems less like a scientist than a bass player with an Ecuadoran rock band. A series of pierced hoops and studs run down both ears, complementing a looped nose ring. His pierced lower lip rests above a frizzy soul patch; a small ponytail brushes his neck.

Dipping down a side trail to trap number one, Javier teaches us the art of adding puma urine to a camera trap. First, you rip chunks of cotton into five marble-sized balls and shove them in a vial. Next, you spray the urine into the vial and onto the cotton. I do ten stinky squirts, but Javier says to do more. I add another ten. My hands now smell of puma urine.

"Great—every female puma in the forest thinks I'm an eligible bachelor," I say to Jade.

"Maybe it's female urine and you're attracting males."

We lodge a stick in front of the camera trap—the camera is mounted on a platform—and tape two vials on opposite sides of the stick with silver duct tape. According to the small orange spray bottle, this is 100 percent pure puma urine.

"One hundred percent *pure*," I emphasize to Wayne and Jade.

"Don't be fooled by lesser-brand puma urine," says Wayne.

The back of the bottle includes a warning: do not drink. Which means that somewhere, some idiot drank 100 percent pure puma urine. Probably a teenager, hoping to catch a buzz. I briefly wonder how one obtains urine from a puma, though I'm not sure I want to know.

Javier says this is much stronger-smelling bait than what he used previously. And I must say, when we return to the lodge for lunch, the smell lingers on my fingers and my thumb bandage even after I wash my hands. We add urine to two traps, and pull memory cards from the cameras, but we can't find the third trap. Javier leads me, Wayne, and Janet down a steep side trail at Nathaniel's farm while Jade, Jean, and Olivia, a marathoner from Maryland, stay up top, secretly taking samurai warrior photos while waving the machete. We pass through a pasture of waist-high grass and ant colonies, swarms of black ants bustling in dirt Manhattans. The itchy African grass is so thick it's hard to see the wavy, potholed trail. We descend past a wire fence and approach a clump of thick trees at the forest's edge.

"Hmmm," says a puzzled Javier, looking in the woods.

There should be a camera trap here. But there isn't. So from a scientific standpoint, we've hiked down this steep, itch-inducing trail for nothing, though from a tourist perspective the view is impressive: the mountains solid with trees, the morning sky free of impending clouds. Javier will later review a map and realize we went down the wrong trail.

So we hike back early to the lodge for lunch. We're supposed to spend the afternoon adding more urine to traps, but Javier is trying to recover data he lost on his laptop. As he scrolls through Windows menus, the clouds roll in thicker and earlier than any day so far. The mountains perish, lost behind a whitish-gray mist; the few visible trees become skeletons. Which means there's nothing to do. I offer to help Helen and Earl pick through bromeliad gunk, but it's a small batch, so they don't need me. I'm so bored I watch.

Yesterday, after work, Natalie took a group of us for a late-afternoon swim not far past the waterfalls. It was about an hour's walk away, and when we reached the swim spot, everyone stripped to bathing suits and shorts. To access the pool, we walked first through a fast-flowing stream, stepping unsteadily, the stones hard on wimpy feet, the water a painful, nipple-hardening, color-draining cold.

The stream grew deeper. And after lumbering through waist-deep water, and exiting to cross slick rocks, we reentered and sloshed to the pool, which is Garden-of-Eden lush: an icy cascade of clear, clean water, surrounded by shimmering ferns. I stood in the stream and admired the simple, stunning beauty, and wondered—

Are my feet going numb?

Seriously—I can't feel my feet.

Swimming required a level of courage I couldn't quickly muster. Brooke, a red-headed University of Sussex student with pale freckled skin, submerged herself for five seconds, gasped as she resurfaced, then couldn't stop shivering. Wayne and a few others bravely swam to the leaping log, as it's called, which descends to the center of the pool: you straddle it, climb up, stand, then jump back into the water. Zachary, of course, did a flip. Phillip leapt twice, though the second time, as he attempted to reach shallow water, panic blanched his face. I thought the water was so cold it drained his strength—his lips were blue—but he later blamed the currents. I reached for his hand and pulled him toward me.

I'd been delaying, but I knew I had to go under. How many times will I swim in a nerve-piercing rain forest pool? Hell, this pool may not exist soon if the snowcaps disappear. So after another few minutes of stall tactics—studying the pretty flowers, marveling at the tall trees—I finally submerged.

How do I describe this.

Back in college, my soon-to-be-former dentist once convinced me that I didn't need Novocain for a filling. The resulting pain was an intense, body-stiffening cold—like a jolt of electroshock therapy.

That's what this was like. Underwater dentistry.

I swam two strokes, resurfaced, and flipped on my back. For a millisecond I thought about reaching the log but the currents were strong and despite my flailing efforts to swim I was shoved back to shallow water. Once I stood up, it was over. I was not going back under.

"You get used to it pretty quickly," Natalie gushed, swimming leisurely as I shivered.

I hadn't realized it until then, but she's mentally ill.

Natalie joins me now in the lodge. She opens the door and fog seeps in, slithering along the floor. It's like we're in Transylvania. As the fog grows so does the chill. I'm sipping a cup of hot tea and writing in my journal. Jason, the local Ecuadoran teenager, is still trying to figure out the guitar, and by my account has played the same minor chord for upwards of fifty minutes.

Natalie sits at one of the picnic tables to talk, her tan pants splattered with mud. She's smiling her usual isn't-life-grand smile and asks about my morning.

"It was good—interesting," I say.

"Camera traps, right?"

"Yeah. We were supposed to go back but Javier is having some sort of computer issue."

I ask her something I've wondered on each of these excursions. Perhaps it's hitting me because we've been sitting around all afternoon, but I'm wondering if we're helping, or if Javier and all the scientists here could work faster without us.

"I mean, I can see the benefits of having us dig through bromeliad gunk. It's like stuffing envelopes. And I can see where you need bodies for Anita's project. But I can't imagine Javier really needed us to spray puma urine."

"Well—sometimes they can do things faster on their own," says Natalie. "It takes a few days for you guys to get used to the walks and the altitude and all that."

"And to learn what the hell we're doing."

"Yes. But something like the bromeliad sorting isn't the best use of the scientists' time. And we're doing five projects now—without volunteers we were doing two." Ellen echoed this over breakfast: her group can do far more surveys with four Earthwatch volunteers on their team.

But our involvement presents trade-offs. Yes, we provide free labor for simple work, and we're paying to be here, which helps fund the research. The researchers, however, are sometimes forced to be hotel managers, dealing with *my room is too cold, I'm out of toilet paper, where's my vegetarian meal* types of issues.

"Tim once had to walk to one of the cabanas and wake up a group of women and tell them it was time to work. It interferes with their research, which annoys them, because that's why they're here," says Natalie.

But really, she emphasizes, the big benefit isn't the work we do, as helpful as that may be. It's hiking the Andes, hearing the birds, swimming the impossibly cold pools. How can people care about saving this place, or all that lives here, if they haven't experienced it? Some people in urban areas—she's seen it in London—are afraid of the forest.

"If you feel that way," she says, "you probably just think it's shit."

Natalie heads upstairs to her room; I write more in my journal. Jason takes a guitar break, so Wayne tunes it. "Bless you," I say.

Javier invites us into the office. Having given up on his computer problem, he's reviewing memory cards we collected from the camera trap. This batch is unsuccessful: the camera was activated by wind-rustled leaves and research teams. So we have no photos of spectacled bears, but several shots of passing Wellies.

He shows us a shot from last month: two pumas stare directly at a camera. Next he pulls up videos of monkeys he filmed in a reserve south of Quito. Their lands are now threatened. Similar monkeys used to live in Santa Lucía, but they're all gone. Javier explains the monkeys' plight in his limited English.

"They have no house," he says.

Earthwatch required us each to submit a medical form, signed by a doctor, testifying that we can handle the rigorous work here in

Santa Lucía without experiencing, say, a coronary seizure. To get that signature, I underwent a physical, my first since high school. The results were positive—blood pressure was okay, cholesterol levels were fine—but I was past the age, I discovered, when men are supposed to have the dreaded prostate exam. Which involves . . . you know. A finger. Up there. Where there shouldn't be a finger.

I was ultrawary because Adam had a prostate exam and experienced a severe case of postfinger trauma.

"How was it," I'd asked him on the phone.

"Dude," he said, "it freaked me out. I still don't feel comfortable."

When he left the doctor's office his wife said he looked ill.

This is the first time I've met the doctor who's giving me the finger, so to speak. Julie frequently refers patients to this practice and it's covered by my health insurance plan. As he slaps on a rubber glove for, you know, I'm thinking, "Shouldn't we get to know each other? Maybe go to a movie? Talk about our feelings?"

"I need you to unbuckle your trousers," he says.

"Oh, yeah—sure."

Like I do this all the time.

"And then just bend over please."

"Okay . . ."

Adam called me that evening.

"How was it," he said.

"You know, what really surprised me—I mean it really caught me off guard—was how much I enjoyed it."

"You're kidding."

"I'm kidding."

Given that I'm pondering a prostate exam upon waking up tells you how energetic I feel. Most mornings here I've felt like a hundred-year-old man. My legs are stiff from hiking. I wake up in the night with calf cramps. My joints crack. Jade tells me at breakfast she's thought about eating wild berries so she can get sick and stop hiking.

I delay getting up by counting my mosquito bites: I have twenty-seven on my feet and calves alone. Some of the bites are from mites, which hang out near the ground and nip your feet. We walk in our socks in the lodge, to avoid tracking in mud, so our mealtimes are probably the mites' mealtimes as well. I also wonder if bedbugs are using my legs for nocturnal nibbling. I've started lifting my blankets every night to check for critters, a habit I developed after seeing the eyelash viper, and the tarantula, and then a worm that was longer by far than my boot. Some worms can grow up to four feet in length.

"That's a big worm," said Wayne.

Wayne has bites on his back, legs, and the bottom of his feet, which are sticking out of his sleeping bag at night and making him a ten-toed buffet. The hiking is a mix of pleasure and pain, he says: it helps scratch the bites on his feet, but it also causes them to swell—and hurt.

My most impressive bite is the swollen-red knot on my left elbow, which looks like a surgeon inserted a golf ball next to the joint.

"Most likely a spider bite," says Nick as we begin our hike to the work site. "You probably got it in the grass." That would be the high grass from our errant puma urine expedition.

"If it gets any bigger I'll have to declare it at customs," I say.

I'm with Nick and Tim today for the "Canopies and Carbon" project. One of the many ways to monitor the effects of climate change, says Nick, is to study how tree species are reacting to rising temperatures (are they growing differently, are their numbers shrinking, and so on). One way to do this, particularly in rugged terrain like the Andes, is with aerial photography.

The researchers' efforts to create aerial images have been more notable for their failures than any successes. First they tried a helium balloon, but they needed something quicker and more mobile.

(And more reliable: it crashed. The altitude affected the balloon's buoyancy.) Next was a remote-controlled helicopter, but low-level clouds interfered with its sensors—and, yes, it crashed, thanks to an inexperienced pilot.

"A vulture came after the wreckage," Mika told us. The helicopter is now buried near the lodge.

Eventually they perfected their use of a second remote-controlled helicopter, and they're now using its images to map the forest. Because if you don't know what the forest looks like now, you can't know how global warming and human encroachment are changing it over time.

"But having hundreds and thousands of photos of forest canopy is useless unless you can identify the species, and no one has the sensory skills or the time to do that," says Nick. Ideally a computer program would do the work—two thousand species of plants are growing in Santa Lucía, so distinguishing what's what isn't easy—but that's possible only if each species has a unique signature that's detectable in photographs. And that's the point of their research: to see if such patterns and signatures exist in the aerial shots—to ID tree species by analyzing their crowns—and to see if the signatures exist in normal photos (as opposed to infrared images).

I confess: I only sort of understand what he's saying. And in a way, that's why, as I write this, climate change still elicits cynicism. The subtleties and intricacies aren't easy to communicate. So when there's a massive snowstorm, the talk-show skeptics smirk in the camera and say, "Well, so much for global warming. It's freezing out! Hey, I'd *love* some global warming—*hahahaha*." Never mind that this is like saying a fat guy can't possibly be obese because he ate a bag of carrots. Many climatologists predicted intense snowfall and other winter extremes as a result of rising temperatures, due to changes in the atmosphere. And temperatures are indeed rising. From 1880 until this moment, as I stand in the Andes, global temperatures have climbed about 1.5 degrees Fahrenheit. Three months after I leave, scientists will declare this the warmest decade on record. A fifty-year U.S. Geological Survey report released a month earlier found that glaciers in Washington and Alaska are shrinking rapidly (cities like Anchorage receive their drinking water from lakes fed by glaciers), while British researchers released findings showing that one of Antarctica's largest glaciers is shrinking four times faster than was expected ten years earlier.

As an inhabitant of this pretty planet, I find this disconcerting, just as I would if a team of home inspectors gave me a well-researched report showing my house may have faulty wiring. Aren't the risks high enough that we should act? Many climatologists compare it to people who buy fire insurance, even though their homes may never burn. You protect yourself against unknown but potentially catastrophic risks.

What surprises me, however, is the skepticism I've heard here from some of the researchers. They're skeptical that anything will be done about CO_2 emissions. They're skeptical that the public and politicians have the stomach, the will, to do anything about climate change. They're skeptical that anything *can* be done about climate change. There's a disconnect: the public is debating whether climate change is happening; the scientists are studying its effects.

"The climate is changing, and it's getting warmer—I find the evidence of this undeniable in scientific terms," Nick tells me. "Mankind has certainly contributed to accelerating this change, perhaps significantly, perhaps not so significantly. Judging by the available evidence and a bit of common sense, I think the contribution is significant. And I do think human society can exert an element of control over the changing environment. But I don't think we'll exert that influence in any way that is useful, partly because the climate is teetering at a tipping point beyond which our influence can only diminish."

He admits he's a cynic by nature. He believes our collective governments are more interested in thriving economies than a healthy environment. To which I say: no kidding. But if governments everywhere took the gazillion dollars they pump into bank bailouts and defense programs—all the billions we spend on new technologies for killing people—and instead invested it in sustainability and clean energy, well, just imagine—

Stop.

"That's never going to happen," he says.

Oh.

"Which is why I say we won't exert sufficient influence to do anything."

To a certain extent, they blame themselves for the public's cynicism since, as Tim notes, scientists frequently aren't the most effective communicators.

"I worked with a guy, Harold, who only focuses on leeches," he says as we march past Nathaniel's farm. "They're leeches that attach themselves to slugs. That's all he talks about."

"He must be popular with the ladies," I say.

"You can ask him, 'So, Harold, what's happening in the news?' He won't know. Leeches."

As we walk, Nick spots a tiny frog on a palm leaf. Its eyes protrude like marbles from its head.

"Nathaniel says there used to be frogs everywhere here," says Nick.

"We're probably walking past them but we can't see them because our eyes are ruined from computers," says Tim.

I mention Javier's spider monkey videos; the monkeys that are losing their habitat.

"They probably disappeared here about twenty years ago," says Nick. "Hunted to extinction for food. They're quite tasty."

Nick studied brown-headed spider monkeys—a rare spider monkey subspecies found only in the northwest of Ecuador and southwest Colombia—in another reserve two years ago, in a project led by Mika and a primatologist.

"If they have no experience with humans, they just look at you. But most of them have been shot at, so they don't like us—partly because you're invading their territory, but mainly because they've had bad experiences. They'll throw branches at you, they'll howl—which is stupid because it makes them easier to spot—they'll throw poo and try to wee on you." It depends on the species. Another type sends one monkey out to stare at you while the others hide.

I ask about repopulating them here in Santa Lucía, but Nick says it's tricky. They don't always adapt or reproduce. Elsewhere in Ecuador, a team reintroduced a pair of howler monkeys to an area, but the monkeys were both male. Which makes reproduction a little tricky.

After about two hours we reach our destination: a patch of steep woods bordered on the left by waves of African grass. Cattle graze near the edge of the trail.

"I'm guessing the cows aren't native," I say to Tim.

"Uh, no," he says.

I consider asking him if there are cows in England.

Nick and Tim have brought a series of aerial photographs in plastic sheets. The plan is to march through the woods, confirming that the trees ID'd in the photo match the trees tagged by botanists a year or so ago. We leave our bags at the trailhead, walking carefully down. A wasp nest like a flaky skull hangs above us; wasps crawl on it, emerging from quarter-sized openings. Nick is soon hacking a new trail with the machete; Helen, Charles, and I follow.

The first tree we check is supposed to be tagged. But it isn't.

"Probably bloody Earthwatch volunteers," Tim jokes. "They're useless."

Nick asks me to work my way to trees 86 and 87. "Work" is the key word here: the trail is a sort-of trail, steep and slick, either barely created or long abandoned. I clamber down, slowly, stepping over logs and plants, ducking under limbs and leaves, using saplings and vines for balance.

"Can you shake eighty-seven?" yells Nick.

I can't see him in the density of the forest; I can only hear him.

"I don't see it yet!" I yell back.

"Do you see a clearing?"

"Yeah—I can see light on the plants."

"See that palm? To the left of the tree with the orange flowers?"

It takes me a moment.

"Okay—got it."

"Can you get over there?"

Well . . .

The ground is a mix of soil, roots, plants, leaves, and twigs. I've been told the slopes are a 30-degree angle, but as I zigzag about thirty feet across, taking the same high steps you would in deep snow, 45 degrees seems more accurate. I drop to my knees and crawl under a massive, mossy fallen tree, then turn sharply to what I believe is 87.

"I'm not sure I can get there!" I yell. "There's another big downed tree in front of me. Give me a minute."

Mosquitoes whine, competing with my stomach's growl. Somewhere a bird screeches, screeches, screeches—nature's car alarm. I feel as though I'm underwater: the murkiness when the clouds move in, the thick fuzz on trees like barnacles on a ship. A large yet slender black spider crawls up my shirt sleeve. I flick him off and look at the tree I suspect is 87 and—

Ah! I spot a tag. A fallen tree dips as I step on a limb, but it seems like it'll support my weight. I heave myself over the trunk. And then I scoot, twist, turn, stretch, hop, crawl, shuffle, and inch my way to the tree and the tag.

"This is tree eighty-seven!" I holler, triumphant.

"Can you shake it?" Nick yells.

I do my best, then move on to other trees, creeping like an infantryman under branches and vines. Near tree 90 my feet slip and I slam on the mountain, clutching a sapling to stop my slide.

But I become quite adept at maneuvering through the cloud forest obstacle course.

At the end of the afternoon, I climb back to the top, pulling myself up with saplings, vines, and roots: it's like walking up a playground slide. Closer to the trail, Nick extends a hand and yanks me up. I smile and I think—

I'm happy to be here.

It's something I don't do enough, something most of us don't do. Savoring an experience. We usually do the opposite, distancing ourselves from the moment, as though no event can be experienced unless you photograph it or text about it. (A year ago I went with Terry to see Bruce Springsteen in Richmond. During one rowdy song Bruce slid across the stage on his knees. The woman in front of us missed it—never knew it happened—because she was texting, "Guess where I'm at!")

As we begin the long trek back to the lodge, I hope I can step back and occasionally revel in the routine. If I could re-create one moment in my life, it'd be that night, as a boy, when I had greasy fast-food chicken with Dad and Granddaddy. As ordinary as life gets. But I want that same flash-second acknowledgment whenever I experience the special ordinary; when I find joy wriggling through the dirt.

Earlier, when Nick shared his cynicism about governments and mankind and the lack of will to save our troubled planet, he said this doesn't depress him. "I'm happy contributing to something I believe in," he said, "whether it's ultimately futile or not."

I'm back in the cabana when Wayne returns from working with Anita's group.

"It's Scotch o'clock," he says, flinging his backpack on the top bunk.

"That makes me so happy," I say.

Like an old married couple, we talk about our days, using the long shelf under the window as a bar. He pours the Scotch as I pull the foil off the water pitcher.

Wayne has just about recovered from a stomach bug he and Charles picked up in Quito. Their mistake, they believe, was drinking the ice in their happy-hour mojitos. They also ate *balon de verde*, a local delicacy made from green plantains and, as Charles put it, "the bits of pig you might normally throw away."

"I actually brought a stool softener here," says Wayne. "What was I thinking?"

Charles is still having issues. Three days ago he switched from Imodium to Cipro, a prescription antibacterial drug. The pills are working up to a point—he can hike the trails without waddling into the rain forest with cramps—but each morning starts with, well . . . explosions.

"Man," said Wayne one morning, groggy, still in his sleeping bag on the top bunk. "It's like the Fourth of July."

The evening Scotch poured, I sit on my bed, and Wayne shoves aside stuff on his lower bunk and takes a seat. He changes shirts. I ask him about the large tattoo on his back between his shoulder blades, which looks like a Celtic cross. "That was a tough time in my life," he says. "I wanted to make a statement about what I believe in."

I decide not to pump him for info, and he doesn't volunteer it. We chat, and instead of the past, he discusses the future. He and his wife want to have children next year. He wants anywhere from two to four, since he came from a family of four.

"Do you have kids?" he asks.

"No, no . . . ," I say, sparing him the history.

I can see that Wayne will be a great father. He's like Adam and Terry in some ways: fun, positive, a strength that comes from a clear sense of self. Before I left for Ecuador, Terry told me that his son Clarence, now three, was starting preschool. Terry writes a blog, and wrote about the day: "As we walked up the sidewalk toward his preschool, my eyes filled with tears as I thought that he is no longer completely ours—he also belongs to others. It was all worth it four hours later when I picked him up—he saw me come to his class, yelled 'Daddy!' and ran into my arms. I love being a dad."

As I take these voluntourism trips, a lot of people—all of them parents—say they wish it were them. That *they* were traveling to Asia or South America. But they would never trade parenthood to see the world. I would trade these travels in an instant.

"I know this is painful for you," a friend once said. I was surprised to hear the P-word, because I don't think of it that way. *Pain* is such an intense word. Pain is for people with real problems: people with cancer, people in war zones, people who see more flies in an average day than food. Before Dad died, Mom would sometimes ask, "Are you and Julie *ever* going to have a baby?" And Dad would say, "Oh, leave him alone—they know what they're doing." I regret not talking to him about it, even though this isn't like my old superhero action figures; it's not something he could fix. And I know what he would have said, what anyone would have said: Somehow you need to make peace with this. You need to accept it by making it acceptable. You need to give of yourself. He would have said what Zhang Tao, the head of La La Shou, said in China.

There comes a time when you must do more than complain.

Flush with a warm, pleasing, Scotch-induced buzz, I walk with Wayne and Charles from the cabana up the dirt trail to the lodge. After dinner, as everyone chats inside, I drift onto the porch, slip my feet into my hiking boots, and shuffle out to the grass, laces dragging behind me. This is the first night—the only night—that the clouds part to reveal the sky. The volume of stars is almost overwhelming, sparkling in clumps, the purple Milky Way glowing. Back home, even though we're in the burbs instead of the city, streetlights and strip malls dim the night, leaving only the most obvious stars: the dippers, Alpha Centauri.

I go inside and find Nick. He'd told me on clear nights you can see three of Jupiter's moons. He joins me outside, beer in one hand, binoculars in the other. We rear our necks back, mouths open; baby birds fed by the night.

"Look there," he says, peering and pointing. "That's it—right there."

He hands me the binoculars. The three moons shine. Jupiter has four major moons, known as the Galilean satellites: Galileo observed them back in 1610. Dozens of smaller moons also orbit the gaseous planet.

The Inquisition famously accused Galileo of heresy in 1633 for supporting the Copernican notion that Earth was not the center of the universe. If only the Inquisition had known that we are the center of *nothing*. Some astronomers hypothesize that multiple universes exist, that universes may appear and disappear with the regularity of popcorn popping in a bag. Which means our shiny blue planet isn't simply a speck in a colossal, expanding universe. We're a speck of a speck on a speck of a speck, residing inconsequentially on a speck of a speck (that sits, yes, on a speck of a speck of a speck). If the universe is a closet, our world isn't even a stray flake of lint. And if our world is less than lint, what does that make humanity? What does that make you or me? Our puniness in the universe—a puniverse?—can be overwhelming. And yet somehow . . . it's comforting. It makes life more precious. Telescopes have identified more than twelve hundred possible planets in our spiral Milky Way galaxy, but some astronomers believe, based on the number of stars, our galaxy could be home to 100 billion Earthlike planets. For now, however, as far as we know, Earth is a cosmic fluke: the only planet where everything is just right. The perfect distance from the sun. The perfect atmosphere. Water. In that same Bill Bryson book that inspired Ellen to change her life, he talks about the conditions that make our universe possible. If gravity had been wimpier or more robust, if the Big Bang had been longer or shorter—everything might be different.

One night, as we sipped Scotch, Wayne pronounced a skepticism of scientific theories. "All these people talk about evolution and the Big Bang," he said, "but I think those require as much faith as mine." I'll spare you the evidence for the Big Bang—it's solid—but the key thing for us small-brained little humans is this:

You, me, our friends, our family—we've all been given that rarest of opportunities, the chance to experience life. About 650,000 hours of life, as Bryson said, in a universe that's 13.7 billion years old; a universe that appears to have only one place where you'll find humans, pumas, toucans, worms, spider monkeys, tarantulas, eyelash vipers, ferns, aroids—all the mind-boggling species in our shrinking family of life.

Shouldn't we cherish this? Wasn't that one of the lessons of Dad's out-of-nowhere death?

If we've been given two uncommon gifts—our existence and our planet, which we've abused with gusto, as though Earthlike jewels are as common as new cars in a showroom—shouldn't we treasure them? Shouldn't we revel in our time on this minuscule, miraculous world? And if our fellow lucky-to-exist beings are suffering, shouldn't we find this intolerable?

I hand Nick his binoculars back, and I thank him, and we watch the sky in silence.

On our one free day after six days of work, eight of us trek to see (we hope) the rare spectacled bears that feed in the mornings at the mountain's base. Our guide, Ernesto, is missing an arm, his right tan sleeve pinned to the shoulder. A one-armed bear guide leads us to wonder, naturally, if the arm was gnawed off in a bear-related incident. Ernesto seems pleasant enough, though I sense that if a bear snacked on his arm, he in turn inflicted some serious carnage on the bear.

We walk along a flat trail, speaking in hushed Elmer Fudd *be vewwy quiet* tones. Ernesto picks up what looks like a green olive. He squeezes it: there's a seed inside, along with greenish goo. He hands it to me, taps his nose. It smells like avocado. This is what the bears eat.

Just when we think it'll be a no-bear day, Ernesto beckons us, urgently waving his hand. There, high in a nearby tree, sits a black spectacled bear. The body seems lean, but his head is huge, white fur around his mouth; the clawed paws are clearly dangerous weapons. He utters Chewbacca-like growls, and exhales like a steam locomotive—*poosh.*

We admire the bear for a while, and take our time before returning to the lodge, walking along a stream nearby. I was sure the hike to the lodge would be easier this time, since we've been tromping around the mountains for over a week. Better stamina! Stronger lungs! But it actually seems *worse.* My right knee flares, a sharp ache that started the day before. Every time we go up one of the manmade wood steps that appear in spots on the trail, it's serious pain.

Earl and Phillip and I go at a leisurely pace, stopping frequently. Phillip says one of the staffers at the lodge has a reputation for romancing female volunteers. The cloud forest Casanova hasn't seduced anyone in our group—as far as I know—but his success rate is legendary. Maybe it should be Birthwatch instead of Earthwatch.

Later I discover something else about the staff. Sofi, the cheerful, quiet woman who greeted us with lemonade our first day, lives in Nanegal. She hikes this trail twice a day: up in the morning, down in the evening. *Every day.* She must laugh when she sees us wheezing and pouring sweat. *Right wussies*, as Natalie said. What's a challenge for one is routine for another.

The next morning, I'm up at five thirty for my last assignment: a daily bird survey. Charles and a few more ambitious souls got up at four yesterday to see the Andean cock-of-the-rock, which sounds like the stage name for a male stripper but is actually a species of bird. The bright orange, bulbous-headed males perform a loud and elaborate mating dance to attract the less-colorful females, squawking and bebopping, taunting rivals, making a scene.

I tiptoe out of the cabana, my steps muffled by Charles's snores, and turn on my headlamp for the dark trail. Coffee. I need coffee. Guzzling a quick cup at the lodge, I head to the porch to find Gabriel, the resident ornithologist. I noticed Gabriel relaxing yesterday afternoon, sitting on the ground, leaning against a bench, legs out, feet crossed, casually reading a book about . . . birds. Why are there no half-assed birders? You never hear a birder say, "Yeah, I might have a beer, watch the ballgame, do a little birding." One volunteer, a typically hard-core birder from California, carriers a recorder and a large microphone at all times: it looks like a curling iron in a holster. He expressed his delight at seeing the Nariño Tapaculo and the long-tailed antbird. Ecuador is home to approximately 1,600 different types of birds, about twice as many as in North America, Europe, or Australia. Santa Lucía alone counts among its population 394 recorded species of birds, some of which are near extinction.

We look like miners with our headlamps as we leave the lodge. This early, it's chilly. I keep my hands in my pockets. Our group includes Helen and the Ecuadoran students, Jason and Julia. We walk to predetermined points, stand for ten minutes—I mark the precise time on my digital watch—and Gabriel calls out birds he hears or sees with and without binoculars; whether they're perching, feeding, or flying; how far away they are.

"Tri-colored brush finch, flying, five meters."

Helen and I record his observations on clipboards. Gray-breasted wood wren. Toucan barbet. Yellow-throated tanager. She did the bird gig previously, so she understands his accent better than I do: words like *crimson* sound like "creem-sone."

As the sun rises, raindrops fall from the previous night's shower, landing in bloops and splats. Julia picks a green centipede-like bug off the arm of my fleece. "*Gracias*," I say, smiling. She's pretty, hair in a black ponytail, shyer and more serious than Jason.

We leave the woods and walk down a narrow trail through grass that comes to my hip. Dew droplets bead on the blades. This area is being reforested: the trees are about seven years old and stand about twenty to twenty-five feet in height. Gabriel peers through his binoculars and calls out more birds, which sound like the names of superheroes. Flavescent flycatcher. Violet-tailed sylph. Red-faced spinetail.

I start to recognize a few calls: the *Woo! Woo! Woo!* of the plumbeous pigeon. Jason has on earbuds, though he and Julia each spot birds. Helen and I jot down more info on charts. "Time," I say at the end of ten minutes. And we move to the next location.

Later, after breakfast—my grumbling stomach could be mistaken for a toucan barbet—Helen and I sit in the office, entering the data into a laptop. We take turns to reduce the monotony: one of us recites the info—"Booted racket-tail, five meters, flying"—the other enters it. As we work, Jason again attempts to play the guitar. He's still dreadful, though awkwardly strumming each chord is the only way he'll get better. Most of us aren't songbirds, singing beautifully from birth. We slaughter the notes, we blister our fingers. We persevere.

On a downward slope behind the lodge are the "washing machines": two slim basins on each side of a concrete block, like podiums for a quiz show, with a square pool of water below. A few days ago, before breakfast, I washed some clothes, dipping a small bucket in the water and dousing one of my quick-dry shirts. The shirts are breathable, allowing moisture to escape, yet simultaneously trapping odors.

Ellen was doing laundry as well. We hadn't chatted in a while; I was working on other projects and she was still with Anita's team.

"Forgive my shirts," I said. "They have a high school gym class smell."

She scrubbed a pair of pants, her hands covered in suds.

"Don't worry," she said. "I've been wearing these clothes for a month."

I dipped a brush in a bowl of congealed green soap and scrubbed as well. We talked about the trip home. Ellen is terrified of flying, so getting on the plane alone at Heathrow, traveling roughly 5,700 miles to Ecuador—it was daunting.

"About halfway across the Atlantic I started to panic," she said.

"So what'd you do?"

"Wasn't much I *could* do except calm down and deal with it. And I ordered a gin and tonic."

Having survived the flight, she expected to be the slowest member of the team since she was the oldest student, and since Anita was an experienced mountaineer. But as the weeks progressed, her endurance improved. She discovered she was one of the strongest.

We hung our clothes on the line with other dangling shirts and pants and undies and socks. Because of the humidity and the daily damp descent of the clouds, clothes dry slowly.

Leaving her husband behind at the airport was the hardest thing she's ever done, she says. They don't have children. At times the distance weighed on her. She wrote to him each morning in a journal, which he'll read when she gets home.

"But to work in a biodiversity hot spot in such a fantastic habitat . . . it's been fabulous."

Sometimes in the cabana, when I'm alone, I stand and listen: the croaking frogs, the calls of exotic birds, the rain. And then the intrusion of man; distant jets, the *whoosh* lingering, echoing off the mountains.

After dinner one night, Wayne and Charles and I brought beer bottles back to the cabana as makeshift candle holders; Wayne shaved the candles so they'd fit. We placed them on the ledge in front of the window. An evening rain tapped the windows and roof. Wayne played reggae on the iPod.

"This is how it must have been in olden times," said Wayne. "Except for the reggae."

He came here, he says, because he wanted to deepen his awareness of threats to the global environment; to find the truth between the rhetoric of radical conservatives and radical environmentalists. "That was my driving curiosity. It's not because I work at an oil company, and not because I'm trying to boost their public relations."

It's surprising to me, but after eleven days here he's still something of a global warming skeptic. "My passions aren't driven by me thinking the world is warming up and we're all gonna roast if don't do something about it, or that humans are one of the primary causes for global warming, if global warming is actually happening. I've seen both sides of the debate, and frankly I don't think there's enough science one way or the other. To me, it's about stewardship. Personal stewardship. Am I being a good steward with what we've been given on Earth. At the end of my life, is my behavior something I can look back on and be proud of."

What did change, he says, is his understanding of the damage humans can inflict on the environment, particularly deforestation. "Walking through those fields of grass . . . I was astounded that those patches were once rain forest, and who knows when they'd actually come back as primary forest—I mean, years and years and years. And looking across the porch and seeing these clear patches of land. When you hear the cloud forest is rising three feet a year in elevation, and then you hear chain saws off in the distance . . . I didn't really want to have mercy on people, even if they weren't educated in what they were doing. It just kind of made me mad."

This trip has taught him he can live with less, he says. Charles had a similar revelation after his Earthwatch trip in Madagascar: "I realized I can't complain about being happy," he said.

The last night is a fiesta. We meet on the porch for our final happy hour; I share a bottle of red wine with Wayne and Charles. We tink glasses. Wayne has brought his iPod and speakers. The tunes are lost underneath the chatter until—

Simple pulsing piano chords. Three-note bass lines.

"Oh my *God*!" exclaims Jade.

As jarring as it was to hear "Mickey" in a Chinese park, it's even stranger to hear "Don't Stop Believin'" in the isolated Andes; the wind, the birds, the bugs, all drowned out by Journey, by loud gringo voices singing of a lonely world.

Dinner is a final-night treat: what appears to be roast chicken, though it could be any of the cloud forest's delicious feathered creatures. After dessert, Nathaniel passes around a plastic milk jug filled with homemade hooch. *Aguardiente*: fire water. His grin seems to say, *you have NO idea what this is going to do to you.*

"It looks like lighter fluid," I say to Wayne as Nathaniel fills my plastic cup.

"They probably use it to power the generator," he says.

We drink. It's sweet, actually. Apparently it's some kind of fermented sugarcane. Nathaniel and his sons play music: a guitar, something like a pan flute, a bongo-esque drum with a one-two-three beat. They sing, off-key, but enthusiastically. The *aguardiente* helps. Natalie dances with Charles, who wears a striped wool pigtailed hat from Otavalo. He spins her underneath her arm. Helen drags me onto the impromptu dance floor, Jade later does the same. Nick, having seen these celebrations before, slips quietly upstairs.

I'm pleased, the next morning, to learn that the Ecuadoran mystery hooch has not warped my sight or central nervous system. We eat breakfast and pay our beer tabs. As our backpacks are strapped to the mules, we hang on the porch and discuss chiggers: those of us who saw the spectacled bears two days ago split into two groups, and everyone in the other group has bites. Olivia shows a few red bumps on her hip. Edward, the English volunteer who was capturing horseflies in his cabana and returning them to the wild, is unimpressed. With unexpected bravado he slips off his shirt. He's *covered* with red bites—on his shoulders, back, arms, chest. We gasp and laugh and take photos.

"I took my clothes off and lay on the floor and Janet got rid of them using a head torch to see," he says. "It took about an hour."

After one final sweaty hike down the mountain—Anita wanders off to study plants and gets lost—we climb on the bus, drop off Jason and Julia in Nanegal, cross the equator, and return to Quito. The concrete and cars and pedestrians make Quito seem like another planet after Santa Lucía's isolation. I check back in at La Casa Sol, then wander the new town, stocking up on bags of banana chips to take home.

That evening, we reconvene at Mama Clorinda, the traditional Ecuadoran restaurant where I'd met Wayne, Charles, and Earl the Australian the first night. Wayne had noticed guinea pig on the menu, and he's talked about it ever since (though he seems uninterested in the cow's foot soup or the potato soup with sprinklings of blood). In addition to our individual meals, we order two guinea pigs for our long table. The body is cut into parts—head, back legs, front legs (complete with deep-fried paws)—and presented on a yellow platter. The back legs have the most meat.

"Let me guess—tastes like chicken," says Olivia, the fitness fanatic.

"Kind of, but more like the dark meat of chicken—it's juicy," I say, holding the bone and wiping my mouth. The skin looks fantastic, but it's chewy. Really chewy. Like beef jerky coated with peanut butter. The rest of the guinea pig—the squat front legs attached to the rib cage—don't have much meat. It's a lot of nibbling without a lot of payoff. As for the deep-fried head, I believe you're supposed to suck the brain out, but I'm not feeling quite that ambitious.

The evening goes fast. Laughter. Toasts. Empty wine bottles.

I stuff myself, enjoying another *llapingacho* potato patty with my pork. We end with goodbyes, with toasts, with cheer.

Six hundred and fifty thousand hours of life. That's what we get if we're lucky. By my estimates, Dad had roughly 572,280 hours. I've used up about 382,440. The question is how best to use the 267,560 hours I have left.

PART FIVE

Palestine

A Palestinian ponders an Israeli settlement
near Bethlehem.

LATE ONE AFTERNOON IN Ecuador, I was peeling off dirty clothes for a shower when something slammed against the cabana's sloped metal roof. My first worried thought: *the cabana's been hit by a meteor.* I opened the door and rushed onto the wood bridge to the path. There in the dirt, a large white bird, bigger than a football, lay on its back, its claws twitching, its neck twisted.

I hurried back to the room, slipped on my boots, not bothering to tie them, and ran up the path to the lodge. Mika was talking to some folks at the table where I'd spent two days dropping larvae into alcohol.

"Hey," I told him, interrupting his conversation—this was the first time I'd spoken to him, I realized later—"some kind of bird just hit our roof—I think he's hurt."

We ran back down to the cabana, along with Zachary, the machete-wielding Robin to Mika's Batman. Edward, the amateur ornithologist, hurried down as well.

The bird squirmed on its back.

"Looks like a quail dove," said Edward.

Mika got down on one knee, picked up the dove, and nestled it in his red sweatshirt, holding it against his stomach.

"Best thing to do is keep him warm," he said.

He took the dove back to his cabana, cradling it. When I saw

Mika at dinner that night, he said the dove was woozy, though it eventually stood on his finger, and its pupils had stopped dilating. Mika left it outside on a stump. The next morning, he stopped me at breakfast.

"I have news on your dove, mate," he said. "When I checked the stump this morning, there was a bit of poo and a few feathers. So I suspect he took off. Though he might have been someone's dinner—he was right at puma height."

Either way, a happy ending. It all depends on how you define a happy ending.

The hour-long drive from Tel Aviv to Jerusalem reminds me of winter in northern California. The mild December temperatures, the mountain highway, the yellow streetlights as evening turns to night. Until my folks moved back to Virginia, Julie and I would visit them once a year, usually after Christmas, landing in San Francisco and heading to my parents' home near San Jose. Julie loves skiing, so we'd drive to Lake Tahoe, my parents gambling in the casino— Mom addicted to slots, Dad playing video poker—while Julie and I hit the slopes at the nearby Heavenly resort.

The first time I went skiing, back in high school, two friends tried to teach me. We went to Ski Liberty in Pennsylvania, riding to the top of the Dipsy Doodle slope, which is about as menacing as it sounds. I dismounted from the ski lift, slowing my momentum by falling face-first in the snow. My friends swooshed to a people-free area by a clump of white-covered pines, and I followed, wobbling and slipping and tumbling, like a gunshot victim on skis. With a little help from their instructions, I developed the following technique:

Ski three feet.

Fall.

Stand up.

Ski three feet.

Fall.

Start to stand up—fall—stand up—ski—

Fall.

I was so bad that I finally removed the skis and walked back down the hill, which was humiliating, though faster than if I'd "skied" to the bottom. After a lesson I improved quickly. Julie never tires of skiing—she'd love nothing more than a monthlong ski trip—but after a day or two on the slopes I'm done. My main objection is that skiing takes place in the cold. I just can't see going out of my way—packing thick clothes, making airline reservations, taking off work, traveling—all to visit a place that's far colder than the cold at home.

Dad enjoyed living in California, and developed what I consider a fairly sane policy about snow. Basically—

If I want to see snow, I'll drive to the Sierras and look at it, and then I'll drive home.

That was probably his only regret about moving back to Virginia: the cold. In February, four months before he died, he and his golf buddies played eighteen holes in 20-degree weather. When the ball hit the fairway, it was like hitting asphalt, he said; the ball would bounce fifteen feet in the air. For me, the cold feels right only at Thanksgiving and Christmas. Maybe I've been brainwashed by the corporate Christmas mythmakers, but Santa was headquartered in the North Pole (as opposed to, say, Pensacola) and the TV Christmas shows were all set in winter wonderlands. Had I watched *Frosty the Strawman* each year I might feel different.

This is the first time I'll be away from my mom and my sister and Julie over Christmas, a separation the mild weather accentuates. In some ways, it doesn't bother me. Because here's a little if-you-want-children-but-don't-have-children secret: Christmas is the shittiest time of year to not have kids. That's when parents go to Christmas pageants or take the kids to see Santa; when the whole family decorates the tree. (Some parents, I realize, might say this is the shittiest time of year *because* they have kids.) And yet I feel Grinch-like for leaving Julie, because she loves Christmas as much now as she did as a kid. She wraps garland around the railings, hangs up lights, wears Christmas sweaters and socks. We own, I'm convinced, the East Coast's largest collection of Christmas music, from the Chipmunks to the Mormon Tabernacle Choir. And this *is* a time of year when you're supposed to be with loved ones.

So what we have here is a classic contradiction: I'm kind of happy to be gone, except that I'm sad to be gone.

Every human being, whether in Santa's workshop or San Jose, the West Bank or Northern Virginia, is a red-blooded, oxygen-breathing contradiction. I was so concerned about climate change that I flew to South America in a carbon-spewing jetliner. In my attempts to help others I've neglected the people closest to me. While in China, I missed my nephew's college graduation. I missed Mother's Day. As I climbed the Andes in Ecuador, I missed the funeral of Adam's dad. And now I'll experience Christmas in the Holy Land—the most contradictory spot in the world—spending two weeks in the little town of Bethlehem, a town of hope and hopelessness; the birthplace of a pacifist savior whose name has justified centuries of killing; missing not just Christmas, but Julie's birthday.

Julie was a Christmas baby. Born on December 25.

And so I arrive in Israel with a sort of guilty optimism: guilty for what I've left behind, hopeful for what I'll find. I'm here because of Jonathan's still-sturdy Costa Rica philosophy—*you only learn about yourself when you're outside your comfort zone*—but also because . . . if you want to make a difference in the world, you need to see the world differently. You need to move beyond your assumptions and experiences. And if you want to understand suffering, you need to go to Palestine. The Palestinians have no monopoly on suffering; they've both endured suffering and inflicted it. We *all* suffer. Rich, poor, Muslim, Jew. But understanding suffering without visiting

Palestine is like understanding the Bible without reading Genesis. Nowhere else on earth do the elements that so make us human—violence, hope, compassion, pain—seem on such stark and jarring display.

It begins in a back room at Ben Gurion International Airport in Tel Aviv. I'm escorted there, shortly after deplaning, by an airport security agent. As security personnel go, she's pretty: formfitting, no-nonsense pantsuit, brown hair in a ponytail, more like a businesswoman than a cop, or whatever her inspect-the-traveler role may be.

The room is for those who are deemed threats. I suppose I should have expected extra attention given the country's reputation for scrutinizing passengers, and given that I'm traveling to Bethlehem, although everything started normally. I left the gate and marched with the masses to the passport control booths, where a bored twentysomething woman inspected my passport.

"What will you be doing while in Israel," she droned.

"I'll be in Jerusalem for two days and then two weeks in Bethlehem."

"What"—sigh—"will you be *doing*."

"Oh," I said with a nervous laugh. "I'll be sightseeing in Jerusalem and volunteering in Bethlehem."

My volunteer organization, Volunteers for Peace, forwarded a warning before I left, a message from our hosts in Beit Jibrin, the sixty-year-old refugee camp where I'll be staying:

> *Even if the situation is calm now, you should expect that the situation may get tense. It is important to know that as a foreigner you are supposed to have freedom of movement (in comparison with the Palestinians) and security. But because your presence in Palestine is embarrassing to the Israelis who*

are committing crimes against the Palestinians you should be aware that you might not be welcome by them.

Not welcome? *Me?* How could I not be welcome? I've come here with what I believe is a typically American view of the Israeli-Palestinian conflict. Yes, it's ping-pong politics. Back-and-forth violence. Back-and-forth outrage. Endless retaliation and blood. But when I see Israelis on American TV news, I see statesmen in suits. When I see Palestinians, I see hoodlums throwing rocks. Israel is our ally. Harry Truman considered recognition of Israel one of his chief accomplishments. The nation is a world leader in science and technology. Its citizens have persevered, and thrived, in the face of hideous terrorism. And yet . . . (This is the land of *And yet . . .*)

And yet . . . the state of Israel was founded on land where Palestinians had lived for a thousand years. Imagine being forced from your home, the home of your father and grandfather, the home of generations. Imagine a life of marginalization and harassment. Since 1967, Israelis have demolished 24,145 Palestinian homes, according to a truth-in-reporting group called If Americans Knew. The Palestinians are branded as militants, yet from September 29, 2000, through December 2009, a period that included the Second Intifada, the number of Palestinians killed was six times higher than the number of Israelis killed. As I write this, more than seven thousand Palestinians are prisoners in Israeli jails.

Always look at the other side, Dad wrote. *Often you don't fully understand things unless you put yourself in the other person's shoes.*

In 1938, Mahatma Gandhi wrote about the Holocaust, and the "Arab-Jew question."

My sympathies are all with the Jews. I have known them intimately in South Africa. Some of them became lifelong companions. Through these friends I came to learn much of their age-long persecution. They have been the untouchables of Christianity. The parallel between their treatment by Christians and the treatment of untouchables by Hindus is very close. . . . But my sympathy does not blind me to the requirements of justice. The cry for the national home for the Jews does not make much appeal to me. . . . Palestine belongs to the Arabs in the same sense that England belongs to the English or France to the French. It is wrong and inhuman to impose the Jews on the Arabs. What is going on in Palestine today cannot be justified by any moral code of conduct. . . . I am not defending the Arab excesses. I wish they had chosen the way of nonviolence in resisting what they rightly regard as an unacceptable encroachment upon their country.

The more I've learned about the conflict, the more conflicted I've become.

I share none of this with the woman in the passport booth, who doesn't appear curious to learn Gandhi's worldviews, let alone my own. She hands me a slip of paper to give a gate guard, the next round of security bureaucrat waiting ahead.

Secureaucrats, I dub them. This uniformed secureaucrat gives my passport to the pantsuit secureaucrat, who immediately asks questions—

How long will you be here? What will you be doing? Where will you be volunteering?

I don't know where we'll be volunteering. It's a series of projects, rather than working at, say, a school. We'll receive the schedule when we arrive in Bethlehem.

"I know at least one day we'll be at a farm."

"A *farm?*" she says skeptically.

"A farm."

The V-word—"volunteering"—is probably the reason for my special attention, because it means I'll be interacting with locals, though "volunteering," to me, seems like a pretty positive word. I try to imagine what other upbeat words might raise concerns—

I'll be making balloon animals for two weeks in Bethlehem.
Balloon animals?
Balloon animals.
I see no balloons in your bags. . . .

I once read a book about post-9/11 U.S. security efforts, called *Fortress America*, which discusses the Israeli approach to security. One tactic is for screeners to ask constant questions, some of them innocuous, in the hope that you'll eventually screw up. It's like someone throwing a bucket of baseballs: the more balls that come, the less likely you are to catch them. I have nothing to hide—the most dangerous thing in my bag is an electric razor—but I don't want to get stuck here, so I decide to be perky, big-time perky, figuring if I'm cheerful they'll assume I'm a dork as opposed to a terrorist. And so I tell her we'll be working at an olive farm, and I say it in an Up With People *golly-gee-willickers* kind of voice.

Guess what, boy and girls—we're going to an olive farm! Hooray!
"What do you do for a living."
"I'm an editor."
"You're a journalist?"
"I'm an editor."
An editor! Yippee!

She says she needs to scan my luggage. It'll only take a few minutes. I pick up my backpack from the carousel.
"Do you get paid to come here?" she asks as we walk.
"No—I wish."
"Your ticket is paid for?"
"I actually pay to volunteer."
She looks at me funny.
"It's screwy, I know."

This is when I notice we're walking—alone—past dormant carousels in an empty corner of the airport. We stop at a closed door. She slides her ID card through a slot to enter. I smile, wondering if I'm about to be interrogated. Inside, another woman runs my backpack and carry-on bag through a scanner. She walks to a machine and pulls out a long blue plastic spoonlike wand with a square cloth on the end that could easily—or not so easily—be shoved up an orifice. Next she opens my bags, rubbing the insides with the wand, checking, I assume, for explosives, inspecting everything—my sleeping bag, shirts, camera, phone, the backpack itself. The top of my electric razor pops off and whiskers spray on my socks.

"What is this," she asks, holding up a small purple vinyl bag, the top tied in a knot.

"Toiletries. You know—brush, shampoo, toothpaste."

She unties it, empties it in a bin, and takes it to another room.

An irritated middle-aged Brit is undergoing the same procedure. His sunglasses are propped on his head; he looks like a jet-setter not used to being detained. A morose dark-skinned couple—they might be from Mumbai, based on a label on one of their packages—sit in plastic chairs. They look like they've been here for hours.

The guard returns the bin from the room behind us, and tells *me* to go to the room.

"Empty your pockets," she says.

I walk through a metal detector. Three times. Finally the pantsuit secureaucrat hands me my passport and says I can leave. My clothes sit in a mound in my open backpack, and on top are the blue underpants I accidentally received from the hotel laundry in China. That's right, I'm still wearing them. Seeing them makes me smirk, and that smirk bloats into a giggle, which I suppress, because giggling at the end of a security shakedown would surely reignite the process, and explaining mystery Chinese underpants to humorless secureaucrats would be a chore—

I'm sorry—these underpants belong to another man—I didn't steal them, though—is it stealing if you wear another man's underpants without his knowledge? . . .

I mush everything in my bag, not bothering to fold my clothes. The pantsuit guard thanks me. I nod and leave, and the Mumbai couple continue sitting with long faces, having no such trouble suppressing smiles.

I'm staying at the Christ Church Guesthouse in Jerusalem, less than a five-minute walk from Jaffa Gate and the ancient city wall. I collapsed on the bed in my clothes the night before; now I enjoy a guesthouse breakfast of pitas, olives, tomatoes, and cheese, and dedicate myself to the things one must do while in Jerusalem. Before heading to the Western Wall, I dive into the Old City, descending down tunnel-like David Street, a claustrophobic hub of stone steps and tourist-shop stuff, the tin-awning stalls lined with postcards, plates, menorahs; scarves and patterned dresses high on hooks; "Guns N' Moses" and "Super Jew" T-shirts.

I pass the Petra Hostel, where Mark Twain once stayed—it'd be easy to miss, a small red sign above the door, the harsh lighting making it seem more like a subway stop—and then a jewelry store and more stalls and more stuff, stuff, stuff. In one shop a man kneels with a black umbrella, until I realize, no, it's an automatic weapon. I'll pass multiple men with weapons. One of the volunteers I'll meet tomorrow, a woman from Spain, says she told an old man in Jerusalem how startling it was to see so many guns, and his surprised response was:

Really?

A shopkeeper sees me and waves his arms. "I have special deal for you." An African woman, part of a small tourist group, haggles with the shopkeeper next door over luggage.

Sixty!

No more than forty-five!

Fifty!

I wander down side streets, the smells shifting as I walk. Baking bread . . . ammonia . . . something citrus (tangerines?) . . . an unknown spice. Soldiers in green uniforms pass with rifles dangling;

a monk strolls by in a hooded robe. Hasidic Jews walk and chat in their customary black suits, white shirts, and long beards.

When I retrace my steps and return to Jaffa Gate, past fruit stands and high tile street signs in Hebrew and English and Arabic, the street feels spacious, the new city extending beyond the open gate. I walk in the sun along the Old City wall through the Armenian quarter, descending a hill to the Western Wall entrance, the golden Dome of the Rock behind it, passing through a security shack with an X-ray machine and metal detector. A sign reminds visitors that the divine presence is here. The shack leads to a plaza, often described as an open-air synagogue, the wall behind it a backdrop to constant photos. A group of children hold balloons above their heads. About fifteen soldiers, college-age, men and women, pose in rows; the women good-looking, earlobes with pierced pearls, brunette ponytails, sunglasses on the tops of their heads; the men with cropped hair, grinning for the photo.

A fence blocks entry to the wall. You can enter if you wear a yarmulke, but I stay back, preferring not to gawk as people pray. So I gawk instead from a distance, admiring the Hasidic Jews as they rock, the cracks of the wall filled with prayer notes. Two boys throw rolled-up balls of paper at each other; kids will be kids, even at one of the world's holiest sites. Near the fence young men in white shirts and white yarmulkes dance in a circle around a table covered by a wine-colored cloth, the table loaded with books and scrolls. It's joyous to watch. Even here in the plaza, away from the wall, people pray.

Through an enclosed ramp near the women's side of the wall I reach the Temple Mount—Muslims call it Haram al-Sharif—again going through security. This is the entrance for non-Muslims. The Temple Mount is quiet, like a park, open and green after the claustrophobia of the Old City's streets. Boys play soccer on the grass near the back. I wander, then reenter the Old City maze, strolling in shadows past merchants and men smoking a hookah pipe. Feeling lost, I go back the way I came, but a cop with a rifle stops me: this is a Muslim entrance. And so I roam, holding my open map like an idiot tourist, before discreetly latching on to an Asian group that asks shopkeepers for directions. When I make it back to the shops of David Street, the sunglasses racks and T-shirts feel like home.

And then comes an *oh shit* moment.

Late in the afternoon, I pay sixteen shekels and embark on the Ramparts Walk: a walk along the top of the ancient city wall. Starting from Jaffa Gate, I stroll for about twenty-five minutes, admiring the views of the Dome and the Old City, the water tanks and satellite dishes on clustered roofs. With the sun setting I turn around, eventually exiting through a tall black turnstile at Damascus Gate. I walk down stone steps, push the gate—

And it doesn't move.

I shake the gate—*clang clang clang clang.*

Nothing. A small silver, U-shaped bike lock is on the handle. I march back up the steps to the turnstile. The bars turn an inch or two, then lock.

As darkness descends on Jerusalem, I am trapped in a prison of seven steps.

I could be caged here the entire night. That's my first thought. And it's already getting cold. My hands are in my pockets; the chill creeps through my sweater. But someone will pass, right? I'm close to Damascus Gate, which is heavily traveled, although as I look through the bars of my unexpected prison, rock-and-cement walls at my sides, all I see is a rising, curving stone street that's rapidly becoming dark.

In front of me is a two-story apartment building. A small girl walks onto the balcony above to collect flapping laundry. I shout up to her—

"Hey—excuse me—do you know anything about this lock? Is a policeman nearby?"

She rushes back inside with a pile of sheets.

I'll wait five minutes or so, I decide. See if a cop or soldier walks by, then attempt to climb out. I could use the gate latch as a step—maybe—lift myself up, put my other foot on top of the gate, and climb over. *Maybe.* The other option is to walk back up the steps and shimmy across the ledge to the gate, though there's precious little room for shimmying. And even if I could stand on the top of the gate without falling, I'd need to leap ten to fifteen feet to the stone steps below, which seems like the ideal strategy for breaking an ankle. I'm about to attempt it, despite the foolishness of it, when a young black-haired boy, maybe eight years old, runs up to the gate.

"Hey!" he says.

He slips his skinny body through the gate bars, first his head, then his chest, green sweater and black jeans, then his white sneakers. It's the kind of thing you can do when you're eight.

His head is about as high as my hip.

"Come," he says.

He runs up the steps.

"Come."

The tall turnstile is a like a revolving door, only instead of glass its four sides are black horizontal bars. He twists it to the right, just enough to slip around the bars before they lock, then pushes it to the left, slipping by the next set.

Why didn't I think of that?

I do the same. It's not as easy for me, obviously, but I manage to squeeze by. He waves. He wants me to follow him on the wall.

"Come."

He walks, I follow. The Muslim call to prayer sings from loudspeakers. He stops, points at the view of rooftops and says something in Arabic; what I imagine is a tour guide spiel. We pass a school below. On an asphalt basketball court kids in gym clothes dribble from one baseline to the other. Two coaches seem to be critiquing their dribbling.

"Basketball," says my eight-year-old rescuer.

"Yes—basketball," I say.

He waves playfully to the people below, and despite the energetic bounce to his tyke-sized steps, the more we walk along the wall, and the darker it gets, the more I wonder if he's leading me to a surprise meeting with his five or six much bigger brothers for a game of separate-the-American-from-his-shekels.

"Here," he says.

I'm guessing we're at Herod's Gate. We descend the steps to market stalls selling fruits and breads under fluorescent lights, the women wearing head scarves, carrying plastic bags.

"Money," he says.

Okay, I'd figured I'd give him something before he even asked, and I'm happy to be free without getting robbed or breaking my tarsal bones. I hand him a few shekels, pat him on the back, say thanks. He scurries off. I walk to a street outside the wall and head back toward Jaffa Gate, following a singing, torch-carrying Hanukkah throng to the Tower of David, directly across from my hotel. As I walk, it occurs to me—

I wonder if the kid is the one who locked the gate.

When Julie decorates our home for Christmas she places a red wooden toy soldier on the narrow mantle above the fireplace. The soldier has a happy Playskool expression, black grenadier hat, swinging arms. Dad brought it home from Denmark. He worked there for a few weeks after I was born, sent by his employer to repair check-processing machinery for banks. I'm embarrassed to say we never discussed what he did there, or what he experienced. Sometimes I wonder: *why didn't we talk about this?* You think you know the people you love until they're gone, and then you realize the questions you never asked, the questions that seem less important when they're here.

I was six months old when Dad went to Denmark. He returned to find me even fatter than when he left. I was so wide when I was born, and so long, that I ruined my mother's insides for future siblings. While Dad was gone, Mom took me to Sears for a baby picture. I wore a little red-jacket suit, but the bow tie wouldn't fit around my too-fat neck.

Denmark was Dad's only trip to Europe. He never lamented this. I think he was grateful, even a little amazed, that he made it to Europe at all; amazed that a poor farm kid could travel to China, to journey so often to Japan. I've had more advantages in life, but I feel grateful as well when I travel. I feel grateful my last morning in Jerusalem as I walk the Via Dolorosa, the route Jesus supposedly followed while carrying the cross; as I enter the dark, loud Church of the Holy Sepulchre, which Christians believe holds Jesus's tomb; as I continue to misplace myself in the Old City's cramped, confounding streets. It's humbling to wander these tight ancient alleys, to know this is the center of faith for so many people, a center of human history.

I eat a simple tomato soup lunch back at the guesthouse, pay my bill, heave my backpack over my shoulders, then head out past tourists, locals, soldiers, and scooters, exiting through Jaffa Gate. The meeting point for volunteers is the Faisal Hostel, just outside the Old City wall, about a twenty-minute walk. When I arrive I'm sent upstairs to a narrow lounge, one wall lined by an orange couch. People mill about, chatting. It's like a UN summit. I hear conversations in French and Italian, the accents of Irish and Brits and Scots. I talk with a Croatian woman and a woman from Spain. A Finnish girl looks like Dora the Explorer. It's a mix of ages—an Italian couple appears to be in their sixties—though more weighted toward the college crowd. The common denominator is that all of the Europeans seem to smoke: the room is foggy, like the Ecuadoran cloud forest on late afternoons.

We board buses crowded with late-afternoon commuters, led by

Perrine, a lovely Frenchwoman who lives in the West Bank. She's here because our Palestinian hosts, given that they're Palestinian, can't enter Jerusalem. Palestinians can only enter if they have permits, like the Palestinian laborers, almost entirely men, who pack the bus.

We arrive at the Gilo checkpoint to enter Bethlehem. The men scramble from the bus: they must pass through the checkpoint—they must be out of Israel—by a certain time or they lose their permits.

The checkpoint is like a prison. We head through a penned passageway, pass through turnstiles, then walk to booths. A soldier with a machine gun waves me forward. I show him my passport, then walk through an outdoor area to another turnstile. Palestinian laborers pass through here twice a day, every day; through this cold, colorless chamber of echoes and insinuations, of metal bars and black weapons, of stern and staid expressions.

As we exit, we see the separation wall. It's overwhelming: twenty-five feet high—roughly twice the height of the Berlin Wall—topped here by metal posts and a chain-link fence, built in vertical planks, one next to the other, concrete and gray.

The Israelis call it a security barrier. And from the Israeli perspective, the $2 billion wall is a success, reducing the influx of suicide bombers and protecting settlements. Another unofficial benefit: although the government states on its official security fence website that the wall "does not annex any lands to Israel," other organizations say the barrier has claimed roughly 9 percent of the West Bank's land—in addition to land already snagged for settlements. For Palestinians, the "Apartheid Wall" has led to the loss of farmland, divided families and towns, made it difficult to reach jobs, doctors, schools—to do the simplest of activities. The wall may make sense militarily for the Israelis, but there's an unhealthy paradox here, like a cigarette that both treats and causes cancer. The short-term cure inflicts a long-term curse.

We walk down an empty street, led by a few locals here to greet us, the wall looming to our right, splattered with graffiti, a mix of slogans ("Build bridges, not walls"), occasional humor ("Can I have my ball back?"), and elaborate paintings. One looks like an acid trip—a scene from *Yellow Submarine:* splashy colors, a wavy rainbow, a giant smiling ladybug and butterfly.

In a red heart with white lettering someone has written, "This wall is a big bullshit."

The slogans continue:

Palestina Libre
Only Love Will End War
Tear Down This Wall

And then a peace sign of black, green, and red—colors from the Palestinian flag; a charging rhino that seemingly crashes through the wall; a silhouetted man and woman, holding hands, a fighter jet descending upon them.

I can never decide if the paintings beautify the wall or stain it. It doesn't really matter, because the gray still dominates, a concrete plague along the land.

I stroll with Aarif, an independent photographer who's carrying a shoulder bag and a camera with a massive lens. He's young— twenty-six—though I would have sworn he's my age. He's one of our escorts, a freelancer who works for a news agency.

"I notice almost all the graffiti on the wall is in English," I say.

"It's mostly done by internationals."

Aarif gives a brief anti-wall summary, which I will hear frequently: five years ago, the International Court of Justice issued an opinion stating that the wall is illegal. The wall has been denounced by organizations ranging from Human Rights Watch to the Red Cross.

"You American?" he asks.

"Yeah—what gave it away?"

"I can tell by the accent."

"That's probably not good . . ."

"No—that's good."

"I just mean an American accent isn't as nice as a British accent."

"No, really—you sound Hollywood. Like Rambo."

"You're not the first person to tell me that."

We talk about the conflict as we walk down stark streets. Like a lot of young Palestinians, he speaks excellent English.

"The problem is you have extremists on both sides, so there's always a cycle of retaliation. People grow up in an environment where family members die."

I stare at the wall. It's grotesque. One of the most grotesque things I've ever seen. "We need a thirty-year truce," says Aarif, "just to clear people's minds."

We reach the refugee camp, dropping our bags inside the Beit Jibrin Cultural Center, our base of operations for the next two weeks. The center is a colorful anomaly on a trash-strewn street—more like an alley, really—the doors a welcoming blue. A mural extends across the building at street level: a man and woman holding hands, children at their sides; the neutral expressions of mannequins modeling clothes. The children wear T-shirts with an image of Handala, a popular comic character. He's a youth drawn in outline form, seen from behind, hands at his back, his round head with nine protruding rays of hair, like a refugee Charlie Brown. "He is a 10-year-old boy who lives in a refugee camp and observes the injustice of the world around him," I read in the cultural center, better known as the Handala Center. "He acts as a symbol of the refugee cause and is a testament to its creativity, steadfastness and resilience." Handala's creator, Palestinian cartoonist Naji al-Ali, was assassinated by unknown assailants in London in 1987.

Black graffiti runs across the mural; black power lines crisscross the narrow street. Everything is hard here. Asphalt and concrete and iron. No grass. No playgrounds. The few trees are almost invisible, consumed by squat structures. The most prominent tree isn't even real; it's painted on the side of a tiny market near the Handala Center, the tree's trunk and bare branches a pencil-lead gray, wrapped in barbed wire, a ringed sun like a dim dartboard behind it.

Of the fifty-nine Palestinian refugee camps in the Middle East, Beit Jibrin is the smallest: roughly two thousand people in a 0.02-square-kilometer neighborhood of three- and four-story apartment buildings, the windows covered by bars. Most families fled here from the Beit Jibrin village about thirteen miles northwest of Hebron, and more than half are descendants of the Azzeh family (which is why the camp is frequently called al-Azzeh). The village was included as part of an Arab state in the UN's 1947 Partition Plan, but was captured by Israeli forces in the 1948 war. Forced from their homes, the refugees and their children, and their children's children, have lived here ever since, along with refugees from the 1967 war.

"These camps have been here for sixty years," says Mahad, one of our hosts, his accent thick as the black beard stubble on his long thin face. "We are guests, but we will return to our villages. It may be sixty more years, it may be one hundred years, but someday we will return."

Mahad works at the Handala Center. Among his jobs: he records the oral history of first-generation refugees, with second and third generations conducting the interviews. He sits with us on plastic chairs in a harshly lit third-floor room, the walls void of posters or pictures, as we eat soft pitas filled with hummus and falafel. Later we each pay a two-hundred-dollar fee to the International Palestinian Youth League, which is running the volunteer program, then shuffle up echoing stairs to the large fourth-floor room where we'll soon have nightly meetings. We sit in classroom-style chair-desks as Adli Daana, IPYL's charismatic secretary general, gives a welcome speech. A handsome man, probably in his late forties, he exudes a politician's aura, the ability to work a room, striding with an actor's self-assurance in a leather coat that looks like a racing jacket, a red stripe with white border across the arms and chest.

Daana accuses the Israeli government of apartheid. "We want volunteers to see this, to see the difficult situations that Palestinians face every day. But we also want you to see the real Palestinian people. We love life," he declares. "We love it."

IPYL was founded, he says, to combat hopelessness, the lack of direction in the lives of Palestinian youth. Eighty percent of young Palestinians are depressed, according to a United Nations Development Program survey. The numbers are worse in Gaza, where 55 percent of youths described themselves as "extremely depressed."

"Jesus Christ was a Palestinian," Daana tells us, this being Christmas. "He was born here, he lived here, he was raised here." Jesus was also a Jew living in what was then known as Judea, lest we forget. Bethlehem still has a large Christian community—by law the mayor must be Christian—though their numbers have fallen from 92 percent of the population in 1948 to under 50 percent of the town's 27,000 inhabitants today.

Once Daana is done, Fateen, who's running our two-week program, passes out a schedule and discusses our work—from building rock walls to cleaning streets—and social activities. He'll try to get tickets for the Christmas Eve service at the Church of the Nativity, but given the region's relative calm, various dignitaries and politicians will be attending, so tickets are scarce. We will, however, decorate a Christmas tree, though instead of traditional ornaments we'll use bomb casings and tear gas canisters and other leftovers from Israeli attacks.

Perhaps alarmed at how Westerners accustomed to boughs of holly might respond to barbed-wire tinsel, Daana rises from his seat and raises his hands in not-to-worry, damage-control reassurance. "It's symbolic," he says, chuckling. "Don't worry. It's symbolic."

In another symbolic gesture, we male volunteers will be not be sleeping in the same building as the female volunteers, unmarried slumber being a no-no in a Muslim community. The women will sleep here in the center, packed together in a ground-floor room, while we men will stay in a second-floor flat across the street. We gather our things and trudge in a masculine pack down a narrow alleyway in the dark carrying backpacks and blankets. The blankets are padding for the floor, which is where we'll sleep. It's a two-room unfurnished apartment with all the charm of the checkpoint: peeling white paint, the floor a spackled linoleum gray. Outside it's cold, probably in the low 40s, though it feels colder in the apartment. As far as I can tell, no building in Beit Jibrin has central heating. Our chilly flat has a sole electric space heater, which sits near the bathroom door.

The bathroom has a toilet and a sink. That means we have roughly twenty men and one toilet. Oh—and no shower, though there's one in the unit next door, which is where Fateen and a few volunteers will sleep, since the flat has quickly filled with bodies and packs. A path extends between sleeping bags to the toilet and a smaller back room, where seven of us will sleep. It's like a room for interrogations: a single harsh lightbulb dangles on a wire from the ceiling. I snag two of the blankets, spreading them under my sleeping bag. There's no carpet, so the floor is hard and cold. I crawl into my sleeping bag and zip the bag up around my head so only my face is exposed. The eye mask I brought to block sunlight warms my nose.

I'm sandwiched between Burt, a boomer-age bearded Belgian,

and Mike, a college-age Brit. Two Italian men snore. Doug, a terrifically nice guy from Philly who's here with his wife, is stuck between
the stereo snoring. "It was like sleeping on an airport runway," he
says the next morning.

I wake up several times during the night, stiff from the linoleum. I dream about Adam and his son Erik: they wear football jer-
seys that stretch to their feet, like nightgowns, and they can't stop
laughing. I wake up after that, and the whole idea of being home,
and being comfortable, already seems strange.

Visitors to Jerusalem are sometimes inflicted with a condition
known as Jerusalem syndrome. Basically, they're so overwhelmed
by the city they believe they're prophets—like visiting Disney
World and convincing yourself you're Snow White.

I felt the opposite. I felt small in Jerusalem. I've felt small on
this entire journey. Small compared to the Andes Mountains and
China's masses; small in my skill level and contributions. I feel even
smaller in Beit Jibrin.

A friend of mine at work sometimes wanders into my office on
Monday mornings, and if it's too early, and we're too out of it, we'll
chat for a moment in a bleary, not-caffeinated-enough way, until
she'll finally say, "I have no personality" and wander back to her office. That's how I feel here. Void of personality. Like my humanity
was quashed the moment I walked through the checkpoint, which
I'm sure is the intent. Less of a man coming out than going in.
Sausage grinder to the soul. And the wall. The life-sucking wall.
How do people face this planked, cold, concrete snake every god-
damn day?

And yet, I'm sure I'd feel different if I were Israeli.

Always look at the other side, Dad had written.

Of course, it's hard to see the other side when there's a twenty-
five-foot concrete wall in the way.

After breakfast we walk en masse to Bethlehem. Tomorrow we'll start our work; today is explore-the-city day. We take a side road past a mosque and an auto repair shop to reach Manger Street, about a twenty-minute walk to Manger Square, passing mom-and-pop restaurants, convenience stores, tourist shops selling olive wood carvings of the manger scene. Mountains rise in the distance, though more prominent are the settlements on a nearby hill, surrounded by security walls, backed by a construction crane. Mahad watches as bulldozers rumble up a twisting dirt road. His eyes are narrow beneath a black stocking cap, a black-and-white Yasser Arafat–style scarf—a keffiyeh—around his neck. He tells us the settlements are like military bases: the Israeli military used them to launch attacks during the Second Intifada.

At Manger Square, next to the Church of the Nativity, a massive Christmas tree stands nearly three stories high, decorated with red bells and clumps of gold grapes and red-and-gold balls. The church resembles an old stone fortress, with thin windows for firing arrows. We crouch through the Door of Humility, a short door designed to keep soldiers from charging into the church on horseback. Inside, the church is sparse but broad, the smell of incense hovering. Light from a high window streams between stone columns. Gold lamps hang from the ceiling, their shiny red tops like a police car's siren.

Beneath the church is a crypt: here, the faithful believe, is where Jesus was born. Portions of the church date back to the fourth century. It has survived threats from the Crusades to the Second Intifada, when, in 2002, Palestinian resistors, some armed, barricaded themselves inside for thirty-nine days.

The Second Intifada devastated the local economy. With political instability came severe restrictions on travel and trade. West Bank camp residents depend on work in Israel—most of the camp's residents worked as day laborers before the Intifada, says Mahad—but now they're severely hampered by checkpoints and the wall. The youth unemployment rate is around 30 to 35 percent, though people here think that figure is low. In Gaza it hovers around 50 percent.

We leave the church through Manger Square and head into an old-town section, ascending tight pedestrian walkways, past jewelry stores and tourist shops and food stands. When we reach the Aida Refugee Camp, Mahad gives a ten-word history of how the refugees lost their homes.

"The soldiers, they come, they say, 'Get the hell out.'"

Established in 1950, the camp is more than twice the size of Beit Jibrin. Aida's original residents came from seventeen different villages, and the camp is struggling even more than Beit Jibrin with overcrowding, with 43 percent unemployment, with poor water and sewage networks. During the Second Intifada, twenty-nine housing units were destroyed and a school suffered severe damage from an Israeli military operation.

The separation wall looms over a graveyard just beyond the camp. Everywhere, the wall is tattooed with images. A single eyeball sheds a tear. Multiple black Handalas stand with their hands clasped behind their backs. *Why?* someone has spray-painted in black.

When the oppressed becomes the oppressor, reads another tag.

More elaborate is a yellow tractor smashing a human heart with a wrecking ball. Nearby is a quote from Gandhi—

VICTORY ATTAINED BY VIOLENCE IS TANTAMOUNT TO A DEFEAT, FOR IT IS MOMENTARY.

We leave the road and scale a hill made of crumbled cinder blocks and occasional chunks of asphalt. The wind flaps a blue plastic tarp, half buried by rocks. Twisted cables shoot up from the debris; a rotting mattress rises from the rubble like a crooked tombstone, its mesh cover ripped. Doug finds a little girl's white shoe. Above the toe are Valentine-style hearts.

"Were these buildings?" I ask Fateen.

"These were Palestinian houses," he says. "They were destroyed for the wall."

Fateen points at the wall. Towns and villages were cut in half, he says.

"There's a couple near here—they were supposed to be married. After the wall was built, they can't see each other because they live on different sides. They go up on top of their buildings and signal each other with hand gestures."

We walk down a side street. The call to prayer blares above; a boy rides by on his bike and yells "Beep!" Children kick a soccer ball. A plastic grocery bag floats over the wall.

Afternoon traffic picks up as we head back toward Beit Jibrin. We take a different route, approaching the back side of the neighborhood's gray buildings, walking past a small one-story house. A dog stands on the flat roof of the carport. How he got there isn't clear; a rickety ladder is the only way up. Two boys and their father pull a chain around his neck, trying to get him down, but the dog is scared; yelping, crying, barking, growling; refusing to move. The father says something in Arabic, and the boys climb down and retrieve a red plaid bag, about the size of Santa's sack. They struggle to put the dog in the bag. The dog's howl is piercing, shrill. Eventually, after some fumbling, they succeed, lugging the pooch down as he flails in the bag. When they release him and attach his chain to a pole, the dog is still crying. The father laughs.

As we walk down the alleyway, past bullet marks on the walls, I can still hear the dog's shrieking, horrible howl.

That evening, we see photos of suffering Palestinians: the widows, the homeless, the poor. The photos are on poster boards, set on chairs in the pale third-floor room of the center where we eat our meals. I look at the photos, then go outside, standing in the cold, in the night, leaning against a graffiti-scrawled alley wall.

I miss Julie. I feel like . . . I've never missed her as much as I miss her tonight. It's Christmastime, her birthday is coming up—

What the hell was I thinking?

My last evening in Jerusalem, before going to bed, I sat at the desk in my humble room and wrote a note in her birthday card. I sealed the envelope, walked to the bathroom, squirted toothpaste on my toothbrush, and started brushing. And then—why *then*, in a bathroom, as opposed to any of the holy sites I'd visited during the day—it hit me.

I don't want to do this anymore. I don't want to be apart from her. Everywhere I've gone—Xi'an, Quito, Jerusalem—I've thought . . . "I'll have to come back here with Julie." Like I haven't really been there if she's not with me.

I feel alone, sitting on the steps, depressed by the wall and the rubble and Aida and Beit Jibrin, still hearing the terrified snivels of the roof-bound dog, feeling my blank personality like a weight behind my eyes. I send her an e-mail on my phone, any qualms about contacting home left behind in Ecuador.

> *I'm sorry for not being there. When Dad died, one of the big things I wondered was how we're meant to spend our limited time. I want that limited time to be spent with you.*

I have an opportunity to do things in life that others can't. I should be satisfied with that. I *am* satisfied with that. Funny, though, how life works. Once you've figured everything out, you're tested.

I noticed Monique the first night. She's French, wavy black hair. I watched her smoke a cigarette with an amused smile as Marcen, a friend she traveled here with, performed a semi-mime routine, waving his arms and grinning like a clown.

I was surprised to hear the French accent one evening after a meeting as I wrote in the notepad that doubles as my journal.

"I want to know what you are writing," she said.

I looked up from my scribbles.

"Me? Oh. You know—just taking notes."

"But why in this horrible meeting."

We'd met to discuss a possible Christmas party, the kind of meeting that makes you want to cancel Christmas forever.

"It was so horrible that in some ways it was funny," I tell her.

"I don't see anything funny. Just horrible."

She's right. It was horrible. Instead of just telling us, "You have three Christmas party options—here they are," Fateen asked for ideas. Given that we have forty volunteers of varying ages and nine different nationalities, that question invited a range of competing ideas and even some anger. A volunteer named Paul, who looks like an English Ted Kaczynski and just arrived at the camp, said that instead of a party we should distribute food and soup to the homeless.

"It's hypocritical to go the Church of the Nativity and not serve others. It's bullshit!" he yelled. "It's crap!"

Everyone, regardless of nationality, wore the same puzzled look that said—

Who is THIS asshole?

"Our presence here is statement enough," said Mary, an annoyed young Irishwoman.

Paul then evoked Jesus, as well as Muhammad, in a speech that, I confess, I found incomprehensible because of his accent, though he infuriated the Irish girl even more.

"Why are you dragging religion into this? I'm not here to be religious—I'm here to be a good person!"

Fateen settled folks down: "Guys, guys . . ."

More Christmas suggestions spewed forth.

We should pass out candy or chocolate.

No, no—tools. That'll make a bigger difference in the future.
The center is hosting us; we should buy something for the center.
"Speak slow," said one of the Italians.
We should work for the elderly.
This is about building relationships—maybe we should play soccer.
We should clean houses or repair them.
"Speak slow," said one of the French.
We should have a party for the children.
It's a refugee camp—you can't have a party for the children.
Why can't we have a party for the children?
Because it's a refugee camp.

A middle-aged Scottish woman and a bossy middle-aged New York woman, who clearly don't like one another, began to argue. Nothing got resolved.

"Horrible," says Monique again.

"Okay, horrible."

"So you will show me what you write?"

"Nah—it's not that interesting."

She smiles, a smile that seems to say *there's more to you than you're letting on*, and heads down the steps with some of the French contingency for an outside smoke.

I stay in the room and talk with Doug and his wife, Kayla, the couple from Philly. They're in their late twenties, and traveled to Paris, and then Jordan, before arriving here. Doug broke a bone in his lower right leg playing Ultimate Frisbee days before they left home; he's wearing a black medical boot. Kayla plays as well. They're fit, and thin, so I was surprised to learn that Doug played the tuba in the Drexel University pep band. He doesn't fit the tuba stereotype.

"You should have brought your tuba here," I say. "Some gentle tuba music might have helped soothe the anger in that meeting."

Kayla decides I'm an undercover CIA agent, since I'm here alone and frequently writing in my pad.

"I bet you're taking notes on all of us," she says.

"It's true—you should see some of the shit I've been writing about you."

"I knew it! You were airdropped into the country."

"Yes—*totally* top secret. To avoid detection I didn't use a parachute."

"And your bag is packed with weapons."

I show her my hands. "These are the only weapons I need."

"You're a dangerous man, *Kenny*."

We had discussed bowling one night—for the life of me I don't know why, other than there's not a lot to do in a Palestinian refugee camp—and I had made the mistake of saying I was in a bowling league as a kid, and had my own monogrammed blue ball that said "Kenny" in script.

Kayla finds this *very* amusing.

There's one other American I chat with from time to time during my two weeks. Benjamin is twenty-eight, looks younger (though acts older), of Mexican descent, now living in New York and going to art school while working at Starbucks. He seems shy, but he's simply soft-spoken, thoughtful. The night I e-mailed Julie, when I was in such a deep funk, I went outside, down to the dark street, hoping the chill would clear my head, waiting for dinner: there was a gas leak, so dinner was cooked on Coleman-style stoves. The Italians made pasta. We didn't eat until after 10 p.m. Benjamin stood near the door, mainly to escape the cigarette smoke. We talked about our time here so far. We were both shocked by the size of the wall, both aware that we're hearing one side of the story. I ask him what he thought of the Church of the Nativity.

"I don't like to take pictures in places like the church," he says. "Too often people miss why they're there. I've seen people at art museums take pictures of paintings without actually looking at them."

"Are you a churchgoing guy?"

"Well, I believe in God, but I don't go to church every Sunday."

"I guess I believe in God. I mean, I could see that God or something so unfathomable that we think it's God created the universe or the Big Bang. But I don't believe in a God who knows whether I brushed my teeth at night. And I have a problem with biblical literalism. You know—insisting that the world was created in seven days."

"You ever read Kierkegaard?"

"No," I say, admitting my ignorance of the father of existentialism.

"Kierkegaard says absurdity is essential for religion because to have faith you need to suspend reason."

"I'm interested in philosophy," I say, "I'm just never sure where to start."

"It all starts with Plato," says Benjamin. "Everything since is just an argument with Plato or just restating what Plato said. The issues never change. Modern times, same issues."

On our first day of work I wake up early and head to the Handala Center for breakfast. As I leave the flat, I carefully open the door, making sure I don't whack an Italian guy's face as he sleeps on the floor. Others rise from sleeping bags, stretching, scratching, putting on clothes.

I walk down the split-level steps past graffiti-sprayed walls. Up high is a black-and-white painting of a bearded martyr, a keffiyeh around his neck; a snarling, sharp-fanged lion behind him. Painted below are two Palestinian flags, rows of barbed wire on each side. Four camp residents were killed during the Second Intifada, says Mahad. Many more were injured and arrested. Fateen says every family has a father or son who's been shot, arrested, or martyred. People here seem resigned to it.

After eating what will be our standard morning chow—pitas, jam, tomatoes, cheese, bologna, tea—we ride in buses to nearby

Nahalin to build rock walls at a mountain olive farm. Nahalin is not only separated from Bethlehem by a barrier, but it's also surrounded by four Israeli settlements, making access difficult. The settlements have pushed the villagers from their farmland, a common practice, we're told. An estimated 90 percent of men age eighteen to thirty-five in Nahalin are unemployed.

The bus chugs to a stop. We exit and walk up a long, steep road of dirt and red rocks, past olive trees and occasional piles of goat dung, the sky a bright blue, the clouds in compact puffs like tanks. The landscape is scrubby and brittle. Two yellow flowers poke from a wall, their stems twisted. On a hill to our left sits a red-roof, white-walled settlement. The settlements are expanding: the clangs of construction crews echo across the valley. In Nahalin, and throughout the West Bank, boxed-in Palestinians expand by building up, since there's no room to build out. Son gets married? Build a second floor. Another son gets hitched? Build a third floor.

The wind blows as we climb, tossing everyone's hair. The stone walls are for the olive trees, to help control spring rains and erosion, though given the stark rocky landscape, I'm amazed that it ever rains, or that anything can grow.

Using nearby walls as a model—they stand anywhere from knee to waist high—we stack rocks, making sure one level is solid before stacking on more. Most of the rocks are the size of bowling balls, some smaller, some larger, some flatter; others are boulders that require five of us to move: we strain to flip them from one side to another. A farmer in a New York Yankees stocking cap gives a thumbs-up when we're done.

An eighty-two-year-old man, skinny but strong, swings a sledgehammer with precision authority, slowly cracking one of the boulders into slabs. Everything about him is wiry and taut: his sledgehammer-like frame; the long, stringy white beard; his ears poking out from a white headdress, which drapes over his shoulder to his orange wool sweater. He is not so much old as ancient; his skin as weathered and parched as the landscape. A fierceness burns in his eyes. He could kick my ass. Without question.

The old man argues with a pudgy Palestinian farmer. They shout over each other in Arabic, pointing, gesticulating.

"The old man thinks the road is too narrow now for cars," says Habib, part of the Handala team. The argument continues as I sit with Habib on one of the newly completed walls. We eat lunch: pitas filled with bologna and pickles. He's nice kid, eighteen, upbeat, smart; disheveled hair and glasses on a Ringo Starr nose. A big reader. He taught himself Russian—he visited a friend there—and also speaks English, Arabic, and a little French.

"So I've been wondering if most Palestinians dislike Americans," I say to him. "Well, not so much wondering. I assume you don't like Americans. It's more like, how bad is it."

Since World War II, no country has received more U.S. aid than Israel. In 2009, the United States gave Israel an estimated $7 million a day. We help bankroll everything from the military that harasses Palestinians to the separation wall that screws up their lives. So I'm not expecting him to sing "God Bless America" or the Mickey Mouse Club theme.

Habib chews his bologna sandwich. "It's not dislike," he says. "Most people distinguish between the American people and American policy—the American government."

I ask him where he lives. Hebron, he says.

"Do you go through a checkpoint to get to Bethlehem?"

"Yes, but I don't always have to stop."

"What about Jerusalem?"

"I can't go there."

"Why—because you need to fill out certain paperwork?"

"Because I'm Palestinian."

"So you can't go at all?"

"I can only go if there's a reason—like family or a job. Sometimes if it's a religious holiday."

We finish our lunches, looking out over the brush and the craggy land. Two months from now, on February 25, Habib will be blasted with tear gas. In Hebron and throughout the West Bank, that date is known as Open Shuhada Street Day. The street was closed by the Israelis in 1994 to protect settlers in the city. The closure wounded the local economy; Palestinians struggle to navigate the city. For some a ten-minute walk is now an hour-long commute.

As Palestinians protest in Hebron on February 25—along with some Israelis and international activists—soldiers will fling tear gas canisters into the crowd. Habib will later write to Kayla about the incident:

> *I was only a few seconds away from being arrested, and am grateful to God I wasn't shot. I did feel myself like I was swimming in a sea of tear gas, unconscious almost, tired and very dizzy by the gas I just inhaled, just minutes before the soldiers tried to arrest me. I had an onion trying to lessen the effect of gas bombs on my face, eyes and respiratory system. They threw a sound grenade at me, and in my shock I threw the onion at the soldiers, unintentionally. That's what Newton says in his third law; maybe Israelis should arrest him for discovering that theory. I went away, as far away and as fast as I could, they did want to arrest me, and all I could do is just walk away!*
>
> *To be honest I was very scared that day. It was the fear of getting shot or arrested, or both, either one is not helpful or good for me. I am a young Palestinian, who loves football, and I also love my country, but I don't know what my feelings become after such incidents. My feelings toward my country become those of a raged, bitter and scared young man. The feeling that I am constantly in danger, the fear that something bad might happen to me all the time. And it does almost happen every day.*

Newton's third law, in case you've forgotten your old science lessons, is that for every action there's an equal and opposite reaction. But in the messier world of humans, the laws of physics are twisted. For every action the reaction is often twice as severe.

In one of Dad's late-night writing moments, he took stock of his strengths:

I am:	*I want:*
-*Dreamer*	-*to be the best*
-*Thinker*	-*to be loved*
-*Sensitive*	-*people to remember me*
-*Different*	-*to contribute*
-*Believer in God*	-*to make people happy*
-*Happy*	-*my family to be happy, healthy*
-*Giver, not taker*	-*to make a difference*

I'm not sure why he did this. Maybe one of the many Stephen Covey–style books he read suggested it. But it's typical for him. He wanted to be successful. And yet the rest of the list is about happiness, helping others, giving. For all the success he attained, his legacy was never that the company shipped *x* amount of units or that he improved efficiency or boosted profits. His legacy was the people he supported, the people he inspired. And I think he knew that.

Dad was always close to his cousin Abigail. She was ten when he was born; his family visited her family on their farm most weekends. "Your father was totally at ease with who he was, and I believe he was like that from birth," Abigail told me at a family reunion after Dad died. "I often rocked him to sleep on those weekends. I would sing hymns to him and he never fought sleep like so many babies do." She smiled thinking back. "He was always just so comfortable with who he was."

I always thought I was, too. I thought I knew myself. Now—here—I'm less sure.

I never asked Julie how she felt about me vanishing over Christmas and her birthday. That's how we are. Part of me thinks it's not a big deal for her. Part of me thinks, "How can it *not* be a big deal?" Mom always says, "You two never talk." She's right, but I like that about our relationship. We're comfortable with each other. Sometimes we don't need to talk. We may be a world apart, but I know she loves me. And she knows, I hope, how much I love her. But I would only realize much later, when I was done traveling, when I fully understood how deeply my introversion had hurt her, that there's a fundamental difference between knowing you love someone and showing that love. I am guilty of knowing and not showing.

Doug and Kayla are spending the night at the Paradise Hotel on Manger Street to celebrate their wedding anniversary. Doug made the arrangements with Fateen, so it was a total surprise for Kayla. For those of us *not* spending the night in a hotel with a real bed and a warm curvy human underneath the sheets, Fateen asks us to clean the center.

I mop the floor in the room where we eat our meals. The activity at least warms me up. Before mopping I was shivering, despite a windbreaker and sweater and long-sleeve shirt, despite two pairs of socks. I poured a cup of steaming water, which is meant for tea, just to warm my hands. It always feels colder inside the Handala Center than it does outside on the street, which is where I find Benjamin after we clean. He's going with Carina, a Spanish volunteer, to talk with a local family for the evening. Several small groups are doing this throughout Beit Jibrin, and I'm thrilled when Benjamin invites me to tag along. We're escorted by Tariq, a local guy who helps out at the center; he's one of the family's neighbors. The few streetlights are dim, the alley graffiti barely visible in the night. The family lives in a ground-floor apartment. Aisha, the mother, smiles, nodding, welcoming us. She leads us to a cramped family room, mauve-and-white-covered love seats against three of the four walls, a table in the middle, matching chair on the other side. A setup conducive to group therapy. A faded painting of a mountain and stream hangs on the wall, like something from a hotel. On a small TV is a soccer game. Palestinian men seem rabid about Spanish league soccer, particularly Barcelona and Real Madrid.

Aisha points at us to sit—her English is limited—then scoots down the hall. On a corner table is a small Christmas tree, maybe three feet high. Later, when Carina comments on the tree, Aisha turns on white lights, which fade on and off. I spot reindeer dishes on a shelf with knickknacks and pottery. I've heard that many Muslim families in Bethlehem, like this one, celebrate Christmas. They seem proud of Jesus: he's the local boy who made good.

Aisha's husband joins us. He's not a big man—thin, at least six inches shorter than me, graying hair—but his handshake is as firm as his presence. Aisha brings a pot of Arab coffee on a tray. It's strong, served in small cups. I haven't developed a taste for it yet.

"What do you think of al-Azzeh?" the husband asks.

"The people are friendly. They have been very nice to us," I say, keeping my English clear. "Very warm."

That's not what he means. I can tell from his serious eyes. What he means is—

Do you think al-Azzeh is a shithole.

And I'm thinking . . .

It's a ghetto.

A not-wholly-unpleasant ghetto—I feel safe walking the streets—but the buildings seem less like homes than factories, bleak and uninspired. Functional.

"Were you scared to come?" he says.

We weren't, we all say, but our families were. One of the speakers at Handala had talked about the perception of Palestinians as villains, particularly in the United States, pointing to movies like *True Lies* and *The Siege*. "Palestinians are not simply Arabs," he had said. "We're the worst Arabs."

My sense is that most Palestinians are baffled by the idea that *they're* considered the terrorists. I explain to the husband something I'd noticed before I left home.

"If I told people I was coming to Bethlehem, they'd picture baby Jesus. They'd say, 'Ohhh, that's so nice.' But if I said I was coming to Palestine, or the West Bank, they'd look concerned. A friend of mine asked me if I was bringing a bulletproof vest."

He asks how Americans view Muslims. I tell him it depends on where you go. You'll find plenty of Muslims in big cities, but less so in rural areas. I'm reminded of Costa Rica; of the rural Minnesota teenager who asked Jonathan if there were cows in England. She had never met a Jewish person until meeting Hannah, and had never met a Muslim.

"Who did you vote for?" he asks me and Benjamin, referring to the presidential election.

"I didn't vote for either candidate," says Benjamin.

The husband nods in approval. "Obama is no different than Bush. He does not care about my people. U.S. soldiers kill people every day somewhere in the world."

"What about Arab leaders?" says Benjamin.

"Our leaders do nothing. Abbas does nothing. We are weak. Arab nations are weak."

We pick up a few details about his life. He works for a Palestinian telecommunications company. He was in jail for four years. Benjamin asks why.

"Because I want freedom," he says. "We live here. We are born here. I want to be free. My people need freedom. My people need a state. We are poor—look here," he says, raising his arms to the tight room where we're sitting. "We have no country. My country is a five-minute drive because of the settlements. My country is stone fence to stone fence."

Aisha has left and returned with a second tray, this one with mint tea and a plate of wafer cookies. I ask her husband if he thinks attitudes will change between Israelis and Palestinians. I tell him about racial attitudes in the American South, that we still have racism, but things have improved radically in the last fifty years.

He seems skeptical. He could accept the 1967 borders, he says, but the Israelis take more land. From his old village, he tells us, he can see the settlements.

"When I was a boy we lived near Jews," he says. I hear nostalgic variations of this on multiple occasions while I'm here:

Our families helped their families, and their families helped our families.

My grandmother spoke Yiddish because she watched Jewish children in the neighborhood.

This is not an ancient conflict, people like Mahad and Fateen maintain. It dates back to 1948. And the problem, they say, is not Judaism, but Zionism.

The father smokes one of Tariq's cigarettes. "I respect the Jewish religion," he says. "I do not respect the Israeli government. What the Nazis did to the Jews was terrible. But what the Jews do to Palestinians is the same as the Nazis."

He is opposed to Osama bin Laden, he tells us, because bin Laden violates Islamic law by killing innocents. Tariq notes, probably to get a rise out of Carina, that Islam allows multiple wives, but you must treat each wife equally.

"Multiple wives seem like a lot of work," I say. "I can barely manage one."

The husband agrees. It is too difficult. "Maybe okay if you have half a wife," he says.

Aisha has left and come back *again*, this time with a bowl of oranges. She is pretty, though I'm sure she was prettier once. Her black sweatshirt makes her look frumpy, but in a pleasing way. Her dark hair is uncovered. Carina asks her if she works outside of the home. Tariq translates. She's a housewife.

"Why are you asking her questions?" the husband asks.

"I want to talk with her because she is so quiet. She hasn't been here the whole time."

"She is quiet because she does not speak much English."

As Carina will note on the walk back to Handala, the husband is left-wing politically—he tells us he's a socialist, and hails Venezuelan president Hugo Chávez as a freedom fighter (Chávez broke ties with Israel after the Gaza conflict, hence his popularity here)—yet he is clearly conservative when it comes to the roles of women.

Carina asks Aisha what she thinks of Palestinian men. She thinks a moment while peeling oranges.

"Rubbish," she says—and she throws her head back and laughs. We all laugh. We talk and talk—the husband sits with his thin legs crossed, smoking another cigarette—discussing everything from the Iraq War to housework, realizing eventually that it's after midnight.

"You are always welcome in my home," the husband tells us. "I open my home to you." It turns out Aisha has a relative who studied in New Jersey.

"I have a friend in New Jersey," I tell them of Hannah.

They escort us to the door and we return to the stark street, trash blowing as we walk, plastic bottles skipping and rolling against our feet. A night like this, I decide, is why dialogue is so important. Because a Palestinian may have softened his views of the United States. And an American gained insight on what it's like to be a Palestinian. That has to be worth something.

Burt the bearded Belgian is in striped cotton briefs, his butt about four feet from my face. He's bending over, skinny pale legs extending from his underpants, looking for socks. Burt is a sweet, gentle man, though seeing his striped-cotton middle-aged behind is not my preferred way to start the day, and on this morning it's literally the first thing I see. Granted, we're in such close quarters that Burt has surely endured an equally unpleasant view of *my* ass in not nearly as festive briefs. There's no space between Burt's sleeping bag and my sleeping bag and Mike's sleeping bag and Emmanuel's sleeping bag, which is stretched behind our heads. I lie closer to them than I do to Julie in our bed back home.

I look away from Burt's ass, staring up at paint peeling from the ceiling in strands, the single lightbulb hanging. Mike, the college-age Brit, sits up bleary, resting on his elbows.

"It's starting to smell like eighteen guys in here," he says in a croaking morning voice.

I unzip my bag, get up, put on jeans, and step over Mike to slide open the window, so we can air out the room with the fresh smell of . . . goats. The family living behind our building has a few farm animals.

"A few more days and the goats will be complaining about us," I tell Mike.

Doug has smartly moved to the flat next door, deciding he couldn't take two weeks trapped between the Italian snorers, though space is equally tight in his new digs. He's sleeping in the only spot he could find: partially under Habib's bed, his legs below, chest and head sticking out the other side.

"Funny how that's a step up from where I was," he says.

Bruno is such an impressive snorer—it starts within minutes of closing his book each night—that a few guys from the bigger room come in at night to listen and observe.

"It's like having a vibrating bed," I tell them.

At breakfast I ask Doug and Kayla about their night at the Paradise Hotel. Turns out the hotel's owner, Joshua, lived just a few blocks from them in Philly. He joined Doug and Kayla for a drink.

"The biggest mistake I ever made was coming back to Bethlehem," he told them over a cup of Nescafé. Bethlehem is his hometown; he moved back because the West Bank, at the time, seemed peaceful. But then came the Second Intifada. And the wall. And the checkpoints.

"They make life hard," he said. Last winter, the hotel was booked from before Christmas to after New Year's. Then the fighting began in Gaza. Joshua lost nearly one hundred thousand dollars in canceled bookings. This year business has improved due to the relative stability, but he plans to sell the hotel in two years, when his son is ready for college, and move back to the States.

"He doesn't think things will get better, even though he's relatively privileged," Kayla writes in a blog for family and friends. "He told Doug, 'Don't tell your coworkers about the boycott. Don't bring up the Palestinians—nothing good comes from it.' He was so adamant about it."

We eat breakfast, then walk to the morning's volunteer gig: a two-story building near the Aida camp that's being converted into a youth and cultural center. Palestinians are building such centers to preserve their traditions, from music to architecture to folklore. A brown wood-grained archway shaped vaguely like a keyhole stretches from one side of the street to the other. Sitting on top is a giant black key—"the largest key in the world," says Mahad. The key, he tells us, is a powerful symbol to Palestinians: when families were forced from their homes, they had minutes to grab essentials—money, photos, and, in many cases, their keys, since they expected to be back soon. Those keys are now family heirlooms.

The building has been gutted. In front is a concrete barrier; on it someone has spray-painted their desire for freedom. We go to the second floor. The steps are gone; it's more like a split-level concrete ramp with two-by-fours for traction. Wind whips through large square holes where windows will eventually be. Cinder blocks are stacked in mounds. A few of the Irishmen pound the jagged remains of a concrete wall with jackhammers, debris ricocheting off of walls (someone says they're using the wrong type of bit). The rest of us form a bucket line to dispose of rubbish that piled up during the gutting process: chunks of cinder blocks, tile, swept-up gray dust, pieces of wood, and wires, which we dump from a balcony into the bed of an orange dump truck below.

The two young Italian guys, who seem like lifelong friends but met right before coming here, sing "Bella Ciao"—*Goodbye, Beautiful*—an antifascist resistance tune from World War II. It's a catchy little ditty, and everyone sings as we work—

O bella ciao, bella ciao, bella CIAO, CIAO, CIAO!

Dust rises from the crash of debris in the truck bed below. My coat is covered, my sunglasses caked; I can feel the dust in my eyes. The truck gets full, rumbles off to dump the trash, then returns. The process starts again.

After a few hours, we walk back to Beit Jibrin for lunch, passing one of the more striking graffiti paintings in Bethlehem: it's a soldier, viewed from behind—hands against the wall—frisked by a little girl in a dress. On another wall is a dove with an olive branch in its mouth, a gun-scope target on its breast. I never see billboard-type ads for products—for cereal or soda or cell phone service. The most-advertised products are cynicism, frustration, harassment.

We take a shortcut between apartment buildings, snaking through trench-like alleys. "Bullet holes," says Habib nonchalantly, pointing at some pipes.

Later he notes some red and green graffiti in Arabic.

"It means 'freedom.' I know who did this—he's in prison."

We enjoy a takeout lunch at the Handala Center: roasted chicken with yellow rice and nuts in Styrofoam boxes. As we eat, Mike and Peter, another Brit, say that a week before we arrived, Fateen was stabbed in the leg during a soccer game. Fateen fouled a guy—

hard—and apologized. The guy was pissed. "So Fateen tells him, 'If you won't accept my apology, and you don't want to get hurt, don't play.' And the guy pulled a knife and stabbed him," says Mike.

"I wonder if the guy got a yellow card," Peter quips.

"It was a red card," says Mike. "It was covered in blood."

I'm a little bloody myself. I cut my fingers today while dumping cinder blocks and other debris into the Dumpster. There's blood on my jeans, my coat, my canvas bag.

"I'm amazed no one's been hurt yet," says Peter.

"Think of that construction site," says Mike. "No masks for the dust, no hard hats, volunteers using jackhammers, we're dropping debris while people are working underneath . . ."

"Apparently a few locals and UN people complained about the dust."

The United Nations Relief and Works Agency operates a school next to the building we were cleaning out, and has offices there as well. Each camp is served by a UNRWA office: the UNRWA handles services a municipality might normally provide, from trash to water to clinics.

"Yesterday at the olive farm I kept getting hit by rocks—this eighty-two-year-old guy was pounding boulders with a sledge-hammer and stuff was flying," I say. "Maybe it's part of the fatal-ism here. Why wear safety goggles given all the other shit that's going on?"

"That's probably why they all smoke," says Mike.

Mike and Peter also visited a family last night. They asked the family what they do for fun on weekends.

"They said, 'We don't do anything for fun,' " says Peter. "They just live day to day and see what happens. They don't plan ahead."

When we were working, Mike and Peter and I manned the end of the bucket lines, like a three-man paddle wheel: get the bucket, dump it, pass the empty bucket back up the row, get in line, receive the next bucket. It was quite efficient. At one point I accidentally dropped one of our buckets into the truck bed. Fateen was down below, and climbed into the bed to retrieve it. He flung it back up; I caught it, thanked him, and tossed it again to the folks in line.

"I want to come up," he said.

As in, *I'm going to climb up the front of the building.*

He can't be serious, I thought. There's no way he'll reach this balcony. It's too high. Why is he even attempting this?

He stepped up onto the roof of the truck's cab.

"Give me your hand," he said, raising his.

"For real?"

"We can do it."

I reached down. Fortunately I have long arms. We gripped hands. He jumped as I pulled him up, throwing his foot against the balcony's corner. I put my left hand under his left arm, heaving. He crawled over on his stomach, rolled himself onto the balcony.

It seemed unnecessarily reckless. But maybe that's what happens when you feel powerless. When there's little hope, there's little fear.

We've started venturing out at night for drinks, a welcome development since there's little to do in the camp. Fateen's only request is that we not return drunk, since we're staying in a Muslim neighborhood. He takes a large group of us to a restaurant on Manger Street, about a twenty-minute walk from the camp. It's Christian-owned, so there's alcohol. A young man croons into a microphone, white shirt with black tie and black jeans, accompanied by a piano player, singing Lionel Richie with an Arab accent, then launching into "I Will Survive" and "Hotel California."

"Oh—I love this song," says Fateen. We settle in at a long table and he sings along. The TV beams a slick, soulless, shoot-'em-up action flick starring John Travolta. After that, it's the campy testosterone of *WWE Raw.*

"He's my favorite," says Fateen, pointing up at the tall, glowering Undertaker, who straddles another half-nude man in tights.

Is this really the Middle East?

We order beers. Shakila, an American volunteer from New York City, scans the hookah menu, then orders a pipe with tutti-frutti-flavored tobacco. She was sick her first day due to a raw goat dish she ate while visiting relatives in Lebanon, but she seems fine now as we discuss the Christmas party. A day or so ago, Fateen suggested a party at a resort—"I have a deal for you: one hundred shekels; dinner, Turkish bath, DJ, one free soft drink . . ."—but some folks didn't want to pay that much, and others felt uncomfortable partying at a resort without our new Palestinian friends, so someone again suggested we host an event in the center, and Fateen again said, "This is a refugee camp—you can't do it here," and people got bored and tried to leave but Fateen made them sit back down, and he said a nonprofit is hosting a party on the twenty-third though it won't have a Turkish bath or one free soft drink, and some people said they want to go to Manger Square for Christmas Eve and someone said it's selfish to have fun when people are suffering—

It went on for forty-five minutes.

I looked up during the meeting and saw Monique watching me across the room as I took notes. I held up my pad and she smiled.

"When Fateen says 'This is a refugee camp,' what he means is that they're Muslim," says Shakila. "They don't celebrate Christmas like us. And they kind of resent Palestinian Christians. Christians are discriminated against, too, but they have an easier time getting paperwork or permits approved."

The hookah arrives. She inhales, water bubbling in the pipe's belly, hot coals burning in foil on top. The Italians have some, I have some—hey, when in Bethlehem, right?—and I must say, the tutti-frutti is tasty. Doug and Kayla enjoy the pipe so much they eventually buy one to take home.

Our more frequent hangout is a restaurant called the Bonjour

Café. It's a shorter walk, up a long hill not far from the camp, past Bethlehem University. Nice place. Modern blue lights over the bar, a menu with pizzas and sandwiches. I'm talking sports one night with Kayla and Doug, and I ask them about Michael Vick, given that they're both from Philly. The Philadelphia Eagles signed Vick, I explain to Monique, who's part of the large party, after he'd served time in prison for participating in a dog-fighting ring. I'm a dog lover, so I'm not exactly a huge Michael Vick fan. Kayla rants about how people get *sooo* upset about dogs yet they don't care about what's happening here in Palestine and some baby got murdered in Philly and people didn't get nearly as outraged about *that* as they did about Michael Vick and just because you have four legs and eat fuckin' Milk-Bones doesn't mean you're more deserving of sympathy than a murdered baby.

"Vick paid his debt to society and he should get a second chance to pursue his chosen profession," she says.

Pause.

"I mean, they're fuckin' dogs."

"Wow," I say. "There's something you don't hear often. 'You know what *really* pisses me off? Puppies.'"

She laughs. "One of my coworkers said, 'You're a cold SOB.'"

I excuse myself to use the restroom. It's a tiled wonderland. A working toilet! That blue cleaning stuff when you flush! A working sink with soap! Hand towels! And it's *clean*!

Back at the flat, we're experiencing the problems you might expect from eighteen guys sharing one tiny toilet and sink. Problems such as, you know . . . getting inside to use it. Want to brush your teeth? Someone's inside. Something more urgent? Someone's inside. The best strategy is to wait outside the door. Emmanuel, the tall young Belgian, knocks on the bathroom door one day, asking in heavily accented English how long the current occupant will be conducting business.

"You take *beeg sheet*?" he says.

The toilet leaks, so the floor is a constant puddle. Add in eighteen sets of dirty shoes, and it's a muddy puddle, with muddy footprints leading out. Bruno the Italian snorer, bless him, is particularly dedicated to mopping it up.

Mike noted the irony that one of the Christmas party ideas was to repair old widows' homes. "We can't fix our own fucking toilet," he said. "We're shit workers. If anyone wants to fix some plumbing, I've got a great project right here."

Though you wouldn't know it from the leak, water is a precious commodity: Israeli authorities, we're told, give priority to the settlements when it comes to water resources. During the summer Bethlehem had water one day a week (and not surprisingly, there's no wastewater treatment, so like Ciudad Quesada and even Xi'an, this is a don't-flush-the-TP zone).

We're experiencing these aqua issues firsthand: the men's flat no longer has running water. As with many local buildings, our flat gets its water from rooftop tanks, and the tanks, at the moment, are empty. The Handala Center gets its water from the reservoir, so we use that as a fill-up spot, bringing over buckets and bottles and lugging them back to the flat. I bought bottled water at the small market down the street, mainly for the bottle, so I could fill it to wash my hair in the sink (I also bought a sponge for sponge baths) or to refill toilet tanks.

Conor, a big, dreadlocked Irishman, suggested a toilet-water conservation policy:

"If it's yellow keep it mellow, if it's brown send it down."

So the handsome bathroom at the Bonjour Café is a plumbing paradise.

"Oh my *God*," I tell Kayla and Doug when I come back out. "The bathroom is amazing. You've got to go use it."

"Jeez—you're like a schoolgirl," says Kayla.

"Go in there. I wish I'd brought my shampoo."

We're soon joined by Akbar, a friend of Mahad's. They greet with

Euro-style kisses on the cheeks. Akbar was studying in Baghdad to earn an MBA, but came home after the U.S. invasion. Despite their day-to-day challenges, Palestinians are among the best-educated people in the Middle East. Akbar works as a special-needs teacher, which he enjoys, though he still hopes to earn his business degree, this time in India. Love, however, may derail his schooling: he and his girlfriend, an Iraqi refugee, are discussing marriage. This leads to a lively cross-cultural discussion about families and marriage and culture. Palestinian society is becoming less conservative, Akbar says: "You no longer hold up a bloody sheet for your family on your wedding night to show your wife is a virgin."

Monique, a regular on these postdinner outings, tells us about her ninety-five-year-old grandmother, who lives alone, an odd concept for the Palestinians. Earlier, when I was writing, she had asked me again, "When may I read your notes?" I smiled, and I made excuses, and I closed the pad so she couldn't see.

We're participating in a weekly Friday protest in the village of al-Masara, at a roadblock manned by Israeli soldiers. I'm not sure how I feel about this. I had thought this trip would be more about volunteering than politics, although the title of the program—"Stop Occupying Christmas"—should have been clear.

On my previous trips, I volunteered through one organization, which took care of everything: placement, food, place to stay. This time, the organization I signed up with—Volunteers for Peace—is one of several orgs funneling folks to IPYL, which is running the workcamp, as it's called here. Multiple organizations has led to confusion about the work we'll do. Two of the Scottish women thought they'd be working with children. The older of the pair looks to be in her fifties and recently had back surgery, so she struggled to walk up the mountain when we built rock walls (and certainly could not *lift* rocks). Her accent is so thick that several of us translate for the Palestinians.

I ask Perrine if the work we're doing is helpful, because so far it seems more symbolic than substantial. "Yes, it is helpful, but the work is not as important as working together," she says, which sums things up fairly well: this is less about volunteer labor and more about exposing us to the Palestinian experience, which the Palestinians appreciate.

The al-Masara protest, Fateen tells us, covers a variety of grievances. It's a demonstration against two nearby settlements, and the construction of a third. It's also a demonstration against the Israeli government not only for building the wall, but for confiscating Palestinian land and water to do it.

This is a nonviolent protest, says Fateen. He and Mahad frequently compare Palestine to South Africa (a comparison many Israelis say is grossly inaccurate). Fateen scheduled a lecturer one night to discuss the campaign to boycott Israel, which includes not simply a commercial boycott—encouraging people and organizations to stop buying Israeli products and investing in Israeli companies—but academic and cultural boycotts: asking musicians, for example, to not perform in Tel Aviv.

"The international community enables Israel. It pays for Israel," said the lecturer. "That's why we believe the boycott is necessary. And it is not just about economic impact, but showing Palestinian youth that they can have a role."

Fateen asks if anyone has questions about the protest.

"Will Israeli soldiers be there?" Bruno's wife asks.

"They will be there," said Fateen. "But they won't shoot you."

"Don't throw stones," Mahad advises.

"Yes. We want to say to the world, 'We are civilians in front of soldiers.' This is the message. They have guns. We are civilians. The soldiers will be on good behavior. They know you are there. And there will be media there."

Kayla tells me later that it's Palestinian media. "Preaching to the choir," she says.

"Can we take pictures," asks Ella from Croatia.

"You can take pictures, but don't put your camera in their face. We don't want to make the soldiers nervous."

Yes—let's not make the soldiers nervous.

Almost as an afterthought, Fateen says we can skip the protest if we're not comfortable. And this is partly what's bothering me: no one asked if we wanted to protest. I'm probably the only one thinking this; everyone else seems more gung ho. I want to go, but I feel like I'm in a new relationship where we've haven't kissed yet and now I'm being pressured to go all the way. This protest may be nonviolent, but nonviolence hasn't always been the preferred method for addressing Palestinian grievances. Hopefully that's changing, at least among young men like Fateen and Mahad. So I'm attending, but I'm attending, I decide, as an observer.

The morning of the protest, we stop first in Bil'in, visiting a small cultural center that is under construction. It's a simple structure, next to an existing school, nothing more than cinder-block walls, and we haul materials inside, again forming lines, passing buckets of cement and more cinder blocks. Afterward we walk up concrete steps to the roof, the cold wind stinging red ears. A local guy thanks us and gives a speech, pointing out the inescapable view of the wall.

"We have faith in our rights," he says, "not faith in weapons."

His breath flashes and vaporizes in the damp air as he talks. An Israeli scientist recently won a Nobel Prize, he says (Ada Yonath, who won in chemistry with two Americans for work on ribosomes that may lead to new antibiotics), and yet the world doesn't care that the Israeli government has uprooted thousands of trees, and thousands of lives, to build the wall. "They try to make our lives more difficult so the people will leave. I could get a U.S. visa like *that*!" he says, snapping his fingers. "But we will not leave!"

We walk back down from the roof and kill time before the protest near the three-room school. No students are there, this being

Friday. I go inside, mainly to escape the chill. I walk alone in one of the classrooms. It's more like a bunker. The walls need painting and patching, a hole lets in the cold. Assignments are taped to the wall: the children are learning French. I'm reminded of a similar exercise that Julie and I did in Costa Rica: the kids labeled body parts of a Dalmatian from a coloring book—the eyes and ears and nose and legs.

I wonder how children can learn in such a frigid, prisonlike room.

On the wall is a stick figure drawn in pencil. The figure carries a Palestinian flag. Behind him, drawn in pen, is an equally crude truck. In the truck is another stick figure, this one with a gun. The stick figure in the truck fires his gun at the stick figure with the flag.

We walk up a barren road, about sixty of us, soldiers visible in the distance. Several marchers carry a large Palestinian flag stretched over their heads. Marcen has one corner, one of the Irish guys has another; two Palestinians take the other two. A little boy carries a yellow Fatah flag; another, maybe twelve years old, holds a sign with a poster-size image of a grinning Yasser Arafat. A few of the protesters are Israelis.

The protest organizers lead an Arabic chant. Kayla says it translates roughly as—

> *Stop the occupation!*
> *Stop the wall!*
> *In Berlin they destroyed the wall!*
> *In Palestine we will do the same!*

The English chant is more hostile—

> *1, 2, 3, 4!*
> *Occupation no more!*

5, 6, 7, 8!
Israel is a fascist state!

About fifteen soldiers, all in green, stand in a row behind knee-high coils of silver razor wire. Two jeeps are behind the soldiers. Buildings that look like warehouses loom on the side. On a hill—more like a cliff—two more soldiers stand.

We pass squatty cinder-block homes and shops, no sidewalks, just dirt and rocks. At the wire, we stop. A farmer makes a speech, shouting the usual rhetoric, first in Arabic, then English: "The Germans in World War II said they were just following orders," he says. "Now the Israeli soldiers say *they* are just following orders."

I'm standing in back with Mike, who seems a tad unconvinced by Fateen's don't-worry-you-won't-get-hurt speech. "We might be more valuable if we were injured," he says.

We've heard the story of Tristan Anderson, an activist and photojournalist from Oakland, California, who nine months earlier was shot in the forehead at close range with a tear gas canister at a nonviolent protest in Nil'in. Anderson suffered a traumatic brain injury. The Israeli Ministry of Defense called the incident an "act of war," thus absolving itself of liability. I assume this means Anderson committed an aggressive act by attacking a flying tear gas canister with his skull.

I move up about three feet from the soldiers. Peter asks one how old he is. Eighteen, he says. Some look older, but they can't be more than twenty-one or twenty-two, the soft faces contrasting with the combat helmets and long black weapons.

A few of them laugh at the speeches. I can't tell if it's nerves or arrogance.

An Irish volunteer snaps a picture of a soldier giving him the finger. Israeli military photographers snap photos of the protesters. Doug walks over to me.

"See the guy in the middle," he says. "He had his finger on the trigger. I was right in front of him and I told him he shouldn't do that. He was the only one. And so the guy next to him put *his* finger on the trigger and laughed."

Palestinian boys run up to the wire. The boys hold black nylon straps that are used to ship cinder blocks. They wrap the straps around the barbed wire and pull.

The soldiers rip the straps from the boys' hands.

This protest may be routine, but the tension is heavy like the damp cold; as though it would take only one small thing to provoke the soldiers; to ignite a massacre.

A few of the kids roll a tire into the wire.

The children shout at the soldiers.

A soldier pushes a kid in the chest.

One spark—that's all it would take. That one soldier with his finger on the trigger.

The kids seem to back down after the boy is pushed. They pose for volunteers' pictures in front of the razor wire, like rappers, trying to look tough. One boy has a keffiyeh wrapped around his head. Only his eyes are visible.

I notice a woman off to the side wearing a beige vest with a dove logo. She looks like some sort of official; blond hair, glasses, retirement age. She's smoking a cigarette. I ask if she's here to monitor the protest.

"You're from the States," she says, a bit surprised. "Where from?"

"Virginia."

"New Jersey," she says.

Her name is Anne, and she's in the West Bank for three months, based in Bethlehem, the only U.S. participant out of twenty-five volunteers with a World Council of Churches group called The Ecumenical Accompaniment Programme in Palestine and Israel. They're here to monitor situations, such as this protest, and to help prevent human rights violations. She also works frequently at the Bethlehem checkpoint. About twenty U.S. churches are participating, far lower than the number from Europe.

"They'll usually behave while we're here," she says of the soldiers, "but sometimes they'll harass people after we're gone."

She takes a drag on her cigarette. The protest seems to be quieting down. One of her colleagues, a German gentleman, talks of a town where he stayed in the West Bank. A settler accused a villager of stealing his goat. At 2 a.m., he says, village residents were pulled from their homes by soldiers, forced to stand outside in the cold for over an hour. In another town, two soldiers took a bath in a pool used for drinking water. "Just for fun," he said.

"Why do they do that?" I say. "Do they want to make life so tough that people leave?"

"You're asking why—who knows why?" says Anne. "Why are some of the soldiers laughing? We planted olive trees and the settlers pulled them up. Why? Why would you do that? I think they just . . . I think they want the land. It's that simple."

I ask her if being here has made her pessimistic. She nods.

"The only way anything will change is if the U.S. government says, 'We're going to stop giving you three billion dollars a year unless you quit harassing these people.' Three billion dollars—how crazy is that? People at home have no concept of what's really happening here. There's no clue about what these people face every day."

She asks if we've been to the Bethlehem checkpoint in the morning. No—only the evening we arrived. The line, she said, extends out the building at 4:30 a.m., as men struggle to reach to work on time, fearful of delays. It's like enduring airport security every day: passing through metal detectors, removing belts, emptying pockets, putting ID cards on a card reader, placing a hand on a scanner to check fingerprints.

As I talk with Anne, one of the volunteers, the bossy New York woman, stands in front of the razor wire—and the soldiers—and begins her own personal chant, shouting "Shame Shame Israel!"

Our hosts are not happy. Then she shouts about Hitler and Nazis. Not at all the message the protesters want to convey. "First of all, she's an idiot," writes Kayla that night in her blog. "Secondly, she hijacked the message of the protest. Apparently she was pulled aside earlier and told not to engage in conversation with the soldiers. General questions are okay but nothing provoking. So she made two mistakes. She doesn't understand that in the end, this isn't our fight. We're here to say we think this is wrong and to support the message that the villagers want to send—mainly, stop building a wall."

I get Anne's e-mail address and say goodbye—we're heading back to the village and the bus. Some Palestinians whistle as we walk. The Italians lead another chorus of "Bella Ciao."

Today, the nonviolent protest remained nonviolent. It didn't *feel* nonviolent, but no rocks were thrown, no weapons fired. Two weeks from now, soldiers will jump over the wire and throw sound grenades at protesters, forcing them back to the village. In February, a group of twenty Palestinians, eight internationals, and seven Israeli activists will be assaulted with tear gas and sound bombs; another seventy-five Palestinians will be stopped by the military before even reaching al-Masara. In July, two protesters will be hospitalized and one detained, along with a journalist.

That evening, Doug tells me the protest depressed him. All that energy and effort and anger, and yet the only people to hear it were eighteen-year-old soldiers who couldn't care less; whose stereotypes were reinforced—the kids causing trouble, the antagonistic banners and shouts. "I wonder if they even listened to the farmer's speech," he says. "They'd already made up their minds about the people on the other side of the barbed wire."

Kayla, who exudes a tomboy toughness, had the same downcast reaction as we left. "I let most of the crowd pass—I kept looking at the soldiers," she wrote in her blog. "And I started to cry a little."

In the afternoon I sit on the steps outside the flat, writing in my journal. It's warmer than it was this morning at al-Masara, and the air is fresher outside than inside. I'd thought about writing on the roof, in the sun, but Devin, a nineteen-year-old Taiwanese-American who seems more like an old wise man (minus the wrinkles), is leading a meditation class. Monique told me I should come.

"I'm already pretty mellow," I said, declining.

As I sit on the steps, some kids wave from a window in the building next door. They hold up a schoolbook, and ask if I speak French.

"English," I say.

Their mother appears and waves. "They learn English and French in school," she says.

"Ah—very good."

"Very good!" repeats her son.

I point at my head. "Very smart," I say.

Unlike my other trips, I've felt distant from the children here, which says more about me than it does about them. We hang out on the streets, and the kids are often there, sometimes playing soccer in the narrow street, the ball smacking walls and cars. Doug and Kayla brought a Frisbee and teach kids to throw. Doug thinks we should write "Happy Hanukkah" on a Frisbee, have everyone sign it, and fling it over the wall. Peace through Frisbees.

A local boy, he can't be more than four, always tries to sell us postcards. The cards are connected, accordion-style, and when they hang from his sticky hand they're almost as tall as he is. He never speaks—I wonder if he has some sort of disability—but grins, walking up to people, raising his postcards. I assume he wants money, but he may just be showing them off. One day we notice his pants are on backward. Another day his shoes are on the wrong feet. Later I learn the boy's father has been in prison since before he was born.

One afternoon, in the fourth-floor room where we hold group meetings, some local children perform a traditional folk dance called *dabke*. Everyone claps as the children march in place, hands on their hips, the girls in gold silk tops with red scarves on their heads, the boys with black vests over red shirts. Their black pants spin in rhythm; they stamp their feet. It's like the Palestinian version of Riverdance. They look serious as they perform. Not nervous, but confident. Businesslike. They learned *dabke* here at the center. The theme of the dances, I'm told, is typically love. It's a dance you might perform at a wedding.

We see the flip side of *dabke* a few days later: Palestinian rap. Three high-schoolish guys mimic the finger-pointing *yo-yo-yo* motions they've clearly picked up from MTV or its international equivalents. They rap about Hamas and Fatah; how Palestinians are trapped between them. One kid raps about settlers who burned his uncle's house.

"They gave us two choices: die or die," a short-haired teen in a sweatsuit pronounces into the microphone. "But we choose life. Many people talk about a two-state solution—"

"A fake solution," says his chunky colleague—

"We want equal status—"

"We want the land that belongs to us! Why should I live in a refugee camp?!"

The chunky kid instructs everyone to clap. Teens in the back of the room chant the main line in Arabic, which sounds to me like:

Ath-eeee-uh!
Ath-eeee-uh!
Ath-eeee-uh!

Distortion disrupts the middle of the rap. Samir, a new addition to our team of Palestinian hosts, fixes the sound system. The audience is a mix of volunteers and local teens, though as Kayla notices, more local girls than usual are here.

"Sorry for the sound system," the chunky kid says, "but money talks, and we make from nothing a big thing."

I have no idea what that means, but he says it with authority.

They rap about Gaza—"Fuck the Arab world and fuck the Arab leaders—raise your hand for Gaza!"—then move on to the boycott, an audience-participation number.

"When I say boycott, you say 'now'! Boycott!"

Now!

"Boycott!"

Now!

"When I say Palestine you say 'free'! Palestine!"

Free!

"Palestine!"

Free!

They end to rowdy applause.

"The camps . . . It's a bad life, bad houses," says the chunky kid. "The kids don't know. They think it's paradise. We give our love to the children in all of the camps."

A group led by Samir takes the microphones. He joined us a few days ago, and he's now sleeping next to Bruno in Doug's old space. Samir handles everything from our bus trips to our grocery lists.

"People don't know about Palestine," he tells us. "You internationals can go anywhere in the world, but we cannot go to our capital, Jerusalem. Hip-hop is a way to speak the world's language." They start to rap—

> *The revolution is BACK! BACK! BACK!*
> *You gotta watch your BACK! BACK! BACK!*

Rafid, an attention-craving boy who hangs out here, dances on the table in the back of the room, waving a Palestinian banner. A Scottish volunteer and an Irish volunteer take photos.

"Hands up for the prisoners!" says Samir.

Hands go up. Rafid dances harder as more cameras rise. A bunch of teens dance on the table with Joe, a Brit who's so tight with his new Palestinian posse that he's been dubbed Joe-hammad.

Marcen is invited to join in; he waves his arms in front of the computer's projector screen; ties his scarf around his head.

The chunky rapper is back, rapping about Hamas. Like most rap, it's angry. But it's anger released. Creative expression as opposed to throwing rocks.

Mahad had told us there's debate among Palestinians about rock throwing, mainly because it provokes the soldiers. But he justifies it. The soldiers disrupt protests before any stones are thrown. The stones are symbolic. People are angry. It's an outlet. Sometimes, he tells us, when the soldiers throw tear gas canisters, the gas isn't released. So the Palestinians pick 'em up and throw 'em back. Some Palestinians make their own homemade tear gas: chicken shit in water, letting it sit in the sun for days.

"Tear gas is bad the first time," one speaker tells us, "but after that you get used to it."

To the Palestinians the symbolism of rock throwing seems obvious:

The Israelis have guns, jets, tanks, bombs. We have rocks.

One evening we watch a video of a nonviolent protest. It's presented by a representative from the Stop the Wall campaign. He's a third stringer: the gentleman who was supposed to speak was arrested in his home eighteen hours earlier ("administrative detention," to use the official term). No one knows his status. The organization's leader was arrested a few months ago as well. So this guy gives the talk then shows the video, which focuses on Nil'in, a small village that was separated from its farming land when the Israeli government built the wall. The villagers vowed to stop construction, blocking roads and causing delays.

The video starts with young men, faces covered, throwing rocks at Israeli jeeps. The soldiers respond with tear gas and rubber and plastic bullets. But I didn't watch the video and think, "Oh those poor outgunned rock throwers." I thought, "Geez—those rocks really pissed off the soldiers." As Kayla noted, the subject of the video becomes the rocks, not the wall. And no one here understands this difference in perception, that when most Americans see rock throwing, they see anarchy—not martyrs.

Many of the videos we see bother me. As they're intended to. They're simply-produced, you-are-there mini-documentaries, no narration, usually no more than three or four minutes long, showing the mistreatment of Palestinians by settlers. Several of the videos are produced by the Israeli Information Center for Human Rights in the Occupied Territories, otherwise known as B'Tselem, which politically is a bit like the ACLU of Israel. In one online video, a farmer returns to harvest his olive trees following a ruling from the Israeli High Court of Justice. When he arrives and picks olives, some settlers walk outside. "What's he doing on our land?" one of them says. Despite the ensuing violence—the settlers force the farmer and the cameraman from the olive trees—this is the primary point of the video: to show a man who's harassed for "trespassing" on his own farm.

What's he doing on our land?

It's the ironic, tragic punch line. But before he's booted from his land, the farmer is confronted by a female settler. She's hysterical, screaming—"Who killed my father? Maybe your nice friends killed my father!"

The pain runs deep. And this woman's pain is as deep as any Palestinian's pain.

I've had a hard time shaking two videos in particular. The first is in Hebron, arguably the West Bank's most troubled city. In the video, a Hebron settler—a woman—torments a Palestinian woman and her children. They live on opposite sides of a dead-end street in the Tel Rumeida neighborhood. A thick screen runs along steps in a Palestinian apartment building: the screen is a shield for residents because the settlers and their children, protected by the soldiers, often throw stones at the Arabs.

"Sit here, in the cage," the settler woman says to the Palestinian in Hebrew, forcing them behind the screen. And she taunts the woman and her children in a cold, mocking voice, her face pressed against the pen, lips pursed, sneering the same words—

Sharmuuuta . . .

Shar-muuuuuuuuutaaa . . .

The word—*Sharmuta*—is Arabic slang for "whore."

One night a few of us sat on the fourth floor—me, Doug, Kayla, among others—waiting for a meeting to start. Projected on the pull-down screen was a video taken several years ago. A group of Palestinian youths had thrown rocks at soldiers. The soldiers opened fire. The video showed an emergency room, doctors treating a thirteen-year-old boy. He was hit with a projectile like bird shot that decimated his jaw and shoulder, lodging metal into his chest. His face and neck were bloody. Doctors huddled over him, shouting instructions.

The bloody teen in the video was Fateen. He would be in the hospital for forty-eight days. Jaw wired shut. Shoulder disfigured. Front teeth replaced.

"How can you watch that?" Kayla asked him.

He didn't answer. Just puffed on his cigarette—he started smoking in the hospital; there was nothing to do but smoke and suck on his feeding straw—slumped in his chair, the cold light of the screen turning his face blue as he stared at his ravaged younger self.

We spend two days cleaning Manger Street, starting near Beit Jibrin and working our way to Manger Square. Along the road is a satirical street sign for a tow-away zone: instead of a car the sign shows a tank. In that same mirthful spirit, Habib tells me a joke.

"Why was Jesus born in Palestine and not Lebanon?"

"Don't know. Why."

"Because God couldn't find any virgins in Lebanon."

Ah, but seriously, folks . . .

The road is divided by narrow curbed islands with bushes. We pick up trash, dig up weeds, turn over soil. Given our size and bright yellow highway worker vests, we're hard to miss. The locals appreciate our efforts. A shopkeeper brings us bottles of water. A restaurant owner brings trays of Arab coffee. Taxi drivers honk horns and say thanks: "God bless you! Very good!"

On a balcony a woman yells to us: "Where you are?" We assume she wants to know where we're from.

"U.S.A.!" yells Tyler, a Minnesotan who's going to school in Scotland.

She applauds and waves. In Hebron, a group of guys will approach Kayla and say, "Welcome, welcome, welcome." Throughout the West Bank, folks are thrilled to see visitors.

Tyler churns up dirt with a pick as I collect wads of trash. The cars pass close.

"I don't know if it's the exhaust or the cigarettes or the hookah pipe or all the dust from the construction site—probably all of them—but something funky is living in my chest," I say.

"I know—I don't usually smoke," he says, digging. "But smoking is such a social thing here. I've probably taken a year off my life." He smiles, eyes hidden behind white-frame sunglasses. "But it probably wouldn't have been a very productive year."

I'm paired with Monique most of the second morning. I use the pick, she plucks trash from the bushes. She finds a BB gun pellet— her nephew wanted a BB gun, she tells me. He finally got one, shot a wall, and the pellet ricocheted, nailing him below the eye. (Dad once shot his older brother Georgie in the butt with his BB gun. "He never teased me after that," Dad said.)

"Why do children play war?" Monique asks.

"Well, it's a boy thing, right? Girls don't play war."

"No . . . but why boys?"

"I don't know. Boys are high-energy and aggressive. You know—testosterone."

"So you think it is hormones."

"I'm sure it's learned, too. Look at their role models."

She mentions the professional wrestling we saw on TV.

"I do not understand why that is popular," she says. "I see boys wear T-shirts with wrestlers on them."

"Most boys are rough; they like that kind of stuff. That's why boys don't play with Dalai Lama dolls."

"I do not understand."

Her English is excellent, but my English, I find, sometimes confuses her.

"It's not worth repeating," I say.

Slowly our group works its way down Manger Street in the direction of Manger Square. I'm collecting trash in a burlap sack—cigarette butts, broken glass, coffee cups, gum wrappers.

"You are the garbageman," she says, "and I am the garbage-woman."

We receive an unexpected treat: a free buffet lunch from the owner of a large restaurant on Manger Street. It's a banquet hall for tour bus crowds: ten-foot-high windows presenting views of parched, sacred mountains. The owner is a large man with a big silver wristwatch, black goatee, and black stubble, hair parted neatly to the side.

"I see you working today," he tells us. "It makes me feel very happy. I invite you to eat here to thank you for what you are doing for Bethlehem."

It's a spectacular spread and I load up: mushroom soup, salad, rice, mashed potatoes, chicken, vegetables, bread. Liters of soda sit on the table. We've been eating conservatively since we're such a big group. Not today. This is a feast.

Conor, the big dreadlocked Irishman, lets out a satisfied *aaah* when he's done. He drops f-bombs with Hannah-like frequency, though with his accent it sounds more like *fookin'*.

"That was fookin' good," he says. "That restaurant owner is the fattest fookin' Arab I've seen since I've been here. That's good, you know—I like a guy who runs a restaurant to be big. It means he eats a lot. He fookin' enjoys it."

As long as we're here I take advantage of the restaurant bathroom. The men's flat still has no water, so we've become restroom opportunists. Peter now carries his toiletries on every trip. When I enter, he's shaving in the sink. A shirtless Mike shampoos his hair. I stay clothed, yet manage to take almost an entire bath.

That evening I chat outside with Doug while Kayla writes her blog, using a small Acer computer she brought. The usual crowd of Europeans stands on the street, smoking. It's a beautiful evening. The weather is suddenly springlike, warm like the pink sunset to the west. A woman in a white scarf pushes a double stroller with twins; Monique and others swarm around them, cooing. The mother smiles with pride.

"Kind of nice to see something happy," I tell Doug.

Back home, the D.C. area was pounded by two feet of snow. Philly got nailed as well, says Doug. Kayla comes outside. She says their pastor e-mailed his sermon to his parishioners rather than trudge through the snow to church.

"What a pussy," she says, laughing.

Julie e-mails me wintry photos of our snow-battered home: our covered cars and bushes, the shoveled sidewalk tunnels. It'll be a white, frigid Christmas. I view these in a T-shirt, in 65-degree weather.

The morning we go to Hebron begins, oddly enough, with Conor playing Johnny Cash's "A Boy Named Sue" on a portable stereo next to his sleeping bag. Conor is a fledgling mandolin player, still teaching himself the instrument, which he brought with him to Bethlehem. He often sits on his sleeping bag, leaning against the wall, strumming chords.

"You like Johnny Cash?" I ask.

"He's the fookin' king, man."

For those of you unfamiliar with the canon of country music, "A Boy Named Sue" was recorded live at San Quentin Prison, a song about a kid whose father abandoned him and gave him a girl's name to make him tough and mean.

Hebron is a town named Sue. Established by the Canaanites almost 5,500 years ago, it's the West Bank's biggest city, with two hundred thousand Palestinian residents, yet dominated by a powerful pocket of settlers and the army that supports them: a combustible mix of dominant minority and impotent majority; of unchecked authority and simmering hatreds.

We exit the bus and merge with ambling pedestrians, Fateen leading us down hectic streets, past small stores and gritty food joints, walking to the office of the Hebron Rehabilitation Committee, which preserves and restores housing for Palestinians in the Old City. Every Palestinian town has seemed run-down, but the HRC office has a sparkling old architecture/new interior shine. We sit in a lecture hall, awaiting a presentation, when Fateen enters and asks—

"Has anyone seen Jerome?"

Jerome is French, and seems like a friendly guy, though he's not exactly the sharpest piece of cheese on the tray. With his buzzed haircut and jutting nose he reminds me not of a Frenchman but of Benito Mussolini, though more like the dictator's goofy yet goodhearted brother. Think Benny instead of Benito. Jerome annoyed the female volunteers by washing his clothes in their first-floor sleeping area—there's a tiny kitchen in the room with actual running water—then hanging them to dry without wringing them out, thus dampening the floor and sleeping bags, leaving a persistent musty smell in the windowless room.

Fateen is worried. And ticked. "Who has their badges," he snaps, making us raise our hands. "This is why I tell you to wear the badges." The badges are clip-on plastic slits with a card inside stating our name and country. On the back is Fateen's name and cell phone number.

Of course, it's not like Jerome can casually wander the city. For security reasons, Hebron has undergone a form of carefully planned inconvenience—urban constipation, if you will. The city is divided into two sections: H1, as it's called, is overseen by the Palestinian Authority, though subject to Israeli raids. H2, which includes most of the Old City—roughly 5,500 Palestinians and 400 settlers—is under Israeli control. H2 is shorthand, I presume, for "twice the hassle." To protect and accommodate the settlers, Palestinians are prohibited from walking on certain streets. Other streets are blocked by concrete barriers and stone walls. If an Arab house borders a settlement street its doors are welded shut: Palestinians climb over roofs to reach their buildings. Eighteen checkpoints are located throughout the Old City, so getting from point A to point B can mean multiple metal detectors and inquisitions. Children walk through metal detectors every day on the way to school, their bags inspected.

Settlers carry automatic weapons on the streets. They shoot holes in water tanks on the roofs of Palestinian homes. Sometimes they attack internationals—this happened to an Italian group, according to the HRC.

"The Hebron settlers are effective because they are strong," he says. "They don't get permission for building work; they just do it. The settlers took over a building, and the Israeli high court said no, you cannot do this. But a commander declared it a military zone. If the soldiers come in, tell us to go, we cannot stay. So the settlers kept the building. The Israelis are strong. We are not."

Since 1996, the HRC has renovated nine hundred buildings, supplying five thousand Palestinians with homes and preventing the military from confiscating empty properties. A range of organizations and foreign governments—including Sweden, Spain, Germany, Ireland, Canada—have provided assistance.

When the presentation is over, Fateen, who has been pacing in and out of the lecture hall, triumphantly raises his cell phone. "We've found Jerome," he says.

Jerome had wandered into a shop almost as soon as we arrived. He left, looked for us on the cramped sidewalk, couldn't find us. Eventually he entered another store and showed the owner his badge. The owner spoke some French. He took Jerome's badge and called Fateen. As the owner made the call, Jerome asked him, "Do you speak Arabic?"

Which would be like traveling to France and asking a shopkeeper if he speaks French.

Hebron's Ibrahimi Mosque, also known as the Tomb of the Patriarchs, is a sacred site to Muslims and Jews alike. The stone structure, roughly two thousand years old, is said to be the final resting place of Abraham and his wife Sarah, along with their son Isaac, grandson Jacob, and the two men's wives. In 1994, on the fifteenth day of Ramadan, Baruch Goldstein, a physician and settler, entered the crowded mosque and opened fire on the nearly 800 worshippers, slaughtering 29 Palestinians and wounding 125 others. Goldstein was eventually hit in the head with a fire extinguisher and beaten to death by survivors. He remains a hero to many Hebron settlers.

The massacre of Palestinian worshippers led to a series of security measures that affect . . . Palestinian worshippers. To pray, Palestinians pass through a series of post-Goldstein checkpoints, which we experience as we visit the mosque: the turnstiles in an old tunnel, the stern guard in an obligatory booth. After that, we head to another checkpoint, walking through metal detectors and providing our bags for inspection. A soldier inspects Peter's bag, and seems puzzled as he pulls out a can of shaving cream, soap, shampoo, washcloth, brush . . .

We proceed one by one, congregating on a walkway to the mosque and waiting for the rest of our group, which annoys the soldiers. They tell us to move farther up. I'm reminded of something the HRC speaker said of the mosque: "It's not a holy place—it's a military base."

Inside, we remove our shoes; the women put on gray hooded cloaks. We pass the women's praying area. It's a series of white arches and gold lamps, the floor lined with red-and-blue rugs. The main prayer area, which is coed, is larger and more open, the design more elaborate, its domes painted in blues and reds and whites. Security cameras, like Orwellian eyeballs, hang in the mosque, watching every person and prayer. We see the green doors where Goldstein entered along a back wall, nubs in the marble from the bullets' spray.

When we leave, Samir, our rapper roommate, is detained by the soldiers. He and Habib were stopped on the way in: they're both from a neighborhood that fought an Israeli incursion during the Second Intifada (ID cards issued by the Palestinian Authority show your religion and your neighborhood). No one knows why Samir is held. He seems like the last guy who'd be singled out for questioning, just because . . . he's preppy. More L.L.Bean than Islamic Jihad.

We stand, waiting for him near the checkpoint. The soldiers yell at us to move.

"Just stand against the wall and wait," Fateen tells us.

"We won't leave without him!" the bossy New York woman barks.

"We won't leave him," Fateen says calmly. "It's better if we're out of the way."

We gather by the wall, again drawing the ire of the soldiers. Fateen tells us to go through the security turnstiles back to the market. He stays and talks with the soldiers while children try to sell us key chains and bracelets with Palestinian colors. Joe-hammad sits on a step, morose. Margaret, a Canadian college student, starts to cry. A Scottish student holds her. Others use the time to buy sandwiches, candy, scarves. We hear theories about why Samir is being held. Someone says he was lippy when we entered. Others say his papers weren't in order. Monique says the soldiers didn't like the Palestinian flag stickers some volunteers wore on their shirts.

Forty-five minutes pass before Samir is released. He holds a document instructing him to report to authorities tomorrow for an interview, which seems a tad odd.

Clearly you're dangerous but, eh . . . come back tomorrow.

He receives handshakes and hugs. He's not sure if he was stopped because of his neighborhood—"Because of that, the soldiers didn't like me," he says—or if it was random: they sometimes stop every third person or so who enters to pray.

Fateen reassures him. He shouldn't have any problems. Samir has never been arrested, he's traveled to Europe (which means he's been approved for visas), and he's never been shot, which is, we're told, another oddity of the region: if you've been shot you're considered a security risk. The day we built rock walls, one of the farmers told Kayla that he wanted to move to Amman—his daughter was engaged to a Jordanian there—but he couldn't leave because he was shot years before.

Now that we have Samir back, we wind through the mazelike market—an open-air souk—following Fateen. An old man sells black-and-white keffiyehs. "Merry Christmas!" he says. "How are you! Merry Christmas!"

Above our heads, from one side of the souk to the other, is a wavy, horizontal, chain-link fence. The market is next to a building where settlers live. From their windows, the settlers throw garbage down on the Palestinians below. The fence serves as a metal net, to block the plummeting trash. Much of the hanging debris is decaying in dead, mysterious lumps. I look up and spot what appears to be a milk carton, rotting and limp.

Since the day I passed through the checkpoint into the West Bank, I've tried to remind myself that I'm only hearing the Palestinian perspective. That I haven't made Israeli friends the way I'm making Palestinian friends. That anguish exists in Israel just as it does in Palestine. Because I know the Israelis are good people. I know the Palestinians are good people. I truly believe, despite centuries of evidence otherwise, that *all* people are basically good. No one is born evil; no one is xenophobic in the womb. We are tainted by hand-me-down hate. Habib says of the settlers in Hebron, "Their only contact with us is to beat us, or throw whatever they can at us." As far as I can tell, the bulk of Hebron's ultra-Orthodox settlers are—and please forgive the lack of subtlety—wackos. Extremist, militant, out-of-control nuts. And that nuttiness is being passed to future generations; to the children who throw rocks and learn cute kill-the-Arabs ditties in school. Even many Israelis think the Hebron settlers are fanatics. But who am I to judge? I don't know these people any more than they know me. And ignorance, and isolation, and fallacy are all twined in hatred's DNA.

I don't believe in taking sides here, because each side can match sorrow for sorrow, atrocity for atrocity, rage for rage. In the months after my departure, Hamas gunmen will kill four Israeli settlers, including a pregnant woman, just outside Hebron. Animosity grows here like olives. But as I walk under a fence installed to catch trash hurled by one people against another, I can at least say here's no equality of power here. Some people have it, some people don't.

Being here has changed my view of oppression. Oppression is not simply about guns and tanks and bombs. Oppression is a thousand daily inconveniences. It is tortoise-speed checkpoints and lines, lines, lines. It's being frisked before you enter a house of worship, and being detained by soldiers when you leave. It's security cameras watching as you pray. It's the lives of an armed few dominating the lives of the unarmed many. It's your neighbors pelting you with insults and stones. It's hanging a fence to stop the falling trash, rather than stopping the trash from falling.

Always look at the other side, Dad wrote. *Often you don't fully understand things unless you put yourself in the other person's shoes.*

We walk past the stalls to a street corner. A teenage boy tries to sell bracelets to me and Monique. He shows us the road behind a gate, the road now closed. Guard towers peer down.

"Please buy," says the boy. "Very hard here. No business. Please buy."

He holds up the bracelet. It's the colors of the Palestinian flag.

Earlier, on our way to the Ibrahimi Mosque, we'd seen a once-thriving market that's now a dead zone due to road closures. Rows of green garage-style doors, all closed, none of the shops open. No trash. No people. Our morning host from the HRC had remembered his boyhood, the souk so crowded that he clutched his father's hand, afraid of losing him forever.

Over 70 percent of Palestinian shops are now closed, he said.

"Please buy," says the boy. "Please buy."

Monique and I apologize. We don't buy.

We walk back to the IPYL office, a thirty-minute trek. Once there we eat sandwiches and watch a documentary, *If Americans Knew*, produced by the U.S. organization of the same name. We take cabs back to Bethlehem. Eight of us are packed in a sedan with one local woman in front. It's dark. Our driver tailgates other cars, blinking his lights. He passes when he shouldn't pass—while approaching blind turns. Mike is next to me, offering concerned commentary.

"Don't, don't . . . please—don't . . ."

The driver roars left past four cars on a two-lane road, a pair of headlights glowing ahead.

"Oh God . . . Don't . . ."

We swerve back to our lane.

The driver keeps shouting, pointing his finger. We can't tell if he's talking with the older woman in front or yelling at other drivers.

"The problem with people who believe in the afterlife is that they don't care about this life," says Mike. "I don't really want to die yet."

We zoom past another car. "I want a Snickers bar after this," says Mike. "Actually, if I go through the windshield, melt it and give it to me intravenously." And then—*screeeech*—we come to almost a complete stop, creeping over inverted speed bumps. Mike shakes his head.

"I don't understand anything about this place."

The closer it gets to Christmas, the more I feel the stinging distance of home. I say this despite hearing "Jingle Bells" in Arabic at a Manger Street tourist shop; despite seeing an inflated sidewalk Santa bouncing in the wind. I've seen Kris Kringle's image in Bethlehem more than Jesus Christ's. Not far from the Stars & Bucks Café—a terrific corporate rip-off; it's the same black-and-green color scheme as Starbucks, with Stars & Bucks T-shirts for sale—a cardboard Santa flashes a peace sign from a restaurant window. Behind the window an Arab family waits for lunch, two older women wearing head scarves, Coke bottles on the table.

I've splurged a few times and bought a Coke from the sparse market near the center, along with the occasional candy bar—a substitute for the usual holiday sweets. Back home, Christmas Eve at my sister's house is all about the cookies: chocolate chip and peanut butter and iced sugar cookies. On Christmas Day Julie's mother makes an early dinner of ham and scalloped potatoes, with birthday carrot cake (Julie's request) for dessert.

I'm part of the team that's responsible for tonight's dinner, so I know we won't be eating anything that tasty. It's me, Conor, Carina, and a Belgian woman. The night before we met with Samir in the kitchen to discuss what we need—and more important, what we can afford. Conor has cooking experience so he's in charge. He wanted five roasted chickens, mainly as a time saver, but Samir says it's too expensive. So after a lot of bargaining—Conor had wanted apples, but if we give up apples can we have chickens?—we settle for five chickens, uncooked.

"Here we are in Palestine and the most contentious fookin' meetings are about the Christmas party and what to have for dinner," says Conor.

The Christmas party has been settled, but not without another contentious meeting—

Turkish bath, one free soda, D.J. . . .

Why don't we combine the parties on the twenty-fifth and twenty-sixth?

I can't make the decision; you make the decision!

I help cut carrots, apples, and tomatoes for dinner. The chickens are full chickens, heads and all. Conor chops off the necks, and cooks a delicious-smelling stew in a giant pot with onions and potatoes. He and I carry it, each of us holding a handle, lugging it down the outdoor steps from the apartment. Skinny feral cats scurry to hide as we walk. We haul the heavy pot through the alleyway into the center, up three flights to where we dine. It seems like a huge amount of food, but it's consumed quickly.

"It is very good," says Mahad with a grin, though he seems like the kind of guy who would say that regardless. Mahad has kept a low profile during the Christmas party nonsense. Everything was finally sorted out: some people will go to a party hosted by a non-profit; others, myself included, will go to a resort, tempted mainly by the Turkish bath. We've agreed to pay extra so some Palestinians can come. Mahad, however, quietly declined the offer. From what I heard, he was uncomfortable with others paying his way. It was a personal choice, made without self-righteous pronouncements. I admire that.

Maybe it's because he's a part-time artist—Mahad painted one of the murals we saw on the wall at the Aida camp—but he seems more reserved than the other Palestinian men. Kayla says Mahad spent three years in an Israeli jail. When he was first detained, his hands were cuffed behind his back for twelve hours, his arms raised to just below his shoulders. The worst thing, he told Kayla, is that the soldiers never asked questions. They just held him. For three years. Given that he's promoting nonviolence, that he talks of boycotts rather than bombs, I assume he was arrested for his political views. You don't really have to *do* something to be arrested. In Hebron, Kayla talked with a Red Cross worker. During the Second Intifada, the military declared almost four hundred curfew days in Hebron over three years. Sometimes the curfews lasted up to seven days in a row, which meant you stayed inside. If you didn't, you could get shot or arrested. Because of the curfews, a lot of Palestinians who worked in Israel lost their jobs.

The Red Cross worker was a teenager at the time. Once, after three curfew days, desperate for fresh air, he snuck from his home for a break, and a soldier saw him by the door. The teenager—fourteen at the time—was arrested.

Three days before Christmas we work at a center for abused women in Bethlehem. It's a nice place: arched pink ceilings, stone walls, Persian-style tile, a needlepoint map of Palestine. In the office are new computers—the center receives government funding, says Fateen—and a framed picture of Arafat. I've seen far more framed Arafats in Palestine than framed Maos in China, even though in 2004, the year of his death, 87 percent of Palestinians believed his government was corrupt. I assume he's remembered more for his defiance than for any lasting deeds.

The women are baking. They roll small balls of dough, and the center fills quickly with a soothing, waffle-like smell. Behind flour-dusted aprons they're dressed in stylish Western clothes. Bethlehem, or at least the parts I've seen, seems moderate. This isn't Saudi

Arabia, where only a woman's eyes are uncloaked. More Palestinian women are in universities than men, a woman from the UNWRA's women's office told us one night, though most jobs are for men, assuming they can find work. The women tend to get married, then earn side income through jobs like cutting hair. At the Handala Center, a group of about thirty women do embroidery, using traditional designs to create everything from handbags to glasses cases. In some households it's the only stable income.

We clean up the gardens and grounds. While others dig up weeds and trim trees, I focus on a trash-filled corner, where a tall stone fence meets a vine-covered cinder-block wall. Pedestrians must toss their trash from the sidewalk above: I collect candy wrappers, soda cans, water bottles, cigarette butts and boxes, chip bags, broken glass, torn newspaper pages—it's like excavating a 7-Eleven Dumpster. Afterward, I help carry cut tree branches and vine trimmings to a dump spot across the street, then dig holes to plant daisies. Conor is building what looks like a well with rocks, which is later filled in with dirt and flowers. He'd prefer flatter rocks.

"It's a fookin' humpy fook," he says, pointing at one.

I'm guessing this is not an actual geologic term. It becomes, however, my mental synonym for a struggle. The Israeli-Palestinian conflict? *It's a fucking humpy fuck.*

Lunch, made by the women who run the center, is our tastiest, most satisfying meal yet. I load a plastic plate with *sfeeha*—mini doughy pizzas with lamb meat and onions and peppers—then dip pitas in a bowl of yogurt sauce, a trail of olive oil on top with basil and tomatoes, and scoop spoonfuls of green olives and a salad of oil-drenched tomatoes and cucumbers. Once we're done the ladies serve afternoon tea. They seem grateful. The grounds are transformed. Clean, neat, welcoming. Bright with fresh flowers.

That afternoon I join Monique and Perrine and a few others for coffee at a local restaurant. In Hebron, on the long walk from the Ibrahimi Mosque to the IPYL offices, Monique and I talked the entire way, discussing everything from the head scarf issue in France (she thinks it's silly) to a previous volunteer gig in Djibouti (very sad) to her job teaching philosophy to high school students. She lives in a depressed region, and the students aren't interested in the class; they don't see the point, or they're only concerned with grades. She thinks often of quitting, perhaps spending a year in the West Bank, though the restrictions on women make her wary.

"I wonder how women deal with the rules they follow and what they see on TV—your American shows."

"You mean the wholesome all-American values portrayed in our fine high-quality network programming?"

She looks ill.

"The problem is that you get all our worst shows," I say. "I was in Paris once and saw *Knight Rider* dubbed in French. You don't get the good stuff."

"I did not know any of it was good."

"Of course it's good. Except—okay, most of it's crap, but some of it's good crap."

"Even if it is good crap it shows a life they cannot live."

"Okay, I'll give you that one."

"I talked with a woman today at the women's center," she says. "She says Islam does not allow men to beat women."

"Well, they must be ignoring that or the center wouldn't exist."

Kayla noticed that girls play on the roofs of buildings, while the boys play in the street. Fateen said it's because fathers want to protect their daughters. Violence is less of a problem in Bethlehem, which is stable at the moment, but more worrisome in cities like Hebron, where hostility can easily erupt.

After coffee we head back to the center, then walk to a protest for political prisoners. The mayor of Bethlehem speaks—the protest is in front of a Palestinian telecommunications building—and he invokes Jesus, calling him a political prisoner (or so Doug tells us after eavesdropping on a translation in the crowd). Women and families stand by a Christmas tree and hold photographs of imprisoned husbands and sons. If protests are a form of political theater, this is not a particularly exciting show.

"I did not know protests could be so boring," says Monique.

Our own near-prisoner, Samir, has returned from his interview at an Israeli military base. Samir's father gave him this advice: "Whatever they offer you, don't accept it." It's a standard strategy: the interviewers deprive you of something—in Samir's case, heat (he waited for two hours in a refrigerator-cold room)—then become your buddy by giving you what you want, or need, so you'll offer something in return. Armed with this insight, he walked through a metal detector, got frisked, raised his shirt for wanding. After that he was taken to a different location. At long last his interrogator arrived.

"Are you nervous?" the questioner asked.

"No—I'm cold."

The questioner, Samir said, spoke better Arabic than he did.

"You're cold—do you want some tea?"

"No."

"Coffee?"

"No."

"If you're cold you must want something. Hot water?"

"No—I don't want anything. Please stop asking."

And so it continued.

Do you want this?

No.

Do you want that?

No.

The offers improved.

"Do you own a car?"

"No."

"You must want a car—you need a car."

"My father owns a car and I'm the primary driver."

"Do you have any friends?"

"No—I have no friends."

"How can you not have any friends—you're in university."

"I live with my cousins."

"What are their names?"

After a few hours, they let him go. Being detained and questioned is almost a rite of passage for Palestinian men. Now he's one of the boys.

Although we've happily regained Samir, we've unexpectedly said goodbye to Patrick, a tall Irishman. Late last night, Patrick returned to the flat drunk, and tried to crawl into Conor's sleeping bag. This was problematic, since Conor was already *in* the sleeping bag. Patrick apologized to Conor the following morning, and to Fateen as well, public drunkenness being a headache Fateen does not need. As we departed for the women's center, Patrick asked Fateen if he could skip work. When we came back, his stuff was gone. According to the rumor mill, Patrick got cabin fever, couldn't handle the stress of Palestine, needed to study for his master's—no one knows for sure.

Rather than mourn Patrick's departure, I steal his mattress pad, and Conor and Tyler spread out their stuff, moving their sleeping bags to create a bit more room. "I just picked up twelve inches of space," says Conor. "I'm occupying it like the fookin' Israelis do."

The last few years before he died, Dad and I would go Christmas shopping together at least once: him for Mom, me for Julie, both of us clueless about what to buy. The trip always involved lunch, usually at Burger King. How this tradition started, I don't remember—it was typically the only day in the year that I'd eat at Burger King—but a Whopper and fries was part of the deal. And it was usually the highlight given that we're both such lousy shoppers.

The first Christmas after his death I was at Fair Oaks Mall, where we would usually go, and I saw a man from behind in a department store: same height as Dad, same green winter jacket, same black and gray hair. For a flash I thought it was him. I actually stopped as I was walking. And just as instantly I realized—

No. Duh. Of course not.

Looking back, as a child, I rarely remember Dad having fun. He was always working, whether it was office work (which to him *was* fun) or chores around the house. I can picture him raking leaves and shoveling snow, walking to the carport in winter for firewood, wearing a beat-up jacket he called Old Blue. Mom always wanted to throw Old Blue in the garbage. Dad refused. He was an even-tempered man, almost impossible to ruffle, so on the few occasions when he *did* get mad, it was shocking. Once Mom nagged him repeatedly to move his briefcase from the top of the stairs. So finally he picked it up—and threw it down the steps.

Whoa.

Dad loved aviation, and had he gone to college, I'm convinced he'd have majored in aeronautics. We'd go the massive air show at Andrews Air Force Base when I was young, marveling at the acrobatic Thunderbirds and Blue Angels, the Hawker Harrier jet hovering above heat waves on the runway. Once, as an adult, I was traveling for work, and stopped in California for a few days to see my parents. Dad and I went to an air show at a nearby base. It was brutally hot, so he bought a Blue Angels hat to protect his head from the sun. After he died, that hat was one of the few things I asked for from Mom.

One year as a kid I received a Vertibird as a Christmas gift. The Vertibird was a small helicopter attached by an arm to a mechanical center. It came with a little controller for making the Vertibird climb and fly in circles. Dad loved the Vertibird. He sat on the floor, piloting the Vertibird round and round, making it go up and down. The copter had a hook on the bottom for picking up a plastic space capsule and life raft. He hovered the helicopter over the life raft, lowering it, lowering it . . . slowly . . . lowering it . . . the hook getting close—

Got it.

I had more fun watching Dad operate the Vertibird than I did playing with it myself.

A mother plays with her baby girl on the street in front of the center. She sets the girl on the hood of a parked car—the girl can't be more than two—walks about ten feet away, turns around . . . and runs toward her! The girl giggles before she arrives, waving her arms, squealing before the mom scoops her up and lifts her—*Wooooooo!*

As usual, we're killing time before working, so I lean against an abandoned white van, watching. The van has a flat tire in back, tarlike gunk on its sides. Garbage lies underneath: cans and plastic bottles. People tend to throw their trash on the ground here. Even Fateen does it; I saw him toss an empty bottle on the street. It annoys me, but maybe that's part of the lingering booted-from-your-village mentality. Discarded people, discarded waste.

A few nights ago, folks at the other end of the street celebrated the release of a camp resident who'd spent five years in an Israeli prison. When he arrived, everyone cheered, fireworks flared; the men embraced him, dancing in the street, the women watching from windows and rooftops above. Banners stretched from building to building with Palestinian flags and strings of colored lights. The residents at that end of the street, I've been told, are members of Fatah.

I keep leaning against the van, watching the woman and her daughter, when finally a jean-jacketed Palestinian gentleman, his head wrapped in a red-and-white keffiyeh, arrives to tell us our work plan. We'll be helping a farmer clear his land in the mountains overlooking Bethlehem. The farmer recently was granted access to his land, but he has to farm it, or he risks losing it (in some cases, unregistered land that is uncultivated for three years can be declared state land and used for settlements). The owner has paperwork saying the land remains his if he clears the brush and builds walls.

Someone asks if soldiers are likely to appear.

"No, *inshallah*"—God willing—"but it has happened in the past. If the soldiers arrive, don't talk to them. The owner will talk to them. He has the paperwork."

It's a roundabout bus trek because of the security wall and settlements. Cameras stare from chain-link fences; jets roar above. When we arrive, stopping on a dirt road, the farmer explains our job: digging out a dry brush called *natsh*. The brush is prickly, surrounded by rocks; a hardy, thorny plant well suited to the harsh, arid, treeless terrain.

We grab picks, using the narrow end to dig up rocks, the wide end to dig out the plant. Once extracted, the brush is thrown into piles. Even with gloves the pointy plants are hard to hold.

It's warm out. I wipe my forehead with my forearm. Swing, swing—hit rock—swing. The brush is *everywhere*.

An old Palestinian man works, red and white keffiyeh on his head, two black cloth rings holding it place. He's wearing a gray *dishdasha*—a gown that stretches to his feet—and a long black vest. At noon, he stops, get on his knees, and prays.

After lunch, a shepherd leads goats and sheep through the rocks. The animals stop and eat some of the brush. When the old man joins him, the scene is almost biblical, except for the number of people (myself included) taking photos, the sprawl of Bethlehem in the distance below. I set my camera on a rock, attempting a timed photo. Julie is normally the photographer on our trips. A red light blinks before the camera clicks.

Monique walks toward me across the hot rocks. We admire the view.

"It looks pretty from here," she says.

"Things always look so much nicer from a distance. It's like those photos of Earth from space. You'd never realize how screwed up the place is from just seeing this big blue orb."

We stare a bit longer at the scenery.

"I hear you bought that little boy's postcards," I say as we walk back to our picks. The boy who was always holding postcards above his head is now holding pencils.

She smiles. "I needed a souvenir," she says.

By the time we're done, our sunburned, sweaty group has cleared three massive piles of the stubborn brush and started a rock wall. The jean-jacketed host boards the bus as we leave.

"Thank you for your hard work," he says. "You do an honorable job because you are the first ones here. In a few weeks, we will plant olive trees."

I hope that's true, though I wonder. Supposedly more volunteers will clear more brush, and professionals will build retaining walls and plant the trees. Kayla talked with a woman from the Palestinian Authority's Interior Ministry who came to observe our work. She told Kayla of the ministry's efforts to track down deeds to the land, which will aid their legal battle. Most of the records date back to the Ottoman Empire, she said, so the ministry is seeking assistance from the Turkish government.

The farmer waves. Everyone applauds as he walks off the bus, facing the parched land that is his land, for now, where he'll keep uprooting the thorny brush, separating it from the dry dirt.

At a meeting one evening, a few volunteers asked for a nonsmoking area in the center, which is like asking for a ban on screaming babies in a maternity ward. Fateen estimates that 99 percent of Palestinian men smoke, and probably 75 percent of women (though rarely in public). I'm not loving the smoke, either, but it's the Palestinians' center, we're guests, they like to smoke—or need to smoke—so who are we to demand changes? Just suck it up—literally—for two weeks or stay outside.

The cigarette brand of choice seems to be Jamal, a Palestinian product, though American cigarettes are popular as well. We may not be giving them freedom or equality or apple pie, but by God we are giving them lung cancer. I've seen Palestinian boys who look twelve years old, if not younger, with cigarettes hanging from their mouths.

The children here sadden me, how conditioned they are to inferiority, the expectation that violence and arrests and bullshit are part of life. Two nights before Christmas, in one of the Handala offices, volunteers and locals make Christmas ornaments for IPYL's ten-foot-tall Christmas tree. It's intended, as Fateen said our first day, as a political statement: the ornaments are Israeli tear gas canisters and bullet cases and mortar shells found in Beit Jibrin and Bethlehem. The tree will also be decorated with plastic cups, each with the name of a village taken by the Israelis in 1948 and 1967.

The office is crowded with people and stuff: a desk and shelves and a table for the ornaments. Above a computer, taped to a cabinet, is a printout that looks like an eye exam:

E

N D

T H E

O C C U

P A T I O N

Local kids help with the decorations, including Rafid, the boy who danced during the rap show. He's maybe eleven or twelve, and desperate for attention. He grabs volunteers' cameras, wanting to take photos. He hangs on people. He's clingy. While folks work on the ornaments, he holds up two Israeli tear gas canisters and yells for Doug to take his picture. Later, outside, he holds a shell on his shoulder. A local takes his photo.

This is how boys get attention and validation. I saw the same thing at the al-Masara protest, the children posing for pictures in front of the razor wire and soldiers, unfazed by the weapons.

One day our flat came under assault from some of the local kids. They pelted our door with cucumbers and other assorted vegetables. I'm not sure if they were provoked or if it just seemed like a fun thing to do. Conor went on the roof another afternoon to play his mandolin, and four kids tried to take the instrument. The black case was open next to him; inside were two cigars he was bringing home to a friend. The kids snapped them in pieces.

Conor smacked one of the kids upside the head.

"They were nicer to me after that," he says.

Are these just a few bad kids? Or is this anger that's lurking in each of them?

Mahad and others carry the long, skinny tree to a street corner. Busloads of tourists are arriving in town for Christmas Eve. The tree is positioned in an old metal barrel and leans against a wall. I wonder if tourists will get the opposite message; if they'll see it as anti-Christmas. Like firing rubber bullets at Rudolph. A big jingle-bombs middle finger to Santa and sleigh rides.

A few reporters document the scene, some cabbies honk as they pass. Volunteers lead a chorus of "We Wish You a Merry Christmas." The next morning, the tree is still there, but some of the armaments are gone. I assume they were taken by the children.

Monique asks if I want to walk along the separation wall. I can't imagine why she wants to see it up close—or why she wants me to go with her—but I walk with her after breakfast. We leave the Handala Center, passing fresh trash on the street: cigarette boxes and orange peels. A bread man pushes a cart through the alleyways, announcing his morning wares.

Khubz . . . Khubz . . . Khubz . . .

We turn left on Manger Street and stroll next to the massive wall and graffiti.

"Mahad does not like the graffiti," she says. "He thinks the wall should be ugly."

"I don't think he has much to worry about."

"I think the graffiti is good. Most of the messages are peaceful."

"Well, I can see his point. If you paint it it's kind of like you're accepting it."

"I like the expression."

"You notice almost all of it's in English."

"It is probably dangerous for Palestinians to write with the towers watching."

We keep walking. I pull my video camera from my canvas bag and shoot some of the graffiti, assuming that I, too, am being watched.

"We should probably head back," I finally say. We're supposed to meet at the center around 10 a.m.—I think—to find out if we're working.

She stares at the wall. "I don't care anymore," she says.

She thinks we have the morning off. I heard we're planting trees. I convince her to walk back, where Fateen tells us that yes, it's Christmas Eve, so the day is open.

"You should listen to me," she says. "You are not so clever."

We go for coffee on Manger Street, in the direction of Manger Square. Across from a traffic circle is the Marvel Restaurant. Inside, we say hello to the owner, who wears a bright orange Marvel sweatshirt.

"May we sit outside," Monique asks.

He smiles and drags a table to the sidewalk. Monique sits in the sun.

"It's like a French café," I say.

She pulls her cigarettes from her purse.

"So I wonder if you are happy you came here," she says.

I'm surprised by the question.

"I don't know if I'd use the word *happy*, but sure—I'm glad I came. I mean, it's good to see this. It's been educational. This isn't the story we hear at home."

She lights the cigarette.

"You look lonely."

This surprises me even more, though I appreciate her concern.

"You always look so serious," she says. "Always off by yourself. You walk from one corner of a room to another."

"I didn't think it was noticeable. I hope people don't think I'm a stalker."

"That is what they think." She smiles and blows smoke.

"I don't know," I say. "The whole place kind of depressed me. Watching those men run to the checkpoint. And then going *through* the checkpoint. And seeing the wall. It's all so . . . dehumanizing. Plus—most people here are younger than me. I could be the Finnish girl's father. And I'm by myself. So I tend to just *stay* by myself."

We talk about Fateen and Perrine. I only recently learned that they're a couple. She's French, and he's fluent: he studied French literature and grammar through a university cultural exchange program in 2003. Perrine is becoming a Muslim today so they can get married. Because they're not yet husband and wife, and because the West Bank is predominantly Muslim, they can't act like a couple. Which is why I was clueless.

Romances are blooming among the volunteers as well. Some of the female volunteers are falling for local Palestinians, and volunteers are hooking up with other volunteers. One couple, Monique tells me, spent the night at a local hotel. They told the owner they were married but the Mrs., oops, didn't have her passport.

"Wow—I didn't even know they liked each other."

She makes fun of the word *like*. Sometimes she'll repeat certain words I use, imitating me in a nasally American voice. *Walking* and *talking* become a flat "waalking" and "taalking."

"The women in our room—they talk about the Palestinian men that are most attractive."

"Forbidden fruit," I say.

"And they talk about showers. They are obsessed with showers." Kayla has said this as well: the women are competitive about taking showers, and lamenting that they can't take more showers and longer showers. If the roles had been reversed—if the women's building had lost water instead of the men's—I have no doubt the women would have commandeered our flat.

"I am so sick of talking about showers," she says.

We pay our bill and walk back to the camp. White trucks packed with Palestinian Authority security forces drive by; men in green uniforms with black machine guns. "Ah, the police with their machine guns," I say. "You can tell it's almost Christmas."

There's a demonstration that afternoon on Manger Street near the camp as tourists and dignitaries arrive in town. I'm not sure who organized it—I assume our hosts—though it's small: mainly our group of volunteers and some local teens; a chance to again remind out-of-towners of the Palestinians' plight. A teenager hands me a sign, poster-sized, tacked to a wood handle. Monique has one as well. The sign is in Arabic, and—I'm sorry. I refuse to hold a sign when I don't know what it says. I hand it to one of the teens.

A motorcade of black cars—presumably Palestinian Authority president Mahmoud Abbas—drives slowly past, men in black suits walking on both sides. Monique talks with a French tourist couple. I ask her what they said.

"I told them about why we are here, and the man said you will not go home the same."

"That's true—you'll stink from the lack of showers."

She whacks me on the head with her sign. She has a charm that seems particularly bright here; a mix of seriousness and playfulness that makes Beit Jibrin seem not so sad. Later, she balances the sign on her head and carefully raises her arms, like a tightrope walker.

"This is so the planes can read the sign," she says.

In 1958, a month or two before Dad graduated from Wakefield High School, he went on the senior class bus trip to New York City. My father had some wild friends back then, though Dad himself was not a terribly wild guy. But on the senior trip, he and his buddies got so drunk that he was kicked off the baseball team, forbidden from attending the senior prom, forbidden from attending graduation. Their behavior was *so* bad that Wakefield actually ended its senior class trip program due to Dad and his drunken pals. Which is impressive in a Bluto kind of way.

Telling you this story is disrespectful, according to my mother. (Which is why she won't reveal what Dad and his pals *did* while drunk.) But I don't want you to think Dad was perfect, or that I've exalted him to some saintlike position in my mind. Dad had failings and flaws like any of us. His steady manner, I suppose, made it seem like he had fewer.

"He didn't need to be the center of attention," said Kevin, Dad's friend. Kevin still maintains that my father was the best manager he ever worked for. "He wasn't someone who had to hear himself talk. He didn't need to be the loudest person in the room. He evaluated people and their strengths and put them in a position to succeed."

Dad became something of a wine drinker after moving to California, not all that surprising given their proximity to Napa. When he and Mom moved back to Virginia, I noticed he was drinking a gin and tonic every evening. One before dinner. Maybe one after. Sometimes two. I never thought it was a problem, but I wondered, at times, if it was the start of a problem. Had he lived, had he become bored by retirement—

"No way," said Kevin, who doesn't drink. "He was too disciplined."

I always admired that discipline; the management books he read, the long hours. But as I got older, I thought his priorities were misguided. He regretted not spending more time with us, and you know what? He *should* have spent more time with us. It's not that I feel cheated; I feel like he cheated himself.

Now that I'm in the Middle East over Christmas, away from Julie, I see more easily how it happens. You tell yourself you'll make up for it. You justify it. Dad balanced his own ambitions by saying my sister and I would never experience a childhood like his own. I've told myself that being here, alone, will strengthen my marriage, because I had to break free of my no-kids funk. One mid-December night, about six months before Dad's death, I turned on the Christmas tree lights—Julie had already gone to bed; I'd worked late that night—and lay down on the couch. I read some Christmas cards, including holiday letters from long-lost friends, the kind with clip art and photos and happy paragraphs about their kids' many accomplishments. And reading those letters about first steps and family trips and report cards and recitals . . . that's the night it hit me. The night I really felt the weight of it.

I'm never going to be a father.

I lay on the couch that night until almost 4 a.m.

I don't have many regrets when it comes to my own father, but one stands out. When I was a kid, Dad worked for a couple of start-up tech companies formed by a friend. Typically the companies failed after a few years. I remember how thrilled he was when he was hired at a Fortune 500 company, because it meant stability and benefits.

When I was in high school, my next-door neighbor delivered the *Washington Star*, an afternoon newspaper. Each summer their family went on a summer trip to Rehoboth Beach and I'd deliver the papers while they were gone. In 1981, while I was handling the route, the *Star* announced it was ceasing publication. "I'm carrying on the family tradition of killing companies," I told Dad. I was joking, and he knew it, and it would continue to be something of a family joke. But it bothers me that I told him *this*, and never how much I admired him.

No man is indifferent about his father. His life is the standard, good or bad, whether he abandoned us, enlightened us, or burdened us with the weight of his deeds. Anger or esteem, resentment or reverence—you may love your father, you may hate your father, but you are not apathetic about your father.

Dad never wanted me to be *him*. He only wanted me to be happy. He only wanted me to do my best. Here in the West Bank, I don't feel like I'm accomplishing either.

On Christmas Eve, after helping Doug and Kayla prepare a group lunch of canned tuna and veggies, the three of us walk to Bethlehem. We skipped most of the early-afternoon festivities in town, letting the crowds thin out. Upwards of fifty thousand pilgrims are arriving, mostly Christians, mostly from Israel and the West Bank. Only a few hundred of Gaza's roughly four thousand Christians were granted permits by the Israeli government. While the streets don't seem too packed—many Palestinians can't get here because of the security and the time-consuming hassles—we felt it best to avoid the mass of Christmas tourists squeezing through the Door of Humility into the Church of the Nativity; the visitors watching the annual parade, with bagpipers and Palestinian boy scouts and girl scouts marching to Manger Square.

Sometimes you know pretty quickly when you've made a friend for life, and I feel that way about Doug and Kayla. A few nights ago the three of us went to the Bonjour Café. While walking up the long hill, we met three teenagers coming the opposite way.

"Hello!" said one as we passed.

We all nodded, but none of us said anything—we each thought the other would offer a chipper response—so the teens must have felt dissed, because behind us we heard a loud "Fuck you!"

We busted out laughing. I always seem to laugh with them, and in Beit Jibrin, laughter is a necessity. That first night at the center, the IPYL leader, Adli Daana, told us that Palestinians have a dark sense of humor. It's a coping mechanism.

We enter the old town. "Think anyone else will tell us to fuck off?" I say.

"Merry Christmas—*fuck you!*" says Kayla.

Doug laughs. "There's a Christmas carol you'll never hear."

We have hours of free time until evening, when everyone's heading to Manger Square for Christmas Eve. As we wander through crowded markets, we run into Monique. The four of us walk, eyeing the multitude of wares—the fruits and CDs and clothes and cloths. Doug and Kayla leave for a tour and an olive-carving shopping trip with Joshua, their hotel owner friend, so Monique and I grab a drink. The restaurant—St. George's—looks out on Manger Square. We sit at an outdoor table, watching the square as it fills, the stage workers preparing for the Christmas Eve concert.

It's getting chilly. The temperature was pleasingly warm when I left the camp with Doug and Kayla—near 70 degrees today, compared to the icy postblizzard conditions back home—so I didn't bring my sweater. I cross my arms to keep warm. Somewhere, though we can't see him, a singer croons "Silent Night."

We order a first round of beers, and then a second. I nod my head toward the blond-haired tourist family at the table next to us.

"Let's play a game," I say. "German or not German?"

She studies them. "What do you think."

"I say German. Note the sandals with socks."

She gets up, stands behind them and pretends to survey the square. The father looks up. Monique nods. Merry Christmas, she says. Merry Christmas, they respond. She chats with them for a moment, then sits back down at our table.

"Canadian," she tells me.

"*Canadian?* No way . . ."

She smiles and pulls a cigarette from the box. I shake my head.

"Canadian. Jeez. That's embarrassing."

"You are right to be embarrassed."

"Maybe they're German-Canadians."

"Or they're lying."

She lights a cigarette as I watch.

"Do you want one?"

"Sure—what the hell."

I have maybe two to three cigarettes a year, usually in Richmond. Tom and Adam and Terry are classic beer-makes-me-want-a-cigarette smokers. Meaning they never smoke unless we're at a bar or they've had a few drinks.

I'm not a good smoker.

"Do I look cool?" I ask.

"Oh yes," she says. "You look so cool as you cough."

I ask her how she would normally spend Christmas Eve. She doesn't answer. I get the clear vibe that she doesn't *want* to answer. So I ask if she's bringing home any gifts.

"Maybe I will bring home a child," she says. "Though I will need to split him up to fit in my luggage."

"You can reassemble him when you get home."

Children occasionally wander by the tables asking for money. Monique gave away her last few coins to one boy, but now another is pestering her. I used my last coins for the beer.

"No—I don't have anything," she tells him.

"Yes," he says.

"No—I'm sorry."

"Yes."

He repeats this.

Yes yes yes yes

"I think it's a lost cause," I say.

We decide to head back. The boy finally wanders to another table.

"You are cold," she says.

"Yeah, I should've brought my coat."

She takes my hand and kisses it. We stand up, and I smile, and I think—

What was that? Was that a French thing?

Julie has e-mailed me Christmas Eve photos from home. She sends photos of my mom, my nieces and nephew, my sister's two golden retrievers. The photos are a lifeline to home, and I view them again and again on my tiny screen.

Christmas Eve has always been one of my favorite nights. When I was kid, we'd go with our next-door neighbors for a candlelight church service—we were one of those families that only went on Christmas Eve—and then back to our neighbors' house, where folks would swing by for cookies and ham biscuits and drinks while we hyper kids ran around the basement.

Here in Bethlehem, most of us make a postdinner trek back to Manger Square. Between walking everywhere and limited food given the size of our group—second helpings are no guarantee—I can tell I'm losing more weight. After the daily hikes in Ecuador I was down to about 180 pounds, the least I've weighed since high school. And I feel thinner now.

Once again I'm Doug and Kayla's third wheel. The square is packed; by the time we arrive, around nine o'clock, the concert is booming under bright colored lights. We squeeze our way through the throng. The concert is not choirs singing church songs, but pop music from around the world; a Latin American singer shimmies with her backup singers.

"Notice anything about the crowd?" says Doug.

"It's, like, ninety-five percent men."

"And the only women are foreigners."

The towering Christmas tree by the Church of the Nativity is bright with strands of white light, a beaming star on top. After the salsa singer, belly dancers perform. Men rush the stage, cell phone cameras raised above heads like digital candles. Guys sit on the shoulders of buddies.

"This is probably as close to nudity as it gets here," I tell Doug.

We missed about three-fourths of the concert, and now all the performers join for a final, swaying, arms-around-each-other, peace-on-earth number. And that's pretty much it. The crowd starts thinning out.

"Now what?" I say.

We kind of thought the celebration would last longer than 10 p.m. While milling about the square we run into some of the other volunteers, including Monique, who joins me, Doug, and Kayla. We walk around the back side of the church, looking in the window of a shop selling religious items. In a small wood cradle is a doll, which I presume is baby Jesus but looks oddly like Bob's Big Boy. The four of us have a beer at St. George's, then walk back.

Though it's not yet the twenty-fifth, that afternoon I'd sent Julie a Happy Birthday e-mail.

"I was thinking earlier that we probably haven't been apart for your birthday since we were in college," I wrote. "I am sorry for that: it won't happen again. But you are very much with me, and I hope you have a wonderful Xmas with your parents and an equally happy birthday. I love you very much—see you on Monday. Miss you . . ."

She e-mailed back.

"So what made you decide to make this trip at this particular time?"

I wasn't expecting that response. And because it's e-mail, I can't tell the tone. Is this sarcastic? Is this genuine curiosity? Julie is smarter than me, she's warmer than me, but she's just as enigmatic. So I can't help but wonder if this is code for a question more like—

How could you leave me on Christmas? And my birthday?

I'm sure my answer was unsatisfying: this was pretty much the only time I could find a volunteer gig in the West Bank.

We walk back to Beit Jibrin. Doug and I leave Kayla and Monique at the center and head back to the flat. I unzip my sleeping bag, sweep out some of the grit with my hand, and crawl in, the floor hard despite the blankets underneath. I look at my watch. It's almost midnight. Back home, it's about six o'clock, Christmas morning.

"How do you feel, United States?"

Monique asks me this, sitting on the curb in front of the Handala Center, leaning against a wall, sunglasses on, enjoying a morning cigarette in the sun.

"I feel groggy," I say.

"I do too."

Our volunteer work is done. Had I known this I would have scheduled my flight home earlier. But I'm here, so today, Christmas, is basically a day to explore. Doug and Kayla are heading to Jerusalem; I give them my maps and my *Lonely Planet* book. They're going even though Doug has caught the Handala cold bug that's infecting us one by one. Sore throat, coughing, lots of nose blowing. I've avoided it so far, though viruses are clearly thriving in our tight quarters. We're also sharing cups and silverware, which only sort of get clean. So this is one helluva happy Christmas if you're an infectious microorganism.

A few other folks have upset stomachs. Having learned my lesson from China, I brought plenty of queasy-tummy tablets, which I'm distributing to needy volunteers.

"I hear you have Pepto," Tyler asks me on the street. I feel like a drug dealer.

I sit down next to Monique on the curb, resting my arms on bent knees, the sun warm on my face. A woman with a scarf over her head stands in the doorway next to us and says Merry Christmas. Thank you, we say—Merry Christmas.

Since the day is free, Monique has organized a road trip. She talked with Bruno the Italian snorer: he said Jericho is only an hour away and it's a beautiful trip. So I'm joining Monique and Marcen and Camille, a Belgian woman. After breakfast, we walk down Manger Street to a garage where cabdrivers congregate. Marcen makes a deal with the driver of a minivan. We take a new route in a new direction, passing a homemade Homer Simpson painting on a wall. Hanging from the van's rearview mirror is a small Arafat image, about the size of a baseball card, and below that an American flag air freshener.

"Hey—check it out," I say, pointing at the Stars and Stripes.

Monique hums the beginning of the national anthem and salutes.

After passing through a checkpoint, our driver becomes a lead foot, screeching on tight turns through twisty roads in the harsh, tan mountains.

"This is like one of your American movies," says Monique as we jerk from side to side.

Finally we reach the exit to Jericho. Just outside the town, our driver stops. Behind a white iron fence, surrounded by dirt, is an ancient sycamore tree, its trunk about four feet wide. According to legend, it's the tree from Luke 19:1–10. A rich tax collector named Zacchaeus climbed the tree because he couldn't see Jesus amid the crowd. Jesus saw Zacchaeus and told him he'd spend the night as his guest, which irked some I'm-so-virtuous members of the throng. "He has gone to be the guest of one who is a sinner," sneered a pious observer.

I like those moments when Jesus defies social expectations. He hangs out with the tax collector. Lets the immoral woman scrub his feet. Tells the self-righteous to go ahead and hurl that first stone if they're free of sin.

I've always wondered how the average American would respond if Jesus appeared tomorrow in Anyburb, U.S.A. My own personal belief—and I have zero evidence to support this—is that in much of America, race is less significant than status. As long as you mow your chemical-enhanced Kentucky bluegrass yard and scrub your oyster-gray midsize Volvo XC90, people don't care about color. It's the melting-pot triumph of credit scores over creed. So if a shaggy Palestinian guy in ratty clothes showed up tomorrow with zero cash and zero possessions, claiming to be the messiah, spouting the message that the rich would have an easier time getting that Volvo through a needle's eye than going to heaven, folks would be suspicious. At best, he'd be disregarded as a homeless hippie kook. At worst, an anti-American psychopath. The second coming would result in a second crucifixion.

It's a lovely tree, by the way.

As for the main drag of Jericho, there's not a whole lot here. Our driver hangs out by his minivan as we stroll on third-world streets past churches and mosques and small packed-with-stuff stores. We wander down a dusty side street, stop for a drink at an outdoor sandwich joint, sitting next to sweet-smelling basil plants. I pop open a Coke can. Cow carcasses hang on hooks in butcher shops. Beneath a beat-up blue cart a cat watches us, protecting two squinting kittens.

Monique, Marcen, and Camille speak French and I'm lost. They apologize and I say no, hey, it's understandable. I share the extent of my French:

Hello, goodbye, thank you, you're welcome, hat, egg, cheese, wine, ham, milk, apple juice, empty, shit.

" 'Shit' is good to know," says Marcen.

Marcen is from Morocco, though his accent is more French than Monique's. The English word *good*, as he speaks it, rhymes with *food* or *glued* or *sued*.

Monique teaches me a drinking term: *cul sec*, which is the French equivalent of "bottoms up." It means "dry ass," she says—to leave the glass completely parched. I like *cul sec* so much I jot it down.

We reunite with our driver at the agreed-upon time, and he takes us to Tel es-Sultan, the site of ancient Jericho. It's anywhere from seven to ten thousand years old, though it's now a series of pits, more interesting for the rocky, Mars-like landscape rising beyond to the mountains. Nearby is a cable car that takes the curious to the Mount of Temptation, the spot where, it's said, Jesus was tempted by the devil. A monastery is there, but it's only open in the morning, and we're watching our shekels. We decide to pass.

"We were tempted," says Monique, as we walk to our minivan, "but we did not give in."

I'm thinking the day was a bust when we decide to see the St. George's Monastery. Marcen negotiates with the driver as we zoom past the desert mountains, leaving the highway for a lonely side road. The road ends at a quasi parking lot. There's only one other car, and nothing but overwhelming desert, yet a man has a shaded stand where he makes orange juice. Monique buys a glass.

We walk through a three-arch archway, a cross on top, and then down a winding stone road. The drop-off from the road is steep, a canyon opening up before us, desolate, the sandy mountains seeming soft, as though they'd crumble if you touched them, and yet gritty enough to survive the ages. When we finally see the monastery in the distance, we almost gasp. It's beautiful, carved into the cliffs, and were it not for a few blue and white domes and small red-roof balconies, it would blend into the mountain face. Greek Orthodox monks still live here, as they have since the sixth century.

It's a solemn, peaceful place. Bethlehem's bullet holes, the wall, the soldiers at checkpoints—they seem so far away. We gaze at the mountains, the canyon, the monastery; the few sparse trees like moss at its base; admiring the stillness and becoming part of it.

• • •

After all the debates, and all the meetings, about twenty of us go that night to the Murad Tourist Resort for a Christmas party. Monique was among those who declined; she felt it was inappropriate to stay in a refugee camp and play at a resort. She may be right, though we're joined by Fateen and quite a few of our Palestinian friends. They seem delighted to be here, laughing and joking and sharing a pipe. My argument—and I couldn't sway Monique on this—is that we're pumping money into the local economy. Multiple times, speakers at the Handala Center discussed the drop in tourist dollars because of the Second Intifada and the wall. When I went to New Orleans, spending money in restaurants was probably more valuable than the work we did. I'm sure the same is true here given the high unemployment rates.

"The money will go to the owner," says Monique. "He does not look like he needs money." He's not the owner, but a resort rep named Fahad, a friend of Fateen's who came to the center one night to answer questions. He seemed like an okay guy, though something tells me Fahad's top priority is to take very good care of Fahad.

I'm sticking with my help-the-economy theory. It's easy to be holier-than-thou on these types of trips, and feel that spending cash on pleasure is inappropriate, but the locals seem thrilled that we're drinking coffee and Taybeh beers and ordering falafel sandwiches. Men are working tonight who wouldn't be if we'd stayed at the center feeling pure.

As is always the case here, the resort's splashy brochure, which highlights the four water slides and the garden and pools, makes a political statement:

The resort provides Palestinian residents, who have been denied access to many tourist places beyond the green line due to the crippling occupation and the separation wall, with a space for entertainment and relaxations. The Palestinian people are deter-

mined to enjoy life despite the bitterness of their suffering and
their dire circumstances.

It's worth all the awful meetings for the pool and the hot tub
and the Turkish bath. Everyone is giddy, swimming, splashing,
then running to the saunas. The Turkish bath has olive oil soap
and ropelike pads for scrubbing. It's the first time any of us feel
clean—especially us men—in almost two weeks.

Dinner is in the al-Day'a Tent, a large party room that could
double as a dance hall. The overhead lights give the room a dim
orange hue; a Christmas tree glows near a corner. We start with
pitas and an assortment of dips; dinner is beef with vegetables and
potatoes. A few volunteers had requested a vegetarian meal. The
kitchen replaces the meat with french fries.

A woman sings with a small band after dinner. Fateen and the
others sing along, clapping and laughing. Some of the Europeans
hit the dance floor, as do Kayla and Doug: he moves pretty well
for a guy with a broken leg and a boot. A few of the young Euro
volunteers make out under the pulsing lights. I stay back at our
long table, drinking my one free soft drink, feeling like a very old
chaperone, though that's not a complaint. Some people pine for
their youth, but I can't imagine wanting to be twenty again; to be
forty and missing high school. A friend once told me a man's best
years are in his thirties, but I think my forties will be my peak. I
have nothing to base this on, just a gut feeling. A persistent belief
in possibilities.

On the ride back, Kayla and Paul discuss music. Paul McCart-
ney's name comes up.

"He's such a wanker," says Kayla.

"A wanker?" I say. "The man wrote 'Hey Jude.'"

"He's a wanker."

"What about 'Eleanor Rigby'? Or 'Let It Be'?"

"Wanker."

I laugh. "Merry Christmas, Kayla."

"Merry Christmas, Kenny."

Our last day, Fateen organizes a trip to the Dead Sea. I'm excited to see it; so excited that I don't mind clambering into yet another minimal-leg-room bus to make the same drive we made yesterday (only farther). When we reach the checkpoint, Fateen asks for everyone's passport. He gives the stack to a soldier.

"Two Palestinian flags are hanging on the windshield," says Monique with a nod of her head. The tiny flags hang from suction cups. "That is very provocative."

"We need the American flag air freshener from yesterday."

"This air freshener is red—they will think we are Communists."

As we wait—the national pastime here—Conor questions the effectiveness of examining our passports and not examining the bus.

"What's to stop us from having a terrorist in here?" he says.

The gate finally rises and we drive past concrete barriers to the highway, passing settlements on a peak with palm-tree-lined entrances. The settlements look down on slums; cluttered clotheslines and rusted roofs with rusting water tanks. We exit the desert highway, then head down a side road to the beach, passing several empty, deserted, neglected buildings.

At the first beach, Fateen gets out, then comes back. We can't go here. Why, someone asks. "Because they don't allow Palestinians," he says.

We go to the second beach. The same thing happens.

At times here I've thought . . . this is what the Deep South was like during Jim Crow. I feel that again as we search for a beach. In June 2008, the Association for Civil Rights in Israel, the country's largest human rights organization, filed a petition with the Israeli Supreme Court claiming that Palestinians are regularly prohibited from entering beaches in the northern Dead Sea, and that the checkpoint we passed—the Beit HaArava checkpoint on Route 90—was established to keep Palestinians away. The reason, according to the petition, was that Israelis managing the beaches claimed a mix of patrons hurt their businesses.

We're finally allowed to enter the third beach we approach. We pay an entry fee and walk through a turnstile. The facilities include a restaurant, a shop selling beach towels and T-shirts, and a locker room with showers. Monique talks me into a cup of coffee before I venture to the shore. I sit, sip, and unzip the bottom legs of my quick-dry pants to make shorts.

"You are a biker," she says.

"Yeah—I bike a fair amount. How'd you know?"

"I can tell by your legs."

I have my father's body: skinny but strong legs, no ass.

Kayla and I walk to the water. She doesn't have a bathing suit, so she's improvising, wearing a black sports bra and underpants, which looks like a bikini. I had reassured her that no one would notice the difference, and now, as we stroll through the sand, I chastise her in my most shocked, most self-righteous tone for wearing undies to a family beach.

"You're an asshole," she says, much to my satisfaction.

The Dead Sea is known for two things: its salt and its mud. The salinity level is so high—almost nine times that of ocean water—that fish and plants can't live here. It also means you're buoyant. I lie on my back and sprawl on the water. Kayla curls up in a ball, floating.

About ten feet in front of us, Ryan, one of the Irishmen, growls in pain.

"*Arrrghh*—I got it in my eyes," he says, standing. "Jesus—it's worse than the tear gas."

Yesterday, Ryan and Jerome and a few others attended a protest near Ramallah. The soldiers fired tear gas and flash-bangs: a grenade that unleashes disorienting sound and light and can cause temporary deafness and blindness. Jerome brought back an empty tear gas canister, showing it off like a souvenir from Six Flags.

The Dead Sea mud is rich in minerals, and good for the skin, which is why beachgoers famously smear it on their bodies. The mud is supposed to treat everything from acne to arthritis to anxiety; from psoriasis to muscle stiffness. Shiny mud-covered people wander the shore, the dim sun reflecting off their metallic sheen.

After coating myself with Dead Sea muck, I rinse off at a shower on the edge of the beach and walk along the water. Two Arab men sit in the sun in plastic chairs, wearing white shirts and slacks. Large crystals of salt are scattered like white rocks along the shore. Conor finds one the size of a small watermelon, which he plans to take home. I pick up a smaller, tennis-ball-sized rock to show Julie.

Monique stands on the steps that lead from the beach to the restaurant and facilities, frowning. "This is a settlement," she says, having wandered the grounds and seen the nearby homes and security. "We have come to have fun at a settlement."

"I'd wondered if those abandoned houses we passed on the way in once belonged to Palestinians," I say.

"Of course they did. I can't believe Fateen would bring us here."

She drags a chair across the sand to the water's edge, and she lights a cigarette, crosses her legs, and looks out at the salty water.

Back near the restaurant are tall shrubs with pink flowers. We congregate there before leaving. Monique walks with me back to the bus.

"My hands are sticky," I say, rubbing them. "I'm not sure if it's from the sea or the mud."

"Use my magic potion," she says, handing me a bottle of hand cleaner.

I squirt some and hand it back; she squirts some and uses too much.

"Smells like vodka," I say.

"This cannot be used in homes for alcoholics."

"So do you regret coming here today?"

"Yes."

"Have a drink of your hand lotion. You'll feel better."

While waiting for the bus we observe a row of international flags: Italy, the United States, Canada, France, Sweden . . .

"There's no Palestinian flag," says Monique.

"And the American flag should be bigger than the rest," I say, to annoy her.

The bus pulls up. On our way back, we stop at Nabi Musa, a site that Muslims believe holds Moses's tomb, then drive through the desert. Not long after we return to Beit Jibrin, Monique asks if I want to grab a beer. There's a six-thirty meeting at the center, but nothing starts on time here, so sure, I say—let me clean up a bit: I'm still sticky from the salt, a Dead Sea film on my flesh. I wash my hair with a bottle of water in the bathroom sink, then scrub myself with a sponge. I sniff my sweater to see if it's tolerable, not that I have an alternative.

We take the usual route: through camp, up the steep road past the Bonjour Café and Bethlehem University to the old market streets. The sun is setting. A few nights ago, Mahad invited Doug and me to the roof of the Handala Center. Doug is a serious amateur photographer, so our hosts encouraged him to photograph the work projects. We climbed up a pull-down ladder, exiting through a hatch to the roof, the three of us looking out over Beit Jibrin and Bethlehem. The Judean mountains rose above the haze and the brown landscape. As the sun dipped from view, the sky turned a piercing pinkish orange, the few clouds a bright sci-fi gray.

Tonight, the sky is sullen. Darkness comes fast, blue then black.

We're on a side street of shadowy buildings. A church rises across the street.

Monique is quiet. She seems lost in thought, lost in the darkness.

She stops.

I turn and look at her, wondering if something is wrong.

"May I kiss you," she says.

My face, I imagine, is blank. Blank with stupidity. Blank with shock. As blank as my ill-prepared mind. In eighteen years of marriage, no woman, other than my wife, has asked to kiss me.

Monique walks toward me. Her arms slip through mine. Her lips are warm.

She nestles her head under my neck, her hair ruffling in the breeze, and we stand for a few moments, together, and then we continue walking toward Manger Square.

When I was in high school my parents separated for a spell. My sister was finishing college, so it was just me and Mom. Dad was living in Maryland, near where he worked. His commute from home was long: almost an hour each way, depending on traffic. We should've moved—we even looked at houses—but they didn't because of me, so I wouldn't switch schools and leave friends.

They'd been married for more than twenty years, since they were eighteen. Dad had a classic midlife crisis. After working so hard for so long, working so much harder than the guys with degrees, he must have thought the usual thoughts:

My life is half over. I'm not going to achieve all I'd hoped to achieve. Is this all there is?

I wasn't much help to Mom. I was a junior in high school, and all I wanted was to see my friends and be with Julie. I was bad about coming home on time, which irritated Mom. If I was supposed to be home at 11 p.m., I'd make it back around 11:30. One night, well past my Mom-imposed curfew, Julie and I stood in her carport, kissing.

"Who's that?" she said abruptly.

A shadow was marching down the street.

"I dunno . . ."

Looks like . . . a bathrobe?

"Oh my God—that's my mother. I better go . . ."

I kissed Julie goodbye and walked down the driveway. Mom was furious. I don't remember her rant, which was justified, but when you're sixteen and in love, nothing else matters. I feel bad when I look back, because her marriage was in crisis and I was no help.

Dad came frequently to the house and moved back several months later. We moved to California when he took a job there, but I soon came back to Virginia for my senior year in high school, living with a friend and his family. Mom and Dad stayed married, forty-seven years in all, until Dad's death.

Manger Square is quiet now that Christmas has passed. Monique and I sit at one of the green plastic outdoor tables at St. George's restaurant. She lights a cigarette. We order two Taybehs.

"We have not discussed our personal lives," she says. "I have enjoyed that, you know? But perhaps we should."

We talk about our parents. Our hopes and disappointments. Children. Relationships. Loss. Her father recently died. I talk about Julie, holding up my hand so the ring is visible as we talk.

Monique would like to have children, but she wonders if she's too old.

"You're only thirty," I say.

I was surprised to learn her age. I thought she was *my* age. And I mean that as a compliment.

I ask her how old she thinks I am. Most people—Kayla, all the teachers in China—guess about thirty-five. Sometimes even thirty. I have gray hair near my temples, but a baby face. She studies me.

"Forty-three," she says.

I'm stunned. "That's dead on," I say. "I mean . . . that's exactly right."

"You are disappointed because I did not think you were younger."

"No, no—it's just . . . no one ever gets it right."

"I've always been good at this."

"At guessing ages?"

"At solving riddles. When I was a girl, everyone would come to me when something was missing, and I would find it."

She takes my hand on the table. Rubs my fingers with her thumb.

"Let's get something to eat," she says. "I'm feeling a little drunk."

We order chicken shawarma from a stand. I tell her we need to go back for the meeting.

"I don't want to go," she says. "Please. Let's stay here. We have time."

Behind the stand is an inside dining room. I check my watch. For two weeks I've shown up on time and sat, waiting. We might as well follow Middle Eastern time.

"Let's stay, warm up, eat, and then we'll head back," I say.

She's happy, and orders a cup of spearmint tea. She takes my hand again on the table; looks at our hands together. I don't know what to say. I don't know if I should pull it away. But then *she* pulls it off, as if remembering—

Wait—you're married.

We begin the walk back to Beit Jibrin. I'm trying to convince her the meeting will be fine. Afterward there'll be a party, and then volunteer performances.

At the top of the hill, the city opens up: the Bonjour Café and homes below, city lights—apartment lights—gleaming to our left, though it's the darkness that dominates. The streets are empty, the sidewalks empty. The West Bank is still.

She stops.

She embraces me.

Back home, I have a lot of female friends. I work with a lot of women. I don't think about it. And I enjoy being with Monique. I love her spirit, her sense of humor. She cares about people. I feel close to her, particularly now, particularly here. But I never saw this coming. And I'm not sure how to handle it. I'm not sure I'm equipped to handle it. I'm in bomb-scarred Bethlehem, I'm holding a Frenchwoman, she's holding me—this is not how my life works. It's like I'm back on the Tarzan swing in Costa Rica, moving too fast, in too many directions, my ego offering internal high-fives—*Damn, dude, you've still got it*—my mind trying to control the situation, and wondering if I really *am* in control of the situation, and if I'm not in control then what the hell might happen here?

And then a calming thought, a reassuring voice, whatever you want to call it, tells me—

Don't do anything you're gonna regret.

Which startles me. Because it's a tether to my real life. Because I know on some deeper level it means—

Remember who you are. And who loves you. And who's waiting for you.

You only find out about yourself when you're outside your comfort zone.

I had wanted, I'd said, to scrape away the layers of myself and discover what's underneath; scrape like I scraped that stubborn shed in New Orleans, peeling off what's dry and chipped and dead.

I know now.

I know, perhaps more than I've ever known, who I really am.

Strip me to my core and . . .

I'm a guy who loves his wife.

The same woman I've loved since I was fifteen.

And that's all I am, and all I've ever been. And it's all I want to be.

"Where have you been?" Kayla asks when we return. Everything started on time. The meeting. Dinner. Of course. Plates of cookies sit on a long table that's covered with a white plastic Christmas tablecloth. The meeting, I hear, focused on how to advance the Palestinian cause once we're home. Kayla says the bulk of the discussion was an argument over what to call the Facebook page.

The mood is festive yet sad. Kayla meets Mahad's mother. She tells his mom how impressed she is by Mahad; what a kind man he is. The mother says this is the first time in several years that all three of her sons are free. And then she cries. Kayla doesn't know what to do. In the time we've been here, I've not heard one Palestinian denigrate Jewish people or Israelis. They emphasize that the problem is not the people but the policies. But as Mahad's mother quietly weeps, she tells Kayla, "I hate them. I hate what they have done to my family."

We move to the bigger room on the fourth floor, the site of many meetings. Fateen thanks everyone for their efforts. Tonight is intercultural night, and as in China, volunteers perform. An older Frenchwoman plays guitar and the Finnish girl sings—a beautiful, vulnerable voice. The Italians lead another spirited rendition of "Bella Ciao," this time with the lyrics projected in English onto a screen. Joe-hammad reads two poems he wrote, sounding on the verge of tears when he's done.

Afterward, almost everyone goes to the Marvel Restaurant for a final shindig. We drink Taybehs and everyone sings. "Bella Ciao" returns *again*. Paul plays a sing-along of "Norwegian Wood"—everyone *la-la*'s the sitar part—and "Give Peace a Chance." Kayla Googles lyrics for "Livin' on a Prayer" and we sing, the Brits and the Irish chiming in on the *Ohhhhhh-OHHH* chorus. We stay until almost 3 a.m.

"It is probably the most business he has in years," says Monique.

I think back to the boy in Hebron. *Please buy. Very hard here. No business. Please buy.*

You couldn't pay me to be a Palestinian in the West Bank, let alone in Gaza. I find it almost comical now when I hear some TV wonk or newspaper opinionator harrumph about Palestinian demands. Why would anyone want to be a Palestinian? What could possibly be appealing about it? The high unemployment rate? The lack of security? The lack of land, water, rights, power, money—*what*? As one of the young rappers said, it's a bad life. If I have to live in the West Bank, I want a home in one of those palm tree and swimming pool settlements, plucking olives from confiscated trees, protected by troops.

Peaceniks have often dreamed of a Palestinian Gandhi. A leader who recognizes that when one side is strong and the other is weak, nonviolence is the mightiest force. It's not too late for a nonviolent shift, I suppose, though it's hard to picture macho Palestinian men joining hands and singing "If I Had a Hammer." But when I hear young men like Mahad speak of boycotts, and when I hear Fateen pronounce, *We want to say to the world, "We are civilians in front of soldiers,"* well, perhaps there's hope, though my cynical guess is that the Palestinians will remain fractured politically and philosophically, and that militants will continue to lob missiles into Israel, and to ignite themselves on buses, and to validate bloody reprisals, and that twenty years from now, maybe more, maybe less, the Israelis will have grabbled most of the land, settlement by settlement, fence by fence, leaving some paltry scraps for a small, symbolic, impotent Palestinian state.

If I've learned one thing from my time here, it's to live by the words of Bethlehem's most famous son—*In everything do to others as you would have them do to you.* It seems obvious, yet in the urgencies of life we forget, though virtually every religion emphasizes the same theme:

Love your neighbor as yourself.
Hurt no one so that no one may hurt you.
One should seek for others the happiness one desires for himself.
Do not unto others what you would not have them do unto you.

(That's Judaism, Islam, Buddhism, and Hinduism, just to save you a search.)

Some philosophers have questioned these golden-rule state-
ments with a simple argument: how do *you* know how others want
to be treated? But I think we all know what constitutes torment,
and we all know what constitutes malice, and we all know when
we've treated others in ways we'd never wish upon ourselves.

Always look at the other side, Dad had said.

The challenge in life is not simply being kind to others. The
challenge is being kind to those who don't deserve it. To be kind to
those we despise. To choose empathy over scorn, peace over cruelty.
Violence is easy. Any idiot can kill. Compassion requires effort,
the restraint of brutal instincts. It is, as Conor so eloquently said, a
fucking humpy fuck.

The next morning Monique and I drink a final coffee, sitting
at a two-person table outside a restaurant on Manger Street, the
one with the peace-sign Santa on the window. It's a warm, T-shirt
morning: I pull off my sweater and drape it on the back of my chair.
In a way, it's like last night never happened. No awkwardness, just
two friends sipping java.

She makes some sort of an anti-American crack, partly for my
benefit, partly because she has a genuine anti-American bias, and I
say, "Listen, just for me, tell me five things you like about America.
Actually, I'll make it easier for you: tell me three things."

She thinks, legs crossed, holding a cigarette. "Well, I like you.
And I like your Noam Chomsky and Michael Moore." She pauses.
"And I like the idea of your national parks."

"Good choice."

"And I like your national anthem."

She hums it again, sounding like a horn, as she did on the trip
to Jericho—

Brr brr-brr brr brr BRRR . . .

"That's five," I say. "You gave me a bonus."

We go back to Handala to help clean up. All the men work on
the flat. Four of us haul the refrigerator out of the kitchen, down

the steps. It's awkward, heavy work, the fridge barely fitting. I hadn't realized it didn't belong in the kitchen. The apartments are normally used by the women's group that creates handmade crafts. I'm sure they'll love returning to a largely unventilated room and the stench of eighteen underwashed men.

A small group of us head to town for lunch, to the same Santa-in-the-window restaurant where Monique and I had coffee. Doug orders the Philly cheesesteak, which—surprise—is not as good as a real Philly cheesesteak. Afterward, some of us head back; others are staying in town. Devin is on his way to Gaza. Monique and Marcen are traveling to Jordan, then returning to Beit Jibrin for New Year's Eve.

Monique and I say goodbye. I'll miss her. I'll miss her *bel esprit*. And yet I'm also relieved.

Back at Handala, we drag our suitcases to the littered street. Doug and Kayla donate their Frisbee to the center; Mahad asks them to sign it. I pull my tall blue backpack over my shoulders and fasten the straps. As we leave Beit Jibrin, the three of us plus Conor, Benjamin, and a few others, Kayla notes that the local boys look bitter. She thinks it's because we're leaving and they're staying.

Mahad escorts us as we walk along the wall, the hideous gray wall, back to the checkpoint. Among the paintings and scrawls are the words "Made in the USA."

A few local guys wave as we walk. "You from Azzeh camp?"

"Yeah, man," says Conor with a grin.

Ma'a salama, they say.

Goodbye.

We reach the checkpoint. Mahad embraces each of us.

It's time to go home. I *want* to go home. I want to see my wife.

PART SIX

Kenya

Outside the Marvel Nursery School: "The journey is over; the journey is just beginning."

"YOU LOOK GAUNT," my sister, Cathy, tells me.

Julie and I unzip our coats and pull off scarves, draping them over the pink living room chairs Mom bought when I was a kid. Mom moved to a fifty-five-and-over community a few years after Dad died; tonight we're here for my belated Christmas dinner. I returned yesterday from the West Bank, and I'm sniffling and coughing from the Handala bug, which I finally caught, my throat turning sore as we left for the Gilo checkpoint.

I look at Cathy and smile faintly.

"I lost more weight," I tell her.

For the first time since junior high—probably since Mom bought those pink chairs—I think I'm too thin. I was back at work this morning, groggy from the travel, achy from the bug, and a female friend said, "Wow—you're a shell of a man." Just what every man wants to hear.

I hug my mom, say hello to my nieces and nephew. I thank my brother-in-law for letting me borrow his sleeping bag. "It's a little funky," I say, promising to wash it.

I devour leftover ham and potatoes and rolls and open a few gifts. Mom has a surprise: she's had all our old home movies transferred to DVD. They're in no particular order, just a jumble of clips, some from my childhood, some from before I was born. One moment I'm on the shore at Virginia Beach, four years old, running from the waves. Next Granddaddy and my grandmother are smoking outside their old apartment. Then Cathy and I run through a sprinkler in summer. The clips are colorful yet faded, grainy like the past itself.

Inspired by the DVD memories, Cathy and I, as we're sometimes inclined to do, relive our country music childhoods. Mom started out as an R&B and rock fan, but *Sgt. Pepper* psychedelics pushed her to country. Flip through her old records and her evolving tastes show, from Elvis and Chuck Berry to Aretha Franklin and Gladys Knight, and then . . . Merle Haggard and George Jones and Tom T. Hall.

Cathy and I sing the chorus of "Louisiana Woman, Mississippi Man" (Loretta Lynn and Conway Twitty, as if you didn't know), and then Charley Pride's "Kiss an Angel Good Morning." She performs an enthusiastic version of Porter Wagoner and Dolly Parton's "Fight and Scratch," a bubbly ditty about domestic violence. We croon tunes from *Hee Haw*.

It feels good to laugh and enjoy the familiar. I've returned from the West Bank with a pessimism that feels as entrenched as my Handala cough. And I'm not sure if working for two weeks in a Kenyan orphanage will help it or make it worse.

When I first plotted this post–Costa Rica attempt to do some tiny bit of good in the world, I wanted to hurl myself to places I'd never been: Asia, South America, the Middle East, Africa. I wanted to work one-on-one with children, hence the Global Volunteers program at La La Shou. I wanted to help the environment, so I chose the Earthwatch program in Ecuador. And I also wanted—needed—to work with infants, which is why we'll be caring for kids at Calvary Zion, a children's home in the Kenyan town of Kiembeni, through a British-based placement organization called Travellers Worldwide.

After a stopover in Rome, we fly to Ethiopia for a connecting flight to Mombasa, Kenya's second-largest city. As we land in Addis Ababa, Ethiopia's capital, Julie is bloated from soda and airline food. Her chin is against her chest. The wheels screech against the runway, and she vomits, ever so slightly, into a cup.

This is how we arrive in Africa.

"You okay?"

She nods.

"That was the daintiest barf I've ever heard," I say.

She's feeling too gross to comment, and stays quiet on our connecting flight.

Mombasa's Moi International Airport is largely outdoors, and given that January is summer here, and we're on the coast—Mombasa is a port town and popular tourist destination thanks to its Indian Ocean beach locale—the air is muggy and thick. British colonialists so disliked the heat they moved the capital to more moderate Nairobi in 1905.

The casual airport vibe is a major contrast to my experience leaving Bethlehem and Tel Aviv. It took nearly two hours to proceed through the Gilo checkpoint to Jerusalem. We stood, a stagnant herd of Palestinians and random tourists, packed in a pair of zigzagging security lines, like amusement park lines, only more crowded, bodies pressed against bodies and blue bars; bodies jostling for position. And then an echoing groan when the other line closed.

The mass of people rushed to our line, pushing for position. A Palestinian man complained. A soldier on a catwalk barked at him, machine gun strapped over his shoulder, telling him to shut up, ordering him to the back of the line. A Christian woman behind me, a cross around her neck, raised her small son above her head, handing him to the outstretched arms of a man near the front. He lowered the boy next to some luggage; the boy disappeared in the bodies. The woman pleaded with me. She wanted to move to her son. She begged.

Please please . . .

"I can't move," I said. Between my backpack and the crush of people I was stuck.

The scrutiny continued at the airport in Tel Aviv. A passport check and terse questions from a yellow-vested guard wielding a machine gun on a shuttle—

Where have you been, what were you doing, for how long . . .

Questions from a drab airport secureaucrat who inspected my passport—

Why were you here, what were you doing . . .

The annoyance of an X-ray operator who snapped at me when I asked if the machine would damage the tapes in my video camera.

"Go—get out," he said, shooing me.

And then a square counter, the size of a large boxing ring. The guard unpacked my backpack, sent my sleeping bag through a machine, rubbed a wand over stinky shirts and undies.

And then a back room.

Remove your shoes and empty your pockets.

Raise your arms, please.

Turn.

A secureaucrat left, then returned with another secureaucrat. They shared the same still-in-college face, the same white shirt and khakis.

"This is my superior," he said. "We need you to lower your pants."

I looked at them. What choice was there? I unbuttoned my jeans and unzipped my zipper, my jeans dropping to my knees. He scanned above my crotch.

After that, back to the boxing ring security area. Back to more lines. When passengers finally started boarding the plane, I was again singled out for extra scrutiny, pulled from the line, along with Benjamin, who was on my flight; the two of us and anyone with a hint of brown skin. Secureaucrats again prowled fingers through my carry-on bags, and wanded me again behind a curtain, and told me to empty my pockets, again; and as I took off my shoes and placed my hands against the wall and spread my legs, I realized that in the eyes of the Israeli government, I was a Palestinian. A suspicious man. I could feel it in the eyes of wary passengers on the fully boarded plane, everyone seated as I walked on, as they stared at me: the last one, the distrustful one, the loathsome one. A West Bank refugee. A child of Bajo de Meco. The underclass. It's a feeling I don't want to forget.

We meet the force that is Karimu outside the Mombasa airport. She's our host in Kenya—we're staying with her and her children—and even upon meeting her, I sense that she's a smart, strong, take-charge woman, which is exactly what we want after traveling twenty-four hours and leaving our brains behind in the overhead bin. Maybe it's her years in the travel biz—she worked for a touring company before joining Travellers Worldwide—but her body language says, *I know where we're going, so follow me*, and even though we're simply trailing her strong-postured, formidable frame through the parking lot I think: *Okay, good—this woman is in charge.*

It's a thirty-minute drive from the airport, past blue views of Mombasa harbor, then through slow, hot, crowded city streets. The cabdriver buys pineapple from a vendor who walks between cars. When we pass a fender bender—two vans stranded in the road—we churn over the median, into oncoming traffic, past the accident, then back over. Other drivers do the same.

In Kiembeni, outside the city, weary metal-shack stores line the flat road to Karimu's home. She lives in a small, newish neighborhood of blue-roof one-level houses, set close together, the community encased by a concrete wall with broken glass embedded on top like spikes. We drive into a bumpy clearing of hard earth and ragged grass, about forty yards long, pulling up to a black, fortress-like metal gate. Karimu's ten-year-old son, Kafil, unlocks it and lets us in. We're led to a guest room with two single beds, blue mosquito netting tied in a knot, dangling over each.

The beds are tempting. Julie and I are bleary, but we're following one of our rules of marathon travel: don't nap when you arrive in a vastly different time zone, because it'll only screw you up more. Better to stay awake and get a semi-normal night's sleep. So when Karimu suggests we join her and the kids for an afternoon trip to Nyali beach, we agree with groggy enthusiasm. And after nearly a full day on a plane, the waves and the salty breeze and the wide-open sky are a treat. Humans were not meant to spend long periods in confined spaces breathing recirculated air and eating plastic-wrapped, microwaved mystery meals.

Karimu enrolls the children—Kafil and Scotty, who's five, and a niece she's now raising named Grace—in a kids' area at the beach. Julie and I grab a table under the shade of a tall bamboo and thatch roof, watching a man in tracksuit pants and a button-up shirt pace the shore with a camel, offering rides. I order a Tusker, the beer of Kenya, which won't help my efforts to stay awake.

Karimu join us in the shade. I ask her if most of the tourists here are European.

"I'll be really honest about who comes here," she says. "It's gross old men who are with really young women."

I'd already noticed that. Next to this white-sand public beach is a posh resort, and almost every retirement-age white guy we see, usually in a Speedo, is drinking with—or leering at—a Kenyan woman, some as young as twenty, if not younger. At least two of the men are Australian; I hear a few Germans as well. One guy has bought lunch for a woman and her son. I don't know if these women are prostitutes or merely opportunistic, though even if money isn't exchanged, the expectations are clear. Later, before we leave, two women in bikini tops and hot pants dance in a sandy square. One clutches a dark wood pole, two-handed, grinding up and down. The other raises her arms above her head, thrusting her hips.

"I think they should wait until dark before they do that," Karimu says. "Wait until seven p.m. It makes me not want to bring my kids here."

She tells us about Calvary Zion, the children's home where we'll be working. Some of the kids have lived there since it opened twelve years ago; the orphans of HIV, their parents succumbing to the disease. Others were abandoned after birth, perhaps because their mothers were sex workers, like the women dancing here on the beach. One mother gave birth on the side of the road, then discarded the baby, his umbilical cord still attached. He was four days old when he arrived at Calvary Zion.

"I don't know how you could do that to your own child," says Karimu. "Some people say it's because of poverty, but I think you have to be emotionally dead to do that."

We eat dinner back at Karimu's house: a bowl of what seems like Kenyan coleslaw, with a lentil dish, and something like a crepe/corn tortilla hybrid. Julie, always a good sport, plays Chutes and Ladders with Kafil after dinner. I join them for a second game on a small fold-up, magnetic multigame set. Kafil wins, though he cheats at the end, moving five places even though he rolled four with the dice. Julie and I give him a break because he acknowledges with a laugh that he cheated. And because we're seriously tired.

We sleep twelve hours. The thumping church service behind the house finally rouses us; the beat that pulses through the walls, the preacher wailing God's word in baritone Swahili. Three repeating organ chords accompany chanting singers: "Amen . . . Amen . . . Amen . . ." It's loud enough to wake up God and any dozing angels.

When we crawl out from under our mosquito netting the house is empty: Karimu and the kids are at church. She left us breakfast on a square green plastic table: bread and peanut butter and jelly, some hot dog–like sausages covered by a plate, a thermos of warm masala chai. The tea is made with a distinctive spice, and Julie and I are quickly hooked.

The house booms with energy when Karimu and the kids return. Kafil speaks excellent English: he's the best in his class, Karimu says. English is common here, a legacy of British rule. Streets signs and billboards are more frequently in English than Swahili.

"I am a human propeller!" says Kafil, spinning.

He chases Scotty, who runs, laughing, throwing himself into Julie's arms.

Now Kafil makes up jokes. He asks Julie: "Why did the old man have white hair?"

"I don't know. Why *did* the old man have white hair?"

"Because he drank so much milk."

Julie laughs, kind soul that she is.

Karimu is taking Julie and me to Mombasa for the day. Her eighteen-year-old cousin Isabel, who lives there and helps with the housecleaning and cooking, will watch the kids. We walk through the field from Karimu's house, past bony cows grazing near the road. The sun is already bake-your-skin hot, and it's not quite 11 a.m. We stand in the shadow of one-level, tin-roof buildings across the street. The buildings sit in rows like barracks, holding shadowy stores: a tiny market with a flapping white curtain for a door, a newsstand, a hairdresser. Down dirt side streets the buildings become homes and schools and more shops. I wouldn't call them slums, but this ain't a high-rent district, either.

We're waiting for a *matatu*—a shared taxi—the most common mode of transportation since gas is expensive and the *matatu* is cheap. It'll cost forty shillings (about fifty cents) for the thirty-minute minibus ride to Mombasa.

"I owe you for yesterday's beer," I tell Karimu, since she picked up the tab at the beach.

"Don't worry about it," she says.

"Well, you shouldn't have to pay for us."

"In Kenya, if I offer and you don't let me pay, I will be offended."

"I don't want you to be offended."

"Good."

"If you want to buy me more beer I won't be offended by that either."

She laughs. "A lot of volunteers don't realize if you ask Kenyans out to drinks, the expectation is that you'll pay."

"I bet they learn fast when they're handed the bill."

"Kenyans are poor," she says, "but we're not as obsessed with money as other people."

A *matatu* approaches, trailed by dust. A guy in a red button-up shirt hangs from the open passenger door, one hand holding a rooftop rail, the other a wad of cash.

"Bamburi, Bamburi, Bamburi!" he yells.

Bamburi is a crossroads town, about a five- to ten-minute drive from Kiembeni. From there we'll take another *matatu* to Mombasa. We squeeze inside. Some *matatus* are pimped-out sleek, others junkyard shabby. This one is somewhere in between: the seats are torn, the shocks are shot, but reggae booms with bass-thumping clarity from shiny speakers.

The red-shirt guy sits in the passenger seat. He's the money man—they're required to wear red shirts—and his job is to aggressively seek customers, shoving passengers inside like clothes in an overstuffed suitcase. When I slide the side door shut, he speaks to Karimu in bewildered Swahili: apparently I've made a *matatu* faux pas.

"He's wondering why you shut the door—I explained this is your first *matatu* ride," Karimu says.

"Great," I say. "Now they know we're from out of town."

"You think that gave it away?" says Julie.

We *are* a tad paler than everyone else.

The van's four rows fill, the smell of armpits mixing with the toxic whiff of burning trash. My knees are pressed against the metal seat back. We transfer in Bamburi, which is more bustling, with street vendors cooking fish, selling vegetables and fruit from wood carts; cars honking, competing to pass each other, angling for space. On a corner, across from food joints and wandering locals, sits a sprawling trash dump. A few men sift through the garbage, poking with sticks, looking for some refuse treasure, as do a handful of scrawny, scavenging cows. Dumps like this start spontaneously, Karimu says: someone unloads their trash, and then more do it, and soon there's a noxious mini-landfill with crisscrossing flies.

Mombasa, when we arrive, feels more like a Western city. Karimu takes us to a sandwich joint, and we drink sodas in the shade next to the city's giant metal tusks, which form arches over two lanes of traffic (and look vaguely like an urban design from *The Flintstones*). The tusks were built for the arrival of Queen Elizabeth in 1952, the same year natives launched the Mau Mau Uprising against British colonial rule. Eleven years would pass before Kenya gained its independence. Here in Mombasa, the city's roughly nine hundred thousand residents are a mix of Muslim Mijikendas and Swahilis, and it's a city that's known violence. In 2002, militants believed to be linked with al-Qaeda ignited a car bomb at an Israeli-owned hotel, killing fifteen. In January 2008, Mombasa erupted in riots following the Kenyan elections. But the city remains a major tourist site, known for its beaches and diverse culture.

Karimu prefers coming on Sundays, when it's less crowded and crazy. I ask again about the old men we saw at the beach—or more specifically the Kenyan women who provide the Speedo-clad geezers with companionship. Unlike the prostitutes we saw in China, who hid behind glass doors, this was more open, more evident, more jarring.

"So do the men come because they know the women are there,"

I ask, "or do the women come because they know the men are there?"

"They both seem to know," says Karimu. "But the men are gross. They can be very crude."

"I saw a German guy grab a waitress on the behind," says Julie.

Karimu nods. "I saw that too."

"*Men,*" I scoff in disgust, before they have a chance.

I have a theory that, thanks to us men, every technology is eventually used for sex. Telephones lead to phone sex, televisions lead to porn channels, airplanes lead to guys who fly to Kenya to hire prostitutes . . . Necessity may be the mother of invention, but sex is its horny father.

"It's not just the man's fault," says Karimu of the butt-grabbing German. "The waitress laughed. So it's partly her fault. I wouldn't let someone touch me like that."

Some locals, she says, recently beat up a foreigner because he slept with a fourteen-year-old girl. "They said, 'If you're going to do that, do it in your own country.'" Online marriage proposals are also a problem, she adds. A girl goes to another country—usually a poor girl, hoping for a new life—and the man takes her passport and puts her in a brothel.

Here in Kenya, Karimu says, divorce is becoming more common, and more acceptable.

"I wonder if people are getting divorced too early now instead of working on their marriage," she says.

"I dunno," I say. "Most divorces aren't fun—the fighting over the kids and the money and stuff. I don't think people rush into it."

Julie and I will never get divorced, I tell her, because we're both too mellow. Neither of us would get around to calling the attorney.

I forgot to call the lawyer. Do you mind doing it?

I'll do it tomorrow.

Maybe we should wait and get divorced next week . . .

After wandering the old town and Fort Jesus—a sixteenth-century fort with torture rooms and holding cells for slaves, now offering history tours and high harbor views—we return for dinner at Karimu's house, eating a Kenyan staple called *ugali*. The closest thing I can compare it to is cornbread, only denser and with less taste. The *ugali* is mainly a vehicle for scooping up other foods: in this case, a kale-like veggie and pork in a tomato-type sauce.

"It's poor people food," says Karimu. Most children—including hers—don't like it, though for adults it's Kenyan comfort food.

We sip some post-*ugali* chai tea once the kids go to sleep and watch a Nigerian movie on TV. In terms of production values, it's like a telenovela. In terms of plot, it's two hours of mundane people doing mundane things. There's an excruciatingly long setup of a happy family eating a meal—cutting their food, chewing, passing a dish, chewing, cutting their food—and then they go shopping, the parents' three daughters singing a dippy song at the store:

> *I like shopping with my faaam-ileee!*
> *Daddy buys the shoes, Mommy buys the toys . . .*

Karimu says these Nigerian movies are popular, even though they're awful.

The kids are still singing, by the way.

> *Daddy buys the shoes, Mommy buys the toys . . .*

"They've been shopping for ten minutes!" Karimu says, exasperated. "This is so stupid!"

The parents eventually croak—perhaps they're sick of the song—igniting a battle over Daddy's money. This is an issue in real life, says Karimu, since inheritance traditionally goes to a son. Because of that, most Kenyans want a male child. But as divorce becomes more common—leading to an increase in single mothers—having a boy can be a disadvantage: potential boyfriends fear that if they get married, their property will go to another man's son.

Traditional Kenyans don't believe in adoption, she tells us. Karimu once thought about adopting a girl, but her mother was opposed, encouraging her to have her own baby, even though she's single. Perhaps that will change, because on our various *matatu* rides, we've seen no shortage of children's homes. Roughly 2.6 million orphans live in Kenya, and nearly half of those are AIDS orphans. Parents, it seems, are a much-depleted natural resource.

Calvary Zion sits on a dirt road, about a ten-minute walk from Karimu's house. It's the last in a row of houses, hidden behind a six-foot-high concrete wall with the obligatory broken glass poking from the top. It's a common security measure in Kiembeni, and I assume throughout Kenya. I can never decide if the glass is to stop criminals, or birds, or both.

The gate to the home is massive: two wide black doors that meet in the middle, like the entrance to a security compound. CALVARY ZION CHILDREN'S HOME is painted in white, though an R and an E and an N are fading, the bottom of the gate infected with rust. Karimu clangs a knocker the size of a cowbell. A young guy, maybe in his early twenties, skinny and friendly, unlocks the gates and lets us in. I never get his name, or his story, and though I see him sweeping and playing occasionally with the kids during our time here, this seems to be his primary duty: he sits in a one-man shack and lets people in the gate.

Inside is a courtyard—"rough, lumpy, bumpy cement," as Julie will write in her journal. A mangy black-and-white mutt lies in the shade of a thin tree, raising his head as we enter: he's interested, but not enough to get up. Karimu leads us inside, past a small white-tile porch, introducing us to the housemothers, who live here full-time: Priscilla, a stout, serious woman in her twenties; gentle, soft-spoken

Alice, her three-year-old son, Daniel, sitting by her feet; and Rose, the newest arrival, and the most natural manager of the bunch. I think of Rose as being big, and yet months later, when I look at photographs, I see she's actually shorter than Julie.

Rose welcomes us and escorts us through the house. We're waiting on Jane Karigo, the founder of Calvary Zion, who's coming to meet us. Jane is essentially Calvary Zion's CEO, so her time is devoted to raising money for day-to-day operations—the home survives entirely on donations—and the new site she's building nearby: close to three acres of land that will have more space for more children. As for the massive daily duties of running Calvary Zion—the cleaning, cooking, laundry, bathing, and surrogate parenting of forty children—that falls to Priscilla, Alice, and Rose. A fourth mother recently left.

We take a tour, poking our heads in the three bedrooms, each packed with bunk beds and cribs, the walls dinged and desperate for paint. Up to ten children share a room, with the smaller kids sleeping three and four to a bed. A mother sleeps in each room as well. The kitchen is tiny, like one you'd see in a small apartment. Behind the house a servants' quarters has been converted to a bedroom for the older boys. A "father" named Gregory shares their room.

And then Jane arrives.

I'm not sure how to say this without it sounding like melodramatic drivel, but Jane Karigo exudes . . . something—a life force, a presence, a spirit. She enters the room, boisterous, welcoming me and Julie. She hugs us. Hugging Jane Karigo, you feel some sort of warmth, some sort of radiance, and I can't explain what it is, but it's beautiful, and inviting, whatever it may be.

"My mother wanted me to be a teacher," she tells us. "Now I teach the word of God."

We sit in comfy yet well-worn furniture. The chipped walls are painted in fading safari scenes, green grass and blue skies with a zebra over one chair, parrots over another, a waterfall over the couch. In the corner a dilapidated china closet seems as abandoned as the children.

A junior-high-aged girl sits on the floor. She was sent home, much to Jane's annoyance, because her teacher thought the braids in her hair looked sloppy.

"They look fine to me," says Karimu, inspecting the girl's head.

"It is ridiculous," says Jane. "This is not a fashion show. She is there to learn."

Jane holds a boy named Christopher in her lap. She's raising him: he was found in a department store bathroom as a baby, abandoned by his mother. Christopher looks to be about three. He doesn't like other children to get near Jane.

The children at Calvary Zion range in age from seven months to eighteen years. The oldest, Elizabeth, will soon start college. Her parents died of HIV in 2003; her younger sister and brother live here as well. About 6.3 percent of adults age fifteen to nineteen have the virus, down from its peak in 2000. An estimated eighty thousand Kenyans died from AIDS-related illnesses in 2009 alone.

The youngest is Jacob. His mother abandoned him in a hospital. Karimu holds him, marveling at how he's grown, then hands him to Julie, who rubs his feet, talking softly to him, bouncing him a bit. He's been sick with a cold.

"His chest sounds a little rattly," says Julie. "He feels warm."

With Jane's permission, she takes off his sweater and overalls, and Jane tells us how she formed Calvary Zion.

"I ask God for my vision, because I am a Christian. God gives me the vision and tells me to take care of the children. This is my mission. If I don't take care of these children, who will? They deserve fulfillment, and they deserve opportunities, like any other children.

"So I work in other children's homes to see how they are run. And once I am ready to open my own home, the government came and inspected it and said I must have furniture and five hundred thousand shillings in an account. I tell them I have nothing. But I get the furniture from donations. Some of it we are still using." She points at the ratty yet durable chairs and couch where we sit.

As for the half a million shillings, she pulled a bureaucratic switcheroo, changing her status to welfare organization instead of orphanage, which allowed her to open without the large bank account.

"I defeat them with my faith," she says. "I trust in God. I know God loves these children. I know He will provide. And people ask me—how will He provide? I tell them some people are vessels. The people who come here, the people who come from so many countries—these people are vessels."

And she looks at Julie, and then she looks at me. And she tells us we are vessels.

After a long chat, Jane waves goodbye and leaves with Christopher, and Julie and I transform into a sweaty cleaning crew. Rose asks me to wash the windows in every room of the house. The windows are a series of horizontal, rectangular panels, which, in theory, would open with a lever, though the levers no longer seem to work. The lower panes are grimy from kids' fingers and hands, the higher levels caked with dust. Clearly they haven't been cleaned in months, though on the list of children's home priorities, I'm sure this isn't high. I dab a rag in the soapy water that's splashed on the floor for mopping, then scrub windows in the living room, the three bedrooms, the two bathrooms, the kitchen, the older boys' room out back. Nearly every window is missing glass.

"Good thing it's warm here," says Julie.

The mornings are quiet because the kids are at school. Only the infants are here. Once the windows are clean, I take Faith for a stroll. She can't be more than ten months old. Great baby cheeks.

And great baby legs; flubby thighs like water balloons. She's learning to walk, and *loves* to walk, though she can't manage it yet without assistance, using walls and the couch for balance. She puts her arms up over her head, so I give her my index fingers, and we walk, me moving backward. We go out of the house, along the front, and then along the side, lap after lap after lap. It begins to strain my forty-four-year-old back.

"Want to trade for a while?" I ask Julie.

She's cleaning cobwebs with a broom and is happy for the switch. They walk some more, and when Faith starts to slow, Julie scoops her up, then sits with her on the white bench on the porch. Faith falls asleep against her chest.

To Karimu, this is the big benefit of volunteers: holding, cuddling, nurturing the infants.

No child needs nurturing more than a two-year-old boy named Elijah. When I'd walked with Faith, Elijah was jealous, trying to step in front of her, whimpering. He's an industrious walker, pattering around the house and the courtyard in a bowlegged, babyish way, but he likes being carried.

"*Ah-dahh*," he says.

It's his one word. I wonder if *Ah-dahh* is Swahili, but no, I'm told it's just a sound he makes. He says it more when he's curious, pointing at a cup or a tree. It sounds happy. But the mystery of Elijah is the anguish that must lurk inside, the pain he can't verbalize, the pain that expresses itself in his lack of expression; the blankness that pulls on his face, widening his eyes.

Every child at Calvary Zion has a sad story, a tragic reason why they're here. Faith, who is so busily learning to walk, was abandoned in the hospital by her mother, and then neglected by her nurses. On her little hand, the hand that held my finger for balance, is a scar from an IV tube. At many overburdened hospitals, abandoned babies are fed with IVs instead of bottles. It's a time-saver. The IV stayed so long in her hand that the incision became infected.

Elijah is a child of incest. His fourteen-year-old mother was impregnated by her grandfather, and the birth brought shame to the village. For the first year of Elijah's existence, he was hidden from others—no human contact, no nurturing, no love. Just silence, and hunger, and isolation. The mother tried to stash the baby under a bush, and witnesses called the police. She is serving seven years in prison. The father is free. Elijah was brought to Jane Karigo and the mothers of Calvary Zion.

Holding Elijah, carrying him around the courtyard and through the house, I wonder about the damage—the effects of the deprivation. At Karimu's house I searched online for info on child development: in the first year of an infant's life, a baby develops bonds of love and trust with a parent. "The way you cuddle, hold, and play with your baby will set the basis for how he will interact with you and others," says the Centers for Disease Control and Prevention's site. There is no medical consensus, however, on how much the first three years of a child's life shapes intelligence and emotional well-being. So maybe Elijah will be fine, as fine as someone with such an unfair start to life can be. He is a sweet, beautiful boy, and if his face at times looks blank, those big eyes never do. Those big eyes make me think there's something fierce, and smart, and thoughtful inside. That he's been hurt in ways he must feel but can't understand. To know Elijah is to worry about him, and to feel protective. To hope for him. To hold him when he wants to be held. When he raises his arms, I find it impossible to say no. And so I hold him. And we walk.

I talk to him not in baby talk, but as I would to a friend. About Julie. About Karimu and her children. About the way the sun shines off the glass shards poking from the wall.

He gets heavy.

"Okay, buddy," I finally tell him. "We need to take a break."

I set him down. And he raises his arms. And I look at his wide eyes, and his outstretched fingers, and I pick him back up.

• • •

Wazungu—white people—are rare on the dirt road to Calvary Zion. Julie and I walk to the home each morning, reaching the road from a rutted shortcut path. Tall grass and weeds poke from the scruffy landscape like stubble on a dry dirt beard; poles for drooping power lines rise above palm trees and scattered garden apartment buildings and two-story under-construction homes. Workers watch us pass, surprised to see our Caucasian selves. They smile and say *Jambo*—Swahili for "hello."

Our routine is quickly set: once we arrive at Calvary Zion's massive gate, around 9 a.m., we wash dishes and do whatever chores or baby-watching is required, and then at noon, we deliver lunch to the Marvel Nursery School, about ten minutes away, down a dusty side street. Six Calvary Zion children, each of them four years old, go to school at Marvel. I lug the lunch—a large metal container, along with bowls, a cup, and a liter bottle of water—in a plastic bag and Julie dishes it up.

"Calvary Zion!" the principal, Angela, announces when we arrive. "Lunch!"

The kids sit at a short rectangular table. The room is cramped; another classroom is visible and loud through an opening in a shared wall. The teacher greets us, a thin young man: he looks like a dance instructor in his silk shirt and pinstripe pants. Taped to a small chalkboard is a drawing of an African man, body parts labeled, along with a list of words and their opposites (front/back, happy/sad) and a photo chart of African wildlife. Today's date and the weather are scrawled on the board: "Sunny."

"I'm guessing they don't change that very often," I tell Julie.

Julie scoops the food, a rice-and-potatoes mix, and taps it into bowls. The kids wolf it down, rice stuck to their cheeks, holding their bowls for more. I walk into a shady outdoor alley between two classroom buildings and say hello to Angela. She is short, round, gray haired, often wearing an apron. Drill-sergeant tough.

"What do you need," she asks.

"Nothing—we're fine—thanks."

"You need chairs."

"No, really—we're good."

"Sit—we are not slaves."

It's hard to argue with that. We each grab a chair and Julie and I sit, watching the Calvary Zion kids through a window. The only boy of the six, Logan, acts like he's going to steal food from a girl, which causes her to scream, which causes the others to giggle.

"We do not talk while we eat," Angela barks, poking her head inside. "Sit up straight."

She is a firm disciplinarian with a soft heart: in Calvary Zion's early days, when Jane couldn't afford tuition, the principal accepted the children for free. She watches them eat.

"They are happy because it is good food," says Angela.

The kids wash their faces and hands outside after they eat. I pour them cups of water. They chug the water, then thrust their empty cups at me, wanting more. Everything is a competition: who can get the most food, the most to drink, the most attention.

We see this as well in the afternoon, when the nursery and elementary school kids come home. Tranquility becomes chaos. The kids rip off red-checkered uniforms, running and squealing in various states of undress as they change into fresh clothes. They're supposed to do homework, though they're more likely to chase or hit or taunt their Calvary Zion siblings. Conflicts follow a reliable three-step process:

1. Child A has an object.
2. Child B sees the object and desires it, grabbing it from Child A.
3. Child A and Child B clash over the object, causing the loser to scream, sulk, sob, or unleash violent vengeance on Child C (who will take out his or her frustrations on Child D).

All children act this way, but it's more intense here. Our first afternoon, in something of a Costa Rica flashback, Julie and I are alarmed to discover we're the only adults outside: the housemothers are involved with their countless other afternoon calamities and responsibilities. Martina, a three-month German volunteer who started last week, left at lunchtime with an upset stomach, her face red from heat and green from nausea. (The family she's staying with doesn't have running water, so the toilet situation is—how shall I put it—less than sanitary.) Things start out okay—I kick a soccer ball with Stevie, an overall very responsible kid, probably in fourth grade; Julie sits on the porch, helping a girl write the alphabet for her homework—but then Jacob starts crying. So Julie gets up and holds him. And then four boys grab Debbie, one of the nursery school girls, picking her up by her feet and hands and carrying her around the concrete yard. She screeches and bawls, eyes wide in what seems like terror. Julie and I try to break it up. But then Faith starts crying so I run back and grab her. We separate Debbie from the boys, but they grab her again, carrying her against her will around the house, and again she cries and screams. Julie and I say "No" strongly—we've been told to correct them—but the boys laugh. The word *no*, we quickly realize, is comedy gold. Say that word and we'll get huge laughs. Say it sternly and it's pee-in-your-pants funny.

I push the boys away, which only encourages them. When I yank a boy by his sweater, it's a game: another boy grabs Debbie just so I'll yank *him*.

I look dumbly around the concrete yard: it's like a domestic *Lord of the Flies*. A boy swings a bag filled with shoes and other miscellaneous objects above his head, ready for launch. Another boy hangs from a bar above the front door, swinging his feet. I'm worried he'll slip and fall, but no, instead, he accidentally kicks a girl in the face. She sprawls on the porch floor, crying.

I hold Faith tight against me. Maybe I can at least protect her.

"I'm surprised there aren't bloodstains everywhere," I say to Julie.

"No kidding—I can't believe no one has stitches."

"We should probably learn the Swahili word for concussion."

And yet despite the children's hockey-enforcer style of play, and the uneven gravelly concrete yard, and the hard-tile porch that seems perfect for cracking skulls, we never see even a single scraped knee.

Our workday ends at four o'clock and I admit it: I started checking my watch around three. When quitting time finally arrives we put Faith and Jacob on the couch, notify Rose, wave goodbye, then slice past racing bodies and exit through the large black gate, relishing the dirt-road serenity on the other side.

We walk back to Karimu's house in shell-shocked silence. Julie rubs her head; some of the girls were pulling her hair (the children are fascinated by *wazungu* hair, Karimu tells us).

"I think we need a new strategy," I finally say.

"We need a new something."

"Did you notice the gate guy didn't seem concerned about, you know . . . head trauma?"

"I think he's just used to it and we're not."

At one point, when a soccer ball sailed into the yard next door, the gate guy, with my assistance, climbed over the concrete wall and the glass spikes in *his bare feet*.

Given that Julie and I have no power and everyone is unfazed by the bedlam, I propose what will be our guiding philosophy: let things happen. Basically, it's a nonintervention policy. Unless someone initiates an activity that might result in, say, a shattered fibula, we'll let the kids resolve situations themselves, or let the mothers handle it. If we get involved, bad behavior grows worse.

"Sometimes they act like that to get attention," Karimu tells us when we arrive home. "And they know the volunteers don't have much authority."

Karimu's house feels sedate in comparison: like the Buddhist temples in Xi'an. Isabel usually brings us a snack when we come home in the afternoon—some sliced papaya, some avocado juice (more like an avocado shake)—and we sit on Karimu's porch. A breeze bounds over the concrete wall, and we people watch, spying the women wearing colorful cloth kanga-like skirts, baskets balanced on their heads as they walk down the street.

I enjoy hanging out with Karimu's kids. Shy, smart Grace warms up to us more each day, asking Julie to watch her jump rope. The acrobatic Scotty likes me to lift him over my head. Kafil arrives each evening in his blue uniform, backpack filled with homework. We eat *matoke*, a typical Kikuyu meal from Karimu's tribe—a stew of potatoes, green bananas, carrots, and a little bit of meat—and Kafil tells Julie and me about atomic wedgies: he just learned about them from a kid at school. If you're not a wedgie aficionado, an atomic wedgie is when you pull someone's undies up over their head. I had no idea the wedgie was an international concept.

"Have you ever had a wedgie?" Kafil asks me.

"You mean have I given one or received one?"

"Both."

"I must have. I don't remember. But I have a friend who used to give wet willies."

"What's *that*?"

He asks in the voice of one who's about to receive great knowledge.

"Well, you lick your finger, and then you swirl it in someone's ear."

He cracks up, then pretends to do it to Grace with his pinky. She giggles.

"Use a bigger finger," I tell him. "Use your index finger. Here—let me demonstrate on Julie."

"Don't even," she says.

"Actually, instead of one finger you could use all five if someone's ear is big enough."

"What would you call that?" he says, laughing.

"I dunno. Maybe a Wet William."

He laughs more, rising in and out of his chair.

"Wait—I've got it," I say. "It's a Wet *Whale*-y. Get it? Whale? Willie? Whale-y? Because a whale is big and wet?"

"That's bad," says Julie of the awful pun.

"Don't listen to her," I tell Kafil. I lean in and whisper: "Deep down she thinks I'm a genius."

"Do you think he's a genius?" he asks her.

She smiles at Kafil, scrunching her nose and shaking her head.

We pass a Muslim woman near Calvary Zion one afternoon, her body and head covered except for her eyes. She says *Jambo* with a surprising jauntiness given the forbidding black attire, but all I can think is . . . *Damn—she must be roasting.* This is the heat of summer at home; the heat of my father's death. The June day that seems increasingly distant, yet still so easy to summon, like pulling a book from a shelf. Dad enters my thoughts frequently here, perhaps because of the heat, perhaps because we've entered a new year, a year that will mark the five-year anniversary of his death.

Two weeks before he collapsed on the golf course, Dad hit the first hole-in-one of his life. My father was not a fist-pumping, chest-beating kind of guy: his golf buddies said *they* were the ones who screamed when the ball rolled in the hole. Dad just walked to the green, leaned down, casually pulled the ball from the cup. We're alike in that way. "You never get excited about anything," Julie has told me. But I know Dad was thrilled. After he died, I used his computer to write the funeral program, and I found an e-mail he sent to a friend. "On Saturday I had my first hole-in-one," he wrote, followed by—I counted—*twenty-one* exclamation points.

I read e-mails he'd sent to his former Japanese colleagues. Once he was dead, and dead so suddenly, I was less concerned with his privacy than with glimpsing his state of mind; discovering some premonition, or some sense that, yes, he was content with his new life. In each note, he encouraged his friends to visit. He spoke of his last trip to Japan, when he was flown to Tokyo for a retirement party, heavy on sake and golf. This was a huge honor, particularly for an American. He wrote one Japanese friend a few months before his death:

> *Retirement life is OK so far and I am enjoying it, but I miss being part of the team and especially my visits to Japan. The retirement party in Japan will always be one of the best memories of my life. I thank you and everyone else for that honor. I hope my retirement budget will allow me to make a few trips to Japan to play a little golf and see everyone. Please tell my friend Suzuki-san that I am taking his advice and "taking care of my family and wife" as he told me to do at the party.*

The day before Dad died, a Japanese friend e-mailed him in broken English—he was pleased that Dad was enjoying life: "I could get good image in my head about every your description in the mail because of your exciting."

My mom took a picture of Dad at home after he hit the hole-in-one. He wasn't happy about posing, but stood on their deck, trees behind him, holding the ball and the scorecard. It was his last photo. The photo that sat on his casket. At his funeral, my sister, Cathy, and I read eulogies. "My dad lived life intensely," Cathy said. "He truly exuded the American work ethic. He believed in working hard and always, always doing your best. We heard many times that nothing was worth doing unless you were going to do it right. But he didn't just say this. This was the way he lived. He truly believed that you could do anything if you tried hard enough.

Now it is our turn to take the lessons he shared, and execute them on our own."

Rose wants us to arrive earlier each morning at Calvary Zion: the mothers do much of their cleaning before 9 a.m. Upon learning their daily workload I vow to never again complain about work. Each day one of the mothers is up at 3:45 a.m. to boil water for tea and start breakfast. The next one is up at 4:30 to assist with cooking and waking the kids. The third is up at 5:00 to help feed, bathe, and dress them. They try to get to sleep at night by 9:30 or 10:00.

"No wonder they like our help for all the mundane stuff," says Julie.

Julie, at the moment, is pondering the CDC's position on chicken shit. We're sifting through rice on the porch bench as two chickens and a few chicks walk by our feet. The rice has pebbles in it, so we pour mounds of rice onto wicker trays and pluck out the rocks and any other foreign objects. The chickens usually stay out back—which means we dodge poop on the backyard concrete while hanging laundry in bare feet—though they use the hallway as a bypass to the front, in the hope, I'm guessing, of pecking at falling rice.

"I'm sure the CDC would frown on that," says Julie of the backyard turds.

"Stepping in turds or the mere presence of turds?"

"The mere presence. You know—disease."

As far as I can tell, the chickens contribute nothing to the house, not that I expect them to help with homework or hang wet laundry. But they provide no eggs. They're here because one of the kids loves animals, so he's raising them. I guess Jane figured that with only forty kids and a dog the house needed more life forms.

Rose gives Elijah a bath outside as we sift. She pours a bucket of water over him as he stands, the water glistening on his belly. It's the first time I've seen Elijah smile. His smile makes Rose laugh, which makes me and Julie laugh. He's a far different boy than when he arrived, Rose says.

"He did not know how to eat. He open his mouth and wait for something to go in. He was half dead. Now he eat and eat and eat. Sometimes he vomits he eat so much. He is getting revenge for not having food."

He climbs into Julie's lap after his bath, still naked, as we continue picking through rice. A girl named Hiari "helps" us. She's probably about seven or eight, tall and gangly, bald spots in her closely cropped hair. Jane told us that Hiari is deaf and dumb, and that she should be in a school for deaf children, but despite many calls to many bureaucrats, Jane has yet to find success. So instead of attending school, Hiari is here with the babies.

She points at the rice, and then at me, nodding. She's mute, though she makes burbling, *blllpppp* types of noises.

"Yes, thank you," I say, nodding back.

Policemen found Hiari several months ago, alone on Mombasa's streets. When no one claimed her, or sought her, she was brought to Calvary Zion. Hiari is certainly not dumb. Her body language exudes a strutting confidence. She's just frustrated that she can't communicate, and because of that, she throws tantrums.

When Julie and I folded laundry, Hiari pointed at the clothesline, showing me where to grab more dry dresses and shirts and pants.

"She should be in management," I told Julie.

Hiari points and *blllpppp*s and waves when Abraham, a cheerful guy who is Jane's brother, pulls through the gate in a pickup truck. Occasionally he's here in the afternoons, and he clearly loves the kids as much as they love him. The truck bed is loaded with thirty to thirty-five yellow canisters of water. I help lug them to a tank out back. Calvary Zion doesn't have running water, so twice a day, Abraham replenishes our supply.

He offers to drive us to Marvel to deliver lunch. Julie and I climb in the truck bed with the empty yellow canisters, the smell of burning trash hitting us on the bumpy, dusty ride. It's a toxic aroma that reminds us a bit of . . .

"Barf," says Julie.

"Yeah, it's a little barfy. I'm gonna keep talking so I don't breathe through my nose."

"Is that what it takes to make you talk?"

"I guess. Try that at home when I clam up."

"What—burn some trash?"

"Sure. Instant conversation starter."

"That's *really* sad."

I haven't told her about Monique, not that there's anything to hide. Nothing happened. And I'm proud of that. You think—you hope—that as a husband or wife you'll thwart temptation, but until it happens, until you face the heat, the attraction—the warm whisper of infidelity—you can't be sure. I was caught up by the moment, but I never lost control. I reconfirmed what I've always known, but perhaps had taken for granted: that I love Julie more than anything on Earth. That I need to do a better job of showing that love, and sharing that love, and caring for her. Hers is the only whisper I want to hear.

Monique and I exchanged some e-mails when I returned from Palestine. I heard from her on New Year's Eve, when she and Marcen returned to Beit Jibrin after visiting Jordan. I had told her to write. But once we started e-mailing, *that's* when it felt wrong. Julie didn't even know this person existed. And I realized how badly I had misread Monique's feelings. When I told her we would probably never see each other again—we live on separate continents, after all—she was hurt. And I understood then that we saw the situation differently. I saw us as two friends who, in a screwed-up place, after two emotional weeks, became close. She saw us, I think, as two friends who were falling in love.

She and Marcen were thinking about traveling to the States;

she e-mailed me and asked if we could see each other. A lake house, perhaps. The two of us.

I can't do that, I wrote. If things were different, if I weren't married, who knows? I might have packed myself in her suitcase, followed her home from the West Bank. But things aren't different. I don't want them to be different. I'm a married man. I'm devoted to my wife.

Her response was angry. She told me I misunderstood, though I can't imagine that I misunderstood. And then, the next day, she apologized. And though she never said the word, I read her message to be . . .

Goodbye.

Which it was.

Before dinner, Julie teaches Kafil some yoga moves. She takes a yoga class once a week, which has cured an achy back, and Kafil is curious. I suspect he thinks yoga will make him elastic, like Reed Richards from the Fantastic Four. Kafil is a great kid: incredibly mature—he came home this evening, started his homework, brought in the laundry, polished his shoes—yet he still has that juvenile, what's-a-wet-willie silly side.

"How would you cure choking?" he asks Julie one night, knowing that she's a nurse.

"Like this"—and she pretends to strangle him. Which he thinks is hilarious.

Equally hilarious (though unintentionally so) is *Storm over Paradise*, a Mexican telenovela dubbed into the overacted, clipped English of an old Godzilla movie. We watch it after dinner: the show's evil heroine, Maura, who will eventually be killed by bees (seriously), is stealing control of a ranch run by the weepy Bravo family. Each character is a caricature—Maura is Snidely Whiplash with bosoms—yet it's so bad it's addictive. After that, the more serious *Nairobi Law* dramatizes real-life court cases. In tonight's episode, a housekeeper is fired when her employers discover she has HIV. She sues—and loses—but Karimu remembers the actual case: an HIV-infected waitress was fired by a catering company, sued for unfair dismissal, and won close to thirty-five thousand dollars in a landmark case.

I miss the verdict because I'm showering: I've been bathing at night to cool off before going to sleep. Most evenings there's a comfy breeze, but the house stays humid and warm. I blame it on the gust-stifling curtains and the mosquito netting.

I wake up frequently most nights, coughing a dry cough from the Handala bug, sticky and warm from the heat. The digital thermometer on Julie's travel clock reads 85 degrees one muggy night (though she doesn't tell me this, assuming the knowledge would make me hotter). I've been wetting a rag and leaving it in the bed, and when I wake up at 2 or 3 a.m., I rub it over my face and arms and chest and think cool thoughts. Slurpees. The air-conditioned ATMs in Mombasa. Swimming pools.

I was swimming the day Dad collapsed, and I've wondered many times if I hit the water at the moment he fell. I can see it . . . I run and leap from the edge of the pool; the squeals of splashing children like sirens. I'm airborne. Diving toward the deep end. Arms outstretched. Legs straight. *This* is the moment when he crumples. We are in unison despite the distance. As my hands hit the water, his hands reach for his heart. As I surge toward the surface, toward the light, his life goes forever black. Alive as I dive in, dead as I come up.

It's a pointless exercise. One I haven't done in quite a while. What does it matter? What does it change? And Dad's death wasn't a tragedy. He was sixty-five years old, young in many ways, but his was a full life, an influential life, a life that changed others.

You are a vessel, Jane had said.

I'm guessing she doesn't recall saying it. She's probably told the

same thing to countless volunteers. So I don't want to overdrama-
tize this, and I don't want to imply I'm on some woo-woo African-
inspired mystical mission, but something about the way she said it
struck me. The conviction. I think it means I'm supposed to help
Jane, to help the children of La La Shou and Bajo de Meco, no matter
how small my contributions compared to the needs, even when I'm
back in my comfort zone: when I'm not in my African bed, warm
beneath the mosquito netting, coughing my Palestinian cough, wiping myself with a rag in the sleepless hours before dawn.

The dog joins us as we walk with Rose to get supplies from Jane's
house. He knows the way, trotting happily ahead of us. Rose asks
where we live in America—and if it's cold.

"The summers are similar to this," says Julie, "but we got almost
two feet of snow around Christmas."

Snow is a foreign concept. Julie explains that it's slick and hard
to drive in and it has to be plowed and snow can be dry and fluffy
unless it's wet and heavy—she accurately and vividly describes
slush—and it sounds like she's making it up, a phony alien world
of salty roads and sand trucks. I'm half waiting for Rose to say,
"Yeah—you put chains on your tires. I'm sure." Instead she simply
shudders and says, "Oh . . . I do not like cold."

The African sun is fierce as we cross the main road, humidity rolling sweat past my ears. We pass a tired, beat-up building,
seemingly abandoned if not for the people inside, broken glass like
diamonds in the road. The dog waits, checks to make sure we're
coming, then walks down the next street. He looks tough: scratches
and scars and torn fur. Rose says he gets in fights. The new site already has three dogs, so I'm wondering how chummy he'll be with
his new canine roommates.

"He does not like to share his food," says Rose. "He stays at the
home, but he leaves to poop and to meet with female dogs."

"Not a bad life," I say.

The same animal-loving boy who cares for the chickens apparently cares for the dog.

"We once had rabbits but they were slaughtered," says Rose.

"I hope the chickens don't know that," I say.

At the house, Jane's adopted son, Christopher, is unhappy to see us. He cries and clings to the leg of a teenager who's washing a car. Abraham, meanwhile, who's sitting on a couch in the cramped living room, rises and grins and waves: "Welcome! Hello! Welcome!"

In the carport we load three big bags of supplies: powdered milk, bananas, onions, cabbage, carrots, toilet paper, a bag of beans, blue industrial-strength soap. Some of the items are quickly put to use when we return: Julie and I cut cabbage and carrots with dull knives. When we're done, I hear Jacob crying on the couch.

"Why are you so fussy?" I say, picking him up.

We walk together outside. I pace in the dirt area, underneath the shade of the tree. He lays his head on my shoulder and drools. A string of spit soon binds us.

I hand him to Julie on the porch. She pulls off his Elmo sweatshirt—he's warm—and feeds him *uji*, a hot cereal made from flour. Jacob was malnourished in the hospital; now he eats with an eager ferocity. Like Elijah, he is getting his revenge. Julie holds him, and when he's finished with his *uji* vengeance, she gives him his medicine, the scrunch of his face revealing his preferences. Zithromax: nasty. Ventolin syrup: better. Orange cough syrup: *oh yeah*.

Elijah sees us and walks to me, arms up, as if realizing—

Hey, wait—tiny humans are getting attention and I'm being excluded.

He's in a yellow polo shirt, no diapers. His legs are covered with dirt from playing outside.

"*Ah-dahh*," he says, pointing as I lift him.

"What—you see the tree?"

"*Ah-dahh*."

"You think?"

"*Ah-dahhhh.*"

"Yeah—good point."

I think *Ah-dahh* is an expression of wonder. Or that's what I hope. It sounds that way, and if you'd spent your first year in confinement, deprived, and if your second year of life was in many ways a second birth, maybe everything *would* be a wonder.

Look at that! A tree! A dog! Sunshine! Food!

The more we walk, the less he talks. We sit on the bench. My left arm is stiff from holding him. He falls asleep, his hand slipping down to his chest.

A breeze gusts, swirling dirt in front of the wall, rustling not only the tree branches but the gate, which clangs and bangs. Across the street, laundry flaps on the roof: bright blue checkered sheets.

"Let's get a more comfortable seat," I say.

We go inside, sitting in one of the beat-up gold chairs. Elijah resettles, nestling against my chest. Out cold.

Rose walks in and smiles. She lifts him from me, puts him on the couch, fastens him in diapers, then flips him to his belly, his cheek against the cushion. He awakens, then is quickly back asleep, oblivious to me watching, oblivious to the flies that land on his back and the soles of his feet.

Since Karimu is an experienced travel-biz pro, we play an after-dinner game on the porch: I read blurbs aloud from a Kenya guidebook, and she says whether they're right, wrong, really wrong, or flat-out ridiculous.

I name a Mombasa nightspot.

"Total whore bar," she says while patching one of Kafil's shirts.

I mention a restaurant.

"I'd rather eat in a prison," she says.

Strike two. I try another.

"Please—the food at Palm City is much better than that. And they probably didn't include Palm City."

"No Palm City," I say, scanning the listings.

The three of us rode to Palm City last night for dinner. It's within walking distance of the Nakumatt, which is Kenya's version of Costco or Super Target or the Ren Ren Le in China. Anything you could possibly want—camcorders, car batteries, blue jeans, goat meat—is available at the Nakumatt, about ten minutes from Kiembeni by *matatu*. We stopped for a pre-dinner Nakumatt trip to scratch off some necessities on Karimu's shopping list. And then came a shock. An honest-to-goodness, holy-cow, I'm-not-kidding-because-I-totally-did-not-expect-this *shock*.

The Nakumatt was brimming with white people.

"Oh my *God*," I practically shouted to Karimu. "Look at all the *wazungu*."

She laughed her boisterous laugh. "A lot of volunteers say that. After living with an African family they forget they're white."

We've been here a week. I guess it doesn't take long to acclimate. And I do seem to be putting the Ken in Kenya rather quickly. Yesterday the mothers at Calvary Zion gave me honorary African status when Priscilla saw me barefoot, peeling potatoes.

"Where are your shoes?" she asked.

"Oh—I'm not sure," I said. "I took them off when I climbed on a bunk bed to clean windows."

"You are becoming an African," said Rose. "Africans can walk for miles without shoes."

The sandal-clad white folk roaming the Nakumatt are primarily German tourists since the store is close to the beach hotels. Germans are prevalent enough in Kiembeni that some of the nearby restaurants advertise bratwursts and *frikandelles* (meatballs). But at Palm City, Julie and I were the only *wazungu*. It's entirely outdoor seating, our round table under a thatched gazebo-like structure, trees and ferns behind us, Michael Jackson wailing "Thriller" from hidden speakers. We ordered *nyama choma*, a group plate of pork and chicken grilled in coals with two sides of potatoes and spinach with onions. A waitress brought a water bowl for pre-meat hand washing; we splashed our hands like surgeons. As with most dishes here, *nyama choma* is an eat-with-your-hands meal. The pork was particularly good, smoky and moist.

"So how many volunteers are a total pain?" I asked Karimu, grabbing more pork.

I'm always curious to hear travel-biz folks confess their dark secrets about problematic clients. On a group bike trip in the Loire Valley of France, I asked one of our French guides about problem bikers. The guide said one woman had never ridden a bike before. A friend had talked her into coming and riding, oh, thirty-five miles a day for a week. It was a disaster. On that same Loire Valley trip, we stopped at a goat cheese farm, sampling cheeses near the barn. Our guides asked a curmudgeonly biker from Sacramento if he was enjoying himself.

"I can smell goat shit at home," he said.

Despite my goat shit story, Karimu didn't take my tell-me-about-big-jerks bait, insisting instead that most volunteers are very nice and very friendly and—

"Gimme a break," I said. "You must've had some morons here."

"Well," she said at last, "one girl thought she was in South Africa."

See? Thank you. That's what I was looking for.

"Oh my God—she obviously did a lot of prep work," said Julie.

"Yeah—that's pretty bad," I said. "I mean, I could see if someone drugged you and placed you on a plane and you had no idea where you landed, but otherwise . . ."

Karimu laughed and poured Coke into a glass. Another volunteer was supposed to stay for two months, then left after three days, without saying goodbye. But most volunteer complaints tend to revolve around mundane stuff: not having running water, or hot water, or not liking the food.

I've enjoyed the food here, tasting traditional dishes, staying in Karimu's home, playing with her kids. I'm enjoying the time with new friends who are already old friends. Enjoying the time to talk and laugh and eat and learn.

Six days before Dad's death, my mom hosted Father's Day dinner. Dad grilled chicken, the smell similar to *nyama choma*. My sister and her family walked home, so Dad and I sat on the deck, barefoot, bellies full, sipping wine; the sunset blackening backyard oaks. He rested his glass against his knee, swatted the occasional gnat. We watched the fireflies twinkle against the trees. One of those unremarkable moments that's now forever idyllic. Father and son. Hanging out. Sitting on the darkening deck, talking, and not talking, and refilling our glasses, enjoying the quiet and the summer breeze, the fireflies blinking, yellow then black, floating like dust.

He didn't do enough of that. *We* didn't do enough of that. So much bullshit clutters our lives. Julie and I split a second Tusker, and I resolve to spend more time gazing at fireflies.

We only work a half day on Friday so we can leave for a weekend safari in Tsavo National Park. Tsavo is Kenya's largest park, but it's less crowded with tourists than other reserves, mainly because the higher brush can make it tough to spot animals. I'm willing to take the risk if it reduces our people-to-wildlife ratio.

We feel guilty skipping out early, but Karimu suggested it. If we leave by early afternoon we can hopefully spot a few elephants and zebras and other Kenyan creatures before dark. Our driver and guide is a friendly, stocky guy named Rudolph: Karimu knows him through her years in the travel biz, and they're from the same tribe.

Lest you think we're shirking our housecleaning duties, Julie and I provide Calvary Zion with plenty of morning labor before embarking on our *Wild Kingdom* weekend. I wash dishes and scrub pots, which are blackened with caked-on, burned-on bits of bubbled gunk, and after carrying Jacob until I can no longer stand the heat we hang clothes to dry out back. Supposedly the home has a donated washing machine, though we never see it, probably because they don't have running water, which means the mothers do laundry for forty children by hand.

At Rose's request, Julie and I attack a floor-to-ceiling closet the size of a bank vault in one of the back bedrooms, organizing and folding all the clothes. We fold for over two hours: shirts, skirts, jeans, slacks, sweaters, undies, and the occasional towels and sheets.

"These sweaters look handmade," says Julie, holding one and inspecting it.

"That makes me hot just looking at it."

Julie and I and the German girls are roasting, and yet when the kids come from school they put on sweaters.

She takes a picture of me folding clothes, then looks at the screen on the camera.

"In every picture you look like you're sweating."

"That's because I'm sweating in every picture."

A few damp clothes must have been shoved in the closet: it smells musty. Fruit flies sporadically flutter from the cloth. We organize the clothes based on gender, size, and type of clothing, putting the heavy sweatshirts and sweaters in back.

Rose walks in and asks if we're tired. They must think we *wazungu* are soft. All three of the mothers occasionally tell us to rest. I appreciate their concern, though it's a little frustrating. I mean, I'm a grown man. Folding undies will not exhaust me.

We're fine, says Julie. Rose nods. "I like the way you work," she says.

Okay, now I feel bad, because that's seriously high praise. That's like Dr. Seuss saying he likes the way you rhyme. These women work *constantly*. Sometimes when we do small tasks, whether it's washing dishes or cutting vegetables, Rose will say, "Oh . . . I am so grateful." And it's not some throwaway thank-you. She means it. These women do so much, every day, that any help, even from slow and soft us, seems welcome.

"I wonder if they ever get a vacation," says Julie.

"They're probably lucky just to get a night off."

We walk the dirt road to Karimu's, past debris in tall grass: plastic bottles and stray packaging; the occasional black grocery bag tumbling in the wind. Rudolph arrives around one o'clock and we're off, free from the clog of Bamburi and Mombasa, racing into the countryside, passing tiny roadside hotels and basketball-sized rocks that serve as pylons for road work. Like all Kenyan drivers, Rudolph is fearless, zooming past a car on a two-lane blind turn with no shoulder approaching a bridge.

We arrive in Tsavo—alive—engulfed by the landscape. It impresses not in a breathtaking, Grand Canyon way, but through its spare, flat simplicity. The light green grass and darker brush. The reddish-orange dirt roads and sparse, frizzy trees. The sky massive above the long horizon.

If you're a human being, Africa is a homecoming. We are all children of Africa. This is where mankind began. Five million years ago, nine million years ago, somewhere in between, our hairy ancestors began to distinguish themselves from other creatures, their posture shifting upright, their bodies and brains enlarging. It was here our *Homo erectus* kin chipped the first barely distinguishable stone tools. It was here they evolved and grew.

Julie and I stand in the van—Rudolph pushed up the top once we arrived—and we scan the level landscape, the wind hitting our faces as we drive. We're thrilled to see elephants, the tusked adults and the lumbering young, unconfined, their wrinkled skin red from the soil. In just a few afternoon hours in Tsavo East, we see jackals, gazelles, and antelopes; impalas, giraffes, and vervet monkeys (which I dub blue-balled monkeys, because of their bright blue . . .); and more birds that I can name: hawks, eagles, herons, doves; red- and black-beaked hornbills. Rudolph points out a kori bustard, which he says is the largest flying bird in the world. It's ostrich-sized—and about as attractive—standing around five feet tall. Nearby, as we drive, a hippo plods through a pond. Later we stop the van as a pack of baboons crosses the road into the brush.

Whether you believe God made the Earth in seven days (and the evidence suggests it took a tad longer), or that He merely yet magnificently produced the elements and acids and proteins that make life possible, we know at least one thing about God as Creator: He digs diversity. Think of the insanely varied trees and plants that rise from the mineral-rich earth. Or the magnitude of marine life swimming in streams and ponds and oceans and lakes. God created platypuses and plankton, cheetahs and cherries, oak trees and orangutans . . . and people! Just think of the wild variety of people. Brown, black, red, yellow, white (or whatever Caucasians are); fat, thin, short, tall, hairy, bald; big noses, squat noses . . . And yet despite the differences, people are all genetically the same.

I can't fathom the idea that God has a chosen people, or a chosen religion, or a chosen anything. Why would a God that values variety offer one route to knowing Him (or Her, or It, or whatever pronoun God may be, if God exists at all)? Why wouldn't there be multiple routes, as different as our cultures and colors? The idea that God plays favorites is more human than divine, more centered in human pettiness than in holy creation.

I've wondered what makes a person good. I wonder each day in D.C. On a nighttime walk to the train station at L'Enfant Plaza, a man and a woman stopped me on the Mall, the lit Capitol to my left, the lit Washington Monument to my right.

"Can you help me out," he said.

I thought he was a tourist until he held up a soda cup. I apologized and said no.

"I'm a veteran—please. Can you help me out?"

I always make eye contact when I say no, sorry, not that this makes it better.

An old bearded guy frequently sits on the train station's steps, announcing trains as they arrive.

Fredericksburg! Fredericksburg!

Manassas!

He has a standard spiel as he shakes his cup, as rush-hour passengers scurry past.

Help the homeless, help the homeless.

Need ten dollars to get that bed at the mission.

It has a rhythm when he says it, like a ballpark vendor yelling, "Hot dogs, peanuts . . ."

He tells us "God bless you" as we pass, regardless of whether we give him money.

Need ten dollars to get that bed . . .

I've wondered if you really pay ten dollars for a bed at a mission. I've thought before about what strategies I would pursue if I were homeless, how I'd spend food money to maximize my nutrient intake, how I'd test-market which pitches were more likely to result in cash.

"That's why you're not homeless," a friend of mine once said.

The old bearded guy recently announced it was his birthday. Balloons hung from his cart. I gave him a couple of bucks. And then several months later he again said it was his birthday. And I was pissed, because I knew I'd been suckered. But I thought later . . . I'd do the same thing if I were him. If I found a scheme that worked, hell yes I'd use it again.

A friend of mine at work said when he was a boy, at Catholic school, the nuns told him you should always give money to the homeless: a homeless man could be Jesus. But as soon as you give cash to one homeless Jesus, another homeless Jesus appears.

What are we supposed to do?

Once, years ago, I was talking with Dad about *Son of the Morn-*

ing Star, Evan Connell's book on Custer's last stand. Dad used to read a lot of Westerns—his favorite writer was Louis L'Amour—and we talked about the mistreatment of Native Americans over the course of our country's history.

"Well, we've done a lot of wrong," Dad said. "But in the big picture, I'd like to think we've done more good than bad."

Maybe that's the best all of us can do. More good than bad.

The African plains are life at its most Darwinian severe. A life of fangs on flesh and the lapping of blood. Survival of the fittest. But perhaps the fittest survivors—at least among humans—are those with compassion. Of all the creatures roaming Tsavo's plains, only we humans kill each other with easy willingness, for revenge or greed or lust—for sheer cold indifference—a trait as unique as our large brains and opposable thumbs. But compassion *is* wired in our brains. Neuroscientists have studied this: helping others sparks the same brain regions that light up when we experience pleasure.

I hope I'm a kinder person than I was forty-plus months ago, when I hauled trash and painted ceilings in New Orleans. I've met people from over twenty countries during my volunteer jaunts, and these encounters with Kenyans and Brits and Chinese—with folks who have far different perspectives from my own—have changed me as much as the work has. The small things in life seem smaller to me now. *I* feel smaller, and yet somehow larger. I see myself less as a Virginian, or an American, and more as, well—don't be ill—a person. A person of the world. A person with ancient African roots.

We are all Africans. We are all human. We are all vessels.

My mom's cousin Lee—the one who wishes my sixty-nine-year-old mother would start smoking pot—once explained to me why he'd like to be a lion:

"They eat, they fuck, and then they sleep for twenty hours."

He'd seen this on a nature show, though I assume that PBS or

National Geographic did not use the f-word. (*Behind the brush, we can see the Tsavo lions fucking . . .*)

Lions hunt at night, so if we want to see them before they sleep, or fuck, we need to start early. So Julie and I are up at 5:30 a.m. and chugging coffee by 6 a.m. A staff member asks if we heard the lion roaring in the night. A lion's roar can sometimes be heard as far as five miles away, but this one was close. Neither of us heard it. We heard one of the Italian guests snoring in the next tent, but not the king of the beasts.

"Figures," I say. "We hear the snoring Italian but not the roaring lion."

"Maybe the snoring Italian *was* the roaring lion," says Julie.

The Ndololo Camp Site may sit in the heart of Tsavo—the sign in front of our tent's entrance flap warns, "Don't Go Beyond This Point"—but we aren't exactly roughing it. Our tent has two large and comfy beds with white sheets and mosquito netting, and a sturdy desk that evokes an image of Hemingway writing his thoughts after a day of stalking kudus. We have a bathroom with sink and shower, and lights throughout the tent, though electricity cuts off at 10 p.m.

"This is more like a condo than a tent," says Julie.

Our tent standards have clearly risen. Sixteen years ago, for our second anniversary, we flew to California to visit my parents, then borrowed their car and drove up the coast into Oregon. We went as far north as Crater Lake National Park, home of America's deepest lake, formed by a collapsing volcano. The lake water is a vibrant blue, reflecting the clouds and surrounding mountains. We camped there a few days. Dad let us borrow his old tent: we'd aired it out in my parents' small backyard, since he probably hadn't used the tent since his hunting days before I was born, or maybe on a Cub Scout camping trip when I was ten.

With the exception of the tent, Julie and I hadn't planned what we'd need. We bought food at a general store before driving to the campground, and for three days we survived on Pop Tarts and peanut butter and bologna (bologna sandwiches one night, grilled bologna sandwiches the next). And since it was summer, we weren't prepared for the cold mountain nights. Our sleeping bags were warm, but my exposed head was freezing. I was then struck by an ingenious idea: I'd sleep with underwear on my head. I put one pair on, the leg holes sitting east and west, and then a second pair over those, this time north-south, thus covering my entire head.

Smart, right?

Julie wanted to take a photo. I begged her not to. But I fully realized: when a woman is willing to spend her wedding anniversary eating grilled bologna sandwiches with a man who sleeps with two pairs of carefully placed underpants on his head, you should never let her go.

The dawn glows orange over gray clouds. We're in the van with Rudolph. He talks with another guide on the radio and zooms down a dirt road, poofs of dust rising in our wake. Yesterday my white shirt turned bronze from the red earth, even though I never left the van.

Up ahead, we see not lions, but five vans like ours, parked, which means lions must be near. And then we spot her. A female in the road. She's glorious, proud and scarred from battles, indifferent to the open-mouthed *wazungu* faces gazing from the various vans. The rising sun paints shadows on her ribs. She saunters to the dry grass, stalks rustling beneath her paws, before lying down, her fur blending into the plains. Farther out, a male ambles, tail curled, his dark mane formidable like the vastness of the land. The lions here have thinner manes than elsewhere in Africa, an accommodation to the heat, perhaps. His body is curved muscles, thick shoulders, and rippled legs, and yet he's lean, magnificent, cruel.

Back at camp for breakfast, a few of the staffers ask if we saw lions. Two, we say.

"Ah—you are very lucky!"

Yes—we are indeed lucky. In many ways.

Our bags packed in the van, we leave Tsavo East for Tsavo West. Tsavo is divided in two for administrative reasons—like dividing Yellowstone in half so it's easier to manage—yet the terrain shifts, the flat plains bulging into mountains, the trees thicker, more plentiful. We pass zebras and impalas—which I now view as lion food—and elephants and giraffes. Piles of elephant dung the size of pitcher's mounds loom near the road. Rudolph points out dikdiks, a type of small antelope, which travel in pairs. He tells us they mate for life—they're rarely seen alone—and commit suicide when their partner dies, sometimes bashing their head against a tree.

"Will you be my dikdik?" I ask Julie.

"Yes . . . except for the suicide part."

"Well, the suicide part is really the key to the whole deal."

If we ever renew our vows we should include a dikdik suicide pact, I tell her. And she doesn't have to bash her head against a tree; I'm cool with other methods.

"That's so sweet of you," she says, and she smiles, the smile I've loved since high school, the smile that says—

Remind me again why I put up with your nonsense?

That night, we stay at the Ngulia Safari Lodge, which looks down on the green valley below. I lie on the bed, still in my clothes, my magazine making me drowsy. Through the mosquito netting I see Julie jump up onto a chair.

"That was a mouse," she says. "A *big* mouse."

The rodent scurries under an extra bed near the window.

"Is that another one?" I say.

"Where?"

"Up on that shelf?"

It's a log shelf running along the top of the wall.

"Something just went running up there," I say.

Julie peeks around the room, but ultimately we're both too tired to get worked up about it. We're in the wilds of Tsavo. Countless critters have surely inspected our room.

The night beats with the guttural snorts of water buffalo and the burps of frogs. After dinner, a Maasai gentleman had escorted us back to our room. The Maasai are Kenya's best-known tribe, famous for their commitment to traditional ways, for drinking cattle blood and *mursik* (milk fermented with cow piss and ashes), for their seminomadic lifestyle, for defining their wealth through cattle. They've lost much of their land due to everything from commercial farming to national parks. This gentleman wore a traditional red *shuka*, a long, blanketlike cloth worn over the shoulders, and carried a walking stick. Economic necessity often requires them to take jobs like this one.

Before we went in the room, the Maasai man asked us, "Do you see the water buffalo?"

We could hear their deep bellows competing against the frogs, but no—we couldn't see them. He could. At least a hundred of them at the bottom of a hill maybe two hundred feet from where we stood, hundreds more below. He flashed a light, illuminating eyes. I realize this Maasai man lives here, that he's more intimate with the creatures and the terrain, but it bothered me that our eyes were so disconnected from the night, our lives so disconnected from the land, so disconnected from creation.

I'll miss the wiry acacia trees. They rise from Tsavo's plains, narrow canopies like umbrellas above long branchless trunks. Giraffe and zebra linger under their shade; flaky weaver nests hang from limbs like ornaments. The trees are Tsavo's most distinguishable feature, particularly in Tsavo East, and I admire them as we leave the park and return to Mombasa.

On our final morning animal quest, we rode with Rudolph and a Maasai guide on a jutted off-road, searching for leopards and lions. Rudolph saw tracks alongside the thick brush and assumed the beasts were hiding. A tree where a leopard often resides was empty. So he drove the van down the pitted trail, our heads jerking, and as the tires hit a sandy ditch about two feet deep, we weren't entirely shocked when the van got stuck.

We sat at a sharp angle. The tires spun. The Maasai guide, who had traded his traditional red garb for jeans and a sweatshirt, hopped out and pushed the van. No good. Rudolph asked us to get out—"Okay by me," said Julie, who wondered if the van was about to crash on its side—and he stayed in the driver's seat, gently pumping the gas, the van rocking forward then back.

I looked out over the tall, green brush. The animals in Tsavo are more aggressive than in other Kenyan parks—more wild—perhaps because they're less accustomed to seeing people.

"Now I'm kind of hoping we *don't* see another lion," I said.

Yesterday, a Kenya Wildlife Service (KWS) ranger escorted us to the killing grounds of the famous lions of Tsavo. In 1898, two lions terrorized British government officials and migrant workers—many of them Indian—as they built a railroad bridge above the Tsavo River. Over thirty people became lion takeout food. The lions may have developed a taste for humans due to Arab slave caravans that trekked through Tsavo to Mombasa: many slaves died from tsetse fly bites, and their corpses became snacks. The project's chief engineer finally shot the lions and sold them to the Field Museum in Chicago, where they remain stuffed and preserved on display. The Kenyan government wants the stuffed lions back, the ranger tells us.

The ranger joined us in the van at an information center. He looked more like a soldier with green fatigues and a thick black belt, his pants tucked in polished black boots, a long black rifle in his lap. Poaching is a long-standing problem. Forty years ago, close to 20,000 black rhinos roamed Kenya. Now the number is down to around 600 (which is an improvement: in the 1980s only about

300 black rhinos were left). Kenya suffered its worst rhino losses in twenty-five years in 2009, when gangs using automatic rifles slayed twelve black rhinos and six white rhinos.

Animals are killed for everything from their tusks to their coats to their exotic meat. Two days after we arrived in Kenya, KWS security agents confiscated four hundred kilograms of game meat on its way to a market in Nairobi. In Tsavo, the elephant population dropped from around 35,000 in the late 1960s to a little more than 6,000 by the late 1980s, the animals suffering first from drought, then poaching. In 1988, the Kenyan government issued a shoot-on-sight order against poachers. The situation stabilized. More than 11,000 elephants now rumble across Tsavo's plains.

The ranger took Julie and me down a hill to an empty streambed as Rudolph relaxed in the van. We stopped by a large round impression, as if someone had shoved the base of a garbage can in the sand. Elephant tracks. He also spotted leopard tracks, and the remains of a zebra kill, the bones scattered by scavenging hyenas. As we walked, the ranger kept his hand on his rifle, alert, watching the brush along the bed. KWS officers killed two elephant poachers and injured two others in the Kubihoke area about two weeks before we arrived in Mombasa.

Fortunately, we were not eaten, here or near the leopard tree, where Rudolph finally rocked the van from the ditch. Now we head back through Tsavo East, back toward Mombasa, cruising by occasional water holes and sausage trees, the fruit shaped like, well, sausage, which is fermented and made into beer. The Maasai man impersonates a drunk in the front seat, sticking out his tongue and rolling his eyes.

We drop off the Maasai man in his town: he works in Tsavo four to five days a week. A trench extends along the road for miles. Rudolph says it's for fiber optics, but it's being dug by hand. To *Uganda*. High-tech network, low-tech installation.

The closer we get to Mombasa, the warmer it feels. Crawling

through the chaotic traffic jam of Bamburi's only intersection, we once again smell hot rotting trash, see mosquitoes swirling above. Tsavo seems far away.

When we arrive back at Karimu's her mother and brother are visiting. Isabel and Karimu make dinner, and show Julie how to cook pilau rice. She sits on a wooden kitchen stool that's round and low to the ground: African women use these while peeling potatoes or cooking on small grills.

Julie has been writing Swahili words in her journal, adding them as she learns them. "Thanks" is *asante*. "You're welcome" is *karibu*. *Mtoto* means "child." That evening, I learn that *safari*, in Swahili, means "journey." I like that. Life isn't a journey. It's a really long safari.

Our first morning back at Calvary Zion, a grinning Rose welcomes us, clasping our hands, kissing Julie on the cheeks. She's so happy to see us, so jubilant, that she asks Julie to scrub the floors. The mothers clean the floors each morning because forty pairs of kiddie feet turn white tile cocoa brown. The home has no mops, so Rose demonstrates her preferred technique: dip a towel in a bucket of water, wring it out on the floor, then wipe the floor using a side-to-side corkscrew motion. Julie is a quick study, bending to form a human triangle: feet out, butt up, hands together on the towel. I scrub a few days later, and I can say with confidence that an orthopedist would not approve of this bent-over, back-straining technique.

Rose watches Julie mop, then hugs her when she's done. Later, out back, near the clothesline, Rose holds her hand. As we finish folding clothes in the closet—a final pile from Friday—Rose takes our picture with her phone.

"I want to remember you after you are gone," she says.

Rose likes Julie. How could she not? Everyone likes Julie. Saying you don't like Julie is like saying you don't like sunshine or candy or bunnies. Not liking Julie says more about you than her. The worst thing I can say about her, aside from being too much like me, is that she's chronically late. Our last morning in Tsavo, we were supposed to eat breakfast at six-thirty, but Julie was photographing water buffalo, so we weren't ready when our Maasai escort arrived, which left me making awkward African chitchat. (*So those red Maasai robes—are they comfy?*) You know how some people panic and rush around the house when they're running behind? Not Julie. She's comfortable with tardiness.

We peel potatoes for lunch out back, using the yellow water canisters as stools. Rose sings while she peels, the chickens pacing behind her, beneath the straining clotheslines. I like to hear the mothers sing. Alice sometimes sings what sounds like a traditional African folk song, the notes matching the strokes of her work.

"At home, you use machines for everything," says Rose, after asking if the floor scrubbing hurt my back. "We Africans. We do everything by hand."

I've seen Priscilla open cans by pounding a large knife with another large knife into the tops, which seems like an ideal way to slice an artery. The knives are dull, which almost makes them more dangerous. Julie used the dull knife to cut veggies and it slipped on a carrot and gashed her finger. She instinctively put her bloody hand under the faucet, but there's no running water. She used baby wipes to clean up the blood.

Despite her bandaged kitchen wound, Julie is elevated to sous chef. She fries veggies in a large pan on a charcoal grill, which is outside, next to the kitchen door. Charcoal and firewood are Kenya's most common cooking methods. Even at Karimu's home, which has running water and relatively reliable power, charcoal is the fuel for cooking. At Calvary Zion, a sack of charcoal lasts just two to three days, says Rose. If there's no charcoal they use wood, but wood is smoky.

The mothers enlist Julie to make *ugali*. It starts as a flour, frequently cornmeal, which you add to boiling water. It thickens quickly, turning gluelike. Julie struggles to stir.

"Use two hands," says Priscilla.

Julie's face contorts, her forearms strain. Within minutes they take pity: Priscilla stirs.

"It wasn't really stirring—it's more like she beat the shit out of it," Julie says as we take lunch to Marvel. "Beating it makes it smooth. Mine would have been *really* lumpy."

Now that she's an expert, I tell her I've got a great name for an *ugali* restaurant. I doubt she remembers, but I once proposed an S&M restaurant specializing in Asian cuisine called *Thai Me Up*. The waiters would spank you while serving seafood curry.

"Think about it—no restaurants at home serve *ugali*," I say, explaining my business model. "Actually, I can't think of any Kenyan restaurants. There's Ethiopian, Moroccan . . ."

"So what would you call it?" she says.

"What would *we* call it. It'd be *our* restaurant."

"Oh, of course. What are we calling our *ugali* restaurant."

"Ready? We'll call it *Ooooo—Golly!*"

She laughs. Of course, she laughs at Kafil's jokes, too. When I suggest a Little Richard–themed restaurant named *Ugali Miss Molly*, she rolls her eyes. "You should've stopped with *Oooo Golly*," she says.

Ugali is not a kiddie favorite, but when Julie dishes out the cabbage and veggie mix at Marvel the kids want more, more, more, interested in accumulating *ugali* as opposed to eating it. Logan competes for a second scoop—he holds his plate up—even before Julie finishes distributing scoop number one. Debbie stands on her chair, bug-eyed.

"Somehow I'm guessing she shouldn't be doing that," I tell Julie in a low voice, since the teacher is sitting on his desk reviewing a handful of alphabet exercises.

We've dubbed Debbie "the Drama Queen." She's adorable in a

Shirley Temple way, frequently making silly faces and silly gestures, but the slightest thing makes her howl and sob.

Two more kids follow her lead and stand on their chairs. It's a test of our nonintervention policy.

"Right now only three of them are doing it," says Julie. "If we say no all six will do it."

Debbie wipes spinach on her face, mugging for the other kids.

"At least they aren't throwing it," says Julie. "I'd have to holler at them for that."

And then Angela, the principal, fills the doorway with her imposing frame, fists on her hips.

"*Sit*," she commands. "We do not eat like animals."

They sit.

Between the tone of her voice and her accent Angela reminds me of Nelson Mandela, which is an idiotic thing to say, since a South African accent is surely different from an East African accent. It's like an African saying a Boston woman sounds like Lyndon Johnson. But in my mind, Marvel's principal is a short, heavyset, female Mandela.

She shakes her head after admonishing Debbie.

"They don't listen to us," Julie tells her.

"That is because they know you can't punish them."

"Smart kids," I say.

We return to Marvel in the afternoon with the German volunteers, Barbara and Martina, to pick up the kids. We've been instructed not to carry them—they need to learn to walk, says Rose—though one girl, Johari, often takes off her shoes and cries. It's the cry of a child actress; a girl who's learned that softhearted volunteers will carry her when tears flow.

"She's a manipulative little bugger," says Julie.

One day Johari pinched Julie, so Julie pinched her back.

"Maybe that wasn't the best thing to do, but she only did it once."

Logan and I tend to zip ahead of the group on the walk home. He takes my hand, which surprises me. He can be a shit sometimes. The gate guy was playing with a boy named Njau the other day, and Logan butted in. Njau sobbed, shuffling to the wall of the house, falling on his butt as he wept. Logan walked away. The gate guy called Njau to come back. Once Njau started walking over, Logan ran and took the gate guy's hand again. Njau sobbed again. Logan laughed. It's like he was tormenting him for sport.

As Karimu noted, it's partly a way of getting noticed. But it's also the lack of individual supervision given the number of kids, and the nature, I suppose, of being strong in a pack. So I'm happy Logan is getting this one-on-one attention, and even though it's hot and our hands are sweaty, we keep holding them, walking at his pace, and when he gazes at walls and trees and birds I steer him around piles of cow shit and holes in the dusty path.

I've thought a few times here about a friend back home. Her ex-husband, Ron, was a carpenter, and during the 1990s, as Internet entrepreneurs made huge and sudden fortunes, Ron developed a niche business building wine cellars. Some customers wanted a wine cellar even though they didn't drink wine. It was a competition of excess: their neighbors built a wine cellar, so now *they* needed a wine cellar, and it had to be bigger, so they'd spend up to sixty thousand dollars even though they wouldn't know a French merlot from Mountain Dew. And because they weren't wine drinkers—this is the part that kills me—they'd sometimes buy wine bottles filled with colored water to stock their cellars. Which means there's a whole industry based on the production of fake wine for people who don't drink the real thing.

I don't want to be self-righteous. People can spend money any way they want. You want a Porsche? Go for it. The desire for wealth unites both rich and poor (though if I can make just one self-righteous and hypocritical comment, the Earth would suffer a planetary stroke if the American lifestyle were followed on a global scale). But fake wine for a wine cellar you had built even though you don't drink wine? That's the definition of more money than you know what to do with. It's just . . . shallow. And I worry that, in some ways, these two-week trips of mine may be similar. Lacking in depth. Because I don't want to be fake wine. To be colored water posing as chardonnay; a bottle that holds nothing. And I don't want to forget these kids. To see their hardships and then disappear forever. It's easy to walk on a dusty road here and think, "Yes, dammit, somehow I will help these kids." But it's harder to actually do it.

Logan and I arrive at the gate.

"We're home," I say.

I bang the gong-like knocker three times.

"We're so much faster than the rest of them," I tell him. "I don't even see them."

I pretend like I'm running hard, pumping my elbows. I'm not sure he understands. The gate opens, and we go inside, and we let go of each other's hands.

"When are you going to tell me why girls are so troublesome?" Kafil asks me one night.

I'd promised him this insight a few days ago. We were sitting on the porch, Julie and I in plastic chairs we'd pulled outside, Karimu sitting on the wide rail in front of us, relaxed, leaning against a wood post. She was disparaging men for their laziness. It was my fault: I'd asked why you never see men balancing baskets on their heads like women do.

"In Kenya, the women work while the men nap," she said.

"Well, I'm sure the men are tired from all the work they did during the day."

"Yeah, right."

"No, really," I said. "It's very hard to be a man in today's world—particularly a white man."

I said this to rile her, knowing that this is a surefire way to rile women of any color, generation, or nationality. After nearly choking, she unleashed a brief but pointed rebuttal, then shifted her condemnation to boys, talking about their hyperactivity and the weird things they do. To be fair, Scotty had just pulled his lower lip like a window shade to the bottom of his jaw, a feat of facial elasticity that I thought looked pretty cool.

"Don't listen to them," I told Kafil. "At some point I'll tell you the truth about women."

"Tell me now!" he said, eager to learn.

"Well, the fact that I don't want to tell you with your mom and Julie sitting here pretty much tells you everything you need to know."

Now, as we sit for dinner, I divert his renewed quest to understand girls by asking about his day at school.

"Do you feel any smarter?"

"Yes—my head is getting very big."

"You know, I was just thinking your head looks bigger than it did last night."

"It keeps getting bigger and bigger and bigger!"

He makes an earsplittingly high-pitched screeching noise, pretending that his head is a popping balloon. (I'm sure Karimu thinks this is weird, too.)

"I'm concerned you're going to need new shirts," I say. "The shirts you have aren't going to fit around your rapidly expanding head."

He makes a clicking sound as he pretends to knock his head with his fist. This is his new shtick. Grace does it as well.

One night, while watching Nigerian soap operas and drinking chai tea, Karimu told us that she's been criticized, sometimes by total strangers, for being a single mother.

"I tell them, have my children ever bothered you?"

They're great kids. Before dinner, Grace shined her shoes. She balanced the shoe shine jar on her head, then walked, like the women we see on the road. Next she balanced the brush on top of the jar. Scotty had been playing with a plastic train, but feeling competitive, he stood on one foot on the porch and hopped.

After dinner, Grace jumps rope.

"Look!" she says to us. She jumps and jumps.

"I counted twenty-three," I say.

Her eyes widen and she jumps again and surpasses that total: 31, 32, 33 . . .

Julie and I each take the ends of a long cord and twirl it so she can jump in the middle. It takes me a minute to get the rhythm and height, a six-foot-two man not being the ideal person to swing rope for a third-grade girl.

"I want to try," says Julie. She switches places with Grace. After getting tangled a few times, Julie trades flip-flops for sneakers, times her entry, then jumps in, doing a one-foot-then-the-other hopping technique—

1, 2, 3 . . .

Left foot up, then the right foot—

6, 7 . . .

And then she reaches 11. Grace and I cheer. And as we laugh I think, *I'm going to miss this.* A lot. Hanging out at home with the kids. The laughter. The precious silliness amid the daily drama.

A few days ago, Karimu conferred with her neighbors about a crow problem: there's a nest with baby chicks in the tree that's squeezed between the concrete wall and her porch. Karimu has worried that Scotty will provoke the crows, since he likes to hang from the branches. Yesterday morning, one of the crows, presumably the mother, attacked the boy next door to protect her chicks. The neighbor decided, with Karimu's blessings, to kill the four chicks to prevent further attacks. Crows are viewed as pests; no better than flying rats. They're plentiful here, probably, as Julie notes, because of the plentiful trash.

Maybe it was because of the crow chicks—because we all knew what was coming—but dinner that night was awkward, almost total silence. Kafil was in a surly mood because he hurt his leg at school. Scotty was pouty. When Julie and Grace and Isabel walked across the street to the store before dinner, he sobbed because he thought they'd excluded him.

We never saw what happened with the crows. Karimu closed the windows and sent the kids to bed. I only heard some squawking, and rustling, and the voices of men.

After a full day of scrubbing and baby carrying at Calvary Zion, Julie and I take our first solo *matatu* trip to Mombasa, where we'll meet Karimu for dinner. The van is shiny and freshly waxed, the inside a mix of blinding colors and bumper-sticker quotes, fluorescent paint splattered Pollock-like on the dash. A bare-chested Tupac Shakur looks down from the ceiling, encircled by spiritual pick-me-ups.

God answers prayers
Miracles really do happen

Next to "The Lord is my shepherd" is "Get rich or die tryin'." Both are near photos of bikini-clad women.

"Maybe that's what they're praying for," I tell Julie.

We switch *matatus* in Bamburi. Cows wander the garbage dump, as usual, oblivious to the flies, noses scouring rubbish.

"I assume the cows can find actual food," I say, watching.

"They don't seem malnourished."

"It's not just that—I mean, I assume they're smart enough to not eat trash. Or that there's some instinct telling them not to eat, you know, batteries."

"I saw a cow eating a big piece of cardboard."

"Really? Wouldn't that make them sick?"

"Apparently not."

"I guess they're okay—none of the cows are barfing."

I tell her this sounds like the title of a book:

None of the Cows Are Barfing—A Memoir

As our *matatu* enters Mombasa's exhaust-choked streets, the red-shirt money guy doesn't give us our ten shillings change. I consider asking for it, but I figure it's pointless; he'd give us some reason I couldn't necessarily refute—*it's rush hour, this is rush hour price*—and besides, he *did* point us to the downtown post office where we're supposed to meet Karimu: a large, gray-cement building lined with rows and rows of mailboxes.

Rush-hour pedestrians clog the sidewalks. "I hope Karimu can find us," I tell Julie above the car horns and voices, looking over the tops of African heads, though the stupidity of that statement hits me as soon as I say it.

"We kind of stand out," says Julie.

Karimu approaches and waves.

"I saw your head from *waaay* down there," she says, as if to emphasize the point.

We walk to Island Dishes, a Swahili restaurant she likes in the old town. The "island" reference is for Lamu, Kenya's oldest town, located on the island of the same name. The food is fantastic: sim-sim bread—circular, cut in quarters, oily and herbed—grilled beef kabobs in tamarind sauce; tikka chicken, which has almost a Jamaican jerk quality; coconut potatoes; and something like a Swahili pizza loaded with Middle Eastern–style flavors.

I sit back in my chair, full. As Julie makes a post-Tusker bathroom trip, a guy in Muslim attire sits alone, drinking tea, talking loudly, perhaps to Allah, perhaps to the voices I suspect he hears in his head.

"I think he's mad," says Karimu, glancing at him.

"Mad angry or mad crazy?"

"Both."

"Maybe I'll go introduce myself. I'm sure he loves Americans."

"I'm sure."

"What'll you give me if I walk up and hug him?"

"I'll visit you in the hospital."

She sips her juice and smiles. "I'm gonna miss you guys," she says. "I'll miss having adult conversations."

"I'm so sorry you consider this adult conversation."

She says we're probably looking forward to getting home and returning to quiet.

"Actually, it's gonna be *too* quiet. I'll miss coming home and jumping rope or throwing Scotty in the air. They're really terrific kids."

She smiles again and thanks me, and we leave shillings on the table and stroll with Julie through the old city streets in search of sweets. Last night Isabel brought out a late-evening plate of mangos and oranges. The kids were slow going to bed, and Scotty noted in Swahili that they *couldn't* go to bed: their doctor said it's important for them to eat fruit. It was essentially his way of saying—

Listen, I'd like nothing better than to go to bed, really I would, but it's in my best interests to stay up and eat this fruit.

"What a great stall tactic," said Julie.

Scotty was bitten by a child at school yesterday. He was a biter himself, Karimu says. Someone once told her that the cure for biting is to put a match near the child's lips.

"You put the flame *just* close enough to feel it," say Karimu.

Not the kind of advice you'll find in *Parents* magazine. It's a cultural difference. Yesterday, Martina again carried Johari home from Marvel. When Rose found out, she whacked Johari on the hand with a switch—*thwack*! Johari cried, tears dripping onto her checkered school dress.

"She knows she is not supposed to do that," Rose said. "It's bad manners."

Karimu and Julie and I stroll to an ice cream place with the giddy name of *Ooh!*. Julie orders mango gelato, which inspires me to robot dance—a subdued robot dance—and sing "mango gelato" using the tune of Styx's "Mr. Roboto"—

Domo Arigato, Mango Gelato . . .

"You're weird," she says. (Trust me—it's a term of endearment.)

We take a *matatu* back to Bamburi, and then to Kiembeni. I usually give my shillings to Karimu and let her pay, so Julie and I don't get ripped off. On the second *matatu*, Karimu and the red-shirt money guy squabble in Swahili. When we get out, he's still yakking—it sounds like a lecture—but Karimu ignores him, walking with us in the dark through the field to her house.

"What was that about?" I say.

"What an *idiot*," she huffs. Occasionally her accent is apparent, as it is here.

Eed-ee-ott.

"He said *wazungu* are rich so we should charge them an extra ten shillings each. I told him he can do that on his own, but I want my change back."

The principal at Marvel said one day that African men often take advantage of *wazungu* women. She mentioned a German girl who taught there and got ripped off, paying too much in rent, buying a man she was dating a flat-screen TV. But compared to most Kenyans, we *are* rich. We're used to comforts. We're used to running water. We're used to stability.

That night, around 10:20 p.m., we lose power, a not uncommon occurrence, though it hasn't happened much since we've been here. It was out most of the afternoon as well, sparing Julie from ironing clothes at Calvary Zion. We sit in the living room, in sudden darkness. I use the light on my digital watch to get around. Isabel lights candles in the kitchen and brings us one. She drips wax onto a plate, then sets the candle in place, with the nonchalance of someone who has done this many times before.

Elijah sits on the floor without diapers, pondering torn furniture, when Hiari yanks his pecker—pulling it the way you'd pull the lever on a pinball machine. He screams, of course, and I nearly scream, because no guy wants to see another guy's pecker get yanked.

"Whoa! *NO NO NO*," I say, grabbing Hiari's hand.

She laughs and does it again. His scream intensifies. Barbara pulls Hiari away; I pick up Elijah and hold him.

"Hey, *hey*—it'll be all right," I tell him.

We go outside and sit on the bench. He cries against my chest.

"That's a good reason to start wearing pants," I tell him.

Slowly he calms down. His sniffling stops, and he leaves my lap to study Julie's shoes. I watch him. It's easy to forget the challenges here; that many of these kids were physically and sexually abused; that they suffer emotional issues evident and undiagnosed. Amid all the good intentions here, and all the good work, there is heartache, the ache of abandonment and loss, and unlike the dirt we clean on the white tile floor, the hurt does not so easily wash away.

At every stop on this journey, I've wondered if I'm actually helping. A common criticism of voluntourists is that we benefit more than those we're supposed to help. It's a fair point. One night I shared my concerns with Karimu.

"It worries me that we enter these kids' lives and then boom—we abandon them," I told her. "I'm afraid we're just reinforcing that abandonment—that they can't count on people."

A 2010 journal article supports that fear. Titled "AIDS Orphan Tourism: A Threat to Young Children in Residential Care," its coauthors—Linda Richter, a distinguished research fellow at the Human Sciences Research Council, and Amy Norman, a researcher at Queen Mary, University of London—studied AIDS orphans in South Africa. "The formation and dissolution of attachment bonds with successive volunteers is likely to be especially damaging to young children," they wrote. "Unstable attachments and losses experienced by young children with changing caregivers leaves [sic] them very vulnerable, and puts them at greatly increased risk for psycho-social problems that could affect their long-term well-being."

Put in a less academic way: small kids can feel quick attachments to volunteers, creating a cycle of abandonment. High staff turnover adds to the problem. Richter argues that "welfare authorities must act against voluntourism companies and residential homes that exploit misguided international sympathies to make profits at the expense of children's well-being," adding that "young people should be made aware of the potential consequences of their involvement, be discouraged from taking part in such tourist expeditions, and be given guidelines on how to manage relationships to minimise negative outcomes for young children."

Karimu takes a different view.

"The children have the mothers, and Jane, and all the other children," she says of the kids at Calvary Zion. "They have plenty of familiar faces. And they're used to volunteers coming and going." Indeed, a steady stream of volunteers has worked at Calvary Zion since December. "They get attention from you guys. And they wouldn't get that attention if you weren't there. No one has time to cuddle the little ones, and if even there *was* time there are too many kids. Would the babies be better off if you didn't hold them for two weeks? And what about the older kids you help with their homework?"

This being my sixth voluntourism gig, I see two main benefits. First, you get to know people from different cultures, and they get to know you. That benefits everyone: it smashes stereotypes and broadens our view of the world. And second, volunteers provide free, enthusiastic, temporary labor for minor but necessary jobs. So here at Calvary Zion, we haul food to Marvel and cut vegetables and fold laundry. When Julie wrestles with a fussy Elijah to change his diaper, the mothers don't care why we're here or how we benefit. They're just glad that somebody else is doing it. When Julie attempted to make *ugali*, Rose and Priscilla laughed as she labored over the pot. At La La Shou, Tom and I broke up the monotony of difficult days with small help and the novelty of our presence.

The same morning that Hiari yanked Elijah's pecker, I helped Faith walk, as we do most days. She took my finger as we scooted around the house outside, though she did most of the walking herself, balancing against the wall. Once or twice she fell, landing on her butt in her little pink dress. I gave her my finger to help her up. She walked again, her tongue sticking out.

In China, Meilin said that two-week volunteers are links in a chain. I'd dismissed that as orientation rhetoric, but I see some truth in that now. Before we came to Kenya, other volunteers helped Faith walk. Once we're gone, someone else will do it. Soon she'll be walking on her own. It's far from perfect, but what is?

On our second to last day, Karimu joins us for lunch at Jane's house, and we arrive on time: a social faux pas. "Jane is going to say something," says Karimu. "In Kenya we arrive thirty minutes later than the actual time." Sure enough, a surprised Jane notes our punctuality. "You are using *wazungu* time," she tells Karimu, laughing.

We settle in the cramped living room. Barbara and Martina, the two German volunteers, are here as well. Above the couch is a sign:

IF YOU GIVE YOUR LOVE, SINCERELY AND UNSELFISHLY, YOU GIVE GOD, BECAUSE GOD IS LOVE.

Jane brings out plates and pilau rice and vegetable stew with beef, plus a big bowl of fruit for dessert. The always-clinging

Christopher follows as she travels back and forth to the kitchen. Finally she joins me on the couch. We bow our heads in prayer before we eat.

She thanks God for the food. She thanks God for Martina and Barbara. "And I thank God for Julie and Ken," she says, "and for the time they have been here, and for all they have done for the children."

Christopher climbs in her lap as we eat. "This is not a good idea," she says, and he spills meat and rice on her leg.

"See what you did?"

She laughs, and shakes her head, and feeds him from her hand. When we're done eating, she presents Julie and me with thank-you letters and certificates of appreciation.

"You are my friends," she says. "You are part of my family now. People from all over the world come to be with us and support these children. I want the children to have the comforts and prosperity that all children should have. This is my mission."

She takes us on an after-lunch drive to the new property. Martina, Barbara, Julie, and I are all crammed in the backseat: it's like a *wazungu* clown car.

"People are staring," Barbara says as we drive, looking out at bemused faces.

We pass a roadside trash dump—"The trash situation is shameful," says Jane—and then leave homes and shops and people for high grass and occasional trees.

"Welcome to the brush," Jane says.

This new location is far more remote than the current home, so we're wondering how the kids will get to school. Jane is hoping to obtain a minibus. And I'm thinking—

How will this woman get a minibus? Who's going to pay for it?

"God will provide," she says, as if knowing what I'm thinking. "I have never gone to the United States. I have never gone to Germany. I have never been to the UK. But God sends these people to me. I put my faith in God. I know He will give the answers. I know—because God has told me. Because God wants me to care for His forgotten children. The home is my calling. When I told my husband what I must do, he says, 'How will we support our own children and all of these orphans?' But at last he says, 'If this is what you must do, then do it.'"

Down a side road is a stone wall, and we churn dust as we approach an impressive blue gate, like entering a military base, the letters bold:

Welcome to
Calvary Zion Children's Home
A home of signs and wonders

The site is beautiful and big: roughly two and a half acres with sprouting crops and newly planted trees, three dogs and a goat roaming the grounds. A gazebo with thatch roof occupies a central spot, like a town square. It feels like a commune, a noble attempt at self-sufficiency. No rent. Solar energy. An irrigation system. Chickens to produce eggs. Homegrown fruits and veggies, from mangos to maize. Any excess food will be sold at a local market.

"This will be the living room," says Jane, as we wander through one of two buildings under construction. Her voice echoes off the concrete floor and cinder block. Unlike their current claustrophobic setup, each building will have two toilets, two baths, two family rooms, a dining area, a kitchen—and no more sharing beds. Ultimately Jane wants one hundred children to live here.

And she started with nothing. No money, no resources. Just faith, and commitment, and friends. Many, many friends.

A German couple, Tanja and Reiner Fischer, raised the money to buy the land, and continue to raise money for the home. Tom Greaves, a former volunteer from England, raised nearly fifteen thousand pounds for building materials by biking from Vancouver to the coast of Mexico, sponsored by family and friends.

And then there's Susan Peattie. In 2005, Susan was teaching English for a month at a primary school near Marvel. At the age of thirty-nine, she had recently left a government job, and came to Kenya before pursuing a university language degree. It was serendipity—or God's will, depending on your viewpoint—that steered Susan to Calvary Zion.

Before she left for Kenya, friends gave her school supplies and cash—around $150—to give students where she taught. Rather than hand all the money to one school, Susan decided to share with others. She saw the road sign for Calvary Zion, stopped by the house, and found that the children were skinny. Too skinny. Several suffered from colds and chest infections. Food supplies were low. Susan took the mothers to the market and stocked the cupboards, and returned several times before heading home. As she got to know Jane, she realized the home was fighting to survive. The rent was behind. They'd been evicted several times, the children moving to Jane's house.

Susan cleared the rent arrears, and paid the gas and electric bills. She returned to Scotland, organizing a rummage sale to raise money. In September 2006, as more people contributed to the cause, she formed the Calvary Zion Trust. Four years later, Susan and her friends in Scotland have raised sixty thousand pounds. Much of the money pays for private school fees: public schools in Kenya are overcrowded and underfunded, sometimes with one hundred or more students in a single class. The trust is seeking sponsors for the kids—thirteen kids have sponsors so far—and it has helped fund counseling sessions for children suffering from extreme emotional issues. Any remaining money is used by Jane for daily expenses. The trust also keeps two thousand pounds in the United Kingdom for emergencies.

It's hard to imagine those earlier, more desperate times as we walk around the grounds. "This is *sooo* much nicer than where they are now," says Julie.

When we leave, we drive a different way, passing a megachurch under construction in a field (its architecture reminds me of the spaceship from *Close Encounters of the Third Kind*). Several other building projects are about to begin. We see monkeys run along the top of a brick fence, and I'm reminded of what Javier, the tattooed researcher, said of monkeys who lost their habitats in Ecuador—

They have no house.

We drop off Barbara and Martina—they're taking a *matatu* to Martina's apartment—hugging and saying goodbye. Tomorrow is our last day at the home; they're getting an early start on weekend travel. Jane drives us back to her house. It's the last time we'll see her as well. She's heading to Nairobi for a funeral. She hugs us both and tells us twice: "You will never forget your time at the home."

Karimu gives us a knowing nod. "I have a feeling you'll be back," she says. "I tend to sense these things."

Before leaving Jane, we tell her we want to do something for the kids on our last day: something frivolous, something necessary—whatever she thinks makes sense. Karimu suggested we bring sweets, but Jane frowned and said the children received *lots* of candy at Christmas. I also know that I, personally, would not want to be responsible for forty wired-on-candy kids.

Instead, Jane suggests we make dinner. It's a good idea: Rose, Alice, and Priscilla could have a cooking-free night. "And you'd get to meet the older kids," says Karimu. We haven't met the junior high and high school kids—roughly half of Calvary Zion's residents—because they arrive in the evening after we're gone.

Enthused by our mission, anxious to provide a culinary thank-you to Calvary Zion, we take a *matatu* with Karimu to the Nakumatt. She suggests pasta: kids love it, she says. We buy twelve packages of noodles—and wonder if it's enough—along with several cans of sauce and a large package of ground beef and four packages of queen cakes for dessert: like cupcake-sized pound cakes, light and slightly lemony.

We also want to help the home. It costs about two hundred thousand shillings a month—close to $2,500—to run Calvary Zion, Karimu told us. Jane relies entirely on donations to cover the expenses, including rent, food, tuition, utilities, health care—a long and daunting list. And the donations she receives aren't always the donations she needs. The home receives too many baby clothes, she told us during lunch. She's planning to give a lot of them away.

We discuss numerous possibilities for helping—the home always needs new mosquito netting, we could buy shoes for the older students—when Karimu suggests new mattresses. I've seen the thin mattresses while climbing on the bunk beds to clean windows. Some are no more than an inch thick in the center, the foam mushed from age and from multiple kids sleeping in each bed. In one of the cribs the foam is disintegrating inside the plastic cover.

Jane approves, and on Friday morning we walk with Karimu to the home, the first stop on our mattress mission. I go from room to room, measuring mattresses with a long piece of string, while Karimu feeds Jacob *uji* from a bottle and Julie feeds Faith from a spoon. Elijah watches blankly from his pink potty. The mothers are trying to potty-train him, so he sits on it throughout the day, scooching around the house, pushing himself with his legs—a vehicle without wheels.

We priced mattresses yesterday at the Nakumatt, but Karimu thinks we can do better, so we trek by *matatu* to a narrow, busy market area in Mombasa, which seems like the mattress district: mattress shops face each other, overflowing, beds stacked against walls like tiled dominoes on the sidewalk. At the Nakumatt mattresses cost 3,400 shillings each; the first two shops here offer prices no lower than 3,200.

"I think we're getting special *wazungu* prices," says Karimu.

We'll get a better deal if she shops solo, so I stand next to an empty cart on the corner of the busy street, attempting to avoid being trampled by shoppers: women in bright head scarves with bulbous sacks and baskets on their heads; women in black Muslim garb—*buibui*—holding shopping bags; a swerving red motorbike stacked with strapped boxes. Julie buys a mortar and pestle in a rustic kitchen shop, bargaining the shopkeeper from 250 shillings to 180 (and probably still getting ripped off). Karimu exits a mattress store across the street.

"He's giving a good price," she says. "Twenty-eight hundred shillings, or two thousand six hundred and fifty each if you buy five."

I give Karimu the cash and lurk on the corner. Jane's husband, John, soon meets us in the city. We give him the receipt so he can pick them up when he has the truck.

Upbeat from helping the home and boosting the city's economy, we celebrate with lunch at a place called Mamba Village for more *nyama choma*. The highlight is grilled goat ribs and fries, the goat fatty and gristle-rich at the bone. As we chat, I mention that the *matatus* here in Mombasa seem newer and sleeker, and Karimu corrects me. I mispronounced it.

"What did I say?"

"You said *matutu*."

"What does that mean?"

"Boob," she says.

Oh—well. That's quite different.

"So if I said *matutus* with an *s* that would mean—"

"Yes."

"So people are probably wondering why I'm talking about all the boobs I've seen."

"Probably, yes."

Matiti, she says, means "ass."

"You saved all the good stuff for when we're leaving," I say.

Instead of a *matatu*, or a *matutu*, we take a *tuk-tuk*—like a golf cart with a bigger engine and less space—to Mackinnon Market, a former slave market now packed with fruit and vegetable stalls. We buy ingredients for our pasta dinner: tomatoes, onions, carrots, peppers, cilantro. Karimu warns us about aggressive hawkers. We're basically left alone—probably because we're with her—until a guy with one bottom tooth insists that Julie peruse his spices.

"Only to look," he says. He's persistent though friendly and pesters Julie to pose with him in a photo.

"Mama—take photo," he says to Karimu. "Where you from?"

"United States," says Julie.

"Ahh! Barack Obama!"

This is how most conversations have gone regarding our nationality, though we haven't seen as much Obamabilia as I'd expected, given the president's Kenyan father. A city craft shop sells Obama coffee mugs, and I saw a bumper sticker on a store window. Near Karimu's house is a barber's shack with a folk-art painting of Obama on the outside wall, "Yes We Can" painted underneath. My favorite is an Obama reggae tune I've heard, usually in passing *matatus*, sung by Jamaican artist Cocoa Tea. Forget politics: it's an incredibly catchy tune. You could replace "Barack Obama" with "Barry Goldwater" and it'd still be catchy.

"A lot of people think the Obama family here in Kenya has gotten a bit uppity since he became president," Karimu tells us.

Julie poses with the spice guy. He puts an arm around her and holds up a scooper of ground saffron. They both smile (though Julie has more teeth). I take their photo. Given all his effort, Julie feels compelled to buy some tea.

As we wait for a *matatu*, we see street kids walking the sidewalks. A few sell bottled water. Others wander without purpose. They don't have a Jane or a Rose or a Calvary Zion in their lives. At lunch yesterday, Jane had said, "I think it is important to get the children before they are six—before they're old enough to know what the streets are."

At times, I admit, I've wondered if the Calvary Zion experience is detrimental to the kids; the way they beat on each other, the lack of supervision simply because of their size. Julie found Faith the other day with a pencil in her mouth. I found her on the floor, alone, playing with a marble. But seeing street children here in Mombasa, the contrast is obvious. The children at Calvary Zion are well fed. They go to school. They go to church. They have shelter and responsible adults who care for them. They are loved. Without Calvary Zion, without Jane Karigo, they would be here—nowhere—selling themselves, scrounging for chemical escapes, wandering, suffering, alone, adrift, reviled. Becoming hard. Children of the streets.

Now that we're slicing restaurant-sized mounds of veggies, cooking a farewell dinner for close to fifty people seems daunting. And foolish.

Everything starts out fine. We arrive around five o'clock, which gives us plenty of time to serve by six-thirty, their usual dinnertime. It takes forty minutes to cut the veggies. Stevie helps us peel onions and garlic. Alice lights the charcoal. Julie cooks the veggies in a large pot, and adds the ground beef and sauce.

Excellent progress! Except the noodle water isn't boiling.

Alice stokes the fire and adds more charcoal.

No bubbles.

At seven o'clock, I think, *Surely the water will be boiling by seven fifteen.*

And then it's seven fifteen. No bubbles.

It takes an hour for the water to finally percolate. As it gurgles we dump in the pasta. Julie stirs.

"I've never stirred twelve packages of noodles," she says.

"It looks thick." I feel her arm. "I think your biceps have gotten bigger here."

While waiting for the water to boil, Julie chatted with Alice and the older girls. The house seems packed now that the junior high and high school kids are here. One high schooler in particular, Honour, peppered Julie with questions about hairstyles, jewelry, jobs, where we live, what music she likes—a friendly interrogation.

The noodles are finally ready but we're not sure how to strain them.

"I help you," says Alice.

She's a small woman, shorter than Julie, yet she carries this tub of hot water and noodles into the kitchen, using an old shirt for a potholder. Julie is convinced the mothers have asbestos for fingers: she's seen them carry hot pots with nothing covering their hands.

We serve: Julie scoops steaming noodles from the pot using two spoons as tongs, placing the pasta on plates. I add the veggies-and-meat sauce. We fill fifteen plates on the counter in rows of five with assembly-line efficiency, like we're chefs in a cruise ship kitchen. Children take plates one by one; we keep dishing until everyone is served. I hope it tastes okay—it's so different from the Kenyan meals the mothers prepare—but I trust Karimu's instincts. Sure enough, kids come back for seconds. Hiari licks her bowl, a noodle on her head when she's done. The older kids bring back spotless plates and thank us. The pot is empty. Alice says it's the first time the children have eaten meat in over a month.

Before we leave, I ask Rose to pose for a photo with Julie in the kitchen. Julie thanks her for helping us and making us feel welcome. Rose thanks us as well.

"Mountains never move, but people do, and we will see each other again," she says. She clasps Julie's hand, and kisses her on both cheeks, then kisses me as well.

I say goodbye to Elijah, picking him up, holding him one last time in the kitchen. He seems focused on the counter; the possibility of food.

"All he thinks about is eating," says Rose.

Finally he looks at me, our faces close, and raises his arms over his head. I raise my right arm. For some reason he laughs.

"That's an image I want to take home with me," I tell him, poking him in the stomach. "That's an image I don't want to forget."

Since it's dark out, a group escorts us back to Karimu's house. Rose comes, and Alice with son Daniel on her back, and some of the older kids. Several are barefoot. Not me. Despite what Rose said, I don't yet have African feet.

Rose and I walk together. Bright gray clouds surround a full moon. "The stars are brighter here," I tell Rose. "Back home we only see a few stars at night."

The dog walks ahead of us, moving off the road as *matatus* rush by, their headlights and the moon our only guide.

"You work so hard that even the dog will miss you," says Rose.

Honour, the teenage girl who asked Julie so many questions, locks arms with her for the entire walk.

"It is so painful to part with friends," says Rose.

"I've traveled a lot the past year," I tell her, "and I'm amazed how attached you can become to people in just two weeks."

"It is true. You and Julie work hard—I will notice it next week when you are gone."

"I wish we could have done more."

"No—you do a lot. I wish I could pay you. But God will pay you a special reward."

We walk through the field and bang on the gate to Karimu's house. Kafil opens it; he's surprised to see the dog and the crowd.

The reward from God will not come to me. Nor should it. It will come to Rose, and Alice, and Priscilla, and Jane, and the children, and all who provide for them.

In Kenyan society, if you're a man and you can't produce a child, it's okay for your brother to impregnate your wife. In some tribes, if a man is sleeping with a guy's wife, he plants a spear in front of the wife's home: a phallic warning system to let the hubby know what's up (literally).

Karimu tells us this as we drink chai tea and watch *Shades of Sin*, yet another ludicrous soap opera, this one Brazilian, about twin brothers, one of whom steals the other's wife (the twins were separated as children, one vanished at sea, the wife knows none of this . . . it's complicated).

Around ten-thirty, the church behind Karimu's house begins a booming late-night service. We missed this last Friday since we were in Tsavo. Voices sing and chant through speakers, hymns barrel through the walls. Julie does a dirgelike dance in our bedroom, dipping one shoulder and then the other, head bobbing to the music. The music stops after midnight, then starts again at one-thirty.

Our last full day is spent at Diani Beach, along the Indian Ocean, with Karimu, Rudolph—he's driving—and Julianna, another Travellers Worldwide volunteer. She's from the Congo, studying medicine, and began working this week at a Mombasa hospital. We drive for about an hour, past glimmering seaside views and horrific roadside slums, which make Bajo de Meco seem like Beverly Hills. Traffic slows: a *matatu* has hit a guy pulling a handcart. His fruits and veggies are scattered over the road; his hand and arm are covered in blood. Because of the surrounding crowd, we can't tell if other people are hurt.

The ocean is a postcard blue with hints of green, the sand white, seaweed scattered about. We sit at an outdoor table, feet in the sand, and order fruit drinks: mixes of banana, coconut milk, pineapple, and mango. I notice more old men and young women, and an almost equal number in reverse: an older blond woman wraps her arm around the shoulders of a taut young Kenyan man. Because this is a private beach, there's more stroking, more holding, more grabbing.

Julie and I walk to the clear, warm water, and though the beach is relatively people-free, we're pestered by roaming vendors selling coconut milk.

Where you from . . . British? Dutch? French?

Oh—America!

Barack Obama!

A few native fishing boats, carved from large logs, bob in the waves.

You are a vessel, Jane had said.

Some of our friends thought we'd adopt a child here. From a purely technical standpoint, the Kenyan government doesn't issue visas for children to be adopted by Americans. But I never expected it to happen. I've come to believe, or I've managed to convince myself, that my role in this world is different. I don't want to make you sick with all this vessel talk, but I can see now: I *am* a vessel, a tiny vessel, a humble vessel, bobbing in the waves. A vessel like that beat-up old car of Dad's, the car with the wheel that fell off. A vessel with one way to turn.

Not long after I returned from China, when I contacted Dad's old friend and coworker Will by e-mail, he told me a story:

In looking back over the larger arc that constituted my invaluable relationship with your father, I really have but one regret. As you may know, some years after my departure, a retirement dinner was held for Bob in South San Francisco. When the time came to supply personal testimonials and tributes to Bob, I errantly remained silent. Others were eloquent and quite likely had better things to say. Nonetheless, in hindsight, I wish I had spoken up in that Bob meant so much to me. I remember feeling bad about my non-performance even as I drove away that night. I also remember consoling myself by thinking there would be another time, and that I'd have another chance to tell Bob in a meaningful way of all he'd meant to me (and my wife, too). Of course, "another chance" never materialized. So perhaps Bob's final lesson to me is one that he has taught me in absentia: When the momentary availability of another is involved, and when there is something really constructive, really instructive, and really important that I want to say, I must find a way to seize the moment and express whatever is on my mind. To do any less means missing the moment and risking a regret that lasts.

I didn't speak that night, either. Like my sister, I spoke at Dad's funeral, uttering words he'd never hear. "When Julie and I were married," I said above the casket, "the minister told us something that stuck with me. It wasn't simply that we loved each other; he could tell that we liked each other. And the same is true about Dad. I didn't just love my father. I *really* liked him. I draw strength from him, because I knew he is inside me, and I know he's in a better place. The Japanese call it *Ano Yo*. Heaven. Dad is there. And as with everything in life, he has earned it."

I don't really believe in heaven. But maybe there is a soul. Maybe there's a spirit that transcends our bodies and the limitations of our minds. Jane Karigo has convinced me there's something, a light, the glow of fireflies, bounding inside us all. Our job is to ensure that the light doesn't dim, in ourselves and in others.

I had wondered how I could live up to my father's life when I'm not a father myself. But we live up to those who shaped us by honoring their strongest values, by caring for those we cherish, and caring for those that *they* cherished. By being our best and doing our best, as Dad so often liked to say.

Every day is "another chance." Every life is our only chance. Success comes from helping others succeed.

Should I live longer than my father and grandfather, should my brain start to wither and fade, I hope I'll remember the first Kiembeni morning when I saw Elijah laugh.

He climbed in Julie's lap, turning so he faced her, sitting as if on a saddle. Julie straightened her legs, cupped her hands behind his head, and lowered his head to her feet.

Woooooooooop!

She swung him back up. He was surprised. He smiled. We all laughed.

He waited for her to do it again.

Woooooooooop!

His smile got bigger. One more time!

Woooooooooop!

Finally, he laughed.

Here's the thing:

If this entire journey, from New Orleans to now, was simply about coming here, and making sure these children got some extra attention, and some extra affection; and buying some mattresses so they'd sleep a little better at night, and ensuring they ate one high-protein, high-carb meal; if it was as simple as making Elijah laugh—if that's the reason I don't have children—well . . .

I'm okay with that.

We say goodbye to Karimu and the kids. Last night, on our way back from Diani Beach, we met Isabel and the kids for dinner at a Chinese restaurant near old town Mombasa. Chinese food was Kafil's enthusiastic request when Julie and I said we wanted to take everyone out for dinner. He ate a *lot*—fried vegetable wontons and fried rice and cashew chicken, prawns in tamarind sauce; sweet and sour pork. Afterward, we walked to *Ooh!* for ice cream, Grace and me and Julie and Kafil holding hands. Kafil and Grace ordered bubble gum and marshmallow ice cream, which looked way too sweet. Back in Kiembeni, when we walked in the dark to the gate of Karimu's home, a satisfied Kafil smiled and said, "This has been a very good day." I was reminded of the shirt worn by Zhang Tao's son at La La Shou.

Today is a good day.

Julie and I take a cab to the airport. I spent most of the morning asleep, hit with a stomach bug. A final purge, perhaps. And so I missed playing with the kids, and I missed our last Kenyan meal.

At the airport, we kill time in the duty-free shops, then board the plane. I sit in the aisle seat, Julie takes the middle. No one, as yet, is next to the window. When passengers stop boarding, Julie moves one seat over to give my long legs more room.

The journey is over. The journey is just beginning.

I look at her. She turns from the window.

"What," she says.

"Nothing."

She raises her eyebrows.

"Are you happy?" I ask her.

She smiles, though surely puzzled by the question.

"I'm happy," she says.

I hold out my hand, and she clasps it, and we hold hands in the empty seat between us.

Acknowledgments

FOR TWO WEEKS IN Kenya, whenever my wife and I finished some minor job at the children's home, one of the housemothers—Rose—would smile and say, "I am so grateful." In that same spirit, I want to express my gratitude to everyone who helped make this book a reality.

Kate Nintzel at HarperCollins is a superb editor whose calm guidance tightened my prose and eased my occasional doubts. One of my favorite geeky joys was reviewing her hard-copy edits and finding she'd drawn smiley faces next to her favorite passages (and only one frowny face: when I ate guinea pig). Thank you, Kate, for your unwavering belief in me and my story.

I also owe an enormous debt to the team at the Brandt & Hochman literary agency. Back in 2007, I needed an agent to invest herself in this project, and Joanne Brownstein Jarvi did just that, bringing energy, ideas, and passion. This book would never have happened without her. Special thanks as well to

Marianne Merola and Henry Thayer for their wisdom, advice, and counsel.

A terrific group of experts and friends shared their input on everything from equipment to translations to the story itself, including Reema Attiga, Melissa Bach, Wang Baoli, Mary Prestera Butler, Cori Canady, David Clemmons, Nancy Davis, Hu Di, Meredith Dunham, Perry Garfinkel, Nicolas Gouffray, Meg Grant, Greivin Guzman, Miranda Harple, Jose Hernandez-Ugalde, Mimi Kirk, Cate Lineberry, Quentin Nardi, Irving Perez, Ben Pizzuto, Sandy Rosenthal of Levees.org, Lorissa Shepstone (and her Being Wicked web design team), Jon Skvarka, and the man who shares my love of greasy food and *Columbo* (as do our wives): Art Taylor. I am indebted as well to Sudha Gallagher and Brenda Casale for their fact-checking work. Here's why Brenda is a great researcher: when I wrote that Handala, a Palestinian cartoon character, had eight hairs on his head, she counted them and found nine, while noting that various pictures she'd unearthed showed him with eight, nine, or ten hairs (just in case there was some secret symbolism in the number of follicles).

Thanks also to my boss, Nancy Graham, and all my magazine colleagues, for tolerating my travel and supporting this project. Back in 2006, when I told Nancy I was thinking about volunteering in New Orleans, she e-mailed back and said, "I sense you are going through one of those 'Who am I and what am I doing with my life' phases we all suffer from time to time. Changing the scenery will help give you some clarity on what makes you happy." It was extremely perceptive, which—as you can imagine, Nancy— makes me cranky.

The nearly one hundred volunteers I met through my travels impressed me deeply, and I am so pleased by the U.S. and transatlantic friendships that have endured. These smart, funny, kindhearted people have enriched my life, and they helped confirm much of the information in this book. Kudos as well to the dedicated teams at Rebuilding Together, the Sovereign Military Order of Malta, Cross-Cultural Solutions, Global Volunteers, Earthwatch Institute, Volunteers for Peace, and Travellers Worldwide.

I changed the names of all the "characters" in this story to protect their privacy, with a few exceptions. Zhang Tao at the La La Shou special education school in China and Jane Karigo at the Calvary Zion children's home in Kenya deserve huge recognition and support for their work. The same is true of Susan Peattie, who created the Calvary Zion Support Trust to assist the home and its young residents, and her fellow fundraisers, Tanja and Reiner Rischer and Tom Greaves. Mika Peck, Anita Diaz, and Tim Cane are adventurous researchers who scale the Andes to study the effects of climate change, and I also retained the name of Señor Blanco, the principal at Escuela Cuestillas, and Adli Daana, secretary general of the International Palestinian Youth League, since these gentlemen are quasi-public figures.

Lastly, I owe a huge and heartfelt thank-you to my mom; Karen and Bill; Billy and Katie and Lauren; Murph; Jean and Jack and the entire Sunday dinner gang; the friendly staff at Caribou Coffee at Kings Park, where large chunks of this book were written and revised; Molly, the much-missed, dearly departed dog who brought so much joy to me and my wife (and who slept by my desk during many late-night writing sessions); John and Andy and Todd—my brothers—and my father's numerous friends, loved ones, and colleagues, all of whom provided stories and insights on his life, and on the qualities that made him such a positive force in the lives of others. I hope his spirit, in some small way, lives in me, and lives within these pages. Thanks, Dad, for always doing your best and being your best.

Most of all, thank you to my wife—for enduring my quirks, my flaws, my occasional wanderlust; for being my significantly better half and my favorite travel companion; for sharing your generosity, your warmth, your love. I can't imagine life without you.

To everyone: I am so grateful.

Take Your Own Voluntourism Adventure

You've read about my experiences as a global volunteer—here's how you can do it, too

TEACHING CHILDREN IN NEPAL, caring for cheetahs in Namibia, building homes in New Orleans—exotic opportunities like these are why many travelers are volunteering around the world and throughout America. Here's a nine-step plan for creating a memorable voluntourism experience.

Pick the Right Organization

Selecting an organization is like getting married: There are plenty of possible partners; the hard part is finding Mr. Right (or Ms. Right, as the case may be).

For basic info on some of the roughly 150 organizations that offer voluntourism trips, check out books like *Volunteer Vacations: Short-Term Adventures That Will Benefit You and Others* and Lonely Planet's *Volunteer: A Traveller's Guide to Making a Difference Around the World*. Also check out some of the organizations profiled on Voluntourism.org and visit sites like Voluntales.com.

To narrow the often-overwhelming options, start with these three essential questions:

- What kind of work do you want to do?
- Where do you want to do it?
- How long do you want to stay? (Most programs range from two weeks to three months.)

Keep the questions coming. Think about living conditions: Do you want a communal dorm-like setting or do you need your own space? Do you want to use your professional skills or do something entirely different? Are you hoping to spend eight hours a day working or are you more interested in lounging on the beach?

These questions may seem obvious, but travelers often ignore them until they're already in a foreign land, grousing about the living conditions or the work assignment. But the answers will help determine the place and the program that's right for you.

Learn How Much It Costs—and Where Your Money Goes

On a travel site called Worldhum.com, a blog about voluntourism led to this cynical post from a reader: "If you pay to volunteer, you are a total sucker."

Snide as that may be, there *is* something odd about paying to perform free labor. And those costs typically aren't low. A two-week trip in San Carlos through Cross-Cultural Solutions (CCS), for example, like the one my wife and I did, starts at $2,923. The Earthwatch trip in Ecuador starts at $2,795.

But there's a reason why most groups charge these "program fees," as they're called. The fees typically cover not only the basics of your trip—lodging, food, security, local transportation—but also help pay the group's basic operational expenses.

To find out how your money is being spent, ask the organization for a breakdown or check its website: most explain how the program fees are used. The fees for most U.S.-based organizations are tax deductible.

Some volunteers raise money to help cover their costs. CCS offers fundraising ideas at crossculturalsolutions.org/enroll/funding-your-program.aspx, including information on scholarships and matching gifts. Travelocity sponsors a contest offering a $5,000 "Travel for Good" voluntourism grant. For information go to volunteerjournals.com/volunteer-travel-grants.

Investigate the Organization

For a from-the-trenches view of a potential assignment—the living conditions, the food, the work projects—contact previous volunteers. "Talk to as many as possible," says Charlotte Hindle, coauthor of Lonely Planet's guidebook. "This is the one of the surest ways of finding out about an organization."

The organization will obviously put you in touch with people who had a positive experience, so if you want an unfiltered opinion, search for blogs that might be commenting on a particular organization, or check travel review sites such as TripAdvisor.com or IgoUgo.com.

Find the Right Fit for Your Skills

A well-run organization, says Hindle, will send you a skills audit or questionnaire before matching you to a placement. You should also ask for a job description.

"It is really important that you volunteer with an organization that wants to spend time with you, working with you on finding the right placement," says Hindle. "I, personally, would never volunteer with an organization that tries to tee you up quickly with a placement online or over the phone and one that doesn't spend proper time understanding your skills and how they can best be used."

Explore the Group's Impact on the Community

One of the big questions with any voluntourism trip is whether the work you're doing actually benefits the people it's intended to help. But certain questions can help you determine how committed the organization is to the local community, says Christina Heyniger, founder of Xola Consulting, a company that focuses on the adventure travel industry. Do the group's leaders speak the local language? Is the local community engaged in the projects (are they contributing time or money)? Is the voluntourism group creating dependency or building a self-sustaining program?

Equally important is why the project was started. Heyniger writes on her website: "Did the operator simply cruise through the village one day and say, 'Hey! Looks like these people need more tennis shoes, windbreakers, and blankets—I'm going to bring some of that through on my next tour!' Or did they take a collaborative approach, and work with local people to ask them what they need and then determine whether and how they might be able to support those needs?"

Don't Overlook Small Organizations

With so many volunteer groups to choose from, the appeal of bigger, more-established (and pricier) organizations such as Cross-Cultural Solutions, i-to-i, Earthwatch, or Global Volunteers is easy to understand. They're safe.

"They do what they do really well, and they've got it down pat," says Doug Cutchins, coauthor of *Volunteer Vacations*.

I stuck with the more established groups because they have longstanding partnerships with local communities. But sometimes the more rewarding experiences come from smaller, lesser-known organizations, says David L. Clemmons of VolunTourism.org. Clemmons points to organizations such as Conservation VIP, Conscious Journeys, Go Differently, and Voluntourists Without Borders, which typically work in no more than a handful of countries.

"You'll likely be traveling with the founder of the trip," says Clemmons. "You get to hear the stories of what it has been like to put it all together—the heartaches, the triumphs, the mistakes, the brilliant ideas. It's like riding with Henry Ford in the first car he built. What could be more exciting?"

Your dollars also have a bigger impact with a small group, says Clemmons, since the organization has fewer overhead expenses, and the volunteers tend to be more adventurous and travel savvy. "They did some serious due diligence to come across one of these organizations, or it was a word-of-mouth referral from the creator," says Clemmons. "There's a positive attitude. You probably won't hear something like, 'Well, this wasn't in the literature about this trip.'"

That's the upside. But how can you make sure a small organization is equipped to follow through on its promises?

Look for nonprofits, says Clemmons. Most nonprofits will have to be registered with a governing body—the Internal Revenue Service, for example—and other countries have similar entities. You can also check up on them at sites like Guidestar.org or GlobalGiving.com.

If you're considering a small for-profit organization or a tour operator, Clemmons suggests contacting tourism authorities or the governing bodies that represent those groups—the United States Tour Operators Association, the Pacific Asia Travel Agency, etc.— to see if they have information on the company. Have there been any complaints? Any reports of impropriety?

Watch for Warning Signs

Clemmons once received a letter from an angry traveler who was complaining about her voluntourism experience. The woman, a college student, was looking for "a cheap volunteer program," which is exactly what she got.

Among her grievances: no running water in the dorms for over a week, no working toilets or showers, and promises that weren't kept—from the placement (she was supposed to work in a hospital but was abruptly placed in a school) to dinners (supposedly covered by the program fee but never provided). She was led to believe that the organization was a nonprofit, then found out it wasn't.

The volunteer missed several warning signs that this outfit was run more like the Three Stooges than 3M. According to Clemmons, the following actions might save you from similar problems:

- Find out how long an operation has been in existence. "If you cannot find this somewhere on a website, or in printed literature, stay away," says Clemmons. A new group may be just fine, but it is more likely to be working out the kinks of its program.
- Realize that you may not get "true" answers from the company that you contact. If you can't find information

about the organization in articles or from other
sources—if you're going to Thailand and the local
tourist authority has never heard of the group—this
should be a clue that the organization is bit, well . . .
mysterious.

- Be aware that an organization isn't necessarily a
nonprofit just because its website has a ".org" address.
If working for a nonprofit is important to you, ask to
see a 990 form or an annual report.

Expect Good Customer Service

A voluntourism trip in a third-world country is obviously not the
same experience as a therapeutic massage weekend at a world-class
spa. But the lack of pampering and plush five-star accommodations
is no excuse for poor customer service.

"The idea that 'roughing it' during a voluntourism trip means
that customer service and hospitality are expendable is a pitfall that
numerous nonprofit organizations fall into," says Clemmons. If an
organization dodges your questions or doesn't respond to phone
calls or e-mails in a timely manner, consider it a clear warning sign.

"Most organizations are small and understaffed," adds Cutchins,
"but they should still be professional."

When You Volunteer, Act Like a Pro

"International volunteering is like taking on a real job," says Hindle. "If you approach it any less seriously, there's a greater chance
that you'll be disappointed."

What's your motivation for volunteering? If you're at a school in
Sri Lanka purely because you think it'll look good on a résumé or a

college application, that's bad for the volunteer organization as well as its partner organization (and you'll probably have a lousy experience, too). The volunteers who contribute the most are energetic, enthusiastic, and respectful. Remember: You're a guest. Don't go into a school or a research project and start barking out orders. If they want your input, fine, but don't show up and tell them what they're doing wrong. Follow their instructions and help any way you can. You'll learn a lot and experience a culture and a place in a way you never would otherwise.

Directory

Here are the six organizations I volunteered with on my journey.

CROSS-CULTURAL SOLUTIONS
2 Clinton Pl.
New Rochelle, NY 10801
   800-380-4777
   info@crossculturalsolutions.org
   Crossculturalsolutions.org

EARTHWATCH INSTITUTE
114 Western Ave.
Boston, MA 02134
   800-776-0188
   info@earthwatch.org
   Earthwatch.org

GLOBAL VOLUNTEERS
375 East Little Canada Rd.
St. Paul, MN 55117-1628
   800-487-1074

email@globalvolunteers.org
Globalvolunteers.org

REBUILDING TOGETHER
Rebuilding Together National Headquarters
1899 L St. NW, Suite 1000
Washington, DC 20036
1-800-473-4229
Rebuildingtogether.org

TRAVELLERS WORLDWIDE
Suite 2A, Caravelle House
17/19 Goring Rd.
Worthing, West Sussex
BN12 4AP
England
+44 (0)1903 502595
info@travellersworldwide.com
Travellersworldwide.com

VOLUNTEERS FOR PEACE
7 Kilburn St., Suite 316
Burlington, VT 05401
802-540-3060
info@vfp.org
Vfp.org